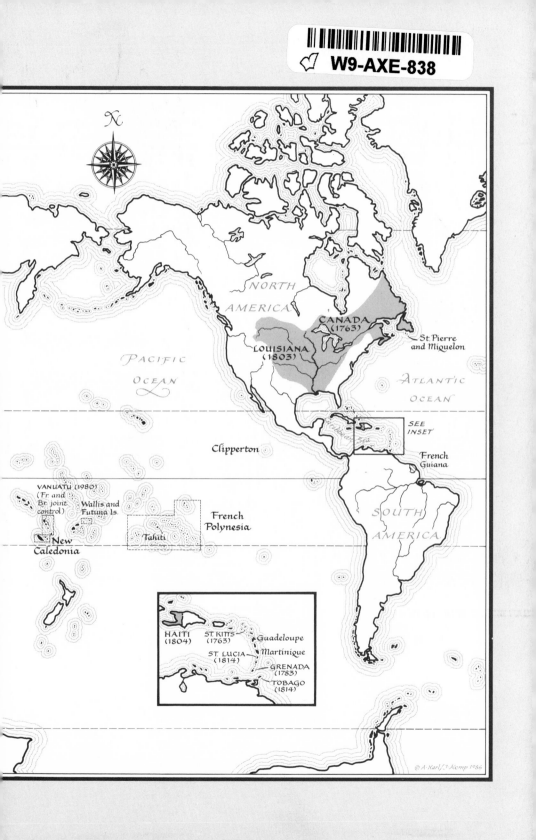

N

NORTH
AMERICA

CANADA
(1763)

St. Pierre
and Miquelon

LOUISIANA
(1803)

PACIFIC
OCEAN

ATLANTIC
OCEAN

Caribbean
Sea

SEE
INSET

Clipperton

French
Guiana

VANUATU (1980)
(Fr. and
Br. joint
control)

Wallis and
Futuna Is.

French
Polynesia

SOUTH
AMERICA

New
Caledonia

Tahiti

HAITI
(1804)

ST. KITTS
(1763)

Guadeloupe

ST. LUCIA
(1814)

Martinique

GRENADA
(1783)

TOBAGO
(1814)

© A. Karl/J. Kemp 1986

MISSION TO CIVILIZE

MISSION TO CIVILIZE

THE FRENCH WAY

MORT ROSENBLUM

HARCOURT BRACE JOVANOVICH

SAN DIEGO   NEW YORK   LONDON

Copyright © 1986 by Mort Rosenblum

Requests for permission to make copies of any part of the work should be mailed to: Permissions, Harcourt Brace Jovanovich, Publishers, Orlando, Florida 32887.

Library of Congress Cataloging-in-Publication Data
Rosenblum, Mort.
Mission to civilize.
Bibliography: p.
Includes index.
1. France—Relations—Foreign countries.
2. Civilization, Modern—French influences. I. Title.
DC59.R67 1986   909'.097541   86-7663
ISBN 0-15-160580-7

Designed by Francesca M. Smith

Printed in the United States of America

First edition

A B C D E

FOR GRETCH AND O.B.
la famille, quoi

Contents

Author's Note

THIS IS A reporter's book on a passionate subject. Reporters pick one of three roads, and they owe their readers some signposts. They can report facts, filtering out any point of view. They can write as editorialists, selecting an argument and then marshaling the facts to support it. Or they can analyze, looking at facts as they find them, and then saying what they think. My choice is the last.

The French like to say *qui aime bien châtie bien*. He who loves well punishes hard. My attraction to France might qualify me for shelter under such a formula. But my purpose is neither love nor punishment.

As a journalist and not a historian, I am tortured by the inability to ring up Richelieu and say, "Come on, you didn't say that?" I have borrowed liberally from historians, with careful adherence to the two-source rule and attribution where possible. For current sources, I have omitted some last names, and some names altogether. I chose their absolute candor over full identification; often, both are not possible. All characters are real.

In the reporting for this book, and over the past nineteen years, I have traveled to nearly every bit of real estate that flies—or flew—the Tricolor. My interest in the French civilizing mission antedates my move to France in 1977: a French mercenary officer taught me how to open a wine bottle without a corkscrew a decade earlier, in the Congo jungle.

Some of the reporting has overlapped my main purpose in life as a correspondent for The Associated Press. Nothing within these covers engages the AP in any way; this work is my own. But I thank Louis D. Boccardi and Nate Polowetzky for having the good sense to keep me on the road.

No one reaches deeply into France without an invitation and a guide. With deep affection, I thank Annie Amirda, Michel Lavollay, Jean-Claude Nuti, Paul Chutkow, Jean-Jacques Sempé, and Hélène Weigand, among others, for sharing the best of their France with me, and occasionally rubbing my nose in it. Sempé, especially, for the cover. And Annie, for the trickier translations and hard work on the galleys.

On the subject of thanks, there is Marie Arana-Ward, for whom my admiration and affection break all rules about how writers are supposed to regard editors; Carol Mann, friend and agent who started me on this project; Joel Donnet, Sylvie Gueyne, Kate Kinstler and others who helped; George Whitman of Shakespeare and Company, for patience. Generous colleagues include Edward Behr, Pierre Haski, Axel Krause, William Pfaff, Jonathan Randal, Scott Sullivan, Paul Treuthardt and, of course, others.

And most especially, for every reason I can think of, there is Gretchen Hoff.

M. R.
Paris

PART ONE

THE MISSION

Civilize: [Fr. civiliser, *1601*] *To bring out of a state of barbarism, to instruct in the arts of life and thus elevate in the scale of humanity.*

—*Oxford Historical Dictionary*

France, France, without you the world would be alone.

—*Victor Hugo*

CHAPTER ONE

France

THE CRUMBLING LITTLE town of St.-Paul clings, half lost in a tangle of lush vegetation, to the western fringe of l'Ile de la Réunion, itself only a tiny patch of volcano and canefield at the bottom end of the Indian Ocean. It might be one of those forgotten cornerstones of empire, essential to a time of sailing ships and steamers but a costly nuisance cast off to the Third World in a jet-powered postcolonial era. But it is blessed with a peculiarity bestowed only upon the most enlightened of settlements. It is among the chosen. L'Ile de la Réunion is France. And St.-Paul is French.

"Ah, but you must not make the mistake of calling this a colony," the political counselor tells visitors to the *préfecture.* "Réunion has never been anything but French territory." The rationale might differ in Guadeloupe, Tahiti, or elsewhere in France, on which, in contrast to Britain's diminishing empire, the sun is not setting. But any Frenchman can tell you the real key: France did not colonize, it civilized.

France itself is strewn across the globe with four overseas *départements,* like American states, and six territories. General Charles de Gaulle, visiting the Caribbean island of Martinique in the 1960s, looked out over a cheering crowd of black and brown people and shouted, *"Mon Dieu! Mon Dieu!* How French you are!"

And in much of Africa, the Middle East, and Asia, former colonies, now independent states, still speak French and glance back toward Paris to check their inflection.

Wherever the French have been and gone, the Gallic stamp

remains indelible. Take Pondicherry, a fleck of palm-fanned seacoast south of Madras which France kept for 250 years. The enclave was a toehold on the Indian subcontinent, just big enough to allow thriving trade and to enrage the British by offering asylum to dissidents of the Raj. France ceded Pondicherry to India in 1954. But they took away only the Tricolor, not Voltaire or Valéry. A recent visitor watched two elderly Indian gentlemen settle comfortably into a ricksha. As it nosed into the throng, a snatch of their conversation wafted back: *". . . Mais, ils sont des barbares, voyons."*

Or Mauritius, les Iles Maurice. After 158 years under the Union Jack, and another seventeen years of independence, its foreign minister calls it "a little France in the Indian Ocean." A community of French-descended aristocrats clings tenaciously to every last preposition in their surnames. Planters and businessmen, they own the best land, frequent exclusive clubs, and marry within their class. They are Mauritian by nationality, but French by nature.

Today a subtly structured empire, as rewarding as any in history, maintains France as a world power, perhaps the only cultural superpower, one that is based firmly and squarely on illusion. Freed of its colonies, it is master. Having killed hundreds of thousands in colonial wars, France is a Third World symbol of liberty, equality, and brotherhood.

That the French can find glory in the irony is the basis of their genius: One can assume any pose, and command any priority, if it is done with conviction and flair.

A FRENCH VIEW of the world is shared by aristocrats, peasants, technocrats, and communists. Gustave Flaubert, in his *Dictionnaire des Idées reçues,* defined the French: "The first people in the universe." Charles Péguy, the Catholic poet who took himself more seriously, observed, "God loves the French best." And Charles de Gaulle put it simply enough: *"La France est la lumière du monde."* France is the light of the world.

In his memoirs, de Gaulle wrote: "Any large-scale human edifice will be arbitrary and ephemeral if the seal of France is not affixed to it." And having created his Fifth Republic in 1958, he pronounced: "France must fulfill her mission as a world power. There is no corner of the earth where, at any given time, men do not look to us and ask what France has to say. It is a great responsibility to be France, the humanizing power *par excellence.*"

Lest anyone think a Socialist government might abandon these cornerstones of Gaullism, François Mitterrand said in his 1981 inaugural address: "A just, generous France . . . can illuminate the path of mankind."

If not always fond of the gaggle of Oxford historians poking around in their psyche, the French received Theodore Zeldin's view warmly enough: "No nation, no democracy can write its own history without acknowledging some debt, or some direct influence to France."

The French world view brooks no self-doubt or diffidence. That niggling analysts might point out that France is no longer a major power is beside the point. France's nuclear arsenal is small but convincing enough. Its Foreign Legion and paratroop units show up regularly to calm other people's unruliness. Only the United States and the Soviet Union supply more arms to the world, and French salesmen penetrate markets of every sort. But true power, as seen from Paris, is not measured in megatons or trade figures but rather in the privileged dialogue among nations.

France illuminates *la bonne voie.* The right way. Moral conflicts, the confounding contretemps that the ungenerous might call hypocrisy, can be set aside for expediency. The greater goal outshadows all. France is the country of choice for nations wishing to distance themselves from superpowers; it is western but not the West. "French is the language of non-alignment," Egyptian foreign minister Boutros Ghali once remarked. It is also the first—or at least second—language of forty nations. Besides the French, 100 million people use it in their daily lives.

The French can find a way to be friends in need to any warlord who does not mind sharing their attentions with his foe. In the case of Muammar Qaddafi's Libya, for one, France has managed to remain friendly with its enemy.

And who is to call that wrong? It is the French way, right there in Descartes. For more than three centuries, French children have been taught to doubt everything but doubt itself and, at the same time, to stack their perceptions in neat little piles. "Descartes made a philosophy the way a good novel is made," Voltaire wrote.

"Everything was plausible but nothing was true." That tends to leave a clear field.

By Cartesian method, what can be seen very clearly is accepted as true. What is not very clear is not very true. "Very" is open to discussion; *donc* anything is negotiable if the goal is worth devising the principles necessary to reach it with integrity.

If you want a dog to look at something and you point at it, the dog will look at your finger. So will the French. France can be led by a logically moving finger to all but the most egregious objectives. Others might forgo their objective if they cannot find the way there among their repertoire of principles. Or they might ignore their self-inflicted restraints which, to the French, would be hypocrisy.

The *Christian Science Monitor* carried an article in 1985 on how the French manage to escape United Nations censure despite bald double-dealing. But it also quoted a senior British diplomat: "Nonsense, duplicity is the very stuff of diplomacy. Every country invokes high principles precisely when it looks after its own material interests. The French are simply more successful at this game than we are."

The view from London has been less charitable on occasion. When Argentina and Britain fought the Falklands War in 1982, each side appealed to France. The Argentines had five French-made air-to-sea Exocet 39 missiles. But they were not able to fit them to their French Super Etendard aircraft. French interests—which is not to say the French government—found a shadowy way to solve that problem for Argentina, well-placed British officials told me. As a result, thirty-six British lives were lost. The missiles sunk two ships. But only two. Being good allies, the French gave the British all the data they needed to defend themselves against the Exocets.

At the height of hostilities, France prepared to send Peru Exocets which, Britain feared, would end up in Argentina. The French desisted, but only after an appeal from Prime Minister Margaret Thatcher to President François Mitterrand. The British ambassador, in his pyjamas for a last-ditch 4 A.M. meeting, had not managed to dissuade top French officials. Immediately after hostilities ceased, despite a lingering climate of tension, France resumed arms shipments.

These are details of history. The weight and the glory of France elude the trifling measures of geopoliticians or the acts of individuals. The nation adds up to more than the sum of its parts. France is an end, says Jean Dutourd of the Académie Française; Frenchmen are merely the means. What really counts is the charge of electricity felt by all benighted non-French, whether Rwandan tourists or American presidents, who approach Versailles to rolling drums. Diplomatic setbacks and fleeting moments of ignominy fall away before an enduring grandeur.

IN PEKING, THERE is a Maxim's, a ludicrous parody of the real thing, opened with a flourish by Pierre Cardin to accompany his implantation of haute couture in the People's Republic. With its sumptuous art nouveau salons underused, it suffers from that most devastating of afflictions that might befall a French restaurant: it is *triste*. But it is Maxim's, and it is approached with reverence. At lunchtime, I asked the Chinese sommelier what wine was featured. He mumbled an inaudible reply. Pressed, he struggled gamely with the booby-trapped *r*'s and silent *t*'s of the long Burgundian name. Finally, he straightened, smoothed his black tails and breathed deeply beneath a starched shirt front. In a voice choked with emotion, he delivered the words that precluded all further discussion: "It is French."

FRANCE FIRST FORGED its overseas empire in an age when it was only natural that it should rule half the globe. Paris had been the capital of the world since the 1600s, for political thought and philosophy, for literature and art. Frederick the Great wrote his bad poetry in French; seeking a name for his Potsdam palace, he chose Sans Souci. French peasants stormed the Bastille in 1789, firing imaginations across Europe. Napoléon added an ironic twist to the new democracy, but he demonstrated the pure power of his nation. However much the French were feared or hated, they were admired. At Napoléon's approach, Russian generals fretted aloud in French.

England set up colonies to expand markets and secure raw materials for its revolutionized industry. France, while also seeking profits, had a different revolution to fuel. With legions of priests and poets,

France ordered itself on a *mission civilisatrice,* a mission to civilize. From Moorea to Mali, redeemed savages learned the stations of the cross and Rabelaisian ribaldry. Black, yellow, and brown school-children studied from books that began, "Our ancestors the Gauls were big and robust."

The word for this is still energetically in use: *rayonnement.* It comes from "rays," the bright beaming of the light of the world. The mission has changed, but it has not diminished.

"La France, c'est la langue française," pronounced Fernand Braudel, the historian of his century, shortly before dying in 1985. Lesser lights belittle the *chien chaud* syndrome, a supercilious mania for translating into French such staple foreign terms as "hot dog." One must not be misled.

Hardly anything is more serious in France than *francophonie.* The word means The Speaking of French. Its pope is the president of the republic and its college of cardinals, the Haut Conseil de la Francophonie. There is a secular arm, the Commissariat général de la Langue Française and a global Holy See, the Agence de Coopération Culturelle et Technique. Missionaries of the Alliance Française work in almost every country. Another 250 separate organizations, some heretical, propagate the word. And nine times since 1635, its bible—a dictionary—has been written and revised by a continually replenished body of forty saints: l'Académie Française.

The watchword is a verb that entered the language in 1568: *civiliser,* to oppose barbarity. Two centuries later, the French coined *civilisation* and never gave up rights to it.[1]

Jules Michelet, the prodigious historian of the last century, defined the French mission:

> The love of conquest is the pretext of our wars, something we ourselves have not realized. Yet proselytism is the most ardent motive. The Frenchman wants to superimpose his personality on the vanquished ... he thinks he can do nothing in the world more profitable than to give him his ideas, customs, and fashions ... this is a sympathetic instinct for intellectual fecundation.[2]

French object lessons included how to find victory in defeat. That came in handy after the Plains of Abraham and Waterloo, and subsequent encounters with the Germans. The empire strengthened, oblivious to humiliations of lost battles and the price exacted on colonies to help wage them.

By the 1930s, every French school displayed a world map proudly ablaze with deep pink blotches, marking an empire twenty-two times the area of the *métropole,* Mother France. The colonies' total population of sixty million was half again that of France. From the age of ten, children knew about the Gauls, Charlemagne, the Crusades, and the other past epochs that made France's civilizing role a natural state of affairs.

A textbook from 1926 tells fourth graders:

> France is one of the world's greatest powers. . . . Heroism shown and services rendered to humanity have enriched its national patrimony and radiance. And yet, in population France is very inferior to the great rival nations. If, in spite of this very grave inferiority, we could keep a considerable place on the earth's surface, it is because of the admirable vitality of the race exhibited in a *brilliant manner,* the expansion of the language outside of France, and the successive formation of two colonial empires. French is the auxiliary tongue of all civilized peoples. Among Europeans, it remains the preferred language of cultivated society. . . .
>
> It is every French person's duty to contribute to his full power in propagating our language by which are spread throughout the world the *generous ideas* that make people love France and increase her moral authority. Beyond that, the spread of our language helps greatly the spread of our products.

The textbook proclaimed: "Modern France cannot do without colonies." But after World War II, shaken by defeat and occupation, France set about dismembering its empire. In a long and bitter war it lost Indochina in 1954. African colonies were turned loose without a fight. Algeria won independence in 1962 after a vicious war of massacre and torture, which brought France to the edge of civil war. Yet officials in Vietnam, Cambodia, and Laos still study the West in French. Independent Algeria is a client and a friend.

In late 1984, in the garden of the French school in Bujumbura,

Burundi, I heard President François Mitterrand fire his countrymen with the message delivered to fourth graders sixty years earlier: "You are projecting the *rayonnement* of our culture, our society, our civilization."

Today the formal structure of *la France d'outre-mer* (overseas France) contains what a Parisian writer dismissed as "confetti of the empire." They are the DOM-TOM: *départements d'outre-mer* and *territoires d'outre-mer*.

The DOM are Guadeloupe and Martinique, in the Caribbean, near Puerto Rico; French Guiana, next to Venezuela on the shoulder of South America; and Réunion off southern Africa in the Indian Ocean. St. Pierre and Miquelon, near Nova Scotia, and Mayotte, near Réunion, are virtually departments, save for a few technicalities. The TOM are French Polynesia, a string of Pacific islands including Tahiti; New Caledonia, a large island, rich in nickel, east of Australia; Wallis and Futuna, a pair of nearby specks; and French Antarctica, an expanse of islands and mainland populated by 200 scientists and a lot more penguins.

The smallest piece of France is enclosed in a four-mile-long stone wall on the British island of St. Helena, southeast of Ascension Island on the way to Cape Town. It is Longwood, where Napoléon fought his last battles on maps of Europe spread over an inlaid billiard table. Queen Victoria designated the estate French property after sending home the emperor's remains, in 1840.

Altogether, they total 1.5 million inhabitants, 2.5 percent of France's population. Discounting the frozen wastes of Antarctica, their land mass is about the size of Pennsylvania, a quarter of the area of France itself. In cold accountant's terms, they are a drain on the treasury.

But, scattered handily about the globe, they are the lynchpins of the new empire. Each is a permanent flagpole for a nation that has grown great by showing its colors. Without asking first, France is free to station troops, refuel aircraft, launch spacecraft, and test nuclear devices. "I was in a cabinet meeting once when a staff researcher announced he had increased French territory by ten times," a senior official told me. "He had worked out how many square miles the DOM-TOM added to France, figuring a 200-mile offshore limit."

And in today's world, the French understand better than anyone the advantages of suzerainty over sovereignty. Twenty-five years after France set free its black African colonies, there are twice as many French in Africa: 300,000. Their currency then was the French African Colonies' franc, the CFA. Today, still freely convertible with the French franc, it is the African Financial Community franc, the CFA. The only two countries that shunned the franc zone, Mali and Guinea, came back to hammer on the door for entry. Spain's only African colony, now Equatorial Guinea, negotiated the right to use the CFA. The countries of Belgium's former empire, Zaire, Rwanda, and Burundi, are members in good standing of the French African Community. English-speaking states attend the annual French African summit as observers. Liberian president Samuel Doe, bemoaning his country's economic chaos, observed that Liberia's worst stroke of bad luck was that it was never colonized by France.

In the late 1960s, the French aided secessionists who nearly tore apart Nigeria, Britain's rich former African colony. In 1986, France, not Britain, dominated the Nigerian market.

France left Syria and Lebanon at the end of World War II, but almost every facet of Middle Eastern politics has its reflection in Paris. French jets and missiles destroy French technology on the ground. The dramas played out in Iran are, more often than not, produced in Paris, by factions loyal to every extreme. Ayatollah Ruholla Khomeini directed his revolution from a sedate village outside Paris. The shah's family fled to the Riviera. And each segment of the Iranian resistance has its French *quartier général*. When Beirut was too charred and cratered to be the Paris of the Middle East, Lebanese moved to the real Paris.

By custom, cities pretending to sophistication and charm were called the Paris of someplace or other. Saigon is no longer the Paris of the Orient, but Vietnamese aristocracy—the cultured class, not the war-enriched officers now in the United States—relocated to the source. The Cambodians and Laotians came as well, often with French spouses. Prince Sihanouk resides in Peking, but in France, he is home. Miniature versions of Southeast Asia, with borders and ancestral homes, have risen on the Left Bank.

Haiti fought off France in 1804 and went its own way. In 1986, Haitians rose again, and the dictator fled. To France.

France did not colonize Eastern Europe, but Poles, Romanians, and Czechs stand against the Soviet Union from the boulevard St.-Germain. Nor were the French in Latin America, but from Paris guerrillas speaking Spanish and Portuguese mounted revolutions against a half-dozen military governments. No self-respecting terrorist group or peace movement is without its French connection.

The literary tradition of Americans in Paris is slipping into history. But Poland's finest literary review is published in France. Eastern European, Latin American, Asian, and African writers work in Paris. When Mitterrand visited the Academia Brasileira on a trip to Brazil, members were upset that he brought a translator. "It is an insult," observed one senior academician. "Any cultured person here learns French as a child."

The British Council estimated in 1985 that France spends 2.3 times more than Britain to spread its culture abroad, nearly $450 million a year. That is well over what the American government spends.

The mission extends to French itself. In a television commercial between "Starsky et Hutch" and "Magnum," a suave gentleman murmurs to his chic companion, *"Un drink dans mon living?"* She slugs him so hard the fenders drop off his Renault. Then he tries again. *"Un dernier verre au coin du feu?"* Success. And a man's voice purrs, "The French language, the pleasure of understanding one another."

Le Haut Commissariat de la Langue Française, the ad's sponsor, uses the slogan: "The common language of 200 million people on five continents." That is pushing it. The number comes from totaling the population of every country with some official French at the top; many of those 200 million can barely manage: *"Oui, patron."*

But in February 1986, presidents, premiers and ministers from thirty-nine nations met in Paris for a festival of *francophonie*, twenty-five years in the planning. They gathered in the splendor of Versailles: Mitterrand and three Canadian premiers in well-cut wool; Africans and islanders in flowing robes, pinstripes and leopardskin; a natty Lebanese president in a silk suit. The audience was postrevolutionary nobility stiffened by republican roughage. And toward the front were a dozen Immortals of the Académie Française, like prehistoric salamanders in green-braided, long-tailed ceremonial cutaways.

Speeches revealed a certain defensiveness. Mitterrand had written only months earlier, "No one continues to listen to a people that loses its words." English was encroaching, and the watchword was neither French nor English: *Angst.* The concern was not without foundation. Reporters asked foreign minister Roland Dumas who would be charged with implementing any decisions taken. He replied, *"Un task force."*

By the numbers, French is not such a major language. A billion people speak English, and 800 million speak Mandarin Chinese. And then come Spanish, Hindi, Arabic, Bengali and Russian. Eighty-five percent of international telephone conversations are in English. The number of articles in French in leading scientific and technological journals dropped from 12 to 7 percent between 1980 and 1984. More people, in fact, speak good German than good French.

But it was *rayonnement,* not numbers, that France was after. Mitterrand reminded colleagues they were each part of a community of equals, free of any "nostalgia." That is, colonial taint. And he set the tone: "We are carriers of a culture that can have the ambition of being universal."

And then President Didier Ratsiraka of Madagascar, a nation that chose Marxism as an antidote to lingering French influence, took the floor. He asked, rhetorically, what he was doing there. And he answered:

"I am French-educated and proud to speak French, and my country uses French to communicate with the outside world, and as the teaching language of our university. . . . I address the French in general, and to the supporters of racism and xenophobia in particular: Know that, whatever you may think, in the four corners of the planet there are people who speak your language, who love your country and who are your friends. The people of Madagascar are among them, despite the ups and downs of history and the vicissitudes of events."

No Algerian was there to echo that message. But it was Cu Huy Can, Vietnamese minister of culture and a poet who spent his early life fighting to eject France from Indochina, who recalled that the first great encyclopedia was written in French. Saint Exupéry de-

scribed the earth as *"la terre des hommes,"* Cu said, and French
promised to be the language of world reconciliation in the next
century.

Thomas Sankara of Burkina Faso did not attend, but he sent
word. In French, he said, he could sing the "Internationale" and
speak to oppressed peoples in New Caledonia. His rhetoric excori-
ates France but not French. For those directing the mission to
civilize, that is good enough.

FOR THE ROMANIANS, among the most avid of Franco-
philes, the cultural lure of France is only nostalgia. Closed borders
keep them from Paris, but memories are undiminished. In Bucharest,
I poked among the back streets looking for a young dissident whose
address friends had given me. He was gone, but I found his mother,
seventy years old and elegant in a threadbare housecoat. She took
my card, with its address on the rue du Faubourg St. Honoré, and
she stared at it for a full minute. Her eyes misted. *"Ah, monsieur,"*
she said, savoring the vowels and consonants which she commanded
perfectly, *"c'est comme si vous veniez d'un autre monde."* I had come
from another world.

IT CAN BE argued convincingly that France is on the wane,
that too many people are looking behind its pretensions. Young
Frenchmen commit the unthinkable sin of expressing doubts aloud.
An Atlantic omniculture, with a strong American accent, is moving
in as the new expression of Western civilization. Japan and Germany
eat away at the markets. Only Washington's and Moscow's doomsday buttons matter in the power balance. Former colonies feel
exploited. French-trained leaders are retiring, replaced by products
of the University of Colorado. Racism is growing, and French
overseas territories are buffeted by currents that are growing violent.

Flexible principles at times humiliate France. In July 1985, two
explosive charges sank the *Rainbow Warrior,* flagship of the Greenpeace movement, moored in Auckland harbor preparing to protest
French nuclear tests at Mururoa. The chief engineer, a Portuguese-
born Dutch photographer named Fernando Pereira, died on board.
Few people suspected France; that would have been too obvious.
And, after all, France condemned international terrorism and re-

garded the peaceful little state of New Zealand as a friend. French
Defense Ministry officials suggested to selected reporters that the
British did it to besmirch France, in revenge for the arming of the
Exocets.

Suddenly French papers found a whole chorus of deep throats
leaking details. Cartesian logic tends to backfire when individuals
see different very clear truths from those up the chain. And an
internal war was raging among French secret services. We will get
back to the *Rainbow Warrior*. But, briefly, it went like this:

After silence and denials, Prime Minister Laurent Fabius admitted
that France was responsible. The head of intelligence was fired.
Defense Minister Charles Hernu took full blame and resigned. Two
arrested French agents were tried and each was sentenced to ten years
in prison. And that was it. Reporters wrestled with the unanswered
questions. The world wagged its collective finger. But France was
prepared to take only so much. Despite a heated run up to the
legislative elections, the opposition all but ignored the subject. No
more questions were asked or answered.

Without French help in the investigation, New Zealand prosecu-
tors had to drop the charge from murder to manslaughter. Most
French believed that meant their government had negotiated a deal
with the judges. When the Wellington government asked for reparations, French papers called it "ransom" and predicted their spies
would be home for Christmas. Commentators decried Prime Minister David Lange as a political opportunist for refusing leniency to
two officers simply following orders in their nation's interest.

The nuclear test, meanwhile, went off as scheduled; in fact,
Mitterrand himself flew out to watch. Greenpeace found another
vessel to send to Mururoa. But it broke down and headed for the
French port of Papeete in distress.

Hernu, who is supposed to have lied about the bombing to his
old friend, the president, did not go to jail. Instead, he received the
loudest and longest applause of anyone at the Socialist Party congress shortly afterward. He outpolled everyone in his district for the
National Assembly in March 1986, and was mentioned as a presidential candidate for 1988.

The opposition did not drop the affair entirely. Alain Madelin,
a deputy and a leader of the Union pour la Démocratie Française,

told a television reporter: "I am very sad for France, a France which haggles, a France which has set an example of terrorist action, a France which has lied, a France bogged down in deceit to the point where a foreign minister, speaking in the United Nations, has to erase in his speech the mention of human rights for fear of making the entire world laugh."

But for most French, there was far less remorse than chagrin that their government had made them look stupid. My greengrocer, a warm and generous man, summed up opinion nicely: "Those jerks, why didn't they wait until it was in open seas and then hit it with an Exocet? *Paf,* gone without a trace, and no one is the wiser. And to make a war minister quit, what for? That's like if I sell a rotten tomato, and they tell me I'm incapable of selling vegetables. I should have known, but so what? Like Watergate, to make Nixon quit. Ha. The *Rainbow Warrior?* That's only the press and some politicians. It doesn't concern the people."

But, I asked, what about the loss of life and the hostile act in an allied country? He looked at me as if I were a questionable tomato and emitted that classic French sound, like a gas bubble escaping from under a lily pad: *"Bofff."*

The whole episode had lacked flair, and it irritated him. But he is forgetting it with conviction.

Proper French style would have been to say nothing, to wait until people just dropped the subject. The columnist Georgie Anne Geyer found out how well that works for France on a trip to Africa. In socialist Tanzania, once a British colony, an editor berated her for American meddling in Africa. After a while, she broke in. The Americans have no African bases, she said. But the French have 8,500 troops and regularly overthrow governments. Why didn't he pick on them? He thought for a moment and replied, "Because they don't answer."

For the French, it is *présence* that counts. One need only look around, on any continent. In Paris, for a start.

PLACE ALIGRE, minutes from the Bastille, is as North African a market as in any casbah on the southern Mediterranean coast. Men with olive faces and flowing moustaches sell overripe figs, comparing them in leering terms to the undulating hips of house-

wives passing by. It is also the Caribbean, the slightest breeze
redolent of mangos and cinnamon. And Black Africa, and Indochina
and the South Pacific. Eyes and noses of every shape and hue take
in the bustling activity. Only the language is the same.

In the center is old France, an antique market of brass coffee
grinders and yellowing prints of ships at rest along Brittany quais.
One Sunday morning at Aligre, I picked up a book from the pile
on a groaning old card table. It was entitled *Visions d'Afrique,* from
1925. The author, Louis Proust, member of the Conseil Supérieur
des Colonies and national assemblyman, described in the tone of his
time daily life in the Ivory Coast:

> And thus is the marvel of our colonial effort. It is not hav-
> ing made cities spring forth from deserts, nor having cast
> across the bush and the forests the long ribbons of railway, nor
> having installed in this virgin country prosperous industries
> and superb scientific establishments; it is not even having
> tamed ferocious races and having imposed our peace. That, any
> European nation could have done; but it is having, in 10 years,
> by our joyous activity, by our serene justice, by our benevo-
> lent firmness, by that powerful attraction that belongs only to
> France, reached deep into these childlike souls, of having
> gently steered them from the mists of their savagery to the
> light of civilization, of having, in the end, made of these indo-
> lent and bloodthirsty populations a real people of merchants,
> artisans and farmers.
>
> By our exhortations, by our encouragements, and above all by
> our example, we have revealed to them the richness of the land,
> we have wakened in them a fecund curiosity. To see us, peaceable,
> hard-working and gay, to hear us speak of order, of work and
> of providing for the future, new ideas stirred among these slum-
> bering intellects. The spears and hatchets, now powerless, are
> rusting at the back of straw huts, and everyone is at work
> planting. . . . and when one looks upon these thousand black
> silhouettes stop[ping] at the foot of each vine to carefully pour
> water carried in a calabash, one can already imagine an immense
> harvest germinat[ing] and flower[ing] under the radiant smile of
> the sweetness of France.

Proust recalls how the French African empire began. The first sixteenth-century trading posts were too vulnerable to attacks by natives and European rivals, so France built an impregnable (except for successful British and Dutch assaults) fortress on the Ile de Gorée, off what is now Dakar in Senegal, in 1677. Proust describes the quaint beauty of the island, its charming stone houses, asymmetrical little squares gay with laughing schoolgirls, like a Normandy village but for the fierce African sun.

He neglects to mention the rank stone cells that filled with water at high tide, where slaves in irons awaited transport to America. Slavery comes up only once in *Visions d'Afrique*, in a reference to Moslem explorations, "somber and destructive," that visited on Africa uncivilized empires which France was forced to strike down.

Nor does he detail the exhortations and encouragements he mentions. During 1927, for example, of 2,850 Africans "requisitioned" for the Sotuba Dam in Mali, 13 percent died, 32 percent were disabled and 24 percent managed to run away.[3]

But why be churlish? If the random glance around falls on Africa today, slavery is not a theme. Rather, the radiant smile of the sweetness of France, or at least the largesse of its coffers, enlightens half the continent.

Time and again, I have watched the colorful clash of symbols —the Tricolor, the Gallic *coq*, the Music of History—reorient those who stray from the natural order of things. In 1979, for instance, I went as a reporter when President Valéry Giscard d'Estaing flew to Guinea to call on President Ahmed Sékou Touré. No one missed the significance of this first visit to Guinea by a French leader. When, in 1958, de Gaulle offered French African colonies the option of total independence or association within a French community, only Guinea chose the former. Livid, departing French technicians took everything they could carry. They ripped telephones and light fixtures from walls. They left machinery too awkward to move, but carried off the instruction manuals. Sékou Touré led his people into a socialism that devastated the economy, isolated Guinea from the West, and filled the jails. Two decades later, he was ready for reconciliation. Giscard d'Estaing was coming down to do the honors.

Half of Guinea waited at Conakry airport, a ramshackle cluster of buildings in a coastal rain forest. At the foot of a red carpet, Sékou Touré stood with his cabinet, his high command, the party leadership, tribal chiefs, and assorted dignitaries. An honor guard, a band, and dancers flanked the officials. In the distance, huge crowds waved the brother nations' flags in the sun.

At the appointed minute, a sleek shape pierced the clouds, flashed in the sun, and settled gently on the runway. The aircraft slowed and wheeled toward the reviewing stand, and an audible gasp rose over the engine whine. Guineans had seen enough airplanes but never a Concorde, let alone one carrying a president of France. The svelte little jet rolled up, its nose sloping elegantly downward. A blue, white, and red flag flew from the cockpit window. Everyone, soldiers, witch doctors, and president, watched transfixed. The plane could have kept on rolling and taken Giscard d'Estaing back to Paris without even a wave. The message had been delivered. *Vive la France.*

Valéry Giscard d'Estaing was defeated two years later by an electorate fed up with aristocratic airs. France brought in the Socialists, men of the people, egalitarians. In 1984, President Mitterrand made a trip to Africa, and I went along to see the difference in style. At the airport in Kinshasa, Zaire, the crowds were waiting. Mitterrand was forty-five minutes late, as was his habit, and people grew restless in the steaming heat. Dancers dragged a bit, and soldiers wavered under the sun. Then a glint of sunlight caught the approaching aircraft. Same Concorde. Same blue, white, red flag in the cockpit window. And same reaction among the crowds. Socialist, schmocialist: *Vive la France.*

Freed of the burden of subduing colonies, France can afford the high road. In the new empire, the president of France arrives not as master but as colleague and friend, a dazzling accoutrement to the image of any Third World leader. And almost any week of the year, France is welcoming at home one of its own to whom civilization was brought as a total package. An army colonel who learned to polish buttons at St.-Cyr, who absorbed Molière for his school play, and whose blood courses at the flash of blue, white, and red snapping to the "Marseillaise," does not stray far when he takes over his country. If his economy collapses, there is the Ministère de la Coopération and the Elysée slush fund. And he never forgets, if he oversteps the bounds of decency, there is always the 2me REP of the French Foreign Legion.

The substance of France in the world, for better or worse, is measured in figures and analysis in later chapters. But, among the French, substance pales against a feeling that is as overpowering as it is intangible.

No visitor to France on a day of national effusion can possibly miss the feeling. Blue, white, and red banners the size of schooner sails hang criss-crossed in the Arc de Triomphe and up the vast sweep of a boulevard, the Champs-Elysées, that only the French could have built. In perfect cadence, strutting and prancing, a phalanx of horses carries the Garde Républicaine, each guardsman in gleaming silver helmet and rich plumage. At some point, unfailingly, brass instruments send the rousing strains of the "Marseillaise" upward into the air, and along the tingling spine of every French person within earshot.

The British might match the ceremony, but it is somehow different, an emotion that turns inward among people who seem reticent to show their pride. The Germans might have, but no longer; anything close would send shudders of past trauma among neighbors and Germans alike. American grandeur seems somehow too parvenu, too brassy, too conscious of the cameras, with too many on the sidelines feeling a nervous embarrassment when their eyes moisten.

I first felt it the night Giscard d'Estaing welcomed Jimmy Carter to Versailles. Guests arrived in their Citroëns, hair worked to exhaustion by master coiffeurs, silks brushed and furs fluffed. They walked across crunching gravel to the rumble of kettledrums slung across the saddles of horses draped in blue, white, and red. On the ornate facade of the Sun King's palace, an engraved legend could be clearly read by all who approached: *A Toutes les Gloires de la France.* Amid the splendor, President Carter's security guards fidgeted uncomfortably, glancing surreptitiously at the awkward spaces between the cuffs of their trousers and the tops of their shoes.

And I saw it on the summer Sunday in 1984 when a million French marched on the Bastille to protest an attempt by the government to control the curricula of church schools. Under fleecy clouds, Tricolors snapped and unfurled against the tarnished copper of the

Bastille column. Parents, priests, politicians from all over France marched to Chopin and Beethoven, and throngs in the square sang Verdi's "Song of Slaves."

At the edge of the crowd, a short, stocky Frenchman stood at unconscious attention, the creases and puffs of his gray face revealing nothing. He wore a three-quarter-length tan raincoat. On his head was a newspaper folded into an admiral's cocked hat, the word *Prix,* in black letters, emblazoned on the side. His wife silent next to him, he watched, the corners of his mouth turned down slightly in satisfied discontent. The music stirred, 50,000 voices rose, and, in a subconscious natural gesture, he slipped his right hand into the front of his raincoat and held it there. Napoléon.

THESE ARE THE people who set out to civilize the old empire and who are hard at work bringing light to a new one. There are only fifty-five million of them altogether, with perhaps 1.5 million scattered abroad; 200,000 in the United States and about that many in West Germany. But they are French.

In the end, it is as Louis Proust put it in 1925, describing St.-Louis, Senegal, the seat of France's emerging African empire: "In a shiver of admiration and pride, one feels all the profundity and eternity that the word, *la patrie,* can express, as it is always the same soul which spans the generations, constantly rejuvenating but always the same, pursuing the same ideal, committed to the same task, and, at every moment, under whatever sky, burning with the same love for France."

CHAPTER TWO

The French

AN ENGLISHMAN APOLOGIZES when you step on his foot. A Frenchman berates you when he steps on yours. Beyond that, generalizing about the French is risky business.

It is easy enough, in France, to base your prejudices on fact. I had resolved to write this book without Alexis de Tocqueville. But here is this, from *l'Ancien Régime et la Révolution:* "France is the most brilliant and dangerous nation of Europe, best suited to be, in turn, an object of admiration, hatred, pity, terror, but never indifference." There are grounds enough for any of the abuse and adulation outsiders heap upon France. But the French, fifty-five million individuals who touch every extreme, defy generality.

Just when you devise nine new circles of inferno for Parisian taxi drivers, a cabbie returns your wallet and waves off a reward: "But it is only normal." A stranger throws open his home to you, and then invites your wife to lunch when you are at work. If France is so mean, where do you place Hélène and Jean-Claude: generous, open-hearted, broad-spirited, and very French? If it is so grand, who is making those raw, greasy, fast-food hamburgers on the Champs-Elysées?

And after centuries of shaping a society from empire, what is French? Annie Amirda, small and brown with an Indian father born in Vietnam, is French to her cuticles. Léopold Sédar Senghor, a poet who expressed the concept of negritude among African writers, was a French national assemblyman and is a member of the Académie

Française. He was also president of Senegal for its first twenty years of independence.

But distinct traits, habits, and patterns of thought shape the French into a society. They explain how France cast itself upon the world as civilizer, for better or worse. Ask any French person who has stepped far enough back to take a look.

My friend Claude, for example. A journalist for fifty years, he has lived in the United States, roamed the world, and observed the French empire from the outside with an insider's eye. Over asparagus in brown butter and *confit d'oie,* with a decent Cahors, he pronounced judgment:

> The Frenchman has to detest someone or something . . . his boss, his work, the state, the Socialists, the capitalists. Nothing is ever one's own fault; someone else is always to blame.
>
> And France lacks the sort of consensus needed in a country that is well off. The spirit is not ample. It produces people who are hostile. They drive like lunatics. Young people glower at the elderly. In the metro, you see old women who can hardly stand. Young men look them in the eye and won't get up to offer a seat. The French are xenophobic, very xenophobic, even among themselves. Many are racist. The famous French tolerance, the ideals of the French revolution: *Liberté, Egalité, Fraternité.* That is pure literature.
>
> When he had money, the Frenchman was the most ignoble tourist in the world. Looking at himself in the mirror, he knows he is the best. But when he goes abroad, and he sees he is not, it vexes him. But he won't say it, covering it with aggressiveness. It is very hard for him to admit that he is not the best. If you tell the French they are the most important, the most intelligent, as de Gaulle did, they tremble with pride. In fact, de Gaulle used to say all Frenchmen are sheep. But never in public.

Claude told me about an aging mechanic living so close to the Swiss border that the road to most of the rest of France went through Switzerland.

I asked him if he had ever been to Switzerland and he got angry. "Me? Those people? Never." It was very simple. Right next door was a wealthy country, where everything worked, clean, orderly, peaceful. It was constant proof to the garageman that his world might not be the best, and he cannot stand it.

He paused, saddened at the hard look I had invited him to take, and he reflected a moment to consider whether he had been too harsh. Then he concluded:

These are a people I love. I was reared among them, and I am one of them. But there are moments when I am so disappointed. I find my compatriots so self-absorbed, so selfish, I am sickened by them. And I want to go somewhere else.

Another friend, Philippe, sees a similar view in a brighter light. A dentist, he keeps track of teeth on a slim Olivetti computer; Bruce Springsteen is piped into his office. He works hard and late, but is always just back from hiking in Scotland or rafting in Utah. He is young, smart, amiable, *branché*—plugged in—and ready to look over borders for inspiration. He separates himself from a not very silent majority stuck in patterns and prejudices dating back to the Middle Ages: *les Français moyens.* The label means average, or middle. But in a language where *pas mal* (not bad) means "pretty good," *moyen* smacks of mediocre. Philippe sums it up neatly: *"Le Français moyen, il est vraiment moyen."* The middle-class Frenchman is decidedly *moyen.*

ALAIN DUHAMEL, A popular French commentator, calls his countrymen narcissistic and vain but not insensitive. "They know well they are not the . . . navel of the world, only a medium-sized power, weakened, but which still matters and does not give up." But, he wrote, they are grandly wrong on one point: "They believe themselves to be loved and respected everywhere. What a mistake! Foreigners prefer France to the French and admire more the past than the present. The 'great nation,' as it named itself before in all modesty, has lost much of its luster and its attributes, its feathers and its clasps."

But many foreigners pass judgment before taking the trouble to know the French.

Outsiders go wrong by looking at France through their own optics. It is always a jolt for veteran travelers to find that culture shock in France is more severe than in Saudi Arabia or Bolivia. Elsewhere, things look and sound different, so you expect them to be different. France looks like home, or at least like familiar old postcards and paintings. Surprise.

French society, even at the ends of the earth, is made up of little overlapping circles. With luck, timing, and patience, an outsider can fall into one of these circles, and hardly anything is more pleasant. In Paris, some years ago, we found ourselves in the Ile St. Louis microcosm a few days before Christmas. We had a turkey and no oven big enough to cook it in. "But, see the baker," offered the cheese lady. "But of course," replied the Martins, the bakers, waving aside effusions of thanks. "It is only natural." Our outlook changed and so, it seemed, did the island's. The lady who howled every time our dog lifted his leg began asking after his health. The fruit and pheasant man told us dirty jokes as he personally selected each tangerine. The butcher spent twenty minutes hand-chopping the beef whenever I made a pot of chili. We met Mimi, the traffic cop, who had given up her job stamping passports at the airport to be posted on the Ile St. Louis, her circle. No kid on the island crossed the rue des Deux Ponts without a kiss on Mimi's cheek and a piece of candy from her purse.

When I first went to the bustling Café St. Louis, I ordered fried eggs and then left the yolks: a peculiar mania of mine. Three weeks later, I went back a second time. "Listen, you don't like the yolks," the owner said. "Shall I make your eggs with only the whites?" Only a Frenchman could do that.

But when a Frenchman strays out of his circle, or encounters an untested outsider, he acts defensively. In France, defensiveness is no more a simple state of unease than cooking is the throwing of a piece of meat into a pan. It is a sport, a high art form, a spiritual fulfillment.

Among the more accomplished, defense joins offense in a dazzling pas de deux worthy of standing ovation. A basic component is *mauvaise foi,* which translates not so much to bad faith as to wrong-footing. The idea is that, whatever the evidence, the other person is wrong.

For example: I was once in a Paris hospital for something requiring rest. At 4 A.M., two nurses, gossiping loudly in the hall, woke me up. I asked if they could please hold it down. One replied, outraged, "We are discussing supplies. If we don't get the necessary supplies, we can't take care of you." It was my fault.

Or: I got into a taxi with the "in service" light on and asked, please, to go to the Ile St. Louis, which was not far away. The driver whirled around. "What?! You don't ask my advice first? This is no longer a republic? Anyone can get in my cab and give me orders? Don't I have the right to eat, too?" He would have preferred another direction, toward his house. But his light meant he was working; by heading toward his cab, I had missed the only other one I had seen in fifteen minutes. Driving off toward my destination, he resumed, "Do I walk into your dining room and sit down and eat? I should have locked the door. Next time, I will, you watch. Do I . . .?"

Mauvaise foi does not necessarily mean *mauvais caractère*. It is a conditioned response, learned in self-defense. Once at Les Arcs, in the French Alps, I left an empty ski bag in the hotel's locked luggage room. A week later, it was gone. I mentioned this to the desk clerk who replied, without a pause, "Well, why did you leave it there?" His lip curled slightly to discourage further comment. According to the game, I should then have demanded to see the manager who would have found another means of proving me wrong. Instead, I said, "You are perfectly right. I was a fool to entrust anything to your care. I won't make a claim. But I'd like you to say, 'Monsieur, I am sorry you suffered this loss in our hotel.' " He thought for a moment and apologized. As I drove away, he trotted along in the snow repeating his apology. Forced beyond his reflex action, he responded in good faith.

Wrong-footing can be harmless. A Californian discovered in his Mexican restaurant in Paris that most French never considered asking for guidance. "People would just point to tacos on the menu and then eat them with a knife and fork as if they had eaten tacos that way all their lives," he told me. Any nearby Mexican who ate with his fingers was pierced with the look of scorn he deserved.

But *mauvaise foi* and *mauvais caractère* can blend into the poisonous mix that so discourages Claude. Late for a meeting, I turned up a side street that was blocked by a truck unloading boxes. Five cars behind, in mid-block, I could only wait and stew. At my back fender, a woman in costly furs and a Citroën CX was trying to pull away from the curb. My front bumper was touching the car ahead, and I gave what was meant to be a friendly shrug of helplessness. She gunned her engine, edged up until she bumped my car and blasted her horn. The noise shot along raw nerves, and I covered my ears in another gesture—still friendly; I hadn't caught on—to ask for a little consideration. With an evil scowl, she leaned on the horn until I got out, and she suspected I might not share the French male's penchant for forgiving anything of a woman in makeup.

The contradictions can be unsettling. At one extreme, there is *la politesse,* courtesy and manners polished to a blinding sheen. The old treatises wax on for pages about when a hand should be shaken firmly, brushed lightly with the lips, squeezed, or waved aside. At the other extreme, there is the postrevolutionary tradition of asserting one's equality by acting with unbelievable rudeness. In *The French,* Sanche de Gramont argues that this does not mean some Frenchmen are polite and others are not. "It means that the same man who kisses a lady's hand in a drawing room will half an hour later be grossly insulting to a fellow motorist at a red light. Such inconsistency is only possible because good manners are considered a form of currency . . . and thus should be used thriftily and not on strangers."

IT IS EASY enough, at this point, to slip into 1,001 Reasons to Hate the French. (The *Village Voice* did it: "For *quiche* alone they should be shot.") That is too easy. The society's harshest critics are those French who live daily with its foibles but who also see its balancing style and richness.

As I was writing this chapter, a friend handed me two letters clipped from the *New York Times.* A Leonore Kuhn of Queens described a pleasant trip to France. Someone had stolen her mother's wallet in Nice but the police were helpful and assured: "In Nice they rob, they don't mug." Later, someone returned the wallet and papers, less the cash. She added, "French civilization also exists on the roads. Although traffic always moved fast, no one tailgated, cut us off, used insulting sign language, blew the horn or ran red lights." And two people named Sneider noted kindnesses by French people who acknowledged their war debt to America. "I think it's pretty marvelous that we have run into two appreciative and gracious people, and write this letter to disprove the myth of the anti-American French."

Few French are surprised to learn, from foreigners rising to their defense, that they are actually human beings like everyone else. (And any Frenchman who drives the *autoroutes* is likely to wonder whether Ms. Kuhn had mistakenly crossed into Switzerland.)

But the French notion of civility helps to define France's place in the world. And there is no arguing the basic point: the French evoke in any outsider in their midst a mixture of admiration, outrage, and often awe. Therefore, back to the generalities.

UNLESS AN ADVANTAGE might be gained by *politesse*, the concept of me-first is defended with elbows, ski poles, bright beams and horns, and studied indifference to anyone already waiting. Lines work only in small confined spaces where crashers cannot avoid eye contact—and possibly scandal—with those they inconvenience.

Airport strikes are seldom prolonged, so as to disadvantage the strikers, or held during the week when businesses are most affected. They come on peak holiday weekends so the people who suffer are other workers' families whose vacations are ruined. A wildcat metro strike over petty grievances paralyzed Paris for eight hours late in 1985; ambulances sat immobile, heating fuel went undelivered, and mothers walked for hours with tiny children. That night on television, a union leader smugly blamed "the bosses" for causing such hardship.

Such obsequious Anglo-Saxon and Germanic standards as "the customer is always right" often fall away as needless obstructions. Witness, for example, my American friend Butch, coming home from university in New York, ecstatic to be revisiting the bakery in the Paris neighborhood where he was reared.

"May I please have three croissants, two *pains aux raisins* and one *pain au chocolat?"* asked Butch, as pleasant a human being as might be found anywhere.

The woman assembled his order, wrapped it in paper, and picked up a pencil stub. "Okay, what did you have?"

When he stopped to remember, she ripped open the paper and angrily enumerated the items: "Three croissants, one *pain aux raisins,* two *pains au chocolat."*

No, he said, gently. "I wanted one *pain au chocolat."*

She flung one chocolate bun back into the glass case, muttering darkly. The lady in line behind, shaking her head at Butch's atrocious behavior, sniffed her judgment: "After all . . ."

A repairman who came to fix my stereo fouled up the wiring. When he finally returned, I was out, and a friend let him in. He deceived her into thinking he fixed it (he fixed nothing) and tried to convince her to sign a paper reading, "The customer does not know how to work his machine."

Such behavior is capricious, not necessarily to be taken as personal or permanent. My friend Jeff bought an expensive piano for his house in Normandy. The distance is nothing, the salesman assured him, organizing a hasty delivery—and payment in full. When a key broke, however, Jeff was much too far away. We are too busy, the salesman sniffed, call back next month. Later on, I asked Jeff about the piano. "Great," he said. "We raised so much hell they came on Christmas Eve to fix it."

In Paris, especially, there is the *engueulade,* the art of pointless quarrel. Visitors who do not encounter it should not boast; it is likely that they are considered too wimpish to play. The Parisian *code incivil,* explained Stephen O'Shea in *Passion* magazine, is that the ruder you are to people, the greater value you give to their existence. "Thus," he wrote, "Parisians who respect you will shower you with pleasant little incivilities from time to time—but only after you've shown yourself worthy of insult." Responses are standard but varied, graduating up to *"Allez vous faire soigner!"* Go have yourself looked after.

"Do *not* stand on the principle of customer service," warns O'Shea. "For most Parisians, Swahili is more easily understood than this principle. Selling in France is an act of charity which a seller performs for a buyer. . . . Nor should you argue from the notion of graduated hierarchy. Parisians work *at* a company, not *for* it."

What counts in France is not one's designated function but rather one's self-conception. Do not, for example, push a gendarme too far. You may think he is a public servant, paid to protect you. He may think he is Robespierre.

A touch of avarice darkens the picture. At the Brasserie Lipp, the menu scolds in advance: "A salad is not a meal." Café owners often refuse to sell tokens for their public telephones to anyone but their customers. "I passed a serious accident the other night, with a guy lying there bleeding, and went to a cafe to call an ambulance," a cabdriver told me. "The guy wouldn't let me use his phone. It was midnight, and everything else was closed. When I told him I would report him to the police, he got real nice."

Me-firsting and wrong-footing are learned early. Competition is fierce at kindergarten, the first elimination heat toward the narrow gates of *les Grandes Ecoles.* A narrow aristocracy runs French government and business. Well-born or not, aspirants need ennoblement from the Polytechnique, a fine engineering school run by the Defense Ministry; the Ecole Normale Supérieure, a teachers' college and seminary for great thinkers; or the Ecole Nationale d'Administration, l'ENA, a boot camp for top civil servants. Few get in, and only the best survive.

For butchers or brain surgeons, there are *brevets, permis, concours,* and *patentes.* A lifeguard is no beach bum on part-time wages; he must qualify as a *maître nageur.* A notary goes to law school, buys a thick carpet for his suite of offices, and acquires a lofty air of importance. There is competition at each of these stages. Once ascended to his chosen goal, a Frenchman then competes for honors to set himself above his peers.

Napoléon created the Légion d'honneur and, with great fanfare, awarded nearly 40,000 little ten-pointed stars in twelve years. More recent presidents have slowed the pace, but there are medals of merit for postmen and healthy children. At Verdun, the army decorated a carrier pigeon gassed in the line of duty. At cocktail parties, any senior official with no rosette or ribbon in his lapel is apt to huddle in lonely mortification back among the canapés.

Who's Who in France weighs seven pounds, with 20,000 entries.

Among the higher levels, every encounter involves a clash of *esprits*. Sanche de Gramont defines *esprit* as "a verbal spark, quick, bright, and ephemeral. It serves, like courtesy, to deflect the thrust of all that is unpleasant in life." If you are particularly good, or tongue-tied, you can do it with the eyeballs.

With so much competition, someone has to lose. But the society takes care of that with a keenly developed sense of self-delusion. To win in the face of clear defeat, one merely stakes claim to the high road, whatever road is actually taken. Self-delusion obliterates any attendant contradiction. This applies not only to individuals but also to the society at large.

A selective view of the past filters out lower moments. Echoes of Charlemagne, Louis XIV, and Bonaparte drown out the small-minded politicians in between. *L'affaire Dreyfus* evokes a tenacious, courageous defense, and eventual clearing, of a Jewish officer wrongly accused of spying for the Germans. Not so many recall why the fight was necessary, that Dreyfus spent eight years on Devil's Island because anti-Semitic officers, too proud to admit error, falsified evidence. He never did get his back pension. Ferdinand de Lesseps is the hero who built the Suez Canal, not the man whose backers in Panama squandered lives and treasure and then hid the facts for years by buying off journalists and politicians.

World War II remains a dull, aching memory in some nations Hitler subdued. But, looking back, the French remember André Malraux's reedy voice etching a portrait of heroism over the remains of Jean Moulin. That the few *résistants* Moulin led were often betrayed by Frenchmen is beside the point. France, in the end, won the war.

These filters apply equally to the present. France is hardly alone in defending its own perceived values. But, whatever the fine points of fact, a woman scorned hath no fury like the French public defining—and then seizing upon—a principle.

In 1984, Jacques Abouchar, a reporter for the state-owned television network Antenne 2, was captured in Afghanistan. He had sneaked into the country with rebels, carrying a letter he could not read urging the resistance movement to intensify its fight. It was a journalist's nightmare. Reporters, in fact, have no right to break laws even though professional canons dictate that they must take risks to cover the news. (In Uganda, reporters have been shot on the spot for clandestine entry.) As Abouchar admits, to his credit, a reporter captured in such circumstances can claim only leniency. But France decided that freedom of the press—and the rights of Frenchmen—were under assault.

For forty days, up to ten minutes of evening newscasts were devoted to *l'affaire Abouchar*. Each night on Antenne 2, a large numeral marked off the days. Fifty thousand letters poured in, and huge crowds marched on the Afghan embassy. Prime Minister Fabius canceled his appearance at a Soviet embassy function, and the French Communist Party admonished Moscow. When Abouchar was freed, a national assemblyman flew to Kabul to bring him home in Mitterrand's personal jet. Fabius greeted him at the airport, with live coverage.[1]

Interviewing Abouchar, a colleague broke into tears, saying, "This is a man whose profession is liberty." Across France, Abouchar's release was heralded as a victory for press freedom. The theme of press freedom dominated the papers and airwaves for days. In a ninety-minute special, a young moderator noted that the Afghans observed that Abouchar's passport listed another profession besides journalist. "After all, all of us who brave such conditions give our professions as anything but journalist: businessman, art historian," he said. Abouchar, again to his credit, broke in to note that such deception was ignoble, and that his passport had been issued before he became a journalist.

Days later, a more practical application of press freedom was quietly ignored. Britain announced that, like the United States, it would leave the United Nations Educational, Scientific, and Cultural Organization, largely because of Soviet and Third World attempts to muzzle reporters. Britain was an outspoken critic of moves within UNESCO to "protect" journalists by issuing them credentials, i.e., licenses. Under such international arrangements, Abouchar would have needed a government-issued press card to prove he deserved protection. But UNESCO's headquarters are in Paris, a source of income and local pride. A Socialist government had seized upon UNESCO as a forum for expressing French solidarity with a Third World oppressed by superpowers.

For the most part, French television and press comment reported

Britain's decision with a note of sarcasm: Britain, a shameless ally of the United States, was simply following the master.

The French press reflects well how France looks at itself and the world. It is the filter the French rely upon to comfort themselves in self-delusion. Some fine journalists are quick to point out when the emperor is wearing fewer clothes than advertised. But they are few enough to be folk heroes on the fringe. Most delight in helping France find faults in others it somehow misses in itself.

Reporters at the Los Angeles Olympics sneered at ABC for focusing its U.S. coverage on American medalists, although pool footage was available on all events. "This only proves that this young nation must call attention to itself," one television commentator explained. Then his ten-minute Olympic report dealt exclusively with fencing and show jumping, the events in which France excelled.

That sort of blind aggrandizement is known among the French who laugh at it as *cocorico,* the sound of a cock crowing. Since the heyday of the Gauls, 2,000 years ago, the rooster has symbolized France. It is fitting enough. The rooster preens and struts and picks fights he thinks he can win. He puffs up and announces his accomplishments loudly enough to dispel any doubts. He dominates his hens. And, in any barnyard, he determines a pecking order and moves as far up the line as he can manage without grievous injury to himself.

Some journalists crow a great deal. Recently, French and American doctors, working separately, isolated the AIDS virus. News reports in Paris dealt as much with the glory attached to the French role as the breakthrough itself. Pasteur was recalled. And there was a fleeting reference to additional work by "certain researchers of other nationalities."

But that is not universal, and French journalists who reject *cocorico* do it with a vengeance.

Once in the Central African Republic, I chatted with a French reporter at a reception behind the Résidence de France. He surveyed the six acres of mango trees and flowering plants and the ambassador's terraced home, guarded by some of the 3,000 French troops based in the former colony. "We are always writing about how other countries act like masters around the world," he said. "You know, 'Hey, have you seen the Russian embassy in Kabul?' or 'Look what the Americans put up in the Philippines.' Hah. Look at this."

We were with the press corps covering Mitterrand's African trip in late 1984. He had attended the annual summit France organizes for its former African colonies—and independent states whose history deprived them of French colonization.

It was to have been a stormy summit. Weeks earlier, France and Libya had announced a mutual withdrawal of their opposing forces in Chad. Foreign Minister Claude Cheysson laid the honor of France on the line: "If they stay, we will stay. If they leave, we will leave. If they return, we will return." Then, his voice tinged with pride, he declared on television, "The French operation in Chad is not the American operation in Grenada nor the Soviet one in Afghanistan. The purpose of the operation was to make the foreigner leave. He has left."

But American officials revealed satellite evidence showing that more than 3,000 Libyans were still in Chad. Mitterrand, after a roundly criticized meeting in Crete with Qaddafi, admitted that the Libyans had not, in fact, gone. The Opposition howled, blaming the government for soiling the image of France. African leaders worried aloud that the French could not be trusted to save them should they face outside attack.

Mitterrand stood firm. He told the African summit that France had no obligation to defend Chad; it was not one of the African nations that had comprehensive defense pacts with France. Privately, Africans called that hair-splitting. They noted that France had promised to drive Libya out of Chad. But discord was masked by civility. The storm was supposed to come when Mitterrand met the press.

The French press corps jostled for seats, and Mitterrand opened the news conference. No hands went up. An American reporter asked about Mitterrand's talks with Chadian leader Hissène Habré, known to be furious that France had acquiesced to de facto partition. "Very interesting," the president said. A French reporter noted that the summit had been forecast to be tense; what was Mitterrand's reading? "Excellent." Another reporter asked about the conflicting numbers of Libyans in Chad. "I did not take my camera and see for myself," the president said. Little more came out of the questioning.

Not only the president was contemptuous of the press. In six days, there were two official briefings, both short and without substance. Minutes into the first, Guy Penne, Mitterrand's chief adviser on Africa, banged the table and stood up. *"Bon,* if you're going to ask questions like that, I am leaving." A reporter had asked whether Mitterrand would exchange toasts with his host, an apparent reference to the possibility of frostiness. Penne stayed but did not answer the question. In the second briefing, he offered a few generalities and announced, *"Voilà,* I've told you everything." Someone asked about Zairean president Mobutu Sese Seko's remarks. "Oh, I don't know, the usual." Pressed, he finally added, "Oh, I forgot. Mobutu asked for a formal declaration on Chad." The only news.

French officials are used to looking downward at the press. With others' leaders, French reporters are aggressive to the point of abusiveness. With their own, they exude gentleness. This allows French policy to exist on the separate levels of image and reality. Accountability to the electorate is a needless obstacle to expedient policy, and few French expect it. At the height of the Chad crisis, a television anchorman remarked, "The Americans have announced intelligence reports that Libyan troops have remained in Chad. French intelligence knew this, too, but it was supposed to be a secret. Why would the Americans reveal this? That is the mystery."

At the summit, a senior official denied that France had agreed to a partition of Chad. "We would never sign such a paper," he said. "And if we did, we certainly would not tell the press."

The arrangement is cozy. The press can raise hell when it counts. Reporters threatened to boycott coverage of Mitterrand's visit when Syrian customs inspectors wanted one of their number to remove his false teeth. If belittled by officials who use them ignobly, they are well treated. On the trip down to Africa, wracked at the time with famine, our menu was: *foie gras de canard truffé du Périgord, chaud-froid de bar sauce Roquefort, magret de canard aux deux poivres, cèpes sautés, pommes cocotte, fromages de France, gâteau Louisiane, corbeille de fruits,* and, need it be added, fine wines and champagne.

And consciences are salved by *Le Canard Enchaîné,* an iconoclastic weekly that is far enough off the wall to be ignored when convenient. A feisty daily, *Libération,* often separates itself from the pack. *Le Monde* has its moments of glory. But the state dominates television, and independent papers, with their own interests, often pull punches.

In 1986, when an *International Herald Tribune* reporter resisted the Elysée's efforts to edit Mitterrand's remarks in an interview, a veteran colleague from *Le Figaro* scolded him: "You don't understand. These are the rules, and things are always done that way here."

That is how Valéry Giscard d'Estaing fended off what might have been a major scandal about diamonds he received from Emperor Bokassa I. He sniffed regally at anyone who raised the subject. And it is why so many of the French wonder to this day how the Americans could turn out of office such a great president, in their estimation, as Richard Nixon.

For those charged with protecting French leaders, the press is just another part of the obstructive rabble. France, explains a range of modern thinkers, has never ceased being a monarchy. Petty officials serve their sovereign and thrill in the reflected glory. Perhaps not, but the wise Frenchman seeks not to give the police a chance to demonstrate their powers. As for the presidential guard, it might as well be protecting the Sun King. I had a reinforcing lesson in this on the African trip.

In Zaire, I joined French photographers taking pictures of Mitterrand with Mobutu. As a reporter, that was not my usual pursuit, but I wanted to illustrate a story I was working on. National photographers who regularly follow a head of state move like a well-rehearsed ballet troupe. Newcomers are slightly out of step, but that presents no problem. Security guards, by international custom, nudge them along. I photographed on the move, sticking with the group, well ahead of the two stationary presidents. Suddenly, everyone else leaped to the left on a subtle cue, and I was a split second late. The beefy Elysée security team leader grabbed me in a manner most civilized societies reserve for mass murderers caught red-handed.

"You don't understand anything, you stupid . . ." he said, using the *tu* form used only to show familiarity or contempt. He gouged my arm, shoved me hard enough to break a pair of glasses, and threw me diagonally between the crowd and the pavement. With a parting shot, I was apprised of my crime: "You are in front of the president."

That is what happened with *Warrior* gate. French journalists dug
and probed, printing leaks and raising questions, until Fabius admitted France had sunk the *Rainbow Warrior*. Key questions remained
unanswered. For example, what happened and who did it? Who else
was involved? Suddenly, the case was considered closed. The day
before the two French spies were sentenced in Auckland, Mitterrand
gave a two-hour news conference. He spent forty-five minutes
discussing an additional state-authorized television channel. Finally,
ninety minutes into the questioning, someone asked about the trial.
He was brief and vague, and the subject was changed. Later, someone asked what his defense minister had told him. "Monsieur Hernu
has been my friend, and he continues to be. . . . He bears objective
responsibility." Without elaboration, or elucidation, he dropped the
matter.

WHAT OUTSIDERS might call cynicism permeates French
thinking. I tried to explain at a dinner party why foreigners were
upset by the *Rainbow Warrior* affair. An eminent guest fixed me
with that gaze meant for children, morons, and Anglo-Saxon moral-
ists. In France, power and self-interest are respectable goals. That
explains why it is not necessarily corrupt to decide beforehand who
should win a competition or, at times, even a court case. If money
changes hands, there may be dishonor. Otherwise, a sort of cosmic
justice applies. In France, power and self-interest may come about
as omelettes do. They may require breaking eggs. At the level of
l'Etat, state services are given the power to break eggs in the interest
of France. What they must avoid, at all costs, is a *bavure*.

A *bavure* is a hitch, a foul-up, notably by officials or police, and
it is so common that a smooth operation is referred to as *"sans
bavure."* At times, *bavures* can be blamed on bad luck or innocent
incompetence. Captain Paul Barril, in *Missions Très Spéciales,* recalls
his first challenge as a commander of the elite GIGN gendarme force
in 1981. Pope John Paul II was in Paris about to say mass in front
of Notre Dame. Police had learned that some students planned to
set loose over the pontiff and his flock a giant helium-filled doll—
with an enormous penis in its mouth. Barril and another sharpshooter perched in the towers with .22 rifles and silencers to deflate
the prank. He confided the plan beforehand to a prominent televi-

sion reporter who did not break the story but had this to say: "You guys are such bunglers you'll end up murdering the pope on live television." Police found the students in time. No shots were fired.

Other times *bavures* stem from the inertia of French officialdom. In Paris, during 1985, a bandit shot a bank manager in the stomach and fled with a bag of money. He forced a passing woman to drive him away. Across town, they were caught in a traffic jam, and he turned her loose. She rushed into a nearby police station; the sergeant there only shrugged his shoulders. If the robbery was on boulevard Voltaire, he said, she would have to go to the Beaubourg station to report it. But you can still catch the man on foot, she pleaded. Lady, he replied, that is not our business.

Often, however, *bavures* are the result of a *guerre des polices*. National police forces, the gendarmes, regional units and security services fight among themselves for power and glory. Sometimes there is tense peace. More frequently, criminals and terrorists are the incidental decor of the battlefield. Barril was a major casualty.

In August 1982, in the midst of murderous terror bombings and machine gunnings in Paris, Barril got an enticing tip: two leading Irish terrorists with Palestinian links were hiding in Paris. His elite gendarmes arrested them, and he preened for glory. The first hitch was that an antiterrorist squad formed nine days earlier at the Elysée wanted credit. Barril, fuming, handed over his prize. Mitterrand's office announced "dangerous terrorists" had been caught in a daring action of exceptional importance. The suspects, however, turned out to be minor actors. One was a British informer. Second hitch: Barril and his gendarmes had been set up in a *piège à cons* (a trap for fools) by rivals in the secret services who had passed along exaggerated information.[2] Barril was not short of evidence against the terrorists. But that was the third hitch: he was found to have planted two pistols and explosives on the prisoners. The Irish terrorists spent nine months in jail, despite the fake evidence, while rivals argued over their import. They were released, but four years later police were still fighting over the case.

Bavure is also a Cartesian euphemism for police brutality. In 1986, a new conservative legislative majority set out "to terrorize the terrorists." And a lot of other people. Police swarmed through cities, making random identity checks more befitting Bulgaria than the reputed cradle of human rights. During the incidents, Paris police held ten minors, mostly girls, incommunicado overnight, treating them roughly; parents who came looking for them were turned away at the door at submachine gun point. A black plainclothes officer was slugged before officers noticed his badge; a 63-year-old man was roughed up for hours. Two journalists and their lawyer were kicked around and told by one policeman, "We don't give a damn about the regulations." On television, the Paris police chief explained, "These incidents have always occurred. Now there is a press campaign, and they are being reported."

But polls suggested a majority of Frenchmen approved of the new measures. Their personal interest was order.

Some call cynical official actions that place a narrow reading of national interest ahead of broader responsibilities. The French closed their airspace to U.S. F-111 aircraft en route from Britain to attack Libya on April 15, 1986. France, critics say, could have disassociated itself from President Reagan's dubious venture without enfeebling the Atlantic Alliance it relies upon for survival. Not that long ago, after all, the French were happy to see American warplanes overhead.

Among other things, the government wanted to protect eight French hostages kidnapped in Lebanon. They did; three Britons were executed instead. French relations with Libya are delicately balanced. The Crotale air defense system that U.S. aircraft had to avoid was maintained by Thomson-CSF, owned by the French government. Libya's public thanks did not help.

Americans brought up France's past humiliations, and mockery of the French was returned in kind. The magazine Le Point asked: "Could the Americans have an inferiority complex toward us? Could they be jealous of our culture, our sophistication, our taste, out subtlety?"

Some French politicians objected to the refusal. Mitterrand let it slip that France would have supported a tougher move if it was certain to topple Qaddafi. French sources floated the version that the plane, in fact, did fly over the French Pyrenees. Prime Minister Jacques Chirac explained that France had already helped the Americans by foiling a Libyan plot to massacre people waiting for visas at the U.S. consulate in Paris. No one mentioned that no Americans wait in that line; Frenchmen do.

Little was made of a detail that might have stirred major outrage. Among the buildings damaged by the U.S. bombing—indirectly but substantially—was the French embassy.

The next month, French authorities sought to ban a radioactive cloud from the Soviet Union. While surrounding countries reported alarming increases in radiation from the Chernobyl accident —and took vegetables, milk and meat off the shelves at heavy cost —France remained miraculously untouched. And then it came out that radiation had been up to 400 times normal in some parts of France, though still below what was considered the danger level. Pressed for an explanation, Pierre Pellerin, director of the Service of Radiation Protection, said, "Quite simply because there were two holidays in two weeks, and it was very complicated to transmit the data." Others added that the government did not feel it necessary to alarm the French public with technicalities it could not understand.

With forty-four nuclear power plants supplying 64.8 percent of its electricity, France is touchy on the subject of radiation. More, the farm lobby is large and loud. On a popular talk show, a French nuclear engineer said specialists around France knew of the high levels but were told, essentially, to mind their own business. A Belgian member of the European Parliament, Anne-Marie Lizin, said she was not surprised. The European Economic Community had been after France for years to supply nuclear data that EEC countries felt they needed in their own national interests.

BUT THESE characteristics of France, even the least admirable ones, reinforce amazing recuperative powers that allow the nation to spring back in full force from the deepest of defeats. France rests on the same old stones and slow-cooking sauces that have survived war, occupation, and economic depression. Its language, rooted in Latin, rich and resonant, carries far when spoken softly. The French way of looking at things—obliquely direct, judgmental from clear but unspoken baselines—is why France remains a seat of empire.

Well past closing time on Christmas Eve, a guide named Gervette

speared his failing flashlight at every last rock and niche to show
us Fontenay Abbey. It was not for the substantial tip he was surprised to receive. He was simply a nice man. And, mainly, he felt
a duty to St. Bernard, who built the place during the Crusades.

France is admired for outstanding service to the palate and the
nostrils, a sophisticated purveyor of luxury, class, and style. The
French tongue is fabled for wrapping around run-on consonants to
pleasing effect and, in private moments, for darting into intimate
places with accomplished accuracy. To the outside, France is slightly
effete, lacy at the cuffs—or red-nosed, walrus-mustached, and ber-
eted behind a thumbprinted bottle of Pernod.

Less known are solid, stalwart qualities that allowed France to
spread itself across the world. Colonial civil servants and settlers
have always represented a small segment of French society. They
brought their civilization in layers, steadily, with increasing numbers to replace those who died along the way. They simply placed
themselves above hardship. For example, malaria, or *paludisme,* was
nicknamed *palu.* The French diminished the disease by familiarizing
it. That it killed many of them was a mere setback.

The technology of empire was the simple, effective method of
the French heartlands. In Paris, researchers probed into biomedical
mysteries, but malaria was beaten by dumping pesticide out of light
aircraft. French aerospace engineers fashioned a supersonic jetliner,
but Upper Volta and Bora Bora, like the Charente Maritime, traveled in tough old Peugeot 404s. Citroën sedans flash down French-
built superhighways in the Ivory Coast, but the back roads depend
on the Citroën Deux Chevaux, which you can repair with a hairpin
in the middle of the desert. Others shaped the mechanics of their
empires in a similar manner, but not the people.

"The Americans go abroad and say, 'Hey, hurry up, watch, and
do it like us,' " Vincent, a French friend, remarked once in Africa.
"We say, 'Take your time, and be us.' "

Where others tried to suit themselves to local mentalities, until
they departed in frustration, the French reshaped local mentalities
to their own way. As a result, new generations see France as the
standard. African students might attend the University of Texas, but
they stop over in Paris on the way home.

For most French, settling the world is merely a noble role they have been called upon to perform. Outside the Chadian capital of N'Djamena, once named Fort-Lamy, a statue of General Lamy is inscribed, "He died for civilization."

The mission to civilize has never ceased. On trips to Africa, Mitterrand makes a stock speech to the local French communities, invited to watch their president up close and tingle to a recording of the "Marseillaise": They are France, and it is up to them to spread the word.

The "Marseillaise" gets 'em every time. Rouget de Lisle, thirty-two at the time, wrote it in 1792. It fit the mood of the French Revolution; but for all its stirring melody, it is drenched in blood. Sanche de Gramont wrote:

> It has always amused me to watch otherwise mild Frenchmen, the kind who wear long underwear in June and droopy cardigan sweaters to warm their livers, grow red in the face as veins in their necks bulge and their voices roar out about throat-cutting, outrage, parricidal projects, sanguinary despots, vengeance, expiring enemies, and impure blood soaking French furrows.

In an audience at Bujumbura, Jean-Marc, a paratroop sergeant-major, stiffened with pride at Mitterrand's words. He was no Socialist, but he was French. Jean-Marc was the archetype of the best in France abroad. Tall and straight, ruggedly handsome with a full black mustache, he spoke of duty and sacrifice with no trace of self-consciousness. He was unhappy that French troops were pulled out of Chad, but orders were orders. He missed his wife and family, he said, but that is life. Two minutes after meeting him, I had the impression he would step in front of a poisoned spear to save my life. He was the sort who would gently pick a fly out of his boeuf bourguignon without killing it but spray machine-gun fire into a crowd if ordered to do so.

I asked him how he felt about fighting to support African presidents who murdered their opponents and robbed their people blind. *"Bof,"* he said, with an easy shrug. "None of them is a saint. This is Africa."

Like most French, Jean-Marc took a pragmatic approach, extracting reality from rhetoric. His line of thinking recalled conversations

I had had with French officials when the United States invaded Grenada in 1983.

American concern in Grenada was symbolized by an airfield the Cubans were building on the small Caribbean island. Prime Minister Maurice Bishop denounced U.S. values with Marxist-Leninist catchphrases. Bishop, trying to see Reagan, was kept waiting for a week and then palmed off on a low-ranking State Department officer. His ambassador approached the U.S. envoy to Cuba, Wayne Smith, who pleaded in vain for permission to listen. Isolated, Bishop was toppled by hard-line associates and then shot. Reagan, on the excuse that American medical students were in danger, ordered an invasion.

The French saw the airfield as a long strip of blacktop necessary to any country, particularly an island. Whether it was to be a civilian airport or an airbase would be a political decision, not a technical one. Had Grenada been in the French sphere and the Cubans had beat them out for an airport contract, they would have cashed in by selling jetways and microwave ovens. Quai d'Orsay strategists noted that for all Bishop's speeches, free enterprise thrived and tourists needed no visas. They have seen the Soviet Union fail time and again in attempts to rent friends. In Grenada, the French would have done what they do in the Congo and Benin, two former colonies. When leaders espouse Soviet-type rhetoric, they roll their eyes in amusement. Whenever those leaders come to Paris, they are paraded down the Champs-Elysées. And French influence prevails.

The French world view fixes Paris squarely at the center. When Lawrence Eagleburger, an American diplomat widely respected for a knowledge of Europe, criticized Atlantic allies, the French daily of record, Le Monde, reported in its news columns, ". . . and he does not even have the excuse of being one of Reagan's inexperienced conservatives." No room was left for the possibility that Eagleburger might have had a point worth considering.

For France, expediency counts, and diplomacy is the art of making it palatable. Suggestions that such pragmatism might include an element of hypocrisy are dismissed with a wave. What, a French diplomat might ask, about the democratic principles of such American friends as Mobutu Sese Seko and Zia ul-Haq?

However they might bristle at real or perceived insult, the French skin is not thin. Foreigners have bashed them for centuries. In *Henry VI*, Shakespeare had Joan of Arc observe, "Spoken like a Frenchman, turn and turn again." Benjamin Franklin wrote, "I know not which are most rapacious, the English or the French, but the latter have, with their knavery, the most politeness."

Obviously enough, such characterizations do no justice to the vast number of individuals who display kindness and loyalty that confounds outsiders who thought they disliked the French. But in the end, whether it is applied with politeness, principle, or arrogant duplicity, the French excel by *savoir faire*. That takes in such vital details as using the right knife. But, more, it means knowing which things are important in life and seeing to it that the lesser orders at least make an attempt to appreciate them. The French are at their best at home, or in spheres abroad still regarded as *chasses gardées:* exclusive reserves. Around the edges, things can get touchy.

MADAME THONG'S Vietnamese restaurant is a hole in a Latin Quarter wall, one room with a tiny kitchen in back. The paint is flecked and the floor, though swept clean, is marked by years of use. Sauces come in cracked saucers and chipped crocks. The food is fabulous and dirt cheap. American friends showed us the place after reflecting carefully on whether to share the secret. Our third time back, something instantly felt wrong. The air was heavy with judgment. Madame Thong was all smiles. But a French civilizing mission had taken charge of the place.

At the large center table, seven people sat around the governor-general, whose lofty gaze commanded the room. He was standard-issue petit bourgeois, but this was his empire. I could hear him organizing the party. "Ah, *mon petit,* I have found the most excellent little *resto, typique mais splendide,* totally undiscovered, only the Vietnamese truck drivers know about it." He sat at the head of the table, burgundy-tinted cheeks puffed, neck slightly back to give his nose sufficient elevation. His voice filled the farthest crevices of the room, the perfect host-raconteur for the masses who oohed over dishes he had selected. "And nothing is more disagreeable," he had just pronounced about something or someplace, in an impressive blend of condescension and pomposity. Just then, an invasion, foreign interests in the colony, and Americans, *en plus.*

His gaze followed us to the small back table, expressing minor outrage and some wonderment that we were seating ourselves without a visa. Every few moments, he glanced over to see if we were preparing to leave. Finally, his eye fell on a copy of a book I had laid on the table, Theodore Zeldin's *France 1848–1945: Anxiety and Hypocrisy.* That was the final straw. He decided on heavy artillery.

"Ah, the Americans," he began loudly to his friends, but in slow distinct French just in case we were still on the phrasebook. "You can find nothing to eat in the United States except fried shrimp." The "fried shrimp" came out in the sort of flat-accented, smeared English of someone who thinks he is imitating an American dialect. At that, he glanced over to check where the shot had landed. I laughed. He paused a moment. Anything further would require direct confrontation. No, this would be too much. And what if he lost? Suddenly, he tossed his head to his friends in a silent declaration of victory.

Peace fell upon the room.

CHAPTER THREE

France d'Outre-mer

CLOCKS ARE NO obsession with the French; there is no Big Ben, no Greenwich from which to fix a mean time. The Eiffel Tower has only restaurants and aviation warning lights. Notre-Dame Cathedral marks time with bells. The eight o'clock television newscasts start whenever the commercials finish. Time is money in France, all right. But clocks don't define life the way they might elsewhere any more than maps do. Wherever the hands might fall on a clock face, night or day, some Frenchman is standing in the sun in his neighborhood park, playing *pétanque*.

When the clocks note dinnertime in Marseilles, the *pétanque* balls are clacking in Réunion. The sun sets in Réunion, but the game picks up in Pondicherry. Some time after, the matches begin in New Caledonia. Then across Polynesia in the South Pacific, into the Caribbean and the edge of South America. By the time the *boules* roll to a stop in Miquelon, players are limbering up in Marseilles.

The game, rooted in southern France, blends bowling with horseshoes. It is taken seriously enough to be a blood sport, but it requires a subtle finesse. Small iron balls are thrown toward one another, launched with the elaborate care a Frenchman uses to deliver an adverb from his palate. But in mother France and the empire, the players have in common only their blue, white, and red *cartes d'identité*. And a state of mind.

In St.-Denis, capital of Réunion, the teams are diverse: tough-looking Malagasys in torn shirts, dark Tamils in red baseball caps and gold earrings, huge Africans from the coast, Chinese in aviator sunglasses. There are also, often in separate clusters, *les z'oreilles*. A *z'oreille* (from "ear," in French) is a Frenchman from the *métropole;* not to split hairs, a colonizer. Creole populations across the empire use the term with varying degrees of affection and scorn. It comes from the newly arrived Frenchman's habit of extending an ear to better capture the colorful distortions of creole dialects.

Creole is a sweeping term for people descended from early settlers. But the French, unlike the English, were hardly reticent about fraternizing with the locals. Their anthropological lexicon is vast. In every corner of the empire, strikingly handsome people emerge in shades from ebony to cream, with eyes and hair that confound categorization.

As it happens, Réunion has no "natives," no descendants of people living there when the colonizers first arrived. The island was uninhabited, and all local residents trace themselves back to Asians and Africans brought in by the French. Similarly, Guadeloupe, Martinique, and Guiana were peopled mainly by Africans shipped over to cut cane. In the Pacific, large native populations remain. Each *département* and territory is a singular microcosm with characteristics all its own. But transfers within the civil service and the military, refugees from former colonies, and free movement have shuffled the ethnic deck completely.

Technically, it doesn't matter. Everyone—Creole, native, and *z'oreille*—is French. But views differ on what that means.

For the black, brown, and yellow French who grew up believing in their ancestors the Gauls, all the pieces are part of the whole. "In Guadeloupe, we say everyone sees midday from his own doorway," a black nurse in Paris told me, meaning France is simply how you see it. That is, in fact, an old French saying. Outsiders who try to use "French" as a euphemism for white risk a reproachful stare.

But for many *z'oreilles,* far from home, each little piece of *France d'outre-mer* is a reductio ad absurdum of France itself. The DOM-TOM are, in effect, bush league training grounds for perfecting those inimitable traits that Francophobes and Francophiles love to seize upon. Distance from Paris seems to exaggerate attitudes and actions, whatever they are.

Réunion is a splendid example. I flew into St.-Denis one afternoon from Johannesburg, after three weeks among people who defined their colors sharply and defended social barriers as though their lives depended upon it. Here was France in shorts and knee socks, racially broadminded yet broadly racist, with social mores that blended modern with medieval.

Driving around, I might have been anywhere else in the country: down rue Pasteur to avenue Charles de Gaulle and rue de Paris, all marked in green-bordered blue and white street signs. The usual cast of characters was enshrined in pompous stone statues, plus the local hero, Roland Garros, pioneer flyer, who is honored in Paris by a tennis stadium. There was, as expected, a somber stone monument reading: "From l'Ile de la Réunion, to its heroic sons in the Great War, 1914–1918. They were worthy of France." Altogether, 607,000 soldiers from the colonies fought for France in World War I.

St.-Denis was clearly built for people who came to stay, by people who had erected other such towns in similar climes. The governor's mansion is handsome and huge, porticoed, white, and spectacularly landscaped. It is near the water, commanding the beach, with walls thick enough to bounce back the heaviest cannonball a Dutch fleet might muster. Straight, narrow streets mark out blocks of what is loosely known as French colonial architecture. Stone rowhouses are painted in light pastels, with a patina of mildew and weathering that obliterates centuries of differences in construction dates. Second-floor balconies hang in front of tall, louvered wooden shutters, fastened by elaborately scrolled iron fancywork. Blazing red and deep purple bougainvillea spill over walls. Palms wound in shiny green vines rise to roof levels.

The oldest buildings show graceful, almost delicate facades; but gates are high, carved doors are solid as iron, stone walls are massive. They were designed to stay cool under the sun, remind civil servants of home, impress the locals, and withstand the odd volley of paving stones should things turn nasty. Not surprisingly, the cathedral and the university were built to last.

The British, in their outposts, leaned toward wood-frame buildings and corrugated tin, as if they did not want the overhead to cut into profits. They were, in essence, camping out. Not the French.

As in any *arrondissement* in Paris, St.-Denis shop fronts bear the large green crosses of pharmacies, the red signs reading *Tabac,* and the usual run of Prisunic and Félix Potin chain stores. And, as in

Paris, there are the slightly skewed manifestations of a U.S.-accented omniculture of self-service boutiques and restaurants: Le Maryland, Big Burger, Kick Self.

From St.-Denis, I drove west, following Highway N1, marked as though it were exactly the same road I would stay on to Paris, if my Renault 12 had pontoons. Off to the left, cracked asphalt snaked over rusty trestle bridges and through rock tunnels, engineering marvels of their time that would serve well on a Third World superhighway. But this was France, and that was an abandoned old road. A new, four-lane divided *autoroute,* smooth as a dinner plate, was built out over the water. And I was battling an afternoon traffic jam of drivers in Peugeots and Renaults, each flashing his lights in the sun, delivering that lovable signal which translates roughly to: move your ass, *connard,* don't you realize *I* am on this road and I don't care if you are already over the speed limit and have engine trouble and don't want to upset your aged grandmother and are caught in this lane by trucks on your right; you are blocking the path between me and my *gigot d'agneau.*

People are not normally at their best behind the wheel. Down the road, at St.-Paul, I stopped to take a closer look. A twenty-four-year-old named Jean-Marie, a dark Creole with Negroid hair, hitched a ride.

"How's life? Awful. I'm a mechanic, but no work. Maybe I get an odd job, a few francs, and then nothing for months. It's bad in France but worse here. No one cares about us. This is no life."

Did anyone consider independence as an option? He smiled uneasily and then seemed to relax, deciding I was merely a harmless simpleton.

"I don't think so."

Had we been in Brittany, or Corsica, the idea of separation from France would have been no more likely, but the question might have provoked discussion. In Réunion, however, such issues are magnified by the distance; you stand squarely on one side of it or the other.

On the next stop down the coast, I had a look at the extremes to which Frenchness can be amplified in the outposts of empire. A lingering sore throat worsened, and I wondered where I could find someone to prescribe antibiotics on a raw, jungle coast in the

Indian Ocean. After St.-Paul, the road narrowed to two-lane black-top and led back in time. It meandered past thatched huts and coconut groves. Then a ubiquitous French stone town marker appeared: St.-Leu.

In a gleaming glass-fronted shopping complex, I spotted the large green cross of a pharmacy. Next door was a clinic; its neon sign offered therapeutic massage and a range of paramedical treats. A lovely blonde in hospital white sat at the receptionist desk inside. Ah, joy, I thought. Hope.

She heard me approach and, with evident pain, wrenched her eyes away from the latest issue of *Marie-Claire*. Her glance would have taken Flaubert a page to describe. That a receptionist's function is to receive is beside the point; I had barged into her circle. She deduced instantly that I had nothing to offer that she might want. And I obviously wanted something from her. Well, okay, dammit, there I was, and there was no escape short of getting up and leaving, which would be unacceptably direct. I would be permitted to have my say. But it had better be good.

Was there a doctor in the neighborhood? I asked, with elaborate courtesy, taking care not to leer at her breasts or the makeup she had elaborately applied to attract attention.

It wasn't good enough. She looked through me as if I were made of glass, and not particularly clean glass, and scowled slightly.

"The other side of the pharmacy," she said, dropping her eyes back to the magazine without bothering to add, "Can't you read, you nitwit?"

It was not, by the way, because I was a foreigner. Thin-skinned Americans tend to make that mistake. I was an intrusion, like some noisome insect to be swatted peevishly aside. Such displays of *mauvais caractère* can be reversed with volleys of gradually lessening hostility. For that, French is essential even if your adversary speaks perfect English. It is not a question of communication but of civilization. Learning French implies that one has sought to be civilized, and learning good French means one has taken it seriously. It gets worse. By speaking a strange language, the Frenchman risks the calamity of making awkward, funny noises or falling short of words, seeming somehow silly. And, symbolically, he—or she, in this case—would be handing you the advantage. For that, you must offer some motivation. A belt in the chops is fastest, but the Napoleonic legal code is even more complex.

The next stop, as often happens, was the other extreme.

"Of course the doctor will see you," replied a cheerful nurse, warmth coloring her features. "Make yourself comfortable there, and it will be just a moment." She said, in fact, *"une petite minute,"* meaning a lot of minutes, but the intention was that it would be as soon as it could possibly be done.

Dr. Bernard Bouchara smiled broadly. He briskly finished the medical business and wanted to chat. I decided to try my independence question. He was pleasant but firm.

"We're in France, only 10,000 kilometers away. No one wants it to be any different. Oh, maybe 1 percent, people who don't have this or that. But this is France and without that, there would be nothing."

He warmed to the theme and grabbed a pile of booklets from his desk. "Look, health cards. Where do you see such medical care anywhere around here? France is doing everything. I came here fifteen years ago, and it is incredible what they have achieved just since then. From Marseilles, for instance, there is very little difference."

Intangibles aside, he had a point. Back up the road at St.-Paul, the island's first capital, the process was obvious.

Outside St.-Paul are a cluster of simple caves where French settlers first sheltered in the 1600s. Nearby, a graveyard of moldering stones and wrought iron-railed monuments traces their history in chipped inscriptions.

"Evaste Feuille, captain of long voyages, killed in a duel." "Olivier Le Vasseur, called La Buse, pirate, Scourge of the South Seas, executed at St.-Paul in 1730." "Leconte de Lisle, poet." Small graves, with legends recalling short life spans, attest to the fevers and epidemics. Ornate mausoleums pay tribute to governors, commandants, and merchant kings.

A colorful poster tacked to the moss-covered wall outside bears a new inscription: "Vote for Paul Bernand, to build the future."

Back in St.-Denis, I met Pascal, a young French disk jockey in a local disco and acknowledged master of the few ceremonies of Réunion evenings. A friendly cook at the pizzeria introduced us.

Pascal started sketching maps for me and then grabbed my elbow. "What the hell, come on." He weaved through the darkened streets in his rattling Cadillac, pointing out every public house that wasn't locked past 11 P.M.

"Anyone looking for a good time has got to go somewhere else," he said. Somewhere else meant Paris. "There's not much for young people to do around here. A few parties, maybe, but it is boring. The local French are very racist. They don't mix much." I asked if local people wanted to separate from France. "Oh, there's an independence movement but it's not ripe. You've got to reflect. If they go independent, then what? There's no industry, nothing."

He wished me luck and went back to his buddies.

I tried the Milord, a dismal basement nightclub. It reeked of the tropical mildew that attacks any establishment that fights its surroundings by laying carpet and overdoing the plush sofas. I was joined instantly by a Swiss lady with skin like a crocodile and teeth to match. Her conversation revolved around a thirst for champagne. "A glass?" "A bottle." I steered her toward beer. Minutes later, I asked for the bill. Just like Paris: two drinks, listed at the equivalent of ten dollars each, somehow came to forty-five dollars.

A few days later, I took my political questions to the politicians.

In the town of St.-André, I found Serge Sinamalé, a dapper little Indian, pottering in the courtyard of his ramshackle home. A former leader of the Réunion Communist Party, he turned in his card and became a founding director of the Réunion Independence Movement, the MIR.

"We never try for big demonstrations, or push for high membership," he said, "because there is too much repression. If a militant works in a garage, or is a domestic servant of a Frenchman, he is kicked out the door. That is economic repression. We are not thousands and thousands. All colonial elections are rigged, anyway."

If there were a free referendum, how many people would choose independence? Ten percent, Sinamalé guessed. Then he thought again. "Well, maybe 5 percent. The colonial situation is in place, and people don't know the truth."

He drew a simple picture. France built a colony to tend the ships plying the spice route to Asia. When that role diminished, the economy was converted to agriculture, and indentured labor was ferried in. Eventually, agriculture was neglected. Réunion, he concluded, was a client state of 550,000 inhabitants, 40 percent Indian, 40 percent mixed blood, and 20 percent *z'oreilles*.

"Now we are only a captive market for the French to unload their finished products," he said, emotion speeding his words along. "We import milk and honey, animals, plants, fruits, coffee, tea, spices, straw. This is a tropical country, and we import straw."

He reeled off numbers from memory and then dug out sheaves of papers to make his points: in 1945, exports equaled imports; by 1977, exports were 23 percent of imports; in 1983, 10 percent.

"Small producers buy animal fats and oils, byproducts, and we spend good money for nicely packaged cooking oil from France in the supermarkets," he fumed. "Rum is sold in bulk here at five francs a liter, cut three times, and comes back at nineteen and twenty francs a bottle. We produce a fine quality of brown sugar that people love in Paris. But they buy it from us at two francs a kilo, refine it to white sugar in France, and then sell it at 12.82 a kilo here. Kids see on television and are taught in school white sugar is better. That is colonization."

Sinamalé had other themes.

"They teach us Europe, the French language, but not what is ours. That is colonialism, even if it is more subtle than before. The form has changed but, at the bottom, it is the same. Some 150,000 Réunion people are in France. They have seen it is not El Dorado. People say, 'Dirty nigger, go home.' They are learning."

Switching the subject, he sprang to a huge map of the Indian Ocean. He jabbed his finger at dots of islands.

"France maintains Réunion as a military base. They have 3,500 men, in all services, ready day and night. Whoever controls the Indian Ocean controls the world. While the U.S. battles for rights on Diego Garcia, France has Réunion, Mayotte, and islands no one knows about. What do we get? They pollute the waters, and we can't even eat our own fish."

He said his movement had expected a change with a left-wing victory in France in 1981 but instead found the situation worsening. At a "point of no return," he said, strategy rests on spreading the word and raising consciousness. The MIR is the only independence movement that operates legally, in the open, he said, but other groups were working clandestinely. An Air France vacation village was burned in 1984, and the odd explosion echoes loudly on the peaceful island. Would the MIR condone violence as a last resort? He shrugged. "If imperialism obliges us, that will come."

An hour later, I was hearing the other extreme, surrounded by the polished wood paneling and tapestries of Government House. Sinamalé seemed farther than twenty miles away.

"Oouuuf, you know there are arsonists everywhere in the world; it is a little premature to refer to an organization, is it not?" said the political adviser to the *préfet* (governor), adding a slight reverse spin of irony to the word "organization." The adviser, Adolphe Colrat, was in his thirties. But he was an ageless, seamless product of a fast-track civil service leadership system which is one of France's highest achievements. His uniform was a well-cut gray suit, with a Bordeaux silk tie. Smooth, charming, assured, he left his interlocutor room to question, but only on pain of severe self-doubt.

Asked about Sinamalé's economic statistics, he flicked an immaculate fingernail.

"You understand, we do these figures somewhat artificially as if there was really a balance to be measured. You cannot categorize these things, from the *métropole* to la Réunion. It is the same economy. We should do more to provide economic activity, I agree, perhaps in meat, cattle, pigs. We are self-sufficient in pork. We must create a new generation of agriculturists, revitalize the higher elevations of the island."

Education is strictly the same in the departments and territories as in France, he said, but in 1983 they added an optional course in creole language and civilization. They might, in fact, welcome new kindergarteners in creole.

Colrat had no figures on movement from Réunion to the *métropole*. "We know 500,000 people a year fly in and out of the airport, to all destinations, but it is, after all, a domestic flight to Paris."

The word "colony," he stressed again and again, was absolutely inapt. Réunion was settled as part of France and was never anything else. And as for separatists, they hardly totaled 100 votes in recent municipal elections. "Here," he concluded, "it is completely different from the atmosphere in the Antilles [Caribbean]."

OR IN THE South Pacific. Whatever Réunion may typify among the departments and territories, it is among the least explosive. All the DOM-TOMs keep French authorities occupied poring over the extensive files of secret services charged with keeping discreet order. When Colrat spoke, the ferment was in Guadeloupe where *indépendantistes* had killed a few people with random bombs to make their point. Caribbean independence leaders organized a meeting for separatists from the DOM-TOMs, Sinamalé included, to jointly denounce French rule. But the real crisis came in New Caledonia.

At the end of 1984, Melanesian natives and white settlers went to war. Before the hard-minded gendarmes from Paris could impose a tense quiet, a score of people died. A few Frenchmen were shot on isolated farms and back roads; ten Melanesians, Kanaks, were massacred in a vigilantes' ambush; police shot dead several *indépendantiste* leaders.

For nights on end, French families sat over their braised endives watching on television wild-haired brown youths stamp on all they held dear. It was Algeria all over again, ran the comment in the cafes. *Alors, ça recommence.* It was not close to being Algeria. But here, twenty-five years later, scenes were repeating themselves. Once again, it was suitcases or shotguns. In living color, frightened housewives loaded bedding, cooking pots, and small children into battered station wagons. French farmers, lean and leathery, declaimed in earthy backcountry accents: "We've been here three generations, and we're not going anywhere. If blood has to flow, let it flow." "Me afraid? I'll cover that fucking roadblock all alone—with my rifle."

And all around the empire, dark-skinned French watched the militant Socialist Kanak National Liberation Front—the FLNKS—win concessions from Paris. With a schedule of referendums and increasing autonomy, the future suggested a choice between independence or bloodshed.

But that was New Caledonia. In Mayotte, not far from Réunion, voters fought to stay closer to France than Paris wanted. With all the feared "contagion" from the Pacific, independence movements elsewhere made modest gains. And even in New Caledonia, Article

88 of de Gaulle's constitution could turn, once again, a French defeat into victory. It stipulates, "The Republic or the Community may make agreements with states that wish to associate themselves with the Community to develop their civilizations." France, freed of responsibility, might continue its mission.

It is not simple. After New Caledonia, partly as a result, the situation worsened in Guadeloupe and Guiana. The threat and the response vary widely; each of the DOMs and TOMs is examined farther on, along with former colonies only figuratively in the empire. Few separatists expect Paris to turn loose the far-flung bits it describes as inseparable parts of France. But those sensitive to the themes of decolonization and peoples' rights see danger ahead. Violence at barricades and noisy strikes tarnish the French image as a champion of developing nations. Bombs in remote marketplaces are heard around the world.

L'Expansion magazine tried to put a price tag on the DOM-TOM in 1985. Together, their trade deficit came to about twenty billion francs. With nickel, New Caledonia's export earnings came to half of its import bill. In Polynesia, however, exports covered 6 percent of imports. Of course, most imports were from France. Education, defense, and government services cost twenty-three billion francs in 1985. And social security taxes from the DOM-TOM cover only 30 percent of what the state pays out. Capital investment and bank loans added billions more to the bill. So did subsidized losses for services such as Air France.

With 2.4 million French out of work, 400,000 people from overseas territories in the *métropole* might be regarded as an expense. The rate of immigration is unsettling. In 1954, mainland residents from the DOM-TOM numbered only 24,200.

Even on Clipperton, where no one lives, the costs are high. The speck of land, named for an English pirate, is 900 miles off Mexico at the center of rich tuna beds. The Mexicans took it from France in 1858 and occupied it with seven men and their families. Then, caught up in a revolution, Mexico forgot they were there. One by one, they died off. Finally, the garrison dwindled to a single man, a tyrannical Indian. The three surviving women murdered him with a hammer. That same day, by coincidence, a passing American ship stopped by, looking for secret German bases. That was in 1917. The

French reestablished their claim in 1931 and now are building a port.

As finance minister, Giscard d'Estaing once murmured, "These are expensive little dancers." But as president, and in the opposition, he argued loudly that each territory is vital to the glory of France.

The return of the right in 1986 brought new emphasis on overseas France. The DOM-TOM Secretariat was given full cabinet status under Bernard Pons, a confidant of Chirac's. He reminded reporters that no other European country was situated in the Americas, the Indian Ocean, and the South Pacific. And he exulted: "Our overseas departments and territories are France's joker in Europe for the twenty-first century."

Pons, just back from the South Pacific territory of Wallis and Futuna, promised changes. For one thing, Wallis would get television. And Futuna would get electricity.

Until further notice the Tricolor goes up every morning. In spite of striking differences, small scenes, vignettes, and recurrent casts of characters stitch the DOMs and TOMs into a single sprawling patchwork that is France in the extreme. Everywhere there is a Restaurant Tonkinois, or Mandarin, or both, featuring red flocking, cheap rosé wine, and *soupe chinoise:* transparent noodles, shrimps, and sliced pork, served up by someone whose roots in Vietnam were severed in the 1950s. There is always a hard-eyed blonde, skin tanned to the texture of a grapefruit, wearing an immodestly short sundress and walking a small gray dog. You can bank on a Café de Paris, most likely frequented by multihued hookers and youths of proven skill at *le windsurfing.*

The pace is always slower than in the *métropole,* but not by much. Direct-dial telephones, daily flights, and satellites swallow up the space in between. A global "regional" television network links all bits of the empire. And life has changed. There is less time for the old colonial qualities of bonhomie and hospitality to ripen under the sun.

In the past, only a small percentage of Frenchmen ever ventured out to live in the empire. When it was tough, the washouts went home or slowly dissolved in their Pernod. They came out by choice, or they were driven overseas by motives strong enough to make them stay and try to like it. Settlers raised families, and each new generation dug in more deeply. The hard, simple life required a strong reliance on neighbors. People often felt a sense of mission, if not to civilize, at least to stand by the land they made flourish. People who came out from the *métropole* for a tour of duty felt a part of their commitment.

Much of the old settler stock remains across the empire. But life is easier now, and *z'oreilles* are likely to be disgruntled city folk who can find no work elsewhere, or who were rotated out by the luck of the draw.

HEADING BACK TO Paris from Réunion, I encountered one guy who did not want to be working on a sunny Sunday in some outpost of the empire. Unfortunately, he was a cop, assigned to airport security. Those who wonder why foreigners do not always rank the French among their favorite people would do well to consult him.

He was short, with a mousy mustache lounging under dark sunglasses. He looked me over with the light smirk of a French bureaucrat anxious to wield his small allotment of power, and I knew I was in trouble. A dull stare and passive resistance would have ruined his fun. But I needed something.

I had brought a dozen rolls of exposed but unprocessed film from southern Africa, along with a few dozen fresh ones. Please, I asked, could he check them by hand? It was a simple courtesy granted in such relaxed places as India, China, and Bulgaria. In fact, only at Roissy Airport in Paris (and once in Vienna, to be accurate) had I been refused before. His smirk widened, and he pointed to the sign over the X-ray machine promising no harm to film.

Yes, I explained, it should not matter one time, if the machine was working properly. But I traveled a lot, and every X-ray built up a cumulative effect. That was what a Kodak engineer had explained once, and I had lost irreplaceable pictures to an X-ray before.

"In there," he said, pointing to the machine, beaming with pleasure at my growing concern.

Look, I explained, I'd love to risk it, but I can't really go back to Botswana and hope that a lion leaps up just when my camera happens to be lying at hand on the breakfast table.

"In there."

The more I insisted, the worse it got. People began to back up in line.

"Listen, I have had film ruined before," I repeated. He lunged for the kill.

"In France?"

Herein was the game. He was playing *mauvaise foi*. I could say, "Yes, France," and prolong the play. I would then demand his superior, who would support him. And they would both amuse themselves all afternoon by sifting through my mountain of hand luggage.

"No," I admitted. "It was not in France."

"Aha," he exclaimed, managing somehow to double the size of his chest. I half expected him to crow *cocorico* and flap his arms. "This machine . . ." with a pause to deliver the word that would brook no further discussion, "is French."

I, like every other passerby and freebooter who had rashly considered making a dent in Réunion, gave up.

CHAPTER FOUR

Corsica: Empire at Home

A FAVORITE THEME of authorities explaining the inherent Frenchness of the overseas *départements* is, "But Guadeloupe (or Réunion) is as French as Corsica." You hear it often. You do not, however, hear it in Corsica.

That little island of breath-catching beauty and blood feuds has flown French colors since 1769. Illustrious Frenchmen have emerged from its ancient stone ports; Napoléon, for one. Corsicans built much of France's empire and died in its wars. The island is ninety minutes' flight from Paris, an afternoon's sail from Marseilles. Everything is there: Prisunic and Monoprix, perfumed poodles, and the kiosks papered in magazine covers of the nation's luminaries of the hour.

But Corsicans in the north revere a man from their mountains, exiled two centuries ago: Pasquale Paoli, who led the island during its only fourteen years of independence in two millenia of resisting outsiders. In the south, they like Napoléon because he colonized France from Corsica.

Corsica is neither a DOM nor a TOM. It is France, pure and simple, as though the 100 miles of Mediterranean between its north coast and the mainland were a bridged river. But it is not French. To test this, drive around in a car with a license plate ending in "75," for Paris. For years, an average of two bombs a day have ripped the fronts off businesses owned by continental Frenchmen.

It is not that most Corsicans want independence from France. But even conservative dyed-in-the-flannel Francophile politicians do their ward-heeling in the blend of Italian, Arabic, Latin, and Catalan that Corsicans speak with towering pride. All parties display the same symbol of Corsica: the black Moor's head—a slave demanding freedom—with a white blindfold pushed up onto the brow, ready to look any executioner in the eye.

Corsica is the most clearly defined of a handful of regions of heartland France where people consider themselves more than just French. Before France was diced into departments, regions grappled with Paris for power. In Brittany, the Basque country, Languedoc, and Alsace, aging farmers and young intellectuals argue their right for a separate identity. They take the issue with dead seriousness. Some want "Basque" or "Breton" written in their French passports; or they insist that their children learn history and arithmetic in their own disappearing languages. They want regional assemblies with more control—and especially more of the taxes they pay to Paris —to settle local issues.

Within these mainland regions, families link themselves tightly together, preserving traditions, cuisines, and languages. Occasionally, Breton terrorists will bomb Versailles Palace or a television relay station so France does not forget they are out there, unsatisfied. Cultural Minister Jack Lang set up a national council for languages and cultures to protect minority tongues. The right wing howled that French was imperiled. But Lang argued the reverse: by preserving disappearing languages, France might encourage other European nations not to dump French as a second language in favor of English.

Mitterrand visited Basque territory and applauded efforts to seek an identity. He said, "I will always be at the side of those who wish to exist at their deepest levels." But, he added, if the question is autonomy, or independence, "I say clearly, face to face, with conviction: No!" He was treated to whistles and a snatch of the Basque tongue: *"Mitterrand kamporat."* Mitterrand out. (And someone stole a police car from his guards, with a secret route map, itinerary, and list of radio frequencies lying on the front seat.)

The Basque problem is bitter and bloody. In two years, the *Groupe antiterroriste de libération* killed twenty-three people in French Basque country, including eight who had nothing to do with the lingering dirty war. The GAL, mainly demobilized French veterans of Algerian War terrorism, fight against the clandestine Basque organization, Iparretarrak. Early in 1986, Iparretarrak set off a fresh round of bombs and promised to pursue an "armed struggle" for independence.

But even with the Basques, identity issues on the mainland have an air of unreality. In a fast-traveling Citroën, Basqueland has no borders. Normandy blurs into Brittany; ancient political and cultural borders are marked by little more than flags in ancient colors or stylized signs on the *autoroute*.

But there is no mistaking Corsica. Its mountains loom straight up out of the water. Vineyards climb up the slopes to villages carved from the rocky peaks, with gates that have slammed shut behind every transient occupier: Phoenicians, Etruscans, Carthaginians, Romans, Byzantines, Saracens, Moors, Genoese, Pisans, Iberians. Its ports are redolent of juniper and oleanders, ripe nectarines, spices and salt breezes, the smoky sweet scent that attracted so many invaders.

In Paoli's old capital of Corte, perched up high at the dead center of the island, computerized tellers dispense 500-franc notes to the passing *pinzuti,* the continental Frenchmen. But up the narrow streets of rough paving stones, the old life goes on. Corsicans smoke their hams, splash out hearty red wine, comment on the sky, and wait to see what new surprise the Mediterranean will pitch up on their shores.

I HAD BEEN fascinated by the idea of Corsica since my first day as a correspondent. I shared a tiny Congolese hotel room with a fearless and good-hearted Corsican photographer named Bodini who ate garlic cloves as if they were apples. "Me, I like fishing, tranquility, and women," he announced, suggesting that that was the first line of the Corsican national anthem. My kind of place.

I flew down next to an immense Frenchwoman in a flowered muumuu who cuddled two Yorkies in a padded basket on her lap. On landing, the steward announced, *"Bonnes vacances,"* as if there were no other reason for being in Calvi. But we had flown far beyond Cannes. The man at the car rental desk wore only satin jogging shorts in Hertz yellow. "This island has produced three great men: Napoléon, Tino Rossi, and Domé," he said, tapping his dark brown bare chest. "Me." Joking over and business done, he stopped a moment to size me up, with sharp gray eyes set among deep crags. "Here," he said, "is a map of Corsica. That way, you also have a portrait of my face."

With Domé's map, I found the village of Pigna. Its little stone plaza hangs off the brow of a mountain, and a wide, fragrant valley sweeps off to the sand beach far below. Toni Casalonga, master engraver and painter, runs a gallery in a medieval house up a twisting cobbled lane from the square.

"In fact," he explained, with a slight chuckle, "we are absolutely like an overseas department, and we don't even have any distinguishing marks to set us apart: no black skin, no unusual way of dressing. . . . But am I against being in France? That is like being against the handbrake in a car. You don't want it until you need it."

Casalonga is an aesthete, dapper and gentle, far from the stock stereotype of the rough, mustachioed Corsican. He has given a lot of thought to his people's dilemmas. "Is someone here first Corsican or French?" he began, repeating my question. "It depends on how you put it to him. The Corsican is highly sensitive to being regarded a traitor, as somehow unreliable or unpatriotic. If he perceives a challenge, he will answer defensively, 'Of course, I am as French as the next guy.' But, in the end, it will come out: he is Corsican.

"These are questions a Corsican must never put to himself."

More to the point, he said, is the question of dependence. With its agriculture crippled by lack of field hands and high transport costs, Corsica depends on France for virtually everything: food, clothing, fuel, even refrigerator repairmen. Economically that is bad; psychologically, it is disastrous.

Casalonga is not bothered by the more than one million tourists who come to the island each year, mainly from the continent. Tourism, he said, might push Paris finally to spend the money necessary to lift Corsica out of its lingering stagnation. "We have a choice between that or nothing at all," he said. "We are not closed to the outside. Among the young, there is more than unemployment; there is social despair. They see no future, no challenge, and they are ripe for extremists." He added, "But we have to be careful to preserve a balance, not to let the numbers become so overwhelming that they destroy the past."

The past in Corsica is the present. The Genoese, driven out in the
1760s after four centuries of occupation, are reviled as though they
left last month. Two clans dominate the island, drawing strength
from family alliances dating back uncounted generations. But the
history books piled high in Casalonga's gallery describe a Corsica
that is going fast.

Early accounts describe how islanders resisted when the king of
France answered a plea from Genoa to help suppress rebellion.
When the French established control, they took over sovereignty.
By now, it doesn't matter whether historical incidents are exag-
gerated. They are the patrimony.

In his pamphlet, *Life of Pasquale Paoli,* illustrated by Casalonga,
René Emmanuelli writes: "This is the response of a militiaman,
fallen gravely wounded into the hands of the French who, surprised
at the lack of any organized medical corps, asked: 'How do you save
yourselves without ambulances or doctors?' The soldier replied: 'We
die.'"

In the early 1800s, when the winds were contrary the island went
months at a time without a single vessel from the mainland. The
first steamship arrived in 1830, an event marred only by an attempt
by Bastia sailors to set it afire as a threat to their jobs. Three years
later, with regular service to Toulon, 2,899 travelers got off in
Corsica.

One early visitor was Alexandre Dumas. He wrote:

> A traveler arrives in a village, walks down the length of the
> main street, chooses the house that pleases him most and knocks
> at the door. An instant later, the master appears, invites him to
> come in, offers him half of his dinner and all of his bed, if he
> has but one, and the following morning, on accompanying the
> visitor out, thanks him for the preference shown. There is, of
> course, not the slightest question of compensation, the master
> regarding as an insult the merest word on the subject.

Such welcomes still apply, or nearly so, in remote parts of the island.
But it is clear that they are reserved for people not intending to take
charge of the house.

A dusty document puts into clearer focus the repeated assertion of modern French administrations that Corsica has been an equal part of the whole since it became a department in 1790. In an 1836 report to Paris, a departing prosecutor general named Mottet noted that Corsica cost France three times what it contributed despite rich agricultural potential.

He warned of a material problem and a moral problem, each linked to the other. Once, Mottet said, he asked a landowner why a river was allowed to run across a wide plain without watering it.

"A canal would be easy," he told me, "but sharing the water would be impossible."

"Why? You could make an ordinance."

"We could never agree to it."

"The authorities could impose it for you."

"Yes, but who would enforce it?"

"The courts."

"The courts!" he said with a bitter smile. "No, *monsieur,* sharing the water would be done by rifle fire."

Mottet continued:

There is the real state of Corsica. Everything is done by rifle fire. Law is nothing; force is everything. . . . Need we have statistics to resume the moral state? I knew of, in 1834, 416 attacks on individuals, including 188 murders, assassinations or attempts and 228 injuries, more or less grave. That is 20 times, 30 times more than in any other area and the population is only 196,000 souls. . . .

The state must not depend on the use of force; experience has shown that 20 times. . . . The Empire and the Restoration have sent generals with full powers: arbitrary arrests, detentions without trial, repeated executions. The Corsicans have seen it all, have suffered it all with impassivity and have remained the same. . . .

It would be folly to expect the country to improve by itself, without the help of money or a modified administration. If nothing is done, Corsica will be in 50 years what it is today, and we will have spent a hundred million francs more with no profit, even for the island. One can discuss the system to follow, but one point remains beyond discussion: It is that we must occupy this unhappy country and occupy it as soon as possible.

Ajaccio, for better or for worse, is occupied. In the palm-fringed capital, wedding cake apartment blocks and office buildings muscle in on the medieval quarter. Traffic chokes the cours Napoléon, a standard-issue Main Street France. But the boom came 125 years after Mottet's report. As predicted, Corsica stayed the same for half a century. Then World War I killed 40,000 Corsicans, one of every five. Thousands of others stayed on the continent or shipped out to the colonies. The island struggled along, moribund.

Then France lost Algeria, and thousands of *pieds-noirs* settled in Corsica. They received the subsidies and credits for which Corsicans had been pleading. Newcomers prospered, bought land, and built businesses. The bad blood still circulates. Today, the ratio of what Paris spends on Corsica to what it earns is perhaps twice the figure of Mottet's time. But Corsica is an assured market, and that is part of the problem.

In Ajaccio today, points of view are as extreme as the architecture.

Paul Bernard, the prefect, was frank but reassuring in a comfortable French prefect's way. He recalled that the Socialist government passed a Special Statute for Corsica in 1982, setting up a regional assembly and offering economic incentives. That, he said, passed its difficult period of apprenticeship and was taking hold. In 1985, Paris contracted to spend one billion francs to the region's 300,000 for specific projects in agriculture and fishing, infrastructure, youth training, housing, and tourism.

"People here have rejected separatism and terrorism," Bernard said. "They have shown their will to manage serenely the affairs of the region."

In December 1984, when mysterious terrorists sprayed machine-gun fire at an elite CRS police unit and killed three officers, 30,000 Corsicans of all parties marched against violence. At 10 percent of the population, the prefect noted, that was equivalent to five million people in the streets on the mainland. Union leaders painted "Jobs, not bombs" on the side of a bullet-riddled van. Separatists and autonomists polled less than 15 percent of the vote in 1983, and they hold six of the regional assembly's sixty-three seats.

But young Corsicans are still discouraged by political and social mores of the past, Bernard acknowledged. Hard hit by the economy, some are attracted to violence.

"Our goal is to demonstrate to the youth that if they work hard and honestly, they will gain from it," he said. "The youth are afraid. But if we can show the state is no longer an accomplice of the system, and it supports the honest citizen, this will disappear."

Also, the prefect added, "We have made the wager of democracy. We preserve essential liberties, no repression, no undue police presence. In the end, democracy will carry the day."

I had already noticed a relaxed approach to security. At the gate, a bored gendarme did not even glance at my ominous-looking black bag. Departing later from Calvi was a refreshing break in my running war with French airport security inspectors. An officer briefly surveyed my huge pile of hand baggage and frowned on finding my portable computer. With sincere concern, he asked, "How can you take work with you on vacation?"

Across the street from the prefecture, however, Jean-Pierre Arrighi had a different view entirely.

"The French colonizers here are at the level they were when taking over the Middle East, as unwanted occupiers. They must come into modern times. People here will sabotage their colonialism, and they cannot stop the steam from escaping. If they try, it will explode, and independence will be inevitable under the worst possible circumstances."

Arrighi speaks for the Corsican People's Party (PPC), a small left-leaning (and legal) group that espouses "armed propaganda" rather than the armed struggle of the clandestine FLNC (National Front for the Liberation of Corsica).

The PPC wants increased autonomy for Corsica, with separate passports and bank accounts, leading to eventual independence. Arrighi is not deterred by the economics.

"When you have this sun and water, and this strategic position, you don't worry." If France paid back what it took from the Corsican economy, he said, the island could balance its budget for a decade. There is the Carbo Sarde deal, for example: France allows

Italy to run power lines across Corsica to its island province of
Sardinia, twelve miles to the south; Italy pays off with electricity
in the Alps. Corsica, Arrighi says, gets nothing.

"Corsica was rich," he insists. "Not only rich, but happy. That
is why we are so angry."

Pierre Poggioli heads the Corsican Movement for Autodetermi-
nation (MCA), the leading separatist party. With 7,000 votes in
1983, it outpolled the more moderate Corsican People's Union
(UPC), for years the most popular rejectionist front. For Poggioli,
that means Corsicans are fast growing fed up not only with French
domination but also with the island's internal politics.

"Our experience in the regional assembly shows the state has no
solution that can interest us," he said. "Nothing works. Unemployment is increasing, and we are ever more dependent. The two clans
run Corsica, and they need dependence, status quo, as the basis for
their power. If the clans continue to dominate it is because Paris
wants them to."

Poggioli maintains that only one voter in three actually went to
the polls. The clans, he said, collected proxies from people who
owed them favors: jobs, pensions, loans, court decisions, land. And
they can afford to dispense favors, he continued, only because state
grants and loans and commercial monopolies are dispensed through
clan leaders.

People disagree on the numbers, but even French authorities
identify electoral fraud and clan domination as a crushing problem
in Corsica. In the old days, small groups took charge of the land
and built up loyal followings to defend it. Vendettas kept accounts
straight and borders clearly drawn. Today, critics say, the clans
operate like Mafia families, but with less bloodshed. François Gia-
cobbi in Bastia and Jean-Paul de Rocca-Serra outside Ajaccio divide
their territory carefully and work in harmony. Both deny any
wrongdoing, but each acknowledges personal followings. Party
labels mean little compared to the name on the ballot.

"The state does nothing to destabilize the clans," Poggioli said.
"If they had no resources, they would wither on their own. They
have no interest in Corsica's development. If there were other
economic means available, people would owe them nothing."

MCA headquarters is in a new apartment block, its walls plastered with posters extolling separatists from Pasquale Paoli to Bobby Sands. Poggioli does not think much of the prefect's idea of liberty. His phone is tapped, he said, and the newspaper he puts out is regularly prosecuted for condoning violence and publishing false information.

The party is widely known as the legal arm of the FLNC, a status Poggioli rejects. "We are a political organization, and we do not feel we can condemn another organization for the means they choose."

What worries the separatists most is numbers. Census figures show that of the island's 240,000 inhabitants, 166,600 are Corsican, 33,600 are continental French, and 39,800 are foreigners. Of the Corsicans, one in three is older than sixty. The MCA argues that the real situation is far worse: 120,000 to 130,000 Corsicans at the most. Uncounted others are scattered from Toulouse to Tahiti.

From the beginning of the empire, Corsica was a reserve of manpower used to hard, hot work. Each time clan leaders placed someone's son abroad, they ensured a whole family's loyalty for a decade. Now that it is time to build a computer-age state in Corsica, others are coming in to do it.

With a million tourists, there is no hotel training program on the island. Civil servants and technicians come from the mainland, sometimes to return home grumbling that Corsicans forced them out.

"Immediate independence would be the worst catastrophe we could have," said Poggioli, the separatist. "First we must put in place a structure. The government's plan to spend money will not work. All that money will be deflected to the clans."

Like separatists elsewhere, Poggioli acknowledges that his is a minority view because people are not aware of realities. "We had 10,000 gather for a rally—in secret, because the television and the papers did not cover us."

There are, it is true, only two significant dailies in Corsica, local editions of papers from Nice and Marseilles. I had asked one local correspondent if he had a telephone number for Poggioli, who was, after all, leader of a key bloc in the regional assembly. "Not really," the reporter shrugged. "I don't know him too well, and it's not the policy of the newspaper."

In the 1986 elections, the MCA kept its six seats in the regional assembly, but its share of the popular vote dropped from 12.73 percent in 1983 to 9.05 percent. Observers from several parties complained of irregularities; in Basta, some contended, electoral lists used for registration were not the same as those delivered for counting.

"The *autonomistes*, the *indépendantistes*, they are finished," remarked a French reporter who knows Corsica well. But who knows Corsica well? On May 16, thirteen hooded terrorists took over a holiday camp at Cargese, tied up the thirty customers and the owner and set fire to bungalows. The owner got loose and tried to dismantle a bomb they left behind. He was killed, along with a gendarme. Such deaths were unusual, but bombings continued at their regular pace.

IN AJACCIO, NAPOLÉON Bonaparte is everywhere. A lot of Corsicans are bitter at the memory of the little emperor, blaming him for nailing down all hopes that Paoli's republic might be restored. But an active Bonapartist Party argues that it was not a matter of a Corsican helping France to colonize Corsica. It was a Corsican who colonized France.

After lunch at Le Petit Caporal—the Little Corporal—next to Le Premier Consul bar and across from an enormous statue of who else, I walked through the medieval quarter to Napoléon's big but undistinguished house.

The tour was fascinating, through a bourgeois house where roomfuls of young Bonapartes grew up, forming their view of a world one of them would soon command. But on a sultry sunny afternoon, the guide could hardly keep his eyes open. In room after room, he droned out his spiel in deadening monotone. "Here is where his mother, returning from the cathedral next door, gave birth to Napoléon. . . . Here is Napoléon's inkstand, Napoléon's documents, Napoléon's sword." Finally, he directed us down the stairs, or so I thought, and I moved toward the exit.

"Halt," ordered a pinched little guide at the bottom, fixing me with a violent stare. "Where is your escort?"

"He is coming, but . . ."

"You must remain at all times with your guide," he sputtered, the Napoléon in him rising with his voice. "When you reach the end of one part, you must wait."

"Forget it, it's not worth the trouble," I said, heading toward the door.

Having paid my eight francs, I had placed myself under his orders until he granted me leave. His face purpled at the outrage; desertion in the ranks at the hallowed shrine. He made a brief move in my direction. But then he stopped and accepted his Waterloo, looking as if he had swallowed Napoléon's cocked hat.

MOST CORSICANS SEEM convinced that the future will make a sharp break from the past and present, but few agree on what shape it may take.

In Pigna, Bill Graham, an international lawyer from Canada who bought a home here in the early 1970s, sees steady progress upward.

"Oh, I suppose the quality of *lonzo* [raw ham] is not as good because the poor peasants don't have to spend their lives slaughtering pigs up in the mountains, but I have seen a better life for people over the past twelve years, with increasing prosperity and respect for the past."

Residents of Pigna got together to save the crumbling facade of their church, for example, doing it on their own with money earned from new economic activity.

Casalonga muses at the outside possibilities.

"You know, there may be a completely new social and political experiment here, something to be tried in a small place and kept if it works or rejected if it doesn't," he said. "Every 200 years, that has been the case, it's a pattern." He ticked them off. In 1133, Pope Innocent II split the island between Pisa and Genoa; the Genoese set up a state in the 1300s; then Sampiero Corso tried something else until Genoa crushed his rebellion. And there was Paoli's republic. "Did you know Jean-Jacques Rousseau drafted a constitution for Paoli? Never put into practice, of course. It is time again, and perhaps the French will try something new."

Not likely.

Buses full of *pinzuti* tourists grind up the mountain, obscuring in diesel smoke the red letters scrawled on rocks: *"Français dehors"* —French go home. At a nearby convent, a priest worries aloud at how Corsican children are losing their values, corrupted by naked bathers on the beaches and television waves that reach isolated mountaintops invaders did not approach.

At San Antonino, another storybook Corsican mountain settlement, Sunday afternoon *pétanque* games are no longer village affairs. Snapping shutters distract the players and braying tourists drown out their patter. Up to now, Corsican hospitality is holding. "Eh, oh, we're going to be on TV tonight," a young player joked when someone's Pentax recorded his pitch. Felix Marcelli, in a blue-striped mariner's jersey, with skin the texture of an overused football, just laughed. I asked if he minded the influx.

"C'est très bien, très bien."

But in Calvi, Les Aloès Hôtel closed its kitchen in 1984, giving up in the face of fifty-seven new restaurants where tourists can eat fast and nasty. These days it is not the menu that counts but the notations on top: "English spoken." *"Mann spricht deutsch."* Maître d's are often rude to young outsiders. Prices are Champs-Elysées. That, many Corsicans fear, is a sign of the times.

All is not lost. At the Aloès, bar talk is still running 1,000 years behind the times. "You know, it wasn't the Saracens who killed Roland [Charlemagne's son], as it says in the *Chanson de Roland,*" the bartender confided to me one night. "It was the Basques."

But the centuries are advancing fast. In Casalonga's stacks in Pigna is a fragment of Flaubert's diary from 1840:

All this is so far from France, so far from our century, frozen in an epoch we dream about now in books, and I asked myself, as I rubbed oil onto my reddened legs, when one travels in stagecoaches, when there will be, instead of these crumbling houses, restaurants à la carte, and when all of this poor country will be miserable thanks to the cupidity that will be introduced, if all of that will be worth more.

PART TWO

THE OLD EMPIRES

Gaul united, forming a single nation, fired by a common spirit, can challenge the universe.

—Vercingétorix, quoted by Caesar,
embellished slightly by Napoléon III

CHAPTER FIVE

From Gauls to Franks

THE FRENCH, MASTER civilizers, started out at the other end of a mission to civilize. Roman envoys crossed the Alps and declared themselves appalled at the barbarity they found. Cicero's remarks to the Senate might have been Louis Proust's report on West Africa to the French Assembly nearly two millenia later. "What could be more filthy than their towns?" the Roman orator sniffed. "What is cruder than their farms?"

Historians quibble over whether France was France back then. But for a century now, schoolchildren have thumbed through primers showing warriors in long blond braids and winged helmets: their ancestors, the Gauls. Ferdinand Lot brooks no waffling. "Before France was Gaul, or to put it better, France continues on from Gaul, and Gaul precedes France. To write the history of Gaul is to write the history of France."

Gaul—France—was peopled first by diverse Celtic tribes, restless and cantankerous enough to move west to the edge of the continent but not driven to build boats and keep on going. By the end of the Stone Age, France was the heartland of Celts whose territory stretched from east of the Danube to the British Isles.

Cicero, in fact, was a little hard on them. The Celts were rough around the edges, but they were in touch with the times. Phoenicians brought their civilization along the Mediterranean coast. Marseilles was colonized from Asia Minor by 620 B.C., and Greek culture filtered northward from the thriving port. Three centuries before Christ, the Celts sacked Rome and invaded Greece.

The Celts lived in timbered clay huts, with elaborate iron cook-ware, forged weaponry, and tanned leather clothing. But the early tribes, too jealous and suspicious to forge any institutions beyond changing military alliances, formed no nation. Gaul—*Gallia*—was the Roman name for their geographical confines. In Latin, the Celts were *galli*. So were roosters.

While the Romans pursued architecture, philosophy, engineer-ing, military science, and belles lettres, the Celts hunted wild pigs and foretold the future by stabbing prisoners and reading the blood flow. The Romans, more civilized, also spilled prisoners' blood and guided their lives by superstition. That posed the obvious question: What is civilization? As in the case of the Romans, and later the French, those with the power to export civilization brought along their own definition.

The Romans colonized southern Gaul by 120 B.C. They built roads and massage parlors and sports stadiums; their ruins today are sprinkled across Provence and the Mediterranean coast. And from fortified outposts, the Romans kept an uneasy eye on Celtic politics to the north.

By 70 B.C., balances began to shift among the Celts. The Se-quanes, to overpower the Eduans, courted a calamity the French would suffer again and again: they brought in Germans. Ariovistus's troops crossed the Rhine and subdued the Eduans—and then the Sequanes who had hired him. The Eduans appealed to Rome for help.

The Senate demurred at first. Ariovistus was an official Friend of Rome, having signed a mutual defense pact. But the Helvetians were also pressing in on Gaul. Hungry German and Swiss warlords meant a threat to Rome's southern colonies. The Eduans, like the Sequanes, received more help than they wanted. They got Julius Caesar and a Pax Romana that lasted four centuries.

Caesar, an able enough general, was a prodigious war correspon-dent. Untroubled by censors, press credentials, or inconvenient facts, he reported his own campaigns in the third person. Today, his *Commentaries* remain the basis for what historians know about the Gallic Wars. He depicts himself as the prudent mediator, driven reluctantly to arms to enforce diplomacy. But his actions suggest a ruthless soldier-politician for whom Gaul was virgin ground for enough glory to earn his next promotion: emperor of Rome.

A first wave of Germans had ventured over the Rhine, Caesar reported. "When the uncivilized Barbarians had acquired a taste for residence in Gaul, with its good land and high standard of life, more were brought over, and there were at present about a hundred and twenty thousand of them."

Ariovistus, brusque and arrogant, challenged the Romans to force him out. They did, handily, and grateful Gauls prevailed upon Caesar to stay, as the *Commentaries* tell it. He was staying in any case, as proconsul. His purple mantle conferred the powers of viceroy, military governor, and tyrant-at-large.

His first news analysis has held up rather well:

In Gaul, not only every tribe, canton, and subdivision of canton, but almost every family, is divided into rival factions. At the head of these factions are men who are regarded by their followers as having particularly great prestige, and these have the final say on all questions that come up for judgment and in all discussions of policy. The object of this ancient custom seems to have been to ensure that all the common people should have protection against the strong; for each leader sees no one gets the better of his supporters by force or cunning—or, if he fails to do so, is utterly discredited.

The Gauls, he noted, were happy to barter for wine at one slave per jug. They were extremely superstitious, given to human sacrifice, and their lives were governed by a mystic fraternity of druids.

Caesar conquered by dividing, playing tribes off against one another. A Friend of Rome was protected and rewarded. Foes were crushed and packed off to the lions. Resisting settlements were razed, and survivors enslaved. The Romans seized hostages to ensure that subdued leaders did not change their minds later. When short of legionnaires, Caesar relied on Gallic collaborators and German mercenaries.

The French today trace the taproot of their glory, the indomitable Gallic spirit, to Caesar's occupation. There is Astérix, a feisty little cartoon character who drinks a magic potion the way Popeye eats spinach. Thus fortified, he and his brawny sidekick, Obélix, dislocate outsized Roman noses, sending legionnaires flying out of their leather-thonged sandals, to the inevitable pronouncement: "They're nuts, these Romans."

Astérix, argues Alain Duhamel in *Le Complexe d'Astérix,* personifies the Frenchman's image of his own political temperament: rebellious, mercurial, courageous, sarcastic, grumbling, generous, individualistic, hungry for adventure and glory, mocking of the powerful, allergic to conformism, sentimental, misogynistic, with condescending scorn for the rest of the world.

And there is Vercingétorix, a Gallic commander whose ten months of glory are celebrated in France 2,000 years after his defeat. Caesar, likely for his own purposes, painted Vercingétorix as a fiery guerrilla chieftain who inspired the colony to rebellion. Events suggest another reading. The Gauls chafed under the Roman proconsul and the Latin civilization he imposed. Their culture was endangered. Bards no longer sang of their ancestors' revered free spirits. Druids could not skewer prisoners for their gods. And the Gauls did not like paying taxes.

Caesar tried to consolidate Gaul by convoking all tribal leaders to Paris, called Lutetia at the time. Some did not turn up. Instead, bitter enemies met deep in the forest to ally secretly against Rome. Among them was Vercingétorix, chief of Arvernes, the son of a leader executed by rivals who feared he would be king of Gaul. Vercingétorix learned early from his father's mistakes. At about twenty, he was a barn-burning orator who could draw first blood whenever challenged.

In 52 B.C., Caesar wintered at Ravenna in northern Italy, fretting over Roman politics, which menaced his position. At the same time, he worried about a restive Gaul. Snow blocked the Alpine passes to France, and most of Caesar's legions were with him on the wrong side.

Gaul seized the moment and arose. The Carnutes stormed Genabum (now Orléans) and massacred Roman civilians. Other tribes followed, united behind Vercingétorix.

Historian Camille Jullian saw this unity as "the result of a universal sentiment, of a desire for the liberty of all, of an accord for the love of Gaul. . . . A collective spirit formed the ferment of a civilization of empire."

Jullian notes, however, that Vercingétorix lavished gold and promises of power on his recalcitrant allies. He commanded loyalty; but, just in case, he kept hostages.

Caesar, ignoring the winter, drove his men into Gaul. The campaign was vicious. Seasoned centurions used javelins and long daggers, attacking with precision strategy. But the Gauls howled down on them with bloodcurdling yells, swinging heavy swords and protected by leather shields. They adorned their horses with the heads of Romans who did not get out of the way.

The Gauls' alliance held, and they built up defenses. Caesar had to besiege Avaricum (now Bourges) until his men finally stormed the ramparts. They were so enraged by then that they slaughtered 40,000 men, women, and children before taking the time to loot. The Romans marched on Lutetia, but it burned before they could take it. At Gergovie, near what is now Clermont-Ferrand, Caesar lost patience with siege tactics and charged the walls. Vercingétorix inflicted so much damage that Caesar fled. It was his first defeat.

Each side craved vengeance, and they squared off for a showdown at Alésia.

For the Gauls, the town of Alésia, 125 miles east of Paris in the Burgundy hills, home of the Mandubiens, was their spiritual center. Legend described it as unconquerable, the cradle of their race. At the fall of Avaricum, Vercingétorix had rallied the tribes with the promise of a united Gaul. They would win the next battle and rule the world. But if they lost at Alésia, it was clear, Gaul would be crushed forever.

For the Romans, heavily outnumbered and far from home, Alésia meant all or nothing. Caesar knew that if he lost the advantage and his dwindling Gallic allies deserted him, his army would be slaughtered to the last man. Triumphant hordes would obliterate the traces of Roman civilization in Gaul, blotting out not only his life but also his place in history.

For both sides, the site was a majestic sweep of a battlefield, designed by the gods for glorious victory. Alésia perched atop Mont Auxois, 1,300 feet over the Plaine des Laumes, behind solid ramparts of hardened logs and earth. Caesar's camp was pitched on facing hills, and he gazed straight across the rolling meadows at his enemies' watchtowers.

Caesar's 50,000 legionnaires faced 80,000 Gauls encamped within the city's walls. He chose science rather than strength. For three weeks, his muscled veterans dug two parallel trenches, each twenty feet wide and nine feet deep, in an eleven-mile circle. Behind them, sharpened branches like barbed wire were rooted in the earth. Then he laid down buried minefields, one of fire-tempered wooden stakes and the other of iron spikes, both masked by leaves and grass. If he could not get in, no one would get out. And then, to defend his men from any rescuing force, he built a second circle, fourteen miles around, with the traps pointing outward. In between, he erected wooden terraces as high as the walls of Alésia.

Vercingétorix was confident. He had food and fodder for at least a month. His cavalry sneaked through the unfinished Roman lines to ride for help; all Gaul was resolved to support him. After three weeks, however, he was nearing desperation. No aid came, and some lieutenants pleaded for surrender. Others urged a frontal assault, preferring impalement to starvation. The relief column was long overdue. But each day the horizon was empty, and the foreground was thick with Romans.

Caesar's nerves were no calmer. Daily, chances increased that reinforcements would thunder over the hills. If Vercingétorix broke out, the Romans would be trapped between two fronts.

Desperate, Vercingétorix emptied Alésia of the people he had come to defend. Civilians at least would eat as Roman slaves; he needed all the food for his troops. The women and children, the sick and weak, streamed out of gates that slammed shut behind them. But they were trapped in the middle. Caesar had enough slaves. Tens of thousands died slowly of hunger.

Just as the besieged troops came to terms with cannibalism, the surrounding hills blackened with 250,000 armed Gauls. The battle, begun the next day, lasted a week. At daybreak, Vercingétorix attacked from the inside, but the relief force hung back. Only the cavalry charged, and the Gauls' best horsemen rode straight into Roman steel. Vercingétorix was beaten back.

The next day, Vercingétorix's allies waited at a safe distance, making only a minor dent with rudimentary artillery. They tried a bumbling night attack, which fell on the strongest part of the Romans' defenses. Gauls fled in terror, seeing comrades lying impaled on the hidden spikes. In a belated council of war, the Gallic generals finally located a weak spot: Caesar's command post on a rock outcropping. They attacked and breached the line. At the same time, Vercingétorix broke through from the other side.

Caesar's lines were cut at two points, and the Romans were outnumbered five to one. Centurions fought on by reflex, convinced that the battle was over and all was lost. But the Gauls' main force still held back, leaving combat to frontline units and the remaining mounted troops. Caesar sensed a turn in the battle. He ordered a massive counterassault behind his German cavalry. The Teutonic horsemen mauled the attacking Gauls. They charged into massed troops and refused to retreat, bellowing war cries and flailing sabers. The bulk of the relief column fled, and Vercingétorix retreated into the Alésia gates.

The next day, the commander of united Gaul threw his broadsword at Caesar's feet. It took six years for Caesar to return to Rome; the proconsul trundled Vercingétorix across Gaul as he accepted the obeisance of chieftains who had vowed to resist him to the death. Finally, Vercingétorix was paraded into Rome in chains as a symbol of Caesar's glory. Then he was quietly executed.

TODAY, VERCINGÉTORIX stands twenty-one feet tall on Mont Auxois, his sword at his side, gazing at the empty space where Caesar camped. French fathers take their children to see him, sweeping by without a look at a smaller Joan of Arc on a horse in the town square below. The statue was commissioned in 1865 by Napoléon III who, in his thick German accent, reminded the French of their ancestors the Gauls.

Not far away, along the *autoroute* to Lyon, expert hands have duplicated the siegeworks that defeated Alésia. An Archeodrome depicts daily life among hearty Celts (Gauls) going back 6,000 years. But visitors head straight for the *pièce de résistance*: the cut branches, the rusty spikes, and the towering ramparts. The replicas are impressive, but the accompanying history lesson is left a little vague.

France's Gallic content is open to question. The Franks, who later overran the terrain and gave it their name, were German, but the

French cling to the glory of Gaul. And if an indomitable Gallic spirit exists, the aura of Vercingétorix exemplifies it. Humiliating defeat converts easily to noble victory. The trick is in how you choose to remember it.

Rome obliterated Gaul. Occupied, it was a prosperous model colony. The Celtic language dissolved into Latin, and traditions melded into what historians call a Gallo-Roman society. Subdued, the Gauls poured wealth into Rome and fought in its legions. In return, Rome held off Germanic forces and kept peace among fractious clans.

In the third century, invaders poured over the Rhine, settling as far west as the Pyrenees. Rome restored peace, but the empire declined and fell. Gallic provinces were left as a loose amalgam of odd-shaped fiefdoms, open to the east. Franks moved in. Their name meant "free"; they were never conquered by the Romans. Frankish and Gallic blood, at first spilled in battle, was mixed in marriage.

And in the late 400s, a Frankish chieftain named Clovis created France.

Clovis murdered rivals, friends and relatives included, to consolidate power. Specializing in deceit, treachery, and military prowess, he forged a kingdom from the Rhine to the Pyrenees. Although a pagan, he acquired a Catholic wife of noble standing and the blessings of a steadily more powerful church. Over thirty years, he sank the roots of unity and order in what is now France. But, after Clovis, three centuries of Merovingian kings tugged hard at these fragile roots.

André Maurois, like most classical historians, depicts the Merovingian period as a black age during which men were at the mercy of their passions. Brothers poisoned one another for succession. Blood poured for bits of land. Bishops were murdered at their altars. Concubines schemed against queens, slaves against masters. Enemies were skewered on the spot. Indeed, Maurois notes with some horror, "Warriors broke into a church in the midst of a council, bellowing at the top of their voices." Other historians say the Merovingians were merely in tune with the times.

The idea of France, in any case, was kept fresh by the church, by culture and tradition, and by diverse branches of the aristocracy. At the end of the eighth century, France approached glory. It was the seat of empire, under a Germanic king known as Carolus Magnus Charlemagne.

For forty-three years, until he died in 814, Charlemagne shaped a cultivated society, faithful to the pope. "The Merovingian dynasty had lost all moral sense," wrote Fustel de Coulanges. "Charlemagne took it as his task to better souls and to make virtue prevail." Maurois thoughtfully advises caution in reading official rave reviews by Charlemagne's official biographer, Einhard. But he allows that Charlemagne "elicited respect through his dignity of bearing, and affection through his friendliness of manner. . . . He was pious, well-meaning, and a hard worker." The church was not enthusiastic about his five wives and four concubines. But his conquests of pagans swelled the Roman Catholics' ranks.

Charlemagne inherited a loosely knit kingdom and a ragtag army to defend it. Frankish troops, allied with the papacy, had driven Moslem raiding parties from the French heartland. As their new commander, Charlemagne chased pagans across the former Roman Empire. He conquered Lombardy and Aquitaine and then pursued barbarian invaders: Saxons, Slavs, Avars, Saracens, and Norse Vikings. He marched on Spain but, sidetracked elsewhere, gave up on Iberia. His empire extended from the Pyrenees to the Vistula, the river Warsaw straddles.

Charlemagne's blood was German, but his court was in France. The seat of the world had shifted from Rome to Aix-la-Chapelle. In 800, Pope Leo III called on Charlemagne, as temporal master of Europe, for help in a power struggle. Charlemagne pronounced the pope innocent of any wrongdoing. The grateful pontiff crowned him Charles Augustus, Emperor of the Romans. The Western Empire was revived, and a Roman pope established the right to crown as emperor a loyal soldier. The Vatican, as a result, had a considerable number of divisions.

Charlemagne's Europe was shaped to his personality. He was not rich; Moslems blockaded eastern routes to gold, spices, and luxuries. Jewish counselors ran his foreign affairs; no one else would treat with Mohammedan infidels. Dukes, counts, *marquis,* and assorted warlords collected taxes. When nudged by Charlemagne's roving inspectors, they passed some revenue upward. Lacking a civil service, the emperor let personal retainers handle government affairs.

Twice a year, notables gathered outside the Aix-la-Chapelle palace
to debate problems of the realm. Charlemagne's scouts and spies
signaled wrongs needing redress.

The emperor had Saint Jerome and Saint Augustin read to him
at mealtimes. The scholar Alcuin, whom he hired from York to
establish an academy, wrote, "During the morning of my life I
sowed in Britain the seeds of knowledge; now, toward its evening,
though my blood may be chilled, I sow these seeds ceaselessly in
France, and I hope that, with the grace of God, they will prosper
in both countries."

The empire collapsed after Charlemagne's death. Barbarians
gnawed at its edges, and the few ships and troops could not protect
long lines of communications. Families partitioned the rest, and the
upheaval resembled the bloody days of the Merovingians.

But Charlemagne's roots held. He had nourished a Latin-based
Western culture, with a landed aristocracy, a permanent military,
and a union between the pope and the king of the Franks. The
empire broke up into separate states. Nonetheless, Ferdinand Lot
observed, "The imprint was so strong that within the bosom of each
new state there would remain, in its institutions, in its law, and in
its ecclesiastical organization, enough common elements for a European civilization to survive into the Middle Ages."

A king of France, 1,200 years ago, had gone far on his mission
to civilize.

CHAPTER SIX

Spreading the Word

BY THE YEAR 1000, France was stitched into a patchwork of fiefdoms and assorted domains. Dukes, counts, and barons ruled wide sweeps of land. At the edges, small-time lords fortified their castles against bandits and tax collectors. Kings ruled in Paris but took along armies when they ventured down the road.

Western migrations had stopped. The Normans, Vikings from Scandinavia, were the last to come, muscling their way in from the north coast as far south as the Loire. They had their own views on royalty. Territorial warfare was constant. The aristocracy chose their king among pretenders who lobbied for support. Noblemen were as much allies as subjects of the king. They wanted a monarch with a generous spirit and a sharp sword.

In 987, Louis V died, the last of the Carolingians. His closest heir was excessively brutal and the crown went instead to the Capets. Hugues Capet descended from Robert the Strong who beat back a Norman advance in 866. He ruled with his son, Robert II, the Pious. They began a 300-year dynasty that sent French knights beyond the edges of Christendom, civilizing infidels at sword point.

Robert II was just, devout, and cultivated. Intellectuals loved him; generals respected him. He ruled for thirty-five years, outlasting rivals in Flanders and Germany. He balanced the independent dukes in Normandy and Aquitaine. But his three sons bitterly contested the succession.

Henri I, the eldest, won the crown. But he owed political debts across France. He split off Burgundy as a duchy for his brother

Robert. The real problem was Normandy, whose duke supported
Henri but demanded Vexin in exchange. When he died, the king
took it back. And then the fragile structure collapsed. Normandy
fell under the control of a new duke, a gentleman known then as
William the Bastard.

THE NORMANS, pagan marauders two centuries earlier, had
settled comfortably in little stone ports and farms. They brought
their own character to the language: *écraser,* to crush, is from the
Norse. But they learned French, and they embraced the church.
William's father, Robert the Magnificent—Robert the Devil, to
some—died on a pilgrimage to the Holy Land.

Faith did not wipe out greed. Armed tourism remained their
favorite sport. Norman bands seized Sicily and chunks of southern
Italy, establishing duchies. Norman mercenaries fought in Byzantine
armies, sharing in the spoils and broadening their horizons toward
the east.

And in 1066, William the Bastard crossed the English Channel
and stamped himself into history as William the Conqueror.

After Edward the Confessor died, William said he had been
promised the English crown. However, Edward later chose Harold,
of the family of earls who owned most of England. A tattered
tapestry at Bayeux, narrow but long as a football field, recounts how
it all happened. William had rescued Harold from a warlord up the
coast, and in return Harold had promised to support him in England. But now Harold was stealing his crown. He was going after
it. Just after Easter, a star trailing fire lit the skies over the Channel.
Halley would identify it 700 years later. At the time, it was an omen
of upheaval among kings.

Like the Allied assault in the other direction, nine centuries later,
William's invasion was carefully prepared. Italian Normans, allies
anxious for spoils, and freelance adventurers streamed up the roads
to Normandy. The latest technology was taken aboard a fleet at
Saint-Sauveur, near Cabourg, a tiny port named for an ancient
miracle.

William packed his men on oversized gondolas, powered by
bedsheet-type sails, on a narrow little stream called the Dives. The

winds were wrong, and his fleet nearly had to conquer Belgium instead of England.

Harold was elsewhere in England when William finally landed and dug in at Hastings. When Harold approached, William rode out to attack. Three horses were killed beneath him; finally, he fought on foot, flailing the English with sword and shield. He broke up massed English forces with a stratagem that has served French legions since: his troops fell back in feigned retreat and then rounded on disorderly pursuers. Harold was killed; God had chosen.

William was crowned at Westminster in tumult; rioting English soldiers burned the town. Over two decades, he imposed his order with brutality and cunning. In the warring French principalities, aristocrats bullied the king. In England, the king was sovereign, and noblemen served him faithfully. William drew up tax and census rolls, taking charge of the island's riches. He seized land and paid stipends to the nobility. Peasants were locked into serfdom, but royal justice reached remote farms. Norman clergymen reorganized the church in England.

When William died in 1087, England and Normandy were split among two of his sons. But the Norman invasion had grafted more branches of French society and culture. The Anglo-Saxon aristocracy held only 6 percent of English land; the old noblemen were mostly dead or in exile. A cluster of Anglo-Norman barons owned land on both sides of the channel. During the next 800 years, England and France would fight interminably, and often English admirals and generals would humiliate the French. But each English sovereign would go to battle under a standard emblazoned in French: *Dieu et Mon Droit.*

SIX YEARS BEFORE William conquered England, Togrul Beg, the Seljuk, captured Baghdad and imposed Turkish rule on the vast Arabic empire. And in 1071, the Turks pushed the Byzantines from Christian Armenia at the battle of Malazgerd. They took Jerusalem from the Arabs. Within the decade, Turks ruled most of Asia Minor. Suddenly, Christian pilgrims could no longer pass among the Moslems to pray at the Holy Sepulcher. By 1090, survivors were telling of atrocities. Infidels rained arrows on them, sweeping from the hills to carry off the women and the pilgrims' meager belongings. Christians were banned from holy places, arrested, or expelled. The sanctified relics of Christ were imperiled.

On November 27, 1095, a French pope, on a visit to the French town of Clermont, demanded holy war. "God wills it," Pope Urban II shouted to an enthusiastic crowd. He toured France eliciting support. The response was overwhelming.

Crusades had already routed the infidel in Spain. French noblemen made twenty-one forays as part of the *Reconquista,* restoring Christian civilization to the Iberian peninsula. They had discovered a side benefit of God's fight. As historian Jean Favier notes, "Of course, the combat for faith fits in quite well with conquest in that the soldier of Christ can install himself in places he has taken from the infidel."

Urbain II's idea was different. Crusaders were to deliver the Holy Land to Christianity at large and to free the faithful trapped under Islamic hegemony. This was the pope's war; kings were discouraged from attending. In any case, Philippe I of France had been excommunicated for an illicit marriage. And in medieval Europe, noblemen commanded the armies. A monk named Pierre the Hermit circled France on a mule and enlisted peasants for a poor man's crusade. They rushed on ahead, but were cut to ribbons barely east of the Byzantine borders. The pope's divisions were headed by aristocrats with enough holdings to pay for the campaign.

According to the few conflicting accounts of Urbain's appeal, the pope drove home his message of the need for purification. Baldric of Dol said that he thundered:

> You, girt about with the belt of knighthood, are arrogant with great pride; you rage against your brothers and cut each other to pieces. . . . You are the oppressors of children, plunderers of widows; you, guilty of homicide, of sacrilege, robbers of another's rights; you who await the pay of thieves for the shedding of Christian blood—as vultures smell fetid corpses.

But he apparently bolstered his spiritual appeal with the promise of reward.

"The possessions of the enemy will be yours, too, since you will make spoil of his treasures," Baldric quotes him as saying. Robert the Monk has him adding, "Wrest that holy land from the wicked race, and subject it to yourselves, that land which, as the scripture says, 'floweth with milk and honey.'" And, Robert adds, the pope reminded listeners that their land "is too narrow for your population; nor does it abound in wealth; and it furnishes scarcely enough food for its cultivators . . . hence it is that you murder and devour one another."

The first to stitch a cross to his shoulder was Raymond de Saint-Gilles, count of Toulouse, who had acquitted himself well in Spain. He was pious but impetuous. Urban II gently resisted his efforts to be field marshal and, instead, balanced his power with that of other noblemen.

One was Godefroi de Bouillon, duke of Brabant, big, blond, and bearded, a hunter of extraordinary force. Arab chroniclers still marvel at the day a Syrian sheik started to challenge him to decapitate a camel with a single sword stroke. By the time the sheik finished his sentence, a camel's head rolled at his feet. Fellow crusaders had few reproaches. One was that he prayed so long at holy places, their dinner got cold.

The crusaders formed an international brigade, largely French but with elements from what are now Belgium and Italy. They chose the common name Franks, evoking the time when Gaul, Germany, and Italy came under the rule of Carolingian kings and the Roman church.

They set off in 1096, following what eight centuries later would be the route of the Orient Express. Within three years, they approached the walls of Jerusalem. Battle, intrigue, and Levantine summers had depleted their ranks. But they took Antioch in Syria and as they marched down the coast of Lebanon, terrified emirs sent out food to speed them on their way.

Franks and Turks quickly learned that neither were pushovers in battle. The crusaders clanked along slowly, encumbered by chain mail armor and heavy siege gear shipped in from Genoa. Mounted knights were the shock troops behind legions of foot soldiers. Preferring hand-to-hand combat, they regarded the infidels' arrows as cowardly, but efficient. Still, the more mobile Turkish horsemen melted away at iron-edged crusader charges. The Franks' smaller numbers usually carried the day.

At Jerusalem, the Franks faced Egyptians who had taken the city from the Turks. Fired with zeal, weeping from emotion, four crusader armies assaulted the ramparts. Arabs poured burning petroleum (the dreaded Greek fire of the Middle Ages) on wooden siege towers.

Godefroi made a bridge to the city walls, and crusaders raced in with flailing swords. "We advanced in blood to our ankles," wrote one soldier, describing the combat for the Al Aqsa Mosque, the Temple of Solomon. Carried away by the victory, crusaders wrought such havoc on the Arabs that Archbishop Guillaume de Tyr wrote, "The city offered such a spectacle of carnage among the enemy that the victors themselves were struck with horror and disgust." The coastal emirs, who had been prepared to negotiate, heard of the slaughter and slammed shut their gates to fight to the death.

With 1,200 horsemen and 9,000 foot soldiers, at odds with each other and facing Egyptian armies of five times their number, the Franks began what was to be nearly 200 years of occupation of the Holy Land.

The crusaders proclaimed the kingdom of Jerusalem and offered Godefroi a crown. He took the job but changed the title from king to guardian of the Holy Sepulcher. If Jesus Christ wore a crown of thorns, he said, he could hardly wear one of gold.

Godefroi died months after the conquest. His brother was crowned Baudouin I. He was an energetic warrior who rallied his men with simple logic: "If you lose, you have a martyr's crown; if you win, immortal victory. As for fleeing, that is useless. France is too far away." He died in 1118 and, by chance, his cousin arrived in Jerusalem on the day of his funeral. Baudouin II ruled well until 1123 when, out hunting with his falcons, he was caught by the Turks. Ransomed, he took back his throne. In 1131, he fell ill and died. The crown went to Foulque d'Anjou, one of the most powerful barons of France.

Foulque ruled for twelve years until the day he went rabbit hunting near Acre. His horse stumbled, and he crushed his skull. His eldest son, Baudouin III, was only thirteen; his widow, Melisende, was regent. In rapid attacks, the Turks seized Edesse, besieged Antioch, and harassed Christian columns.

By then, generations of Creoles (called *poulains*), although considering themselves European, were no longer fired by the zeal of Pope Urbain's words. The chronicler Foucher de Chartres recorded, "The colonist is becoming a native, the immigrant an inhabitant. Each day relatives and friends come from the West to join us. They do not hesitate to abandon there all they owned. In effect, who was poor there attains opulence here. Who in Europe owned not even a village finds himself in the Orient lord of an entire city. Why return to the West when the East fulfills our wishes?"

It was time for a new Crusade. Saint Bernard, a tireless French monk, preached renewed fire from a hillside at Vézelay. He was a giant of his age, a founder of 1,200 abbeys. Among others, he moved King Louis VII of France and Emperor Conrad III of Germany. Not a day too soon, they set off with separate armies for the Holy Land.

Conrad III went first, following Godefroi's route. Byzantine guides took him into Turkey, where he lost three-quarters of his army. The Christian emperor of Byzantium had sold him out because peace talks were underway with the Turks and, crusader or not, the meddling German was in the way. Louis VII fought his way through Asia Minor but had to continue by water. The Byzantines delivered few of the ships they promised. Louis's troops waited for the next transports; none came. Betrayed by the Byzantines, they were decimated by the Turks.

The two sovereigns eventually reached Jerusalem and charged off in the wrong direction. A Turkish force at Aleppo menaced Antioch, Jerusalem, and everything in between. Pressed to the wall, the crusaders depended on an alliance with the Arabs in Damascus.

Louis and Conrad attacked Damascus, on bad advice. Conrad was killed and Louis went home, leaving behind a fractured alliance, an outraged Creole aristocracy, and a strengthened Turkish threat.

"The failure of the second crusade brought a grave diminishing of the Francs' prestige in the Moslem world," historian René Grousset wrote. "The two most powerful princes of Christianity had come and gone, having done nothing."

Baudouin III grew up and saved the day. He fought battles,

forged alliances, chastised unruly barons, and restored the faith. He won over the Byzantines by marrying the Byzantine emperor's beautiful young daughter. He was a model king, but only for a short while. His physician prescribed too much medicine and he died in 1162, at thirty-three.

Baudouin's brother, Amaury I, made another mess. He tried to conquer Egypt and, in the process, allowed power to pass to Islam's greatest general, Saladin. Amaury died of typhus at thirty-nine, leaving his fourteen-year-old son as Baudouin IV. The young king, according to Guillaume de Tyr, was charming and remarkably talented, handsome, lively, open, agile in physical exercise, and a perfect horseman. He had an excellent memory, never forgetting a slight or a favor. He was also a leper.

As his body wasted away, Baudouin led his armies in stunning feats of arms. Near Ramallah, the seventeen-year-old leper took 300 knights on a wild charge that routed Saladin and thousands of Turks, Kurds, Arabs, and Sudanese. The Moslems fled to Egypt, tossing away baggage, helmets, and weapons as they galloped away. Baudouin consolidated the kingdom; but, with no heir, he left the succession in shambles.

The crown went to the vacillating commoner who married Baudouin's sister Sibylle, Guy de Lusignan. As Saladin amassed his strength, Guy allied himself with the greediest and cruelest of noblemen against the advice of his last few capable leaders. The end was swift.

Despite warnings, Guy led his entire army north to Tiberias. Their water ran out. Saladin, camped between the Christians and the water of Lake Tiberias, exulted, "Allah has delivered us." When Guy's army stopped to rest, collapsing under their armor in the baking heat, Saladin attacked. He set an arc of fire to the prairie, trapping the crusaders inside. Nearly all perished, burned alive or cut down by Moslem weapons.

The survivors, Guy included, reached Jerusalem. But soon Saladin was at the walls. He allowed the Christians safe passage to Tyre. With thunderous cries of *"Allahu Akbar"* (God is great), Saladin entered Jerusalem in 1187. The crusaders' kingdom of Jerusalem was reduced to a few coastal towns and scattered fortresses like the impregnable Krak des Chevaliers in Syria.

AS CHRISTIANS struggled to hold onto the Holy Land, the kings of France and England fought over real estate at home. Philippe Auguste, a Capet, ruled in Paris, using all the stealth, treachery, and artillery he could muster. What he could not win in battle, he won by playing off one English Plantagenet prince against another. In 1189, he broke Henry II by spurring the English king's sons against him. The English crown went to Richard I.

Richard Coeur-de-Lion, the Lion-Hearted, was nearly as French as Philippe Auguste. He was born in France, he spoke French, and he spent less than a year of his life in England. His main contact with the English nobility was to raise taxes for his constant campaigns and occasional ransoms.

Shortly after Richard was crowned, he and the French king, then allies, set off together on the Third Crusade. By the time they reached Acre, they were at each other's throats. Richard, insulted in Cyprus, had stopped to take over the island.

Their armies recaptured Acre, and Philippe Auguste went home. Richard stayed long enough to cover himself in glory. He stood fast against Saladin, raised the crusaders' morale, and then he also headed back to his kingdom. But the trip took longer than he planned.

Richard's lion heart was matched by a rhinoceros temper. When aroused, he trampled headlong over diplomatic niceties. After the crusaders took Acre, the duke of Austria flew his flag from the ramparts alongside the English and French banners. Richard snatched it down and flung it in the moat. Dukes' flags, he snarled, do not stand with kings'. The incident might have been forgotten had Richard not passed through Austria in a flimsy disguise.

The duke threw Richard in prison, and Philippe Auguste urged him to lose the key. In his colleague's absence, the French monarch seized chunks of Richard's land. That sat badly with the aristocracy and the pope, who recalled that crusaders' property was sacrosanct.

Richard bought his freedom. With his brother John he fought a five-year war with France in Normandy, beating the Capet king back to where he had started twenty years earlier. But Richard was pierced by an arrow near Limoges, and John inherited the throne. Philippe Auguste won back Normandy. John invaded France and spent so much money on a fruitless campaign that the English nobility rebelled. In 1215 John signed the Magna Carta, limiting the rights of kings in England.

LATER CRUSADES stirred political forces but did little to strengthen Western presence. From 1239, a scrap of verse by the knight-poet Philippe de Nanteuil recalls a campaign against Egypt:

> *Ah! France, douce contrée,*
> *Maudite soit la journée*
> *Où tant de vaillants chevaliers*
> *Sont devenus prisonniers!*

(France, sweet country, damned be the day when so many valiant knights became prisoners.)

An Egyptian sultan gave Jerusalem back to the Christians in 1240, in a political deal, but Turks grabbed it again four years later.

Then Saint Louis appeared. A Capet, king of France since 1226, Louis IX set off on a crusade from the French port of Aiguesmortes he built for the occasion. It was strictly a French operation: he took along his three brothers, and shiploads of dukes, counts, and barons. His goal was to capture the heart of Islamic power, and he sailed for Egypt.

Saint Louis fought his way up the Nile, but typhus and dysentery crippled his army. Captured, then ransomed, he led his forces to Acre. Jerusalem was too well defended, but the French legions pacified the Syrian hinterlands. Louis went home after four years, leaving the crusaders united, with their rear guards safe. But as soon as he left the Franks' colony began to collapse.

Crusaders fought a street war among themselves in Saint-Jean d'Acre for possession of a church between the Venetian and Genoese sectors. Armed quarrels spread to other towns. Meanwhile, the crusaders botched their foreign policy.

Mongol hordes from the Asian steppes had seized most of Syria. With a thin claim to Christianity and a respect for European swords, they sought an alliance against the Moslems. The crusaders, frightened at the idea of Mongol neighbors, instead banded with the defenders of Islam.

Mamelukes, Turkish slaves from the Caucasus who rose to power, reigned in Egypt. With the crusaders' help, they routed the Mongols; then they turned on the Franks. In lightning succession, Mameluke sultans attacked the last colonies. Prince Edward of England negotiated an eleven-year reprieve for Saint-Jean d'Acre, but crusaders used the time to carry on internal quarrels. Pisans and Genoese fought naval battles in the port.

In February 1289, 40,000 horsemen and 100,000 foot soldiers besieged Tripoli. A month later, Venetians and Genoese, whose conflicts had sapped the city's strength, slipped off with their riches at night in ships, leaving the French alone. Sultan Qalaoun stormed the city, slaughtering most of the men and taking women and children as slaves.

In Saint-Jean d'Acre, an Italian people's crusade sought revenge. Like Pierre the Hermit's army, it was formed of peasants, not soldiers. Zealots fell upon Moslem farmers and merchants, in the fields and markets, slitting throats with abandon. That was all the Mamelukes needed.

Sultan el-Ashraf Khalil sent 60,000 horsemen, 160,000 foot soldiers, and batteries of catapults to attack the city. Acre's population totaled 35,000, counting crusaders, Creoles, pilgrims, and Italian sailors on shore leave. Of that, 14,000 were foot soldiers and 800 were horsemen.

Saint-Jean d'Acre fell after a furious fight. A few Christians escaped by boat, but most were killed. The fortress-convent of the Knights of the Temple held for a month and a half. Finally, the sultan offered safe passage for the few defenders left inside. They came out, and he beheaded them.

Tyre, Sidon, and Tortose were evacuated without a fight. The Templars held out on the island of Rouad, facing Tortose, until 1303. Only in 1914 did the Franks—French forces—again reenter Syria. From the island of Rouad.

HISTORIANS, CHURCHMEN, and romanticists draw conflicting conclusions from the First Crusade and the five others that followed.

Paulin Paris notes how the Orient influenced Europe. Crusaders' chronicles were the first writings in French, which Dante had dismissed as "that language of wet nurses." Paris wrote, "People would have long seen Latin as the only written language had the Crusades not . . . made them feel the need to correspond with relatives and friends without having to call on an intervening cleric." From private letters later developed the great novels about the Round Table and Merlin, Arthur, Lancelot.

Contact with the East broadened the European medieval outlook. Tapestries, silks, and brass fittings found their way to dingy castles in Normandy. More than one crusader remembered Saladin's rosewater sherbets from the snows of Mount Hermon.

But Marshall Baldwin emphasizes Western impact on the Levant. "When their goal had been achieved some warriors elected to remain in the east, and they and their successors faced the manifold tasks of a 'colonial' administration. Vastly inferior in numbers to their heterogeneous native population, they created in an eastern environment a civilization which was fundamentally western."

Ships linked the Holy Land to Europe, and Italian merchants set up commerce.

André Maurois notes, ". . . the French tongue and civilization in the Near East acquired a privileged position."

Sir Stephen Runciman, the English authority, observes:

> The determination of the Westerner to conquer and colonize the lands of Byzantium was disastrous for the interests of *Outremer*. It was more disastrous still for his European civilization. Constantinople was still the center of the civilized Christian world. . . . Knights could not believe that so superb a city could exist on earth; it was of all cities the sovereign. . . . Greed and clumsiness led [the men of the Fourth Crusade] to indulge in irreparable damage.

Runciman argues that the crusaders broke Christian defenses and allowed the infidel to penetrate the Balkans. He concludes his three-volume work:

> To the Crusaders themselves their failures were inexplicable. They were fighting for the cause of the Almighty; and if faith

and logic were correct, that cause should have triumphed. In the first flush of success they entitled their chronicles the *Geste Dei per Francos,* God's work done by the hand of the Franks.

It was less surprising that the enterprise collapsed, he wrote, than that it lasted 200 years.

> In the long sequence of interaction and fusion between Orient and Occident out of which our civilization has grown, the Crusades were a tragic and destructive episode. . . . The historian . . . must find his admiration overcast by sorrow at the witness that it bears to the limitations of human nature. There was so much courage and so little honor, so much devotion and so little understanding. High ideals were besmirched by cruelty and greed, enterprise and endurance by a blind and narrow self-righteousness; and the Holy War itself was nothing more than a long act of intolerance in the name of God, which is a sin against the Holy Ghost.

René Grousset, the French arbiter of the period, drew similar conclusions. But he cuts straight to the center with an essential point: the crusaders established the first French colony abroad, and they were the early epitome of a mission to civilize.

FOR THE NEXT CENTURY, France was in conflict— against the English, the Spanish, the Flemish, the Italians, and among its own provinces. Philippe VI established the House of Valois in 1328. French ships took the Canary Islands in 1402. Black Plague was followed by a wave of anti-Semitism.

In 1415, France floundered in the hands of half-mad Charles VI and nobles warring to rule in his name. Henry V of England invaded Normandy with a thin claim to the throne. His small army killed ten thousand Frenchmen at Agincourt, one of the bloodiest of medieval battles. Treachery and assassinations among the French helped consolidate his position. Henry V died in 1422, and so did Charles VI. France had two kings: Henry VI, only ten months old and worse, not French, and the Dauphin, Charles VII of Bourges, who could not wrest Paris from the English regent, the Duke of Bedford.

Then a seventeen-year-old shepherd girl from Lorraine showed up at Chinon and asked to see the Dauphin. Her name was Jeanne d'Arc, and she heard voices. She amazed Charles by picking him out of a cluster of lords. He gave her some troops. She captured Orléans and then rallied Charles' followers under a cross and the *fleur-de-lis*. Bedford called her a witch—on his way out. Charles VII secured the throne. But rivals captured Joan at Compiègne. The savior of France was sold to the English who, after a decent interval, burned her at the stake in 1431.

A lot of Frenchmen since have regarded Jeanne d'Arc as proof that patriotism, faith and genius can produce a miracle whenever France needs one. Charles VII came around to that view fifteen years after her death. At the time, he did nothing to save her.

Crippled by the One Hundred Years' War, France floundered on. And in 1515, François I shifted the nation into another age.

France had taken its hexagonal shape, with a largely homogeneous people who saw common political and economic interests. And France was seen that way from the outside.

"The horizons are broadened," writes Jean Favier, concluding an exhaustive study of the period. "The history of France is from now on linked with a world that encompasses as much the Eastern Mediterranean as England and Scotland, where vital parts are played in the Germanic countries and Italy, where borders are before Granada and Budapest."

Favier adds, "But the French have missed the opening that others find toward Africa, toward the Atlantic. They have sought too late the silk road, and they have also missed the road to gold."

France, soon enough, would find its own roads.

CHAPTER SEVEN

Building an Empire

FRANÇOIS I'S FAVORITE passions, of many, were power and glory. His neighbors included Henry VIII of England and Charles V, a slack-jawed little monarch with brilliant eyes who ruled Austria, Spain, the Netherlands, Naples, and enclaves in between. France was the strongest nation in Europe but not the richest. It could use all the power and glory its king could muster.

Competition was bitter for Flanders. England wanted it as a commercial foothold on the continent; France needed a buffer to protect its northeastern flank. But Austria held Flanders tightly as a bargaining chip. Italy had long attracted French kings, but the new wealth and beauty of the Renaissance fired lust across Europe. Italian city-states, accustomed to invasions, made the best of them. They remained free by pitting one foreign power against the others. Sovereigns perched precariously atop shifting alliances.

In this climate, one of the first of many diplomats and travel writers tried his hand at describing the French character. He was Niccolò Machiavelli:

> These French are perfectly insupportable: always worried, preoccupied only with the moment, forgetful of others' good deeds as well as outrages, little concerned with their blood but terribly avid for money.... Since the time of Caesar, the French have hardly evolved: changeable and lightweight, weak in adversity, insolent in good fortune; you cannot count on them. They

keep their promises poorly and their own interests always predominate.[1]

In his *Rapport sur les Choses de France,* Machiavelli declares the French to be thieves. He wrote:

> They are by nature partial to the belongings of others. A Frenchman is capable of stealing coolly whether to give himself the stolen object, or to squander it, or to present it to the one from whom he stole it. As opposed to the Spanish, you will never again see what the French have stolen from you.

France was difficult to beat, Machiavelli wrote. England was but a shadow of its former self, out of practice at warfare. Spain could not muster the strength to cross the Pyrenees, nor could any Italian state attack across the Alps. Flanders depended economically on France, and Switzerland could manage only border raids. The counterweight, he concluded, was that the French were lousy soldiers:

> They are by nature more impetuous than resistant or skillful; and, if they encounter an enemy who can withstand the fury of the first shock, they lose their bite and lose heart, so much so that they are then more cowardly than women. They suffer so badly from fatigue and lack of comfort that, in the long run, discipline breaks down and it is easy, if one surprises them in this disorder, to triumph over them.

But François I was an imposing adversary, adept at the hard pragmatism Machiavelli later prescribed in *The Prince.* He was six-foot-six at a time when five-foot-five was not short. He stood as solidly as Henry VIII, with an intense stare and a powerful sword arm. He loved art, learning, and copulation. Louis XII had tried devious means to will his throne to someone other than his son-in-law and cousin once removed. But, just before dying, he threw up his hands, saying, "We busy ourselves in vain; that large young man will ruin everything."

Once crowned, François I hired 26,000 mercenaries and rushed off to conquer Milan. He also made permanent peace with the Swiss, bringing the Swiss Guard into the French court and securing rights to recruit soldiers in Switzerland. In Italy, he struck a deal with Pope Leo X over naming bishops and taxing the French church. As a result, France was able to resist the Reformation. André Maurois observed, "Henry VIII broke with Rome in order to despoil the monasteries; François I had despoiled them by previous agreements with Rome."

François I wanted most the title of king of the Romans, emperor of Christian Europe. By custom, seven archbishops and noblemen elected the emperor. They were open to bidding. And Charles V also wanted the job.

The Austrian monarch was the grandson of Ferdinand of Aragon and Isabella of Castile, who had outfitted Columbus. He was backed by the rich mine owners and merchants of southern Germany. Ruling the Germanic empire, with his other domains, Charles V would encircle France. If he lost the crown to François I, his vast territories would be split in two. The heat was on.

Henry VIII parleyed with François I at Calais under tents stitched in gold thread, but decided against backing the French king. English merchants sold wool; Flemish weavers made cloth; and Charles V was master of Flanders. Thus, England toppled the careful balance of power in Europe.

With all Europe lined up against him, François I attacked, marching east against Charles's forces. He was beaten and captured but, in fine French style, emerged triumphant. "All is lost, save honor," he wrote to his mother. Schoolchildren today study his verse: "The body conquered, the heart remains the victor."

France remained united, and Charles V did not know what to do with his prisoner. If François I died, a new king would come looking for revenge. The Austrian could not pay off allies with chunks of France, or keep any himself, without his prisoner's approval. Finally, François I agreed to give up Burgundy as ransom. At home, he repudiated the deal and launched a world war.

The king found a new ally: the Turks. Only two centuries had passed since Saint Louis had crusaded against Moslem unbelievers. But it was no time for encumbering ideology; France was in peril. François I relied on Protestants and Moslems to fight Catholic Austria abroad while he put to death heretics at home. Such contradictions worked out smoothly in France over the next centuries. Church and state remained close; principle and practice did not.

The war was punctuated by separate peaces and split alliances. By the time François I died in 1547, France was fighting not only in the Old World but also in new ones halfway around what only recently had been determined to be a globe.

Occupied close to home, François I had let upstart adventurers raise flags across the oceans in the names of Spain and Portugal. Iberians had the luxury of looking for easy ways to China and India. Portugal, with a million inhabitants, sent out the first probing voyages around Africa. The New World was beginning to speak the language of the ten million Spanish. France, the most powerful single nation of the age, with twenty-five million inhabitants, was out of the game.

It was a double bind. France could not afford to explore and colonize because wars and old war debts ate up most of its revenue. Yet weaker nations suddenly found themselves rich from transoceanic plunder.

Spain's galleons carried gold and silver. France brought back codfish, the catch of a few adventuresome Bretons and Normans off the Newfoundland Banks. Freebooting pirates carried French colors, but they did not always pay their taxes.

French intellectuals, unimpressed with new worlds, put little pressure on the king. They were building glory at home with such seats of excellence as the Collège de France. But François I was losing out on the title to much of the world, and he was not happy. After the Vatican's Treaty of Tordesillas divided all but the Old World between Spain and Portugal, he grumbled, "Show me the Act by which Adam made his legacy of the earth."

It must be noted, in the interest of sound journalism, that François I possibly said nothing of the sort. In fact, Louis XIV probably never said, "L'Etat, c'est moi." History has a way of placing well-turned phrases in mouths long silenced. More, colonial history was recorded largely by impassioned men, rich in ink and imagination, whose purposes were other than to reflect reality faithfully. A French seaman named Jean Cousin, off course from Africa, may have discovered America four years before Columbus, as some will swear. But historians, French and otherwise, have blown off a good deal of mist. Some sources are cited in text and notes, but readers are directed to the bibliography.

FRANCIS PARKMAN, a precise Bostonian of the last century, argues that France's early achievements in the Americas are little appreciated:

> While the Spaniard roamed sea and land, burning for achievement, red-hot with bigotry and avarice, and while England, with soberer steps and a less dazzling result, followed in the path of discovery and gold-hunting, it was from France that those barbarous shores first learned to serve the ends of peaceful commercial industry.

Breton and Basque fishermen steadily worked the cod banks off Newfoundland, perhaps from as early as the 1490s, and Norman explorers probed the St. Lawrence gulf in 1506, 1508, and 1518.

The king's character pushed France onward, Parkman concludes:

> Chivalry and honor were always on his lips; but Francis I, a forsworn gentleman, a despotic king, vainglorious, selfish, sunk in debaucheries, was but the type of an era which retained the forms of the Middle Ages without its soul, and added to a still prevailing barbarism the pestilential vices which hung fog-like around the dawn of civilization. Yet he esteemed arts and letters, and, still more, coveted the *éclat* which they could give. The light which was beginning to pierce the feudal darkness gathered its rays around his throne. . . . Among artists, philosophers, and men of letters enrolled in his service stands the humbler name of a Florentine navigator, John Verrazano.

France sent Verrazano west toward China in 1523, but America stood in his way. He poked around, left his name on the Narrows at New York, sailed north, and then came home to Dieppe.

Eleven years later, François I tried again with Jacques Cartier, from the ancient walled port of St.-Malo, bastion of pirates and traders who, for centuries to come, ranged the seas for France. Cartier explored the mouth of the St. Lawrence in 1534 and brought back two Indians. A year later, with three ships, he returned to sail up the St. Lawrence to China. Indians warned him that the god Coudouagny would visit freezing agony upon the French if they persisted upriver. Coudouagny, Cartier replied, had obviously not heard of Christ.

The explorers climbed an imposing hill named Mont Royal (as in Montreal), and saw that a great deal of narrow river and forest lay between them and Cathay. They turned back, but the river had frozen. Trapped in frail wooden ships, they relied on friendly Indians to deliver food. Friendship dwindled, along with the food stores, and scurvy killed twenty-five men. Miserable with cold and disease, the Frenchmen kept the Indians away for fear they might seize the advantage and attack.

Spring came, and Cartier took home the tattered remnants of his party. Bereft of other treasures, he kidnapped the Indian chief, Donnacona, and his chieftains, to testify to François I about riches yet undiscovered. The Indians died soon after reaching France.

Cartier found another adventurer smitten with the idea of Canada, a Picardy nobleman named Jean-François de la Roque, sieur de Roberval, with enough royal cash to outfit five ships. He set off again in 1541, and Roberval was to follow. The Indians were not pleased to see him without Donnacona. Cartier built a fort in which to sit out the winter. But then, mysteriously, he abandoned New France. Roberval, finally arriving, stopped Cartier on the way out. Against orders, Cartier sneaked away to France; Roberval soon followed.

Cartier's seven-year struggle in Canada left only a few flagstaffs and *fleur-de-lis.* And he added to the French language the expression, "False as the diamonds of Canada."

Samuel de Champlain and France's great conquering voyages were still years away.

HENRI II TOOK power in 1547 and shifted French attention back to the neighborhood. His defense strategy served for four centuries: keep Germany as divided and troubled as possible. France's interests lay along the Rhine; Italy was a luxury to be left alone. The Treaty of Cateau-Cambrésis, a reshuffling among sovereigns in 1559, shaped modern France. By renouncing designs on

Italy, the French secured Metz, Verdun, and Toul to the east and Calais to the west. France, more defensible, was knit more tightly together. And the French were happy. They did not necessarily love a king for winning foreign ground; but they were bitter about anyone who lost a square centimeter of French soil.

Henri II seemed about to be a great king, if a little bloodthirsty over heretics. But he insisted on jousting in a tournament with the son of the captain of his guard. A spear in the eye left France in the hands of his widow, Catherine de Médicis. For the next thirty years, while overseas empires were taking shape, France was ruled by three mediocre kings: a François, a Charles, and an Henri.

Under Henri III, in 1582, Norman merchants occupied the island of St.-Louis in Senegal. But it was only later that St.-Louis became the capital of vast African holdings. France had dealt in Africa as early as the 1300s when Normans from Dieppe set up three trading posts on the Guinea coast. Ships from Dieppe, funded by merchants but protected by the crown, were searching for a western route to the Indies a few years before Columbus. Under François I and afterward, however, the early momentum stalled.

The French were bled by wars of religion, at home and with neighbors, while the court was preoccupied with intrigue and financial chaos. The aristocracy rankled under the informal regency of Catherine, described by one as "that fat daughter of Florentine peddlers."

Frenchmen began shifting allegiance to an Henri from the house of Guise, which worried the Valois king, Henri III. Henri de Guise appeared at the castle of Blois, invited by the king for a council, and was chopped to bits by halberds. Catherine, appalled, knew grief would follow. It did. Soon afterward, a Dominican monk assassinated the king with a dagger, thus extinguishing the House of Valois.

That was in 1589. The France that François I had begun to shape fell again into capable hands.

As Henri III lay dying, he clutched a former enemy, Henri de Navarre, a relative only in the twenty-second degree. "I die happy at seeing you by my side," Henri III told him. "The crown is yours. . . . I order all officers to recognize you as their king after me."

Henri IV took the job. He was a Bourbon and a descendant of

Saint Louis. But he was also a Protestant in a country that bled half to death fighting to preserve Roman Catholicism.

The new king steered a careful course. At first, he rallied the French, saying, "We are born not only for ourselves, but above all to serve the country. Those who honestly follow their conscience are of my religion, and as for me, I belong to the faith of all those who are gallant and good."

He held out against the church. He would search his conscience, he said, but would anyone respect him for converting with a dagger at his throat? Those unwilling to wait could forsake him, he added. "Among the Catholics, I shall have with me those who love France and honor."

But the nobility of Paris hung back, refusing to follow the king unless he converted. Paris, in the 1590s, was already large and lovely, the heart of France. And completely Catholic. Elsewhere, dissension grew, and the council of nobles, the States General, was summoned to Paris.

Finally, Henri IV dressed in white and kneeled in Notre-Dame to embrace the religion he had renounced years before. "Paris," he said, "is worth a mass."

He put together a tense armistice, codifying tolerance under the 1598 Edict of Nantes. Then he threw himself into restoring French grandeur. He told the Rouen notables:

> You know to your cost, as do I to mine, that when God called me to the crown, I found France not only half ruined, but almost entirely lost to the French. . . . Through my care and toil I have saved the heritage; I shall now save it from ruin.

Parkman described his impact:

> To few has human liberty owed so deep a gratitude or so deep a grudge. He cared little for creeds or dogmas. Impressible, quick in sympathy, his grim lip lighted often with a smile, and his war-worn cheek was no stranger to a tear. He forgave his enemies and forgot his friends. Many loved him; none but fools trusted him. Mingled of mortal good and ill, frailty and force, of all the

kings who for two centuries and more sat on the throne of France
Henry IV alone was a man.

The king brought in an old friend, Maximilien de Béthune, later
the duc de Sully, who rebuilt France's crippled economy. Par-
simonious, hard-nosed, and a lunatic for work, Sully rose at 4 A.M.
to pore over intelligence reports in his office decorated with portraits of John Calvin and Martin Luther. He hunted down corrupt
tax collectors and slashed budgets. Steadily, he built up a reserve to
fund his other great love, beside penny-pinching: artillery. French
ramparts and marketplaces bristled with cannons under his command.

"Here was Calvin turned artilleryman and financier," Maurois
observed. Henri IV, more progressive, stopped him from setting up
an inspectorate of morals in each bailiwick to poke into families'
habits. But Sully blocked the king's hopes of reviving the French
manufacturing industry which, at the beginning of the seventeenth
century, was growing much faster than England's. He preferred
agriculture.

Neither the king nor Sully thought much of the New World.

"Tilling the soil and keeping flocks—these are France's riches, the
real mines and treasures of Peru," said the finance minister. He
resurfaced roads, lining them with elms, and built bridges. Transport
and irrigation canals were laid out across France. Forests and fields
were marked out; feudal lords were ordered to eliminate wolves and
wildcats. Breeding studs produced fine herds. Paris bloomed with
such triumphs as the Place des Vosges, admired across Europe.

Quebec was founded in 1608, but Sully was more interested in
the Pont Neuf over the Seine, inaugurated the same year. He counseled the king: "Things which remain separated from our body by
foreign lands or seas will be ours only at great expense and to little
purpose."

If Henri IV did not aggressively export France, he built French
civilization into an exportable commodity. In his name, sea captains,
merchants, and adventurers roamed the new worlds.

Champlain and Pontgrave charted the mouth of the St. Lawrence
up to the Great Lakes, founding Acadia and a handful of settlements.

To back it up, Henri IV claimed for France all American territory north of the fortieth parallel.

A French expedition settled Madagascar in 1601; three years later, La Ravardière claimed for the king Guyane—French Guiana—on the South American coast. In 1604, a company was formed to push trade with India.

Whatever else Henri IV might have done remains speculation. In 1610, a man named Ravaillac leaped onto the running board of the king's carriage and stabbed a knife through the window. Henri IV died instantly, his aorta severed.

Of all the French kings between 1515 and the French Revolution, only Henri IV reaches historian Jean Meyer's category of "good or very good"; François I and Louis XIV made it to "rather good."

Henri IV awakened a feeling of patriotism and a sense of unity that would never again leave France. During his reign, literature flourished, enriching the language. Thought and philosophy expanded, in French and throughout Europe. Henri IV had implanted firmly a Renaissance in which the mind and nature, rather than the Bible, would define the world.

Maurois concludes, "Henri IV remains, together with Charlemagne, Jeanne d'Arc and Saint Louis, one of France's heroes. He typifies not France's mystical aspect, but its aspects of courage, good sense and gaiety."

LOUIS XIII was king at nine, under the regency of his haughty Italian mother, Marie de Médicis. She, in turn, was dominated by a swarthy and mysterious Florentine, Leonora Galigai. And Galigai was married to a foppish schemer named Concini. They enlisted support from the clergy through a young bishop with an arched nose, a goatee, and a long cavalry moustache over thin lips: Richelieu. The young king, unsociable, a daydreamer, was left to his tutors.

One morning Louis XIII, at sixteen, announced that he was king. Concini had been put to death overnight on secret orders to the guard; Galigai was burned as a witch. Marie de Médicis was exiled to Blois. And the ambitious, proud prelate, Richelieu, went back to his diocese.

Before long, however, Louis XIII began to make use of Richelieu's skill at oratory, administration, and punishment. In 1624, already a cardinal, Richelieu was named chief minister. He grumbled that the French were hard to govern, with "more heart than head." He frequently bemoaned "the apathy of France," but he marveled at its recuperative powers. A writer and thinker, he founded the Académie Française and gave lasting form to French ideas of logic and tradition.

Richelieu burned to rebuild a strong army and a navy, but finances were short. Spain, flush with Inca and Aztec booty, was developing the strongest infantry in Europe. In 1636, Spanish armies penetrated deep into France. The king and cardinal appeared in the streets of Paris, and the French rallied. Money and men were thrown into the field. Spain retreated, and Richelieu was awash in glory.

Louis XIII's philosophy was not far from Henri IV's: what mattered was France's greatness within safe borders. Richelieu sought to trim "the great tree of Austria," not to build an empire but rather to keep a rival power from gaining enough strength to threaten France.

Like most French leaders, the king worried about sending abroad too many strong arms and agile minds needed at home. But the ambitious cardinal was not about to let France pass up wealth and glory.

Richelieu set up a system of state colonization through privileged companies. The Compagnie des Indes later built France's first colonies in India; the Compagnie des 100 Associés developed trade with Canada. Under the cardinal's aegis, merchants settled Martinique and Guadeloupe, St. Kitts, Grenada, the Grenadines, St. Lucia, and a string of smaller islands. He sent pioneers to Réunion, then l'Ile de Bourbon, and reinforced colonies in Madagascar and Guiana.

These early colonies were mostly collecting points for exotic riches: beaver pelts, cloves and cinnamon, silks and cottons. Some were plantations for sugar, tobacco, and coffee. But hard behind the traders and farmers, priests carried the word to whatever heathens they found. Montreal, founded in 1642, was a missionaries' outpost.

Moral judgments on these first missions to civilize reached absurd

extremes. In the 1940s, the Académie Française lauded Marius Leblond for a whole shelf of histories of the period. Some excerpts:

> Our action was dominated by the concern for evangelism
> infinitely more than commerce. . . . Our worthiness and initiative
> flourished in the Pacific Ocean which in the 18th Century was
> made *a French sea.* . . . Heroism is the dominant character of our
> action in the New World.

Writing on the Caribbean, Leblond notes that native Arawaks and
Caribs sometimes resisted French settlement:

> The indigenous problem posed itself immediately with as
> much instability and cruel drama as in Canada: our deep Christian
> genius was not the only quality summoned up against it; an
> incredible power of spirit, of invention, of flexibility and imita-
> tion pushed to the level of art was quickly demonstrated in our
> brand new mission of Colonization. . . . France, in its ensemble,
> tried to be soft with the Caraibes.

Except, of course, for the settlers who massacred Indians by the
thousands. Leblond skips over the decimation of the natives, amply
documented elsewhere. He mentions slavery as an economic fact of
life after carefully asserting that France did not start it. And piracy,
by his accounts, was a noble effort to adjust a balance of trade
skewed against France.

Like many, Leblond is fascinated by the buccaneers, *les boucaniers,* named for the spits on which they smoked their meat. "Since
Gaul the French have been great lords of the hunt and bleeders of
wild boar," he writes of the freebooters' main off-duty passion.
He describes their filthy, blood-caked tight breeches, pigskin shoes,
and pointed hats and adds, "The fantastic aspect is completed by
an arsenal of knives, bayonets, a long rifle made in Dieppe or
Nantes."

Their main base was Haiti, ". . . a very Great Island bristling with
rough and wild beauty, with ravines and powdery savannahs
. . . which we denuded before rearming with rich plantations of

coffee, sugar cane, and tobacco. We had to throw in millions of blacks with filed teeth, ferocious eyes, and calloused hands who quickly became one with the land, as sun-varnished, hard, and fecund as they were."

RICHELIEU DIED in 1642, Louis XIII a year later. Again, France was left with a child king. Louis XIV was an infant.

Queen Anne of Austria, a Spaniard of flaring temper, was regent. She convinced the Parlement of nobles to rescind Louis XIII's will, which subjected her to a council handpicked by Richelieu. Then she surprised everyone by naming as chief minister one of the dead cardinal's close cronies, an Italian named Giulio Mazarini, or Mazarin. He pursued Richelieu's colonial policy, setting up a company to trade with China and another to dig deeper into Cayenne, the capital of Guiana. But domestic affairs dominated the regency period.

Frenchmen were not thrilled at being governed by two foreigners. Finances were in shambles. The Parlement, an assembly of hereditary magistrates, wanted more power. Rumblings among nobles and common folk crystallized into the Fronde. A *fronde* is a sling for heaving rocks, David-style. And occasional whizzing projectiles kept Mazarin on his toes. The Fronde, a series of upheavals, was a dress rehearsal of the French Revolution. Most of the royal family fled Paris. Insurgents stormed the palace and demanded that the regent show them the king in his bed so they could be sure he had not sneaked away. Disorganized, half-hearted and sometimes cowardly, the Fronde never rose to revolution. After some compromise, tension subsided. By 1652, when young Louis XIV rode ceremoniously through Paris, the Fronde was quelled. But the prince never forgot the humiliation and fear.

Mazarin ran the government until 2:30 A.M. on March 8, 1661. Gravely ill, the cardinal was going over France's books with a favorite assistant, Jean-Baptiste Colbert. Then he died.

Louis XIV's nurse broke the news to him in the morning, and the king shut himself in his study to meditate for two hours. He never revealed what went through his head. But he emerged to begin a strictly personal rule. He was the Sun King. And the indefatigable Colbert, as everything but war minister and secretary of state, directed his rays.

VOLTAIRE CONCLUDED that for anyone of taste and reflection, world history produced only four centuries of note: those of Pericles, Augustus, the Médicis, and Louis XIV. "Europe has owed her manners and her feeling for social life to the court of Louis XIV," he wrote. True, novice footmen at Versailles knew twenty-seven ways to fold a table napkin, and guests at better French tables learned to turn their heads delicately when spitting, but Louis XIV ate with his fingers until he died in 1715, at which time Voltaire was barely twenty-one years old.

The king's reviews were mixed.

Like François I and Henri IV, Louis XIV devoted himself to the glory of France. He fashioned the pursuit of glory into such a high art form that the French of today still bask in his radiance. He also, as historian W. H. Lewis notes, "rode roughshod over Europe, sowing that crop of hatred which was to bring him fifty years later to the very edge of complete disaster." In the end, he survived by flanking his polished haughtiness with the finest military hardware and architecture of the age.

A year after taking personal charge, he set the tone. The French ambassador to Rome, the duc de Créqui, so antagonized the city with swaggering insolence that on August 20 the Corsican Guard fired on his coach. Louis received the news at dinner. He stalked from the table and ordered an assault on Italy. Later the king relented, on a few conditions: that the Vatican surrender Avignon to France, that the pope raise a pyramid in Rome bearing details of the crime and its expiation, and that the pope's nephew, Cardinal Chigi, come to Paris to read a full apology to the entire court. Finally, the pope disbanded the Corsican Guard. (A century later, Louis XV went his great-grandfather one better and took over Corsica.)

Louis XIV fashioned Versailles with such grandeur that every self-respecting monarch from Peter the Great to Roi Christophe of Haiti tried to copy it. Not the least of his motives was to leave downtown Paris, to make sure no more importuning masses barged in on royalty. He turned down plans by his genius military architect,

Vauban, to fortify Paris with concentric ramparts. Paris, he decreed, should be defended at France's borders. Instead, he developed the intelligence network inherited from Richelieu, planting secret agents, devising codes, and laying the groundwork for three centuries of French dirty tricks abroad.

And to underwrite the costs of glory and arrogance, Colbert built France's first overseas empire. His idea was simple: the colonies were to make money.

Colbert had the same thick wavy hair as Louis XIV, with similar puffy cheeks and hungry eyes. But he was a technocrat, a financial wizard and master organizer. He gathered together the ragtag bits of private enterprise around the globe under a single ministry at Versailles. He built ships to carry goods and fight off rivals.

In 1664, he commissioned the Compagnie des Indes occidentales and the Compagnie des Indes orientales. The first was to settle both Americas and the Caribbean; the second, to colonize Madagascar and dominate trade with China. He backed the first French establishment in India, at Surat, in 1668. Two years later, he created the Compagnie du Levant to import silk and cotton from Asia Minor. He revived Richelieu's efforts in the Indian Ocean, sending colonizers to Réunion.

Colbert encouraged adventuresome Frenchmen to poke around unmapped territory, especially that coveted by Britain. His governor in Haiti, Bertrand d'Ogeron, encouraged the *boucaniers,* "the brothers of the coast." The king commissioned some freebooters who roamed far to the south. Largely from St.-Malo, they were called *Malouins* (the French name for the Falkland Islands is still *les Malouines,* after its discoverers). Leblond, yet again, sings their praises:

> Les Malouins! Honor of French commerce. . . . Their Duguay-Trouin took Rio de Janeiro in one of the most sumptuous exploits of naval history and imposed a ransom . . . which helped save the Great King from bankruptcy and disaster . . . the ladies of Peru danced for them in golden capes and skirts embroidered in triple rows of lace; the Spaniards who they drubbed so many times revered them. . . . We find in them the most complete and creative genius, honored in all the Empire.

Colbert's crown company brought new life to Martinique and Guadeloupe, each settled in 1635 by Norman explorers who found it hard to keep the colonies afloat without help from Paris.

A globe-girdling empire was no mean feat, given the rigors of seventeenth-century sea travel. Fortunes were consumed by it and a fair number of voyagers never reached their destinations. An account from 1644 describes an effort to sail the queen of England across the Channel. After a nine-day gale, she was landed in Holland. During the voyage, she "suffered the terrors of almost certain death, tied down in a little bed, with her ladies tied down around her in theirs."

Robert Challes, quartermaster and "king's writer" aboard L'Ecueil, bound for the Far East in 1690, left an account of life at sea. The 500-ton ship, with 350 men and thirty-eight guns, was "a farmyard," the bullocks, ducks, and pigs making it all but impossible to walk on the deck. Wine was so short he had to sneak on deck at night to supplement his ration. The six-ship convoy sailed past the Cape of Good Hope. France was at war with Holland, and L'Ecueil ran up Dutch colors when an enemy fleet passed.

But the ship attacked the Dutch vessel Montfort off Ceylon. Challes rages for two pages at the boatman who did not get him across in time to pick over the spoils. Then, in an abrupt fit of morality, he notes that the dignity of his position as king's writer places him above looting. The admiral shared the loot with him nonetheless, and he is pleased. He observes: "So I keep my reputation as a man who does not loot, while I in fact get a reasonable share of the booty."[2]

ENTHUSIASM FOR EMPIRE was hardly total. America, for example, was no great prize. Père Jacques Marquette and Louis Joliet pushed down the Mississippi as far as the Arkansas River, but hostile Indians blocked their way. They returned in triumph to Quebec—bells pealed the entire day—and then everyone forgot about the Mississippi. Then Cavelier de La Salle located a channel through the delta. He found a dry spot and claimed the place with all the pomp of the era.

A stone column was painted with the king's coat of arms. La Salle's exhausted company sang a "Te Deum" and "Domine Salvum fac Regem," shouted, *"Vive le Roi,"* and blasted muskets into the trees. La Salle read a wordy proclamation and raised a cross. Everyone sang "Vexilia regis" and a lead plaque detailing the proceedings was buried in the ground. Finally, more shouts of *"Vive le Roi!"*

Then La Salle returned to France for his fame and fortune. But Louis XIV was not impressed. He received the explorer but turned down his request to go back. Later, the king changed his mind. La Salle went back to start a colony.

La Salle assembled a dozen gentlemen, 100 soldiers, a handful of priests, artisans and laborers, enough stores to start a small city, a frigate and three other ships. He set sail for the Gulf of Mexico, missed the mouth of the Mississippi, and spent two years lost in Texas.

Disease, despair, and desertion reduced La Salle's company to thirty-six. He took sixteen of them north to try to find Illinois. A few finally made it, but not La Salle. One of his last remaining lieutenants killed him during a mutiny.

France's start in Louisiana presaged its on-and-off tenure there and its ignoble end. It was a decade before anyone came back to add substance to the lead plaque and the royal standard left to remind the Indians that they belonged to France. Louis XIV, with most of Europe to fight, had other priorities.

The king still had France to unite, culturally as well as politically. The French language was refined during the splendid century, but it spread only slowly. Racine traveled to the southern duchy of Uzès in 1650. By Lyon, he said, he was intelligible only to himself. "My misfortune grew at Valence. As fate would have it, I asked for a chamber pot and a small stove was placed under my bed. You can imagine the results of this damned adventure when a very sleepy fellow used the stove for his night's needs. But in this part of the country things are even worse. I swear that I am as much in need of an interpreter as a Muscovite in Paris."[3]

Colbert himself slowed colonization, except in Canada, for fear of depopulating the *métropole*. France had twenty-two million inhabitants at the start of Louis's reign; at the end, after seventy-two years of war and epidemics, the figure remained the same.[4] The crown awarded 2,000 *livres* (about $5,000 today) to any nobleman who produced more than ten children.

By the time Colbert died in 1683, however, the *fleur-de-lis* flapped in Canada, the Caribbean, Guiana, Senegal, the Indian Ocean, and in India itself. Foundations were laid for commerce and farming, mining, trapping, and fishing. And he had set in motion a permanent wave of Frenchmen anxious to shine their light abroad. In exchange, of course, for some modest return for their efforts.

CHAPTER EIGHT

Into the New World

COLBERT LEFT BEHIND the most powerful navy in
Europe. And Louvois, who had taken over the War Ministry in
1664 at the age of twenty-four, transformed a corrupt and sloppy
militia into Europe's strongest army. Frenchmen were spreading
through the New World, Africa, and beyond, raising the royal
colors and fulfilling dreams of further glory. Louis XIV devised a
land-sea strategy to dominate the world.

It didn't work. English and Dutch ships ganged up on the French
off Normandy in 1692 and pounded Colbert's fleet to driftwood.
A year later, famine ravaged Europe, hitting France the hardest.
Enemies pressed on all sides. Louis XIV, his maritime power lost,
concentrated instead on his victorious armies close to home. Rather
than build colonies, he settled into a duel with England that would
last 120 years.

But the mission to civilize flourished, with the king's distracted
blessing. French freebooters, *les flibustiers,* prowled the Spanish
Main. Baron Jean de St. Jean Pointis relieved the Spanish colony of
Cartagena, Columbia, of twenty million pounds worth of assorted
loot. In northern waters, French pirates seized so much from English
and Dutch ships that Nantes merchants declared them the greatest
financial asset France had yet known.

Brisk trade brought slaves from Africa to the West Indies and
sugar back to France. Stone forts protected Louis XIV's island real
estate. To the north, trappers brought beaver pelts from remote

rivers, and a few troops defended France with scattered outposts and tenuous alliances with Indian chiefs.

If Louis XIV funded few settlements, his dubious statecraft sent French pilgrims around most of the known world. He revoked Henri IV's Edict of Nantes and proclaimed, once again, open season on Protestants. Non-Catholics were commanded to stay home and convert. Instead, huge numbers slipped away. Incorrigibles were deported en masse.

French Huguenots took their skills and fortunes to Holland and Germany, to England, and beyond. Today, their descendants are everywhere. In South Africa, an Afrikaner named Du Toit leaped to his feet on seeing a French address on my card, ecstatic to receive a visitor who might not call him "Doo-toyt."

Louis XIV forced thousands of the French to pay nominal homage to the church, and he proved he was king. But he lost 100,000 of his most industrious people, who smuggled out fortunes, along with trade secrets and specialized tools. W. H. Lewis estimates that 9,000 sailors, 600 army officers, and 12,000 troops left France. Lewis added:

> And what of the invisible items . . . of infinitely greater moment? Loss of honor and good faith on the part of the Crown, misery, fear, hatred, delations, bribery, savagery, the enmity of all Europe, the disapproval of the Pope—who shall say at what price these were estimated when the account finally came up for audit?

European sovereigns found their colonies to be useful pressure points for triggering responses elsewhere, like a global Japanese foot massage. Britain, for instance, routinely defeated France in some far-flung harbor and handed back the spoils for renewed trading rights at Antwerp. Colonies were not jewels of the crown but pawns on a chessboard.

But Louis XIV felt bound by his duties as leader of the world's most enlightened nation. Missionaries sailed first class in his vessels. He gave each one a mattress and bedding, a white suit and six shirts, a cassock, six pairs of drawers, twelve handkerchiefs, twelve nightshirts, twelve pairs of thread stockings, a hat, three pairs of shoes, a sea chest, and one spirit case for every two priests. And some pocket money.

He sent the Abbé de Choisy to convert the Siamese court—and to secure a French base and commercial ally in Asia. Choisy liked to dress richly as a woman, draped in jewelry, and gossip with the ladies. In Paris, as "la comtesse de Sancey," he kept mistresses but insisted they wear men's clothing. But he flung himself into Christianity after a serious illness, and he accepted the Siam mission.

More than Asia, the king concentrated on America. Long after La Salle's Louisiana fiasco, a Canadian-born officer named Lemoyne d'Iberville persuaded the court to outfit a small fleet to the Mississippi. On March 2, 1699, struck by the beauty of the site, he set up a capital at Biloxi.

The river was too shallow, the soil too sandy, and the sun too hot. Dysentery ravaged the settlers. Thugs and outcasts were rounded up in France to bolster the ranks, but a colony of 400 Protestant families, leaving the Carolinas, were turned away. The governor told them, "The Sovereign did not chase the Protestants from his kingdom in Europe to have them set up a republic in his American domains."

Biloxi was abandoned for Mobile. Louis XIV sent out twenty-three young ladies, "raised in virtue and piety," to help populate the colony. But by 1708 an outraged nobleman reported:

> The colony is composed of 279 persons, including six sick people, plus 60 errant Canadians who are in savages' villages along the Mississippi without permission of any governor and who destroy by their evil libertine life with the savage women all that the gentlemen of the Foreign Missions and others teach about the mysteries of religion.

Liliane Crété, in her *La Vie Quotidienne en Louisiane,* noted that Bienville, governor of Louisiana, complained that he was so short of food that he was obliged to give "the largest part of his men to feed the savages." She did not elaborate.

The king, busy with a lingering war of Spanish succession, ceded Louisiana to a merchant, Antoine Crozat. His meager earnings fed 100 infantrymen and seventy-five Canadians in five dirt and log forts spread over the vast territory. Crozat gave up his fifteen-year concession after five years.

Louis XIV died in 1715, ending the Splendid Century. Another Louis would follow; meantime, Philippe d'Orléans, as regent, governed France and the empire.

Suddenly, Louisiana was on everyone's lips. A Scottish financier named John Law swept away the regent with visions of a prospering colony. "The land abounds in gold, silver, copper and lead," Law's agents reported. His Compagnie d'Occident was given control of Louisiana. Law obtained virtual control of the French economy, which he intended to fuel with profits from the colony. Frenchmen lined up to buy his stock, which soared to dizzying heights. Adventurers and gold-seekers rushed west in 1718. But neither farmers nor entrepreneurs followed.

Two years later, the bubble burst. No one found gold or any other wealth; the stock plummeted, taking the fledgling Paris market along with it. Law's paper money was worthless. He fled France, while remnants of the company kept Louisiana limping along.

Planters were given land but they had to find labor. White farmers wilted in the sun, and most tended to cut corners on their employers' time. So the company brought slaves from the Guinea coast. By 1724, Bienville had a code for the blacks, with a first article banning Jews from the colony. It stayed on the books for more than a century.

Bienville decided the colony needed a decent capital. He picked a narrow strip where Indians had to portage their canoes and named it Nouvelle-Orléans, after the regent. The place flooded so often that a levee was built along with the first houses. It attracted such dregs that the court decreed, "Henceforth, no more vagabonds and criminals will be sent to Louisiana."

But the company dispatched *filles de cassette*—"hope chest girls" —who were educated by Ursuline nuns and then matched with husbands of good family. Their parting gift was a *cassette* containing a modest trousseau. Liliane Crété observes, "Judging from the number of Louisiana families who flatter themselves today by claiming to descend from these virtuous creatures, these girls must have been extremely prolific." Short of prospective wives, the company also sent over *ribaudes* gathered up on the streets of Paris. One governor complained that a dozen young women shipped out for marriage were "so ugly and so badly made" that local bachelors preferred Indian women.

The Indians were growing restive for other reasons. France and Britain both exploited rivalry among the tribes. Each had allies and enemies, and neither was above inciting Indians to lift scalps of the other European tribe.

Such tactics were a specialty of the French in Canada to discourage English forays north. Francis Parkman recounts an incident of 1694 on the Oyster River, near what is now Durham, New Hampshire. A French lieutenant, Villieu, and a priest helped 105 Abenaki Indians massacre 104 people, mostly women and children. Twenty houses were burned and twenty-seven prisoners taken. "This stroke," observed Villebon, the French governor of Canada, "is of great advantage because it breaks off all the talk of peace between our Indians and the English. The English are in despair, for not even infants in the cradle were spared."

An Abenaki chief, Bomazeen, taken prisoner in Boston, said missionaries had told him Jesus Christ was a Frenchman, the son of the Virgin Mary, a French lady, and the English had killed him. His death must be avenged to gain his favor, Bomazeen said he was told.

Parkman notes, in balance, that French Canadians often paid ransoms for English prisoners taken by their Indian allies. Some were made to work off the debt, he said, but "they were uniformly treated well."

In Louisiana, Bienville boasted that his Choctaws had razed three Chickasaw villages, bringing back 400 scalps and 100 prisoners. The Chickasaws had disturbed commerce along the river. He wrote, "It is an important advantage in the state of things, particularly since this result was obtained without risking the life of a single Frenchman by the care which I took to make these barbarians act against each other."

After a while, the Indians caught on. The Natchez, fed up with settlers taking their lands, massacred 200 Frenchmen on November 28, 1729. The French mounted a punitive expedition to recover their women, children and slaves. They took along 200 Choctaws and some blacks who did most of the fighting. The Natchez took refuge with the Chickasaws and, together, declared war on the French.

Allied, they harassed the river and the hinterlands. A wall went up around New Orleans, and settlers upcountry, at the least, lost sleep.

The Compagnie d'Occident finally collapsed in 1731, and the crown took over the colony. By then, the English were poring over maps with concern. French settlements formed a thin but unbroken line from the mouth of the St. Lawrence to the Mississippi Delta, and on down through the Caribbean. The thirteen English colonies were encircled. Increasingly, pioneers probing west found themselves hacked to bits by Indians inflamed by the French.

Louis XV, who had taken the throne, was no great empire builder but a proud king of a nation that believed itself the natural leader of the world. He knew that French holdings in Canada and the Caribbean islands disrupted Britannia's plans to rule the waves. But, since Cartier, France had been divided over Canada. Quebec grew slowly, partly stifled by jealous fur traders who feared competition. In 1664, Louis XIV had made the moribund territory a crown colony, and Colbert sent out 10,000 settlers to defend it. But enthusiasm was muted. Voltaire dismissed all of Canada as "a few acres of snow."

The 1713 Treaty of Utrecht, a crucial settling of accounts with Britain, had left the French Canadian map in tatters. France lost Newfoundland and Acadia at the mouth of the St. Lawrence as well as the vast Hudson Bay. The treaty also gave Guinea and West Indian islands to Britain, altogether four million square kilometers of Colbert's empire.

After that, French pioneers held fast in Canada against paralyzing winters, shortages of food, tools, and supplies, and a dubious regard from Paris. Louis-Antoine de Bougainville wrote home in 1754: "What a country, my dear brother, and what patience is needed to bear the slights that people go out of their way to lay on us here. It seems as though we belonged to a different nation, even a hostile one."

That year, five years from a final showdown with Britain, French Canadians numbered 55,009 against at least a half million in the thirteen English colonies to the south.

A SHORT SAIL from New Orleans was Saint-Domingue (Haiti), one of the richest properties of the New World. Its plantations produced sugar and tobacco. It had no minerals, but its ports sheltered pirates who mined gold and silver from boats headed back to Spain. And it helped protect France's other Caribbean islands.

France and England started off amicably in the West Indies, from 1627, sharing the tiny island of St. Christopher (St. Kitts to its friends). In one of their few successful joint enterprises, the French and English exterminated the Carib Indians on the island.

But each power moved off in a different direction. Belain d'Esnambuc, a ruined Normandy gentleman turned freebooter, took to the sea "as one sets forth on Crusade." He settled Martinique from St. Kitts in 1635. That year, Liénart de l'Olive and Urbain du Roissey sailed from Normandy to claim Guadeloupe.

It was tough going. Of the first 550 pioneers to leave Le Havre, 350 died at sea; Richelieu's company had skimped on food. Later, of seventy passengers on Roissey's ship, the *Catholic,* sixteen landed, alive but barely strong enough to build shelters. When Colbert took over in 1664, Martinique and Guadeloupe had fewer than 8,000 white settlers between them. By contrast, Britain's Barbados, half the size of Martinique, had 10,000 inhabitants by 1640, as many as Massachusetts or Virginia.

The Compagnie de Rouen sent 400 men to Guiana in 1643; within two years, all but twenty-five had died. The population grew but dropped again with every British and Dutch raid. By 1670, it was 300 whites and 1,000 black slaves.

France had already lost out on the tobacco market. In 1540, the French ambassador to Lisbon, Jean Nicot, as in nicotine, sent Catherine de Médicis tobacco from Florida. By the time the crown decided to plant the crop, however, Spain, England, and Holland had cornered the market. That left sugar. From 1651 to 1700, the French brought 152,000 slaves to Caribbean sugar plantations. The British, ever pushing their advantage, brought 242,000.[1]

The Treaty of Utrecht gave St. Kitts to Britain but nailed down the French claim to a small string of islands. An economic boom had begun, punctuated only sporadically by the less figurative boom of naval guns. Real estate changed hands frequently. France sold Saint Croix to Denmark in 1733 but later relieved Sweden of Saint Barthélemy. Grenada, at first French, became British.

In the wars to follow, Britain sent a small party onto the imposing Diamond Rock just south of Martinique and for eighteen months blasted away at every French ship trying to negotiate the straits. To this day, the rock is commissioned in the Royal Navy as H.M.S. *Diamond Rock.* Passing British ships salute it, sending the French into fits.

RIVALRY EXTENDED around Africa, through the Indian Ocean, and into Asia, where European powers raced to establish permanent settlements. Had things gone according to Colbert's plan, France, not Britain, would have civilized India. Neither, of course, consulted the Indians.

Europe had craved Indian silks, precious woods, and spices since the Middle Ages. In the 1400s, Portugal and Holland set up trading posts on the subcontinent. The Parmentier brothers reached India for France in 1529, followed by navigators from Rouen and the ubiquitous *Malouins.* Henri IV organized a trading company, and Richelieu gave it form. But only under Colbert, twenty-six years later, was the first French *comptoir* (trading port) established in India, at Surat, north of Bombay. Five years later, Pondicherry was founded near Madras. Chandernagore, outside Calcutta, was ceded to France, and then Calicut, south of Bombay.

By 1701, the French governor had flags planted strategically along both sides of the Indian peninsula. By alternately wheedling and strong-arming, France broadened its hold. And in 1741, the new governor, Dupleix, went for broke. He artfully played off nabob against maharajah, shifting alliances and dangling promises. No general, he nonetheless picked fights with the British who wanted to expand their own *comptoirs* near Bombay, Calcutta, and Madras. Dupleix brought in La Bourdonnais, French governor of Mauritius, who had the nearest convenient fleet.

With the excuse of the War of Austrian Succession, France and Britain battled at Pondicherry. Dupleix lined up the Nabob of Carnatic, who threatened to besiege the British at Madras if they attacked Pondicherry. Meanwhile, La Bourdonnais scattered the Indian army and captured Madras with hardly a fight. Then he gave it back in order to ransom prisoners.

Dupleix was incensed. The admiral merely wanted to stamp out British interests in India; Dupleix wanted India. He had La Bourdonnais recalled to France, but his public relations suffered when the admiral got there.

Without a fleet, Dupleix defended Pondicherry against thirty British ships and an army of Indians. After fifty-eight days of bitter attacks, the English gave up. French historians call that victory, on October 18, 1748, one of the finest military episodes of the eighteenth century. The only problem was that on that same day Louis XV signed the Peace of Aix-la-Chapelle, which restored all conquered territory in Canada and India. He said he sought peace "as a king and not as a tradesman."

Although India was up for grabs, France and England had promised not to fight over it. Dupleix sought instead to conquer by diplomacy. With a crafty aide and a striking Creole wife, he amassed land titles by promising protection and collecting on political debts. His empire extended along 500 miles of coastline and totaled thirty million inhabitants—as many as in France.

The Compagnie des Indes, however, wanted profit and not power. Finally, Dupleix spread himself too thinly to neutralize his enemies in India and France. He was recalled in disgrace in 1754, and his successor signed trade accords with the English. Lord Clive, according to French historians, immediately put to good use the fallen governor's tactic of divide and conquer. Dupleix died in France, broken and miserable, and the fate of French India was sealed forever.

LOUISIANA, MEANWHILE, was still struggling. Into the last half of the eighteenth century, New Orleans' population numbered only 800. The upper crust wore powdered wigs and brocade to gala balls, stocking gilt-carved buffets with fine wines. The master dance instructor was a Parisian named Baby; authorities found it necessary to limit the cabarets to six. And, when it rained, the streets were ankle-deep in mud and alligators. The town was desperately short of carpenters and bootmakers.

Devastating tornadoes alternated with periods of drought. Yellow fever was endemic. Indian wars continued, and disgruntled Choctaws threatened to join the more generous English. The army was so ill-disciplined and cowardly, one local authority grumbled, that he would have sent blacks to fight if they weren't so expensive.

Governor Kerlerec asked for Swiss troops since Frenchmen had disgusted local inhabitants "for the horrors of which they are capable."

The colony might have prospered. One sixty-man French army unit performed so well that each was discharged and given land, a wife, and farm animals; they prospered. Acadians filtered into the colony, thriving after their exodus from Nova Scotia. But Louis XV, battered in Europe and elsewhere, ignored repeated pleas for help. By the time he noticed, Britain's western settlements cast a dark shadow over Louisiana.

France pushed Spain into helping to counter British advances. The Spanish immediately grabbed Cuba. Louis XV worried that Spain might desert him, so he tossed King Carlos III, "his very dear and well-loved cousin," another chunk of territory: Louisiana.

The act of cession was signed secretly at Fontainebleau on November 3, 1762, but it was not until 1764 that Louisiana settlers learned they were to pledge allegiance to a different flag. Frenchmen already had a great deal more to mourn.

William Pitt took power in Britain in 1757 and set out immediately to evict France from North America. His fleet seized the fortress at Louisbourg, in Cape Breton, and a land force overran Fort Duquesne in the Ohio Valley. In a third swift stroke, he sent troops against Montreal. But a smaller French army under Louis-Joseph, Marquis de Montcalm, blasted the British into disarray. Pitt ordered a final multipronged attack at the heart of New France. For the crucial assault on Quebec, he chose James Wolfe, a slight, untested, rheumatic thirty-two-year-old colonel with a weak chin and a receding forehead. Wolfe was given a general's commission, 8,500 experienced regulars, and a well-armed fleet of forty-nine ships.

At Quebec waited Pierre de Rigaud, marquis de Vaudreuil, born a French-Canadian and, at sixty, governor-general of New France and former governor of New Orleans. He was not modest. "My firmness is generally applauded," he wrote to the court in 1759. "It has entered all hearts and one and all say loudly, 'Canada, our native land, will bury us in her ruins before we yield to the English.' This is the course which I am firmly resolved upon and which I shall maintain inviolable."

He had at hand Montcalm, at forty-seven one of the most courageous and efficient officers of the French army. But Vaudreuil
outranked Montcalm and did not let him forget it. Before the
British appeared, Montcalm cursed in his journal the governor's
"ridiculous, obscure and misleading orders."

In response to Montcalm's plea for reinforcements, Paris sent 400
men and some cargo, including brandy. Warships could not be
spared. The court also directed Vaudreuil to defer to Montcalm on
military matters. There is no evidence, however, that the governor
advised the general of the order.

Quebec today, built up the side of dramatic cliffs like the prow
of a ship, appears impregnable. In 1759, after a century of costly but
bungled attempts at fortification, the badly designed and half-
finished walls were less imposing. Corruption and jealousy among
the engineers had taken their toll. The city was still more vulnerable
because no one had fortified the south bank, 1,000 yards across the
St. Lawrence River. In battles past, river currents had deterred the
British, and complacent French strategists counted on similar future
help from nature. With Wolfe nearly at their door, French commanders debated what should be done about fortifying the city.

"There had been much inefficiency and much dishonesty, and
France—and New France—were to pay for these things now,"
observed C. P. Stacey in his account of the battle.

The French found, at the last minute, that they could not block
the Traverse; the tricky channel was too long, and no one had yet
charted it properly. "Our best seamen," Montcalm observed, "seem
to me to be either liars or ignoramuses."

But Montcalm was able to deploy 15,000 regulars, militiamen,
and Indians against the invading force. Wolfe had little intelligence
about his objective beyond a faulty map drawn by his chief engineer, a former prisoner at Quebec. The French drew first blood,
capturing a British cutter. Wolfe was bitter at what he called the
timorous and somewhat uncooperative Royal Navy.

For two months, Wolfe maneuvered off Quebec to little effect.
He bombarded the city and, in retaliation for past massacres of
Britons by the French and Indians, he burned riverside villages. But
he had only a month before winter threatened. He had already lost
850 men in battle, including fifty-seven officers, and more to disease.

Bedridden with kidney stones, dysentery, and fever, Wolfe was in a bind.

Montcalm, too, was hard pressed. Flour from France was exhausted, and Quebec lived on short rations from the local harvest. The British had cut the river above the capital, burning emergency stores.

Finally, in mid-September, Wolfe made his last move, what Stacey calls his eighth plan. At night, aided by the navy he had abused, Wolfe landed a heavy force at an undefended cove upriver. Officers scaled a cliff face the French thought impregnable. Warned of this eventuality, Montcalm had remarked, "We need not suppose the enemy have wings."

Sentries were dispatched in a brief skirmish, and troops scrambled up a steep narrow path. When dawn broke on the Abraham heights, the French-Canadians found an unbroken line of scarlet tunics advancing toward their capital behind the Highlanders' wailing bagpipes.

Wolfe formed six battalions and the Louisbourg Grenadiers, 4,441 men by British count, and sailors lugged two brass cannon up the path. The French had an equal force, with heavier guns, but they suffered from the surprise. Montcalm probably should have waited for help. But at 10 A.M., a hastily formed front unfurled silk banners, cheered, and ran at the British. Disciplined musket volleys cut up the French lines. Wolfe was shot dead in the chest; Montcalm was fatally wounded a few minutes later. The British lost 640 dead and wounded; the French, probably double that.

It was no more than a major skirmish, Parkman notes, but in terms of what it meant, it was one of the greatest battles in history. The French-Canadians held out for another year, besieging the British at Quebec and defending Montreal, but Louis XV sent little help. For France, Canada was lost on September 13, 1759, before lunch, on the Plains of Abraham.

THE TREATY of 1763 could hardly have been more galling. Signed in Paris, it excised in a single cut four million square kilometers of the French empire. It was the same territorial loss that the Utrecht treaty imposed a half-century earlier, but it was far more devastating. France lost Canada and Cape Breton; all of India but for five small trading posts which could not be fortified; Grenada, the Grenadines, and Tobago; and Senegal, its main foothold in Africa. Britain had humbled France.

For Fernand Braudel, French grandeur ended in 1763.

In the New World, France kept a tiny foothold in the far north: St. Pierre and Miquelon. The English could afford a slight flourish of magnanimity. After all, some day a stronger France might seek revenge. But elsewhere in North America, trappers and farmers would have to learn to love a new king or face very cold winters on their own. Along the Mississippi and in Louisiana, the French would have to start hardening their r's and living without Bordeaux reds.

France stayed in the Caribbean, but its little island paradises bristled with cannon behind thick stone ramparts. Spanish and Dutch ships made occasional raids, official or otherwise. But the constant threat was British.

The remaining empire was strong enough in few places to resist a determined push from an English fleet. It comprised Madagascar, Réunion, Mauritius, and the Seychelles in the Indian Ocean; and in Africa, France held scattered slaving and trading posts on the western bulge.

In 1763, Choiseul, Louis XV's foreign minister, took charge of the navy and raced to rebuild the fleet. Bougainville, who escaped from Canada, sailed to Tahiti in 1768 and staked out the vast stretches of the South Pacific that France still controls. La Pérouse followed him five years later to solidify the French presence in the South Seas.

But scandal marred success.

Choiseul decided to build up Guiana as a southern American base to replace Canada, lost in the north. Jesuit missionaries had settled in from 1709 and, by the mid-1700s, priests counted 10,000 "civilized Indians." The colony had 1,200 whites, 5,000 black slaves, and 2,000 mulattoes. Gabriel Hanotaux noted that its promise of natural wealth was attracting "the attention of civilized humanity."

A colonist named Préfontaine fired Choiseul's imagination. The minister ordered a pioneer venture, down to thousands of straw hats with chin ribbons and tambourine players to entertain the settlers. To avoid attention, volunteers were sneaked out of Paris at night, in closed carts, and dispatched to ships. It was the most ambitious attempt France had yet made to people a colony.

At Kourou, Préfontaine cleared a town site and built fourteen rows of straw huts around a statue of Louis XV. Within months, 8,000 settlers arrived. Ship captains unloaded their passengers and left, stranding them without shelter in the pounding rain. Authorities at Cayenne, four miles down the coast, refused to help. Within two years, 10,996 settlers were landed; of those, 918 lived to go home. Scarcely twenty families remained to farm in the region. The exercise cost an estimated thirty million *livres,* about six million dollars in currency of the time.[2]

Abbé Guillaume Reynal brought harsh judgment in his classic work of 1772, edited by Denis Diderot, *Histoire philosophique et politique des Deux Indes:*

> When a prince, a minister, is guided by the public opinion of enlightened people, if he encounters misfortune, neither heaven nor earth can reproach him. But enterprises undertaken without the counsel or wish of the nation, events hidden from all those whose lives and fortunes are exposed—is it anything but a secret league, a conspiracy of a few individuals against an entire society? Up to what point does authority feel itself humiliated? To what point does it exhibit such scorn for men not even to seek to excuse itself for its faults?

LOUIS XV DIED in 1774 in a lingering climate of national humiliation, loss, and lust for vengeance. Yet another Louis took the throne. Soon afterward, his court received secret envoys from a national liberation front. Americans sought revolution against Britain and they needed help. Might France be interested? Might it, indeed.

Foreign Minister Charles Gravier, comte de Vergennes, reported to the king: "The inveterate emnity of [Britain] imposes upon us the duty to lose no occasion of weakening it, so that we cannot but gain by seizing the one now being offered; we must, therefore, give support to the independence of the insurgent colonies."

Before any American reached Paris, Louis XVI had already directed that one million *livres* be loaned through Pierre-Augustin

Caron de Beaumarchais, author of *Le Mariage de Figaro,* poet, salon star, and sometime secret agent. Beaumarchais had argued that if France did not help the Americans, it would lose the West Indies. He set up a phony mercantile company, Roderique Hortalez and Company, and bought munitions from the French arsenal. Spain matched the amount, and the next year, France paid out another million.

American freedom, orators of all extremes tend to forget, was paid for largely with clandestine foreign aid to the rebels.

In 1777, the French dispatched eight chartered ships with 200 brass cannons, 300 rifles, 100 tons of powder, 3,000 tents, heavy stores of bullets, mortars, and cannonballs, and clothing for 30,000 men. All but one ship made it.

Benjamin Franklin and Silas Deane, a Connecticut merchant, bought supplies under the unseeing gaze of a neutral French government. The Americans tried to pay for their arms, but their exports of tobacco and other crops were too bulky to avoid a British blockade. French subsidies and loans made up the difference. Deane worked the deals. Franklin solicited cash from the court at Versailles. The total ranged near 15,400,000 *livres*—worth $2,852,000 at the time—up to the beginning of 1781. That year, new grants added $1,000,000.

France was short of cash, but there was more: a further loan of four million *livres* and a gift of six million. The court guaranteed a Dutch loan of ten million. Spain sneaked some money to the Continentals but stayed out of the war until France promised to help get back Gibraltar and Florida. Spanish leaders feared an independent United States as yet another threat in the New World. Prussia, Austria, and Tuscany slammed the door on American envoys.

By the end, France had paid out an estimated $8,167,500—or $9,600,000, by some counts—compared to Spain's $611,328.[3] In addition, France paid heavy costs for deploying its army and navy. The difference, in the end, was not money.

American morale soared with the first tangible foreign ally. Gilbert du Motier, marquis de Lafayette, was only twenty in 1778 when he rushed to aid the rebels. At the time, he was chafing under garrison life in Metz, living elaborately on his wife's vast inheritance. And he hated the English, who had killed his father in battle.

Lafayette bought the vessel *La Victoire* in Bordeaux and prepared to sail. Louis XVI heard of his plans and forbade the voyage. But Lafayette slipped away a few steps ahead of the cops, helped by a French agent of Franklin and Deane's. As soon as he reached America, the Continental Congress made him a major general, without pay. Washington, at forty-five more than twice his age, adopted him as evidence of French support.

Soon afterward, Vergennes negotiated a "conditional and defensive alliance" which protected the French West Indies but gave up claim to Canada, Bermuda, and all of the United States east of the Mississippi. The minister met secretly with Franklin, who was loved in Paris despite his clumsy French.

Alexander Hamilton wrote in 1780, "Our countrymen have all the folly of the ass and all the passiveness of the sheep in their composition. They are determined not to be free and they can neither be frightened, discouraged, nor persuaded to change their resolution. If we are to be saved France and Spain must save us." Not Spain.

At first, a French naval force under Admiral Jean Baptiste, comte d'Estaing, accomplished little and sat sheltered in port. But in the spring of 1780, France sent 5,500 troops under Lieutenant General Jean-Baptiste-Donatien de Vimeur, comte de Rochambeau. Then Admiral François Joseph Paul, comte de Grasse, arrived with twenty ships of the line and headed for Chesapeake with 3,000 troops from the Saint-Domingue garrison.

They were welcomed warmly. One merchant wrote, "The French officers are the most civilized men I ever met. They are temperate, prudent, and extremely attentive to duty. I did not expect they would have so few vices." And another: "Neither Officers nor men are the effeminate Beings we were heretofore taught to believe them. They are as large & as likely men as can be produced by any nation."

The war was heading for a showdown. Britain's Cornwallis had massed his army of 7,200 at Yorktown. Washington moved 7,000 men, half of them French regulars, overland to Virginia. Comte de Barras broke out of a British blockade at Newport, behind Rochambeau's heavy guns, bringing a twelve-ship French squadron to the battle. De Grasse unloaded men near Yorktown and sent transport for Washington's and Rochambeau's forces.

Benedict Arnold, the traitorous American commander of West Point, nearly ruined the preparations. But the cooperation among generals, admirals, and colonial authorities was unparalleled in eighteenth-century military history. Britain was slow to send reinforcements and patrols, leaving a small French force in control of the Caribbean. At Yorktown, the British admiral, Sir George Rodney, assumed the French would melt away as they had in the past. He sent fourteen ships and found that de Grasse and de Barras had thirty-six.

The decisive battle for American independence was fought by 18,000 French seamen and 7,800 French foot soldiers against 8,000 British and German mercenaries. Only 5,700 Continental regulars and 3,200 militiamen took part. Today, in Bar-sur-Loup, not far from Nice, a statue of de Grasse is inscribed: "To our native son, victor of the Battle of Yorktown, who gave the United States its freedom." Yorktown, Pennsylvania, is the twin city of Bar-sur-Loup, and its mayor visits France occasionally to observe that the inscription is not far from correct.

Rodney, of course, later captured de Grasse in the Antilles. And France got little out of the war beyond heavy debts. The Americans' immediate gratitude was overwhelming. Not long afterward, however, Louis XVI's young ally was at the point of declaring war on France to preserve its right to trade with Britain.

The humiliating Treaty of Paris of 1763 was replaced by a new one—at Versailles. Signed in 1783, it gave Senegal back to France, along with five *comptoirs* in India and the islands of St. Lucia and Tobago in the Caribbean. The French navy, with its honor partially restored, was ready to try again to spread the *fleur-de-lis* around the globe.

But Louis XVI did not have long to weigh what he had won from George III. The French king was about to face his own revolution, and it would sweep away him, his throne, and a centuries-old idea of *la France*.

CHAPTER NINE

Revolution and the Emperors

JULY 14, IN PARIS or Papeete, is no day to miss. Aging couples ignore their swollen joints at neighborhood firehouse dances. Island bars, awash in rum, throb with drumbeats. Exploding lights color the skies over the Eiffel Tower. It is Bastille Day.

From the distance of two centuries, the French Revolution seems fairly simple. Fed up with a bloated aristocracy and a dithering king who ran up bad debts, France erupted. Parisians armed with pitchforks stormed the Bastille; lopped off the heads of Louis XVI and Marie "Let Them Eat Cake" Antoinette; chiseled *Liberté, Egalité, Fraternité* on coins and building facades; and then set off to beam light elsewhere in the world.

In fact, it took the Revolution three and a half years to execute the king, and fifteen years later he was replaced by an emperor. Before the Revolution wore itself out, after a decade, more than 40,000 people passed under the guillotine in Paris, or were drowned in the provinces, in the name of liberty, equality, and brotherhood. But the French Revolution changed the world in 1789. Some argue that it is still changing the world.

Historians spend lifetimes tracking the Revolution as it smouldered at the gates of Versailles and then burst into flame, consuming instigators, followers, and very nearly the nation it was meant to save. Jules Michelet's seven tomes on the Revolution alone augmented his seventeen-volume history of France.

The idea of change had been in the air. In England, a parliament, not God, determined the rights of kings. And John Locke rubbed it in with treatises on the rights of man. Voltaire brought Locke's views to France in 1734, adding his own appreciation of England, "where the prince, all-powerful to do good, has his hands tied against doing evil." His *Lettres philosophiques* were burned, but not soon enough. Jean-Jacques Rousseau evoked the noble simplicity of life without an idle class crushing the peasants. "Voltaire and Rousseau," declares historian Jean Tulard, "were responsible for the downfall of the monarchy." Among others. Diderot's *Encyclopedia* catalogued new concepts of equality. Montesquieu's *Persian Letters* ridiculed the king and his 600 pastry chefs.

Later, the Industrial Revolution lifted England with steam. The Americans threw off outside masters, building a nation on equality and freedom, with the French watching from ringside seats.

Feudal France comprised three *états*. The First Estate was the clergy; the Second, the nobility. Both ran up staggering expenses but paid no taxes. The burden fell on the Third Estate, the commoners. From 1604, anyone with enough money could buy into the nobility and, as an officer of the crown, steal back his investment with substantial interest. Purchased titles were hereditary, but they did not guarantee high breeding.

An intelligent aristocracy might have lightened up and eased toward reform. But in France, the privileged few squeezed harder, hoping to stamp out revolutionary tendencies before they grew dangerous. Caught up in the elaborate minuets at Versailles, they had little contact with the peasants who struggled to pay the bills. Louis XVI, meanwhile, hunted and puttered with locks.

The Etats généraux (States General) had represented all three sectors as a consultative body, but it had not been convened since 1614. After the Fronde, noblemen in the Parlement de Paris arrogated legislative power to themselves, so much that Louis XV abolished the body in 1771. Louis XVI reinstituted the Parlement four years later, thus bumbling headlong onto a slippery slope.

The Parlement blocked each attempt at reform and, at one point, lectured the king:

> Any system which, under the appearance of humanity and benevolence, would tend, in a well-ordered monarchy, to establish among men an equality of duties, and to destroy the necessary

distinctions, would soon bring disorder, the inevitable result of absolute equality and would produce an overturning of society.

They may have misread the causes, but they predicted the effect with stunning clarity. In his priceless *Story of Mankind,* Hendrik Willem Van Loon notes:

> It was the royal habit to do the right thing at the wrong time in the wrong way. When the people clamored for A, the king scolded them and gave them nothing. Then, when the Palace was surrounded by a howling multitude of poor people, the king surrendered and gave his subjects what they had asked for. By this time, however, the people wanted A plus B. The comedy was repeated. . . . And so on, through the whole alphabet and up to the scaffold.

An impasse forced Louis XVI to convene the Etats généraux, ignored for 175 years. The Third Estate demanded to meet jointly with the first two. The nobility objected, and the king ordered the commoners out of Versailles until they agreed to meet separately. Mirabeau, hero of the hour, told the aristocrat who brought the news: "Go tell your master we are here by the will of the people and will be expelled only at the point of bayonets."

That was on June 28. On July 8, the Third Estate, supported by most of the clergy and much of the nobility, formed a Constituent Assembly. Louis XVI refused to accept limitations on his power and amassed 25,000 hired foreign troops around Versailles; he wasn't sure of Frenchmen. On July 13, a crowd of demonstrators clashed with the Royal German Cavalry in the Tuileries Gardens. That went down badly among French commoners already chafing at the power of Louis XVI's Austrian queen, Marie Antoinette. A militia was formed. Within hours, it grew to 12,000 men.

On July 14, a group of the new guardsmen, along with stray workers and some irate *bourgeois,* seized rifles and cannons at the Invalides. Picking up supporters, they marched off to collect more weapons at the Bastille, a symbolic but disused political prison. They negotiated for arms but, as one leader joked later, the Bastille commander "lost his head before it could be cut off." Someone fired on the crowd and started the French Revolution.

FRANCE AT THE time was the strongest state in the world, with 16 percent of Europe's population: twenty-six million, compared to barely twelve million in England and eight million in Prussia. The French, victorious in the American war, had never been more powerful at sea and on land. French art and philosophy dominated the continent. France prospered from its colonies. At home, the fields and farms flourished. But national borders were vulnerable. Foreign powers controlled bits of the left bank of the Rhine, Savoy, Nice, and Avignon. The Revolution twisted and turned, weakening the state. Louis XVI, still on the throne, was made king of the French rather than king of France. The divine right was abolished. But his royal associates in Europe, worried by the precedent, negotiated in secret to come to his aid. Diehard aristocrats expected to rout the *sans-culottes,* revolutionary troops in raggedy breeches. The Austrians penetrated deep into France, but a people's army turned them back. Louis XVI's foreign dealings were discovered, and he went to the guillotine in January 1793.

Revolutionary leaders sought to strengthen the empire. In 1789, the Etats généraux declared itself in favor of colonial enterprise. Two years later, the legislature abolished all trade monopolies with India, the West Indies, Senegal, the Levant, and the North African Barbary Coast. "Commerce with the colonies," it said, "is commerce among brothers, commerce of the Nation with another part of the Nation." And in 1794, the government abolished slavery and decreed that "the colonies are an integral part of the Republic and are subject to the same constitutional laws."

But while France was in turmoil, England grabbed Tobago, Saint Pierre and Miquelon, and Pondicherry. In April 1794, Guadeloupe and Martinique fell. A black army under a former slave named Toussaint-L'Ouverture saved Haiti from the British. But that set in motion forces that soon brought the island independence from France.

Bordeaux, Nantes, and Le Havre were starved of colonial trade. French industry, spurred at first by war, stagnated. Invaders probed

French borders, anxious to pick over the spoils. By 1795, France was pressed to the wall.

Enter Napoléon. Three French armies headed east in 1795 to face Austria and the Italians. The army of Italy was commanded by Napoléon Bonaparte, a young general from Corsica. His victories were dramatic, based on strategy, speed, and surprise. He slipped between two armies waiting for him and crushed the Sardinians, winning Savoy and Nice for France. Then he chased the Austrians home, conquering northern Italy and bringing rich tribute back to the dwindling French treasury. He attacked again, reaching nearly to Vienna, and Austria capitulated. Pope Pius VI ceded Avignon to France. The revolution had passed to a Directoire of five men who began to consolidate France. They secured the left bank of the Rhine and signed peace treaties with Holland and Spain. By 1797, France was at peace, and largely in control, on the European continent.

But there remained England. French ports wanted peace so they could resume their lost colonial trade. In Paris, however, merchants argued that peace would give England a chance to trade in the European markets which the French monopolized. The only answer was war, but Bonaparte dared not try an amphibious landing. Britain's lord admiral of the moment had it right: "I do not say the French cannot come. I merely say that they cannot come by water."

The naval stand-off with England brought another complication: the Americans. At first, Americans had thrilled at the news of revolution. They saw Lafayette emerge to head a people's militia in his own country. The 1789 French Declaration of the Rights of Man read like their own Bill of Rights.

Not long before, Patrick Henry had recalled "a dreadful precipice from which we have escaped by means of the generous French, to whom I will be everlastingly bound by most heartfelt gratitude." He added, "Surely Congress will never recede from our French friends. Salvation of America depends upon our holding fast to our attachment to them."

But the Americans wanted to restore some goodwill with England, build an economy, and make some individual fortunes. The French wanted gratitude. It was not a period about which to write fulsome speeches about undying friendship.

"Dragon's teeth have been sown in France and came up monsters," John Adams observed. Americans were torn between deploring revolutionary excesses and standing by an ally. Commerce prevailed, and they chose strict neutrality, infuriating the French who needed American bases for their weaker navy. France's envoy, Edmond Genet, tried to bypass George Washington and appeal to the people. He was bundled back to Paris amid acrimony. The United States was caught in the middle: Britain confiscated cargo and impressed U.S. seamen in the French West Indies; France seized U.S. ships bound for England.

John Jay negotiated a treaty with Britain which France denounced as a willful sellout; to mollify the French, a U.S. commission went to Paris. They dealt with Charles-Maurice de Talleyrand-Périgord, the foreign minister, who had returned from thirty months in the United States convinced that Americans were crude, simple, and greedy.[1] The result was the XYZ affair.

The French flattered and bullied the Americans, seeking a loan while plundering U.S. commerce. As negotiations continued, the Directoire decreed that a ship's nationality would be determined by cargo, not flag; a pair of English-made boots on board was grounds for seizing a U.S. ship. One of Talleyrand's diplomats insisted on a *douceur*—a bribe—to ease along diplomacy. "No, no, not a sixpence!" retorted Charles Pinckney. (This, amplified by a South Carolina Federalist, was reported as, "Millions for Defense but Not One Cent for Tribute.")

The Americans refused to repudiate neutrality, so the French punished them for "betrayal" by threatening war. The commission reported back in full, detailing insults, and warning that weak, spiritless nations could expect to be trampled by France. Their dispatches were made public, called the XYZ cables, and they touched off a jingoistic storm. "At no time in America's national history have her people so heatedly denounced or so thoroughly detested France," historian Marvin Zahniser wrote.

The United States squared off for war with France. In subsequent years, harsh embargoes and seizures embittered merchants. In 1812, some Americans were surprised that it was the English, not the French, whom they fought.

TALLEYRAND, meanwhile, had an approach to England that suited Bonaparte well: choke the British empire by seizing Egypt. The ambitious Corsican suspected that France might be ripe for a military dictator. But he first needed more glory, such as a dramatic victory beyond Europe. He could block England's Suez route to Asia and mount an assault on India. Egypt, an important new colony, would replace lost territory. Bonaparte landed 35,000 men in Egypt, after seizing Malta on the way. He announced as his pretext: "It is long enough that the beys who govern Egypt insult the French nation and cover its merchants with affronts. The hour of punishment has arrived."

He explained he was there to liberate Egypt. "Is there good land? It belongs to the Mamelukes. Is there a hearty slave, a handsome horse? It belongs to the Mamelukes. If Egypt is their farm, let them show the lease God has given them."

Hostile Egyptians and dysentery left the French miserable. Admiral Nelson shot up the fleet, leaving Bonaparte's men no transport home. Then Turks amassed in Syria to counterattack. Bonaparte pushed north to meet them, but at Saint-Jean d'Acre, he was beaten by a French mercenary commander behind walls that once had protected French crusaders. France, meanwhile, was crumbling fast. Bonaparte delegated his command and rushed to Paris.

Austria, Russia, and Naples, with British funds, had armed 350,000 men. France clamored for a savior. Bonaparte arrived just after news of a French victory over the Turks. Crowds went wild. The Directoire made him first consul and then consul for life. In 1804, he changed his title to Napoléon I, emperor of France.

NAPOLÉON, a symbol of Gallic genius, grew up short and sickly on an island that fought to remain free of Paris, the son of a social-climbing notary public. His French sounded Italian, and he could hardly spell. His flash of glory lasted less than twenty years. But he conquered more ground and killed more enemies than Alexander the Great or Genghis Khan. Paris exalts his memory. He is even on brandy bottles, right hand fondling his sternum under a loose tunic, hat cocked jauntily over a furrowed brow. His code of law still prevails. Avenues radiate from his Arc de Triomphe, bearing names of his victories, his generals, and his Grande Armée. His noble *N* is emblazoned on the bridge to Notre-Dame. Les Invalides, where he is buried, is a museum to his splendor.

Van Loon, after cataloguing Napoléon's faults, muses:

> Here I am sitting at a comfortable table loaded heavily with books, with one eye on my typewriter and the other on Licorice the cat, who has a great fondness for carbon paper, and I am telling you that the Emperor Napoléon was a most contemptible person. But should I happen to look out the window, down upon Seventh Avenue, and should the endless procession of trucks and carts come to a sudden halt and should I hear the sound of heavy drums and see the little man on his white horse in his old and much-worn green uniform, then I don't know, but I am afraid that I would leave my books and the kitten and my home and everything else to follow him wherever he cared to lead. My own grandfather did this and Heaven knows he was not born to be a hero. Millions of other people's grandfathers did it. They cheerfully gave legs and arms and lives to serve this foreigner, who took them a thousand miles away from their homes and marched them into a barrage of Russian or English or Spanish or Italian or Austrian cannon and stared quietly into space while they were rolling in the agony of death.

Why? Van Loon admits that he can only guess:

> Napoléon was the greatest of actors and the whole European continent was his stage. At all times and under all circumstances he knew the precise attitude that would impress the spectators most and he understood what words would make the deepest impression. . . . At all times he was master of the situation. . . . Even at the end, an exile on a little rock in the middle of the Atlantic, a sick man at the mercy of a dull and intolerable British governor, he held the centre of the stage.

In sum, a French ideal.

Napoléon's ups and downs went quickly. He conquered in the name of *liberté, égalité, fraternité,* but he oppressed the masses with a talent Louis XVI never approached. Flushed with victories, he amassed ships to attack England in 1805. Lord Nelson annihilated the fleet at Trafalgar. Without a navy, France all but abandoned its colonial empire.

He took Louisiana back from Spain; the vast territory would supply his sugar islands. But he needed Florida in order to command the Caribbean, and the Spanish would not budge. In 1803, he sold Louisiana to Thomas Jefferson, and America went into the empire business.

The Egyptian campaign withered away. France had nowhere to go but east, by land. Czar Alexander I of Russia had tried five times to defeat Napoléon, aligning himself with any sovereign willing to fight. In 1812, a French army headed toward Moscow. Within two months, Napoléon seized the Kremlin. But he stayed too long. The city burned, and the French retreated into the Russian winter. Cossacks reduced the Grande Armée to a mob fleeing in panic.

Back in Paris, Napoléon raised an army of teenagers. He met the Russians at Leipzig, lost a bloody battle, and fled. Then he abdicated in favor of his young son, but victorious allies placed Louis XVIII on the French throne. The king sent Napoléon to rule the Mediterranean island of Elba. Within two years, he landed a tiny band of loyalists at Cannes. Soldiers deserted the indolent Bourbon king to serve him. France resented Napoléon's depredations, but he had made Paris the capital of the world.

Emperor again, Napoléon sought peace, but his enemies wanted war. His old fire was gone. He defeated a Prussian army in Belgium but let the main force escape. Two days later, about to conquer Wellington at Waterloo, Napoléon saw what he thought was his cavalry galloping up for the coup de grâce. It was the Prussians. The emperor was crushed again, 100 days after his triumphant return. He handed his crown to his son and made for the coast, bound for America. But Louis XVIII, back on the throne, expelled him from France. Napoléon knew the Prussians would shoot him so he informed the English court that the former emperor of France wished "to throw himself upon the mercy of his enemies and like Themistocles, to look for a welcome at the fireside of his foes." He got St. Helena, the rocky Atlantic island where he died seven years later.

The 1814 Treaty of Paris again reordered the Caribbean. France got back Guadeloupe and Martinique, along with Guiana and St. Pierre and Miquelon. But Tobago and St. Lucia went to Britain.

Haiti was lost for good. Toussaint L'Ouverture, after defeating the British, demanded a better deal from the French. Napoléon did not like his tone; in 1802, he sent his brother-in-law, Leclerc, with a huge army and secret orders to restore slavery. Napoléon told the Haitians that only France and its revolutionary ideals could defend their liberty. But France restored slavery in Guadeloupe, and Haitians suspected duplicity.

Leclerc invited Toussaint to meet him under a safe conduct. The Haitian leader, seized and deported, died miserably in a freezing stone cell in the Alps. But insurgents battered the French force. In months, yellow fever killed 29,000 men, including Leclerc. Napoléon promised another 35,000 troops but they could not penetrate a British blockade.

THE RESTORED Bourbons slowly rebuilt the colonial empire. The 1814 treaty had also cost France the Seychelles and Mauritius. But there was still Réunion (l'Ile Bourbon) and, farther east, Pondicherry and other Indian properties. France colonized the east coast of Madagascar, and kept African trading posts at St.-Louis and the Ile de Gorée. From there, they established rights far up the Senegal River.

And then a Barbary Coast potentate had the temerity to slap the French consul, and North Africa was on its way to becoming part of Europe.

Louis XVIII had died in 1824. An ineffectual but moderate remnant of the *ancien régime,* his imposed reign had caused no great unrest. But his brother, Charles X, was a religious zealot, anxious to reimpose an absolute monarchy. He made the theft of sacred objects punishable by death. Charles X was not nearly as widely loved as he would have liked to be. But he kept trying.

In 1827, Charles X's consul, Pierre Deval, guided his horse through Algiers up to the Casbah to salute Dey Hussein. Relations were tense. Since the Turkish occupation of the sixteenth century, the French had leased trading posts on the North African coast. But there was bickering over rent. Also, Hussein wanted the payment due an Algerian Jewish merchant whom he had backed in a grain sale to Napoléon. Twice he had written to King Charles X asking for settlement of the debt.

We have Deval's account of the meeting.

After paying his respects, the consul asked about a papal vessel under the French flag which had been seized by Barbary pirates. Hussein exploded.

"Instead of raising a subject that does not concern you, you had better hand me a reply to the letter I have addressed to King Charles. Has it arrived, this reply? When will you give me the money? If you do not, I will throw you in prison."

"Ah!" retorted Deval. "Don't touch me. If you touch me, you will be dealing with my government."

Hussein slapped the consul across the face with his peacock-feather fly whisk.

"It is not me you insult, but the king of France," Deval said. "The king of France will avenge it."[2]

The dey ejected him from the palace with unkind words for the king of France.

Six weeks later, France declared war and blockaded Algiers for three years. The effect was minimal. Two crippled French vessels drifted ashore; their crews were massacred, and the Sardinian consul had to buy back their severed heads in order to bury them. A French envoy, La Bretonnière, went to negotiate and Hussein's cannons fired at his ship.

It was all too much. Charles X sent 37,000 men. England objected vehemently, fearing a French colony between Gibraltar and Malta. French newspapers ridiculed the venture, warning of a debacle. Within a month, the *Provence,* which had evacuated Deval and then La Bretonnière, sailed into Algiers harbor. A French force landed unopposed and fought its way into the narrow, twisting streets of the city. The Arabs' guerrilla tactics confounded the commanders, used to orderly European formations. But firepower made the difference.

In his *La Vérité sur l'Expédition d'Alger,* Amar Hamdani suggests premeditation: Deval had proposed two weeks before his meeting with Hussein that Charles X should blockade Algiers. Eyewitness accounts, Hamdani adds, say that Deval was rude, provoking Hussein deliberately; the consul abused the purpose of the audience. And the fly whisk was not made of peacock feathers; it was straw from a date palm.

The king's purpose was as much survival as vengeance. Not long before, such victories had brought Parisians into the streets bellowing, *"Vive l'Empereur."* Charles X hoped something similar would shore up his sagging monarchy. But he went to Notre-Dame to celebrate in near silence. A few weeks later, Paris rose again. This time revolutionaries and king alike benefited from hindsight. The July Revolution took only three days. Charles X abdicated and Republicans averted civil war, naming the duke of Orléans, Louis-Philippe, as constitutional monarch, king of the French.

Louis-Philippe pushed on into Algeria. Alfred de Vigny reflected the predominant mood: "If one prefers life to death, one must prefer civilization to barbarousness. No people henceforth will have the right to remain barbarous at the side of civilized nations."

The war, however, was barbarous on both sides. General Thomas-Robert Bugeaud adopted *razzia* (scorched earth) as a tactic. One officer, Louis-Adolphe Saint-Arnaud, wrote, "We have burned everything, destroyed everything. How many women and children have died of cold and fatigue!" Another noted, "The carnage was frightful. Houses, tents, streets, courtyards littered with corpses ... in the disorder, often in the shadows, the soldiers could not wait to determine age or sex. They struck everywhere."

The Arabs responded in kind, provoking the French to even greater excesses. One French officer lighted fires at the mouth of a cave, asphyxiating all but ten of the 500 men, women, and children seeking refuge inside. The incident raised a scandal in the Senate, and *Le Courrier Français* condemned "this cannibal act, this foul deed which blots our military history and stains our flag."

Two months later, Saint-Arnaud asphyxiated 1,500 people in another cave and sent a confidential message to Bugeaud: "No one went into the cave; not a soul . . . except myself." On Bugeaud's advice, the government hid the details from reporters, deciding that they were "evidently easy to justify, but concerning which there is no advantage in informing a European public."[3]

By 1837, France had imposed sovereignty over Algeria except for a part of Oran held by Abd-el-Kadar. Ten years later, Abd-el-Kadar surrendered. In 1848, Algeria was carved into three *départements* and absorbed into France. Arabs fought sporadically against French settlers taking their land, but peace held.

Few French knew how Algeria was subdued. Victor Hugo visited Bugeaud, then governor-general, and found him depressed. France could not hold its head high, the governor said, and Algeria would be hard to colonize. Hugo disagreed:

> Our conquest is a grand and happy thing. It is civilization marching against barbarousness. It is an enlightened people finding a people in the night. We are the Greeks of the world; it is up to us to illuminate the world. Our mission accomplished, I can only shout, Hosanna. You think differently from me; it is simple. You speak as a soldier, a man of action. I speak as a philosopher and a thinker.

Later, Hugo described a peaceful dockside scene interrupted by hubbub around a mysterious cargo, with a long frame and a heavy iron blade: "A spectacle more interesting, in fact, than the palm trees, the aloes, the fig trees, than the sun and the hills, the sea and the sky: it was civilization arriving in Algiers in the form of a guillotine."

The Arabs were mystified. Here was an occupying power that might fall upon a suspect, arrest him and, after trial, release him for lack of evidence. But attacking officers might wipe out a score of Arab men, women, and children without a second thought.

"The Arabs . . ." reflected Alphonse Daudet, "a people we civilized by bestowing our vices."

PUSHY AMERICANS limited French movement in the Western Hemisphere. James Monroe enunciated his Doctrine, prompting *L'Etoile* in Paris to reflect on the cheekiness of a temporary president of a poorly armed republic, independent for only forty years. Tension grew serious over compensation for shipping seized by Napoléon. France agreed to pay but didn't. Charles X, short of cash, delayed and came up with counterclaims. Finally, Andrew Jackson blew his stack. "I know them French," he was quoted as saying. "They won't pay unless they're made to." Paris agreed to settle but only with an apology. "France will get no apology," thundered the *Washington Globe*. In 1835, envoys were recalled and navies were put on alert. Jackson finally came up with something close enough to satisfy France.

"These people seem to me stinking with national conceit," Alexis de Tocqueville wrote to his mother. "It pierces through all their courtesy."

LOUIS-PHILIPPE FACED pressure to expand the empire. Alphonse de Lamartine pointed to England's successful colonization which, he said, "has given birth to children who will perpetuate her name and her influence." The king colonized slowly, anxious to avoid conflict with Britain. But he pushed ahead, nonetheless. "What does it matter if 100,000 shots are fired in Africa?" he remarked. "Europe does not hear them."

Missionaries clashed over who would civilize souls in the South Pacific. Admiral Dupetit-Thouars planted French colors on the eastern Society Islands, the Marquesas, Gambier, and Wallis. French forces occupied the Gabon estuary and the Ivory Coast in 1838 and, later, northwest Madagascar, Mayotte, and scattered Indian Ocean properties. Intrepid Frenchmen set out on their own. René Caillié, obsessed with the ancient desert city of Timbuktu, walked there alone in 1838, disguised as a pilgrim.

In 1848, Louis-Philippe's July Monarchy melted away. "It died," observed Maurois, "for lack of *panache*." Accustomed to glory, France found the complacent, peace-loving regime dull and ridiculous. People seized on Lamartine's judgment: "France is bored."

And nothing cuts boredom like another Napoléon.

NAPOLÉON I had left his crown to his son, but Napoléon II, the duke of Reichstadt, disappeared into history. It was Louis-Napoléon who took the name Bonaparte most seriously. His mother, Hortense, was the daughter of Joséphine de Beauharnais and Napoléon's stepdaughter. Hortense married Louis Bonaparte, becoming at the same time Napoléon's sister-in-law. No one is certain if Louis was actually Louis-Napoléon's father. But the blood lines were clear enough for royalty.

Louis-Napoléon studied in Switzerland with an affable but indolent tutor and nearly ended up as yet another Bonaparte wastrel. But

at the age of twelve he came under the tender mercies of Philippe
Le Bas. From dawn to late at night, he absorbed Latin, German,
Greek, history, science, mathematics, and the rights of kings. Le Bas
cured his nightmares by cutting out the more violent subjects: riding
and dance.

Banned from France as a Bonaparte, Louis-Napoléon sneaked
into Strasbourg and instigated a few officers to mutiny. Louis-
Philippe laughed it off and sent him to the United States. In 1840,
however, Louis-Napoléon invaded France. It was not the way his
uncle would have done it. He landed at Boulogne in a fragile boat
with a few followers. Officers on shore had been bought off, but
not very effectively. The garrison was waiting. Louis-Napoléon
fired a pistol shot at the commander but fortunately, and probably
deliberately, he missed. This time, he was locked up in a humid stone
cell near the Belgian border.

In prison, he wrote books on Bonapartist ideology. By 1846,
fearing for his health, he sneaked out of his cell disguised as a
workman. He fled to London to wait.

Then thirty-nine, the "Little Eagle" was short but ponderous,
with drooping mustaches, a red beard, and dull grey eyes. He spoke
French like a German and weighed each word. "At first glance, I
took him for an opium addict," one visitor remarked. "Not a bit
of it; he himself is a drug, and you quickly come under his influence." He had wit. His cousin, Prince Napoléon, once remarked,
"The Emperor? But you are like him in nothing." He replied, "You
are wrong, *mon cher;* like him, I am saddled with his family."

Louis-Napoléon came back to be elected first president of the
Third Republic by a landslide. When his term expired, the law
forbade reelection. So he rallied the army to demand that he stay
on as president. Mysteriously, crowds began chanting, *"Vive l'Empereur."* By popular acclaim, as he explained, he had himself
crowned Napoléon III.

"THE EMPIRE means peace," Napoléon III declared, and he
fought half of Europe to prove it.

He courted the English, who had quashed the First Empire and
still commanded the seas. Britain vowed to defend the Ottoman
Empire against Russia, and he proposed an alliance against the czar.

After a disastrous start to the Crimean War, Britain and France won. But even the emperor's victories brought him grief.

In Italy, he reversed his loyalty to nationalists and sent troops to defend the pope's temporal powers. But after Italian patriots fire-bombed his carriage, nearly killing him and Empress Eugénie, he backed their cause to push Austria out of Italy. The Italians triumphed, with Napoleonic aid; they gave France Nice and Savoy as spoils. But they then rose against the pope. The French clergy, and even the devout empress, rounded on the emperor.

Prussia, showing no gratitude for Napoléon III's help against Russia, joined his enemies. Then the emperor made peace with Austria, infuriating the Italians. He advised the pope to yield, outraging his own clergy. By the time he yielded to pressure to back the Vatican, Pope Pius IX was allied against him. King Victor Emmanuel united Italy and seized most papal lands. Napoléon III had lost all over the board.

At home, he enraged capitalists and conservatives by signing a free-trade accord with England. He secured lower tariffs, fewer embargoes, and more concessions for French products. But industrialists were angry that he did not consult them first, and many cursed the emperor for bringing their ruin. That was the pattern. He brought France to a state of unparalleled wealth; railroads, ports, and factories were built. New banks encouraged people to save. He brought prosperity to the colonies and abolished most of the remaining slavery. But people rankled at his heavy hand and his ubiquitous secret police.

Overseas, the empire expanded. Napoléon delivered from the throne, in November 1863, the watchword of his lucid if erratic march toward free trade: "To civilize the world with commerce."

From 1853, France peopled New Caledonia with gold seekers, smugglers, deserters, and other hard cases. Despite objections by native Melanesians, a penitentiary was built. One of the first inmates was a terrorist named Berezowsky who had shot at Czar Alexander II as he and his host rode through the Bois de Boulogne to the 1867 World's Fair.

The emperor moved into Indochina. French priests had cast about the area for souls to save since the sixteenth century, and French traders probed the coasts. Annamese rulers resented the meddling.

The court at Hue beheaded two missionaries; one was French. Napoléon III sent ships to fire on the city, but two more Europeans were executed. So Admiral Rigault de Genouilly, fresh from bombarding Canton, shot his way up the Saigon River and demolished the local citadel. French sailors were still carrying loot from Peking where, in rare concert with the English, they had burned the Summer Palace and blackened their names for generations to come.

One officer described the 1859 Saigon assault:

> Major Delavau bashed in a door with a rifle butt and bayonet, and I did the same at another side. We penetrated the enclosure but we were stopped by a structure inside, three meters from the door from where they rained down on us a hail of firepots and rockets which, plunging us into a chaos of flames, smoke and explosions, forced us to retreat. I changed my plan of attack.

A city was shaped by men in wool and boots, protected only by funny-shaped sun hats from the steaming humidity and insects. Ten percent of Saigon's early settlers died from dysentery, malaria, cholera, or mysterious causes. At first men slept in open huts. Wrote one: "All animals of creation enjoy easy access, and you must grow accustomed to the sound at night, around you and over you, of innumerable reptiles, rats, and bats reaching sometimes an incredible wingspan." And another: "We slept in barns with no lack of scorpions or snakes, not to speak of an evil-doing insect that no one ever caught, nor saw, whose bite swells the skins and causes fever."

But there was mosquito netting and red wine. Within three years, French Cochin China covered three provinces of southern Vietnam, with 260 miles of telegraph line and a lighthouse beaming radiance into the South China Sea. Saigon had a girls' school, sidewalks, a decent hotel, and an urban plan for a city bigger than Paris. In 1860, 110 European trading vessels called at the city, along with 140 Chinese junks.

Steam had made the difference. Of 120,600 Frenchmen who embarked on Compagnie des Indes ships from 1644 to 1789, about 35,000 were lost at sea. But by 1862, the Messageries impériales began bimonthly service east with a railroad link across the Suez.

The trip from Marseilles to Saigon took five weeks, instead of thirteen around the Cape of Good Hope.

The French had found Indochina divided among ancient peoples who defended their borders with armies and diplomacy. The Annamese (Vietnamese) controlled what is now Vietnam from the Citadel at Hue. China cast a shadow over the northern Annamese in Hanoi and surrounding Tonkin. The Khmer, pushed across the Mekong to Cambodia, kept a fragile independence from the neighboring Siamese. The Lao court sat at Luang Prabang.

Cambodia soon slipped under French protection; King Norodom preferred Napoléon III to the closer-to-home perils of the king of Siam. A young officer named Francis Garnier, as worthy a candidate for the label "intrepid" as history might produce, explored the Mekong River and routes to China. He brought France to most of Tonkin.

Meanwhile, yet another French officer-explorer began settling vast tracts of African hinterland. Louis Faidherbe, with a stiff collar and a huge mustache, sank French roots on the little island of St.-Louis; it is now connected to the mainland by Pont Faidherbe. Senegal, no longer exporting humans, needed cash crops. He developed agriculture and administration so prosperity could follow.

And on November 17, 1869, the Suez Canal was opened, a triumph of French diplomat and engineer Ferdinand de Lesseps, linking Europe directly to the East.

As soldiers and traders established outposts of empire, Roman Catholic missionaries settled in to civilize them. From 1822 to 1870, twenty-two new missionary orders were organized in France. By 1870, the French colonial empire covered 900,000 square kilometers, with 2,820,000 inhabitants. Napoléon III had some cause for pride. But there was also Mexico.

IN THE 1850s, French and English residents had been harassed— robbed and raped—by troops under the latest Mexican revolutionary, Benito Juárez. Lord John Russell proposed an Anglo-French force to stabilize Mexico and set up a government that would pay off its debts. Napoléon III was anxious to fight again alongside England. And he was fascinated by the idea of a canal across Central

America. But, under the Monroe Doctrine, the American president would likely object. Then the United States went to war with itself, and the picture changed.

France needed cotton from Mexico since the South stopped its exports, and it was desperately short of silver. Mexico had both. A Mexican victory would have foreign policy benefits. Napoléon III could share spoils with Austria to ease enmity over Italy. By taking along Spain, he could open the Spanish market to French merchants. And he would satisfy his Spanish wife, whose Mexican monarchist friends badgered him for support.

Also, Napoléon III saw Mexico as vital to the balance of what he called "the current state of civilization of the world." A strong United States fed European commerce and industry, he wrote. But if Washington controlled Mexico and Central America, it would be too strong. The balance would shift, endangering French interests.

Napoléon III wanted to conquer Mexico. The English, though less ambitious, made no objection. If the emperor succeeded, they would also benefit. If not, he was on his own.

The invading army melted under the coastal heat, battered by guns sent from the United States. Juárez agreed to pay his debts, and England and Spain were ready to go home. Napoléon III had named Maximilian, the brother of Emperor Franz Joseph of Austria, to be emperor of Mexico. But Maximilian agreed to the job only if backed by all three allies.

France, however, was not deterred. Marshal Bazaine pushed on with 23,000 reinforcements and the only map of Mexico he could find in France. The French waited five months before attacking Puebla, en route to the capital. There French forces gave Mexico its beloved Cinco de Mayo by getting themselves clobbered on May 5. But the French finally marched into Mexico City. A general reported back: "Sire, soldiers are literally crushed under flowers and wreaths. . . . The return of troops to Paris after the Italian campaign can alone give an idea of the triumph."

Maximilian and Empress Carlota took the throne in May 1864, and French troops were soon covered in more than flowers. Mexico needed an emperor even less than France did, and resistance was violent.

Napoléon III, in the meantime, had backed the Confederacy, confident that it would win. He needed Southern cotton and he preferred a divided America. In nearly a century of French-American friendship, the alliance had twisted and turned. But this was a severe blow. When Washington won the war, it threw its full weight behind Juárez.

The situation deteriorated fast in Mexico City. Bazaine mocked Maximilian and talked of taking the throne himself. Finally, Carlota made a desperate trip to Paris to plead with Napoléon III for more help. He refused. She then went to the pope and, after that, went mad. Soldiers deserted until the garrison shrank to 5,137 men, and Maximilian surrendered to Juárez.

In May 1867, Napoléon III received the crowned heads of Europe and huge crowds at the *Exposition universelle* of French industrial and technological triumphs. Moments before awarding the prizes, he was handed a telegram from Vienna: "Emperor Maximilian has been shot."

BISMARCK DROVE in the last nail. He annexed Danish provinces and dominated Germany. Napoléon III acquiesced, expecting a close alliance in exchange. Bismarck promised he would expel Austria from the German Confederation and take sides with Italy. If France remained neutral, he said, it could expect territorial compensation. Bismarck marched on Austria, leaving Germany exposed, but the French did not cross the Rhine. When the German prince returned, victorious, Napoléon III claimed his rewards, but Bismarck laughed him off.

The emperor demanded Belgium; Bismarck informed the English, who threatened war to keep Antwerp. Luxembourg and Mainz were German, Bismarck said. Venice went to Italy.

Napoléon III lost out, and the French do not like losers. The emperor admitted to "black spots which darken the horizon." Adolphe Thiers told the imperial ministers, "There is no mistake left for you to make." There was, of course.

The Spanish throne fell vacant, and a Prussian was invited to occupy it. But Napoléon III objected, and the Prussians informally deferred. The French emperor wanted a more formal renunciation of the throne, and sent an envoy to Wilhelm, the Prussian king.

Bismarck, who knew his media, issued separate communiques on that encounter. He told the Germans that an arrogant little Frenchman had insulted their king. At the same time, he told the French that the German monarch airily dismissed their envoy. It was clever news management. Bismarck provoked a war that Napoléon III half wanted anyway.

"Never," said Maurois, "had an international cataclysm been set in motion on a flimsier excuse."

Germany was ready; France was not. In two days, the Germans won two decisive victories. Napoléon III, suffering from bladder stones so painful he could barely walk, led an army toward Sedan. Bazaine, weak and indecisive, lost a main force. Within a month, on September 2, 1870, the emperor was a prisoner. He was allowed asylum in England, where he died in pain and was buried.

The Germans took Versailles and surrounded Paris. But a new Third Republic held the capital. Léon Gambetta floated out of Paris in a balloon and raised an army in Tours. Parisians, under siege, were reduced to eating zoo animals and rats, and by January they gave in.

Bismarck negotiated a humiliating peace, accepting huge indemnities—and Alsace and Lorraine. Just for good measure, a German army marched down the Champs-Elysées. The broad avenue, leading from the Arc de Triomphe of Napoléon I, was silent and draped in black.

CHAPTER TEN

Mission in Full Glory

AS USUAL, THE recuperative powers of France turned doom into triumph. Beaten badly, the French had no prospect of European adventure. Instead, they set out to colonize whatever real estate was left unclaimed—and some that wasn't—in the rest of the world.

For the first time, colonial policy was more than a haphazard, often reluctant reaction to circumstances. Colbert might have attempted more with swifter ships and telegraph; Napoléon III was headed in that direction. But it was the Third Republic that marshaled bankers and bandits, masons, teachers and preachers, public relations experts, soldiers of fortune, and soldiers of every other sort.

France flung itself headlong into its mission, with all its extremes. Some men and women died miserably pushing through the puff adders in pursuit of lofty goals. Others grew fat at home on the profits of mercantilism based on colonial monopolies. French ingenuity, sacrifice, and greed during the seventy years of the Third Republic shaped vast tracts of modern Africa, Asia, and the oceans.

A best-seller of 1874 was *De la Colonisation chez les Peuples modernes* by a thirty-one-year-old economist named Paul Leroy-Beaulieu. "The foundation of colonies is the best business in which one might engage the capital of an old and rich country," he wrote. Colonization, he added, was "one of the highest functions of societies which have reached an advanced state of civilization. . . . Colonization is the expansive force of a people . . . the submission of a universe, or a vast part of it, to its language, its mores, its ideas, and its laws. A people that colonizes is a people that casts the bases of its grandeur into the future and assures its future supremacy."

Others disagreed. Gustave Flaubert defined the subject in his *Dictionnaire des Idées reçues:* "Colonies (our): To be afflicted when one speaks of them."

Enthusiasm grew slowly. Admiral François Page, laying out the streets of Saigon, wrote:

> This country is strange, but full of resources. If France had a shadow of common sense, it could found here a magnificent colonial establishment, which would bring in money, a great maritime movement, and jobs for a multitude of layabouts who know only how to waste their time and degrade themselves. But these are dreams I don't wish to pursue. *Gaulois,* my friends, I know you too well; stay under your gray or blue sky, chat, gossip, and we'll let the earth turn.

Soon after Cochin China was established, Paris nearly gave most of it back, including loyal Annamese who would be punished for having accepted French protection. Prosper Chasseloup-Laubat, minister of the navy, spiked the idea with a memo that set the tone for colonial policy to come. He weighed potential income and money already spent. African slavery was finished, he noted; low-paid Indochinese could replace them throughout the empire. He pinged lightly on the triangle of glory; the Cap Saint Jacques lighthouse shone as "a dazzling symbol of the possession of France." Then he rose to a crescendo:

> France alone was absent (in Asia), but Providence seems to have reserved . . . not only one of the most beautiful and richest countries in these parts, but even more the one most prepared to receive the seeds of our authority . . . to be the center from which will radiate Christian civilization in the Far East.

Francis Garnier, the soldier-explorer, echoed his appeal:

> This generous nation, whose opinion rules civilized Europe and whose ideas have conquered the world, has received from Providence the highest mission, that of emancipation, of calling to the

light and to liberty races and peoples still slaves to ignorance and despotism.

Providence carried the day. In 1867, the French seized three more southern provinces, explaining that they were a refuge "for all the malcontents, all the agitators, all the enemies of our authority."

The war in Europe left the colony to fend for itself. News of Napoléon III's downfall reached Saigon September 27. But, just to be safe, the governor left his picture on the wall until official word arrived October 21. Six weeks after France, Cochin China left the Second Empire for the Third Republic.

In desperation, Empress Eugénie had offered Bismarck the young colony in return for Alsace and Lorraine. He laughed. "Oh! Oh! Cochin China. That is a big piece for us. We are not rich enough to afford the luxury of colonies."

Garnier found that the Saigon River went nowhere. For an access to China, France would have to go farther north, and the opportunity soon arose. A merchant named Jean Dupuis had set up shop in Hanoi to trade with the Chinese on the Red River. Tu Duc, the emperor at Hue, asked the French to remove him. Garnier took a small force to Hanoi to bring back Dupuis. But his secret orders were to open the river for the French.

Garnier blasted into the Hanoi citadel and seized Tonkin. But local mandarins hired the Black Flag, Chinese bandits, to murder him. Garnier chased a Black Flag band to the outskirts of Hanoi and ran headlong into an ambush. He emptied his pistol into the Chinese but was cut to ribbons.

In 1874, France agreed to abandon Tonkin and the Mekong Delta; in exchange, Hue granted a clear title to Cochin China and Annam was made a protectorate.

A college in Saigon trained colonial administrators. Later, moved to Paris, it grew to be the prestigious Ecole Nationale de la France d'Outre-mer. Eliacin Luro, the first director, defined its goals:

In the matter of colonization by domination, by assimilation, one must not go too quickly; one must count on time. Mores, languages, laws cannot be changed in a few years, under pain of disaster. One must understand, penetrate the civilization of the conquered, know their language, let them function first as they functioned before, then, little by little, patiently direct their steps, modify their pace. Finally, to the degree that an exchange of ideas among peoples has been made, that an economic revolution born of free competition has come to change mores, one must slowly modify and change laws.

First, of course, one must conquer. The Chinese did not recognize Tu Duc's treaties with the French and continued to massacre French traders and travelers.

Paris was in no timid mood by 1882. Pushed by Minister Jules Ferry, the navy dispatched Commandant Henri Rivière with orders to seize Hanoi and hold it while the diplomats did the rest. He took the city easily and then calmly wrote novels. At fifty-five, he wrote to his friends Flaubert and Alexandre Dumas *fils,* he was getting a little old to be a conqueror.

The Chinese sent more troops to Tonkin and refused to give way. Like Garnier, Rivière sallied forth after Black Flag thugs. He did not bother with forward patrols. When an aide advised caution, he replied, "Bah! You are made for the great wars. Me, I know about this. Let me take care of it. You will see." He was ambushed at the Bridge of Paper, where Garnier died. Rivière leaped from his carriage and charged with a cane. A bullet dropped him, and he was beheaded.

The French held Hanoi, but a hothead commander moved north toward the Chinese border. At Lang-Son, a messenger handed him a dispatch he could not read. He attacked, and his force was decimated. Later, it was learned that the Chinese were leaving; the message asked only for a few days to pack.

In Paris, reaction was violent. *Bon,* the Chinese were advised, no more Mr. Nice Guy. The French Tonkin force, totaling 3,750 men in 1883, swelled to 40,000 by July, 1885. France called out the nastiest of the Foreign Legion: the Turcos, sharpshooters from Algeria; the Zéphyrs and Zouaves, hard veterans of Africa. And there were regulars from the *métropole,* sweating in heavily ornamented parade uniforms under giant campaign sacks.

The French learned Vietnamese jungle tactics the hard way. Buried bamboo staves took a toll. Fast strikes surprised men used to orderly conduct of battle. But a bitter, brief war settled the Tonkin affair by treaty in 1885. War erupted again and then subsided. France still had to fight for trading posts in China, but it was master of Tonkin, Annam, Cochin China, Cambodia, and Laos.

IN PARIS, the political war was just as bitter. Jules Ferry, called *le Tonkinois,* fell over Lang-Son in a national upheaval over the whole policy of empire. Ferry, premier and then foreign minister, imperious and cutting, was not widely popular. Some thought he was too close to Germany. Catholics resented his sectarianism. His zealous defense of colonization had a following. But from November 1883 to late March 1885, he was called to the legislature twelve times to justify his Indochina policy.

During a heated exchange in the Chamber of Deputies, in July 1885, Ferry said: "Gentlemen . . . it must be openly stated that the superior races have rights in relation to inferior races. . . . I repeat that they have rights because they have obligations—the obligation to civilize all inferior races." To shouts that he was justifying slave trade, Ferry replied that the French Declaration of the Rights of Man was not written with African blacks in mind.[1]

Ferry's nemesis was Georges Clemenceau, spokesman for the left with a personal grievance against the minister. He said France was sinking into war with China, a nation of 400 to 500 million inhabitants. "While you are lost in your colonial dream, there are men here at your feet who demand useful expenditures to develop the genius of France," Clemenceau said in the National Assembly. He saw no predestined role for France. Germans, he said, tried to crush France to prove themselves a master race. "Since then, I must admit, I look twice before turning to a man or a civilization and pronouncing: inferior man or race."

Economist Frédéric Passy railed against spending "the blood and the gold of France" in fruitless global enterprise. If France seeks to radiate greatness, he argued, it can only do it by growing strong.

After the Lang-Son debacle, Ferry had to ask the National Assembly for more money to win the war.

"We need it . . . for our honor," Ferry started.

"Who compromised our honor?" demanded Georges Périn.

Things went downhill from there. At one point, Clemenceau thundered:

"We do not wish to hear you any longer; we do not wish to discuss with you the greater interests of *la patrie*. . . . We do not know you anymore, we do not wish to know you. . . . These are not ministers before me, but men accused of high treason."

Funds were approved—it was too late to back out—but Ferry had to sneak out the back to avoid crowds outside waving fists and yelling, "Get out, *misérable!*" "To the gallows!" And, "Into the water, Tonkinois, Prussian!" Some saw Ferry cry.

Léon Bloy, in his gutter style, fumed: ". . . This man would turn, by the urine stink of his tears, more fetid than the sexual impurity of the Whore of the prophet, the fertilizing mayonnaise of the sewers of Pantin and Bondy."

"And all of this for Tonkin?" reflected Guy de Maupassant. "It is written therefore that our colonies will be, for us, always fatal."

De Maupassant reasoned that some lands should remain uninhabited by Europeans. "The human seed grows like that of plants in land that is good for it," he wrote. ". . . I would put all our colonies in a suitcase, Senegal, Gabon, Tunisia, Guiana, Guadeloupe, Cochin China, the Congo, Tonkin and the rest, and I would find Mr. Bismarck. I would say, 'Sir, you're looking for colonies . . . here is a complete assortment, of all types, of all nuances. . . . I ask of you, for each, one kilometer of Alsace and one kilometer of Lorraine."

Right-wing deputies also insisted on recuperating Alsace and Lorraine as a first priority. Paul Déroulède thundered, "I have lost two sisters, and you offer me twenty chambermaids!"

But the race was on. Gambetta and Ferry had already planted the flag in Tunisia in 1881, with the treaty of Bardo. Troops went to Madagascar in 1883 for the ostensible purpose of protecting missionaries. The French obtained a protectorate accord two years later, but only a decade of blood and bitterness brought the island firmly under control.

Pierre Savorgnan de Brazza, an Italian count of dash and endurance, explored the rain forests of central Africa. He was a naturalized French army officer who funded much of his own expeditions. He had claimed Gabon. Then, marching barefoot with Senegalese troops, he raced to the Congo River ahead of Henry Morton Stanley and his Belgian flag.

The Bateke king, Makoko, chose the French. He handed Brazza a sack of dirt destined for "the great white king" (a president, in fact) to remind him that he owned the Batekes' land. Makoko dug a pit for his chiefs' arms. Brazza planted a tree on top and declared, "May peace last until this tree gives forth iron and powder." He left behind three Senegalese to protect a new settlement called, not surprisingly, Brazzaville.

Brazza wrote, "The Moslem element being unknown in the region, European civilization need not expect to encounter the hostility, hatred, and fanaticism which oblige the French to advance only with armed force from Senegal to Niger. There is nothing to be feared except the natural opposition to whatever is new."

But farther north, Frenchmen in growing numbers were buried beneath the sands, their bodies tilted toward France. Expeditions pushed up the Niger River into the Sudan, now Mali. Joseph Galliéni, a hero of Indochina, led the way. After two years on campaign, his kit was so ragged that he had to borrow pants from the surgeon and boots from a gunnery lieutenant in order to negotiate with an emir. There was also Aimé Ollivier, who never took off his gloves, bathed each morning, dined with flatware, armed himself only with an umbrella, and regarded as essential survival gear his library of Racine, Montaigne, Plutarch, and Ronsard.

In 1888, a Peul emir, Almamy Hamadou, signed Guinea over to France and then chortled to aides about the European mania for meaningless treaties. He would accept arms and gifts and let the termites take care of the paperwork. It took more blood, but France made the treaty stick.

Pieces of the patchwork were sewn into place. The Foreign Legion, fresh from Tonkin, marched into Dahomey. They took literally their slogan, "March or Die." Bullets and spears killed 100; dysentery and malaria killed 200. But they hunted down Zinc-Beak, the "Shark King," and replaced him with a friendlier monarch. Other parts of the coast and the desert were brought under the French flag.

In most of West Africa, France aligned friendly tribes against hostile ones, mainly northern Moslems who trafficked in slaves.

French protection meant lost independence but a certain freedom from slave raids and looting.

Timbuktu had been terrorized for centuries by Tuaregs, the fabled "blue men" of the desert. René Caillié, a lone Frenchman, had smuggled himself in and out of the ancient Islamic center, disguised as a pilgrim, but until 1893 the city was forbidden to Europeans. That year, a young naval officer named Boiteux sailed up the Niger under orders to do no more than look around and leave.

Boiteux tied up at Kabara, the port five miles south of Timbuktu, and sent a message to town authorities. Their promised emissaries did not appear; Tuaregs on camels ranged the dunes between port and town. French guns routed a Tuareg assault, and Boiteux could wait no longer. He fought his way to town and dug in on the outskirts. Local leaders, meanwhile, were frantic. If they leaned to the French, the Tuaregs would sack Timbuktu the moment the foreigners left. If not, the French would do the sacking. While they waffled, word came that Boiteux had better return to his boat.

Tuaregs had killed twenty Frenchmen, the worst debacle yet in West Africa. Boiteux faced excited Tuaregs and 10,000 restive townsfolk with fourteen men. He pleaded for help from Colonel Bonnier downriver. Across the shimmering dunes, he could see the billowing robes of nomads gathering for the kill. The French position grew desperate. Then Bonnier rode in with the cavalry. Boiteux ran to greet him; the colonel cursed him as a dolt and sentenced him to forty-five days' arrest on his own boat.

The battle was bitter. Evaporating and reappearing over the dunes, the Tuaregs dispersed Bonnier's straggling column into disorder. They swept in on camels, thrusting swords and firing at close range. A third of the French force was killed: eleven officers, two sergeants, and seventy-four riflemen. Bonnier, shot square in the chest, was among the first.

A fresh column arrived under Joseph Joffre and methodically subdued the nomads. The French governor, seeking news, dispatched message after message into the void; he recalled Bonnier, already dead; he reassigned Joffre to the railroad as punishment. Joffre fought a last battle, leaving sixty Tuaregs dead without losing a man, and returned to find a frantic request for news. He dictated a response to the governor: "All is quiet in Timbuktu. The sanitary situation is satisfactory."

He reflected a moment and added, "Satisfactory enough."

There was more desert to pacify. For thirty years, an emir named Samory pillaged farming tribes and eluded French forces. Finally, in 1899, he was on the run. The French knew if they killed him in battle he would live on as a martyr. They caught him and paraded him in chains.

That left Chad. The reigning emir, Rabah, wanted Europeans out of his vast desert at the center of Africa. But France needed Chad. A freelance colonizer named Ferdinand de Behagle attacked but fell into Rabah's hands. A 1941 history, *Sous le Casque Blanc,* by Roland Dorgelès of the Académie Goncourt, gives these as Behagle's final words (without indicating how he happened to know them): "I must die, *c'est bien.* A Frenchman does not fear death. But remember I will be revenged."

There is no disputing the last part. Emile Gentil, from the French outpost of Fort-Archambault, dispatched forces to chase Rabah across Chad. Major Lamy ran him to ground. But the emir's men fired from hiding, killing Lamy on his horse, and then fled. Later the French found Rabah's body. A bullet fired at the disappearing nomads had struck him in the head.

The skirmish was on the Chari River, where Gentil situated the new capital of French Chad. He called it Fort-Lamy, and a statue to Lamy was inscribed, "He opened the way for civilization. . . ."

That last piece in place, France had an unbroken stretch from the Mediterranean across the Sahara to the Congo. With enough stamina, you could travel 4,565 kilometers, from Algiers to Brazzaville, without leaving French territory.

EUROPEAN POWERS met at Berlin in 1884 and for a year they drew arbitrary lines on an African map, dissecting ancient tribes, separating arid hinterland from potential farms, and ignoring natural divisions. Geographers could only guess at the terrain. Philosophically, the dominant approach was Victor Hugo's: "What a land, this Africa! Asia has its history, America has its history, even Australia has its history; Africa has no history." Colonizing powers divided up the continent with every intention of bestowing history.

Bismarck encouraged French colonial adventure, reasoning that an otherwise occupied France would not threaten him on the Rhine. Morocco, as a result, joined the French sphere.

Conflicts were numerous. France battled over the Congo River where Brazza and Stanley, in the pay of King Leopold of Belgium, glared at one another across the water. But the last great standoff was on the Nile.

Britain planned to lay a railroad track from Cairo to Cape Town, marking in iron their mastery of Africa. France wanted a road from Dakar to Djibouti. An east-west axis, with a spur to Brazzaville, would give the French domination. Both sides felt they had earned the right to command the continent. For each, the missing central link was Sudan.

Paris sent Captain Jean-Baptiste Marchand to Sudan in 1896. His minister's last words, he noted, were, "Fire a pistol shot over the Nile; we will take care of the rest." Almost immediately afterward, London dispatched Sir Herbert Kitchener up the White Nile in the first attempt to reoccupy Sudan since the Mahdi overran Charles "Chinese" Gordon at Khartoum twelve years before. From opposite directions, Marchand and Kitchener were racing for an abandoned, swamp-bound little outpost called Fashoda.

Kitchener moved down from Egypt with one major obstacle ahead of him: he had to subdue a vast desert full of Islamic fanatics who had already slaughtered a British army entrenched behind walls. Marchand, meanwhile, only had to walk across Africa from the Atlantic through the nastiest bit of jungle on the earth's surface, carrying 500 tons of baggage.

The proud and prickly French captain cut 120 miles of road through impassable rain forest, spanning ravines with logs. He commandeered the river steamer *Faidherbe* on the Ubangi; for most of the trip, the boat had to be broken into sections and rolled along over tree trunks. Hostile tribes ambushed his column; porters deserted; disease decimated his ranks. Finally, on the Nile, his ragtag band bogged down in the mud, moving scarcely 500 yards a day. Supplies dwindled and mosquito nets were in shreds. His men awaited orders.

The moment is described in Dorgelès's paean to French explorers: "He raises his eyes. This illuminated gaze which penetrates you.

'They have asked us the impossible. *Eh bien.* We will give them the impossible, or we will give our lives. God will decide.' "

It took the French two years to reach Fashoda, and they won the race. Kitchener, pinned down by Dervishes, had to await reinforcements from Egypt. Marchand found a gun platform in the crumbled old citadel and ordered the flag raised. In mid-ceremony, a rotten rope broke and the Tricolor tumbled to the ground. "At that omen," remarked a French officer, "Romans would have turned around and gone home." But Marchand rebuilt the old walls and held off Mahdist attacks, using 12,000 cartridges. He had 28,000 left when Kitchener's huge force steamed up the Nile.

The meeting was gentlemanly. Kitchener had orders to raise an Egyptian flag for the khedive at the fort. Over our dead bodies, Marchand said. Given the numbers, that was likely, Kitchener replied, not to speak of certain war between England and France.

Marchand had sent a flash message to Paris for instructions and expected an answer in ten months. Kitchener had better communications, but the French did not trust them. The Tricolor still hung limply in the humid air, and Doctor Emily's zinnias bloomed. "These French," muttered an English officer. "Flowers at Fashoda."

The atmosphere was icy cold on the White Nile, but in Paris and London it was scorching. Newspapers screamed for war, evoking national honor, manifest destiny, and every other Anglo-French issue back to William the Conqueror. Fleets were mobilized. But Foreign Minister Théophile Delcassé knew the real threat was Germany; a war with England would be fatal. King Edward VII and his minister, Lord Lansdowne, were no enemies of France.

Delcassé ordered Marchand home. The captain, seeking confirmation, sent his deputy, Baratier, to Paris. It was true. Dorgelès reports this exchange:

"And the minister?" asked Marchand.
"He asked me why we were still at Fashoda."
"What?"
"Yes, he greeted me with those words. . . . He then said that if England declared war, our mission was lost."
"What does that matter, our lives!" Marchand said.
"That's what I told him. That our fate should not count if the

honor of France was at stake. He replied, 'You don't understand
very well the honor of France.' "

The French backed away not only from Fashoda but from all of
Egypt and Sudan. Colonial rivalry ended, more or less, all over the
globe. England and France reached an entente cordiale, an informal
friendship that, so far, still holds. It was finally the swamp itself, not
the French, that blocked a link from Sudan to the south.

THE FRENCH set about consolidating the empire they had
staked out. But they were thin on the ground almost everywhere.

"The truth is that in the Congo our authority stops at the range
of the rifles of our outposts," wrote Pierre Mille in 1899. The
Belgian Congo colonial army numbered 12,000, he said; the French
Congo army, in an area four times the size of France, had 1,400.
"In this sense, the word 'impossible' continues not to be French,"
he said. "Individual initiative is, in our country, admirable. It is the
collective initiative and the practical sense of the utilization of effort
that is lacking."

An entertaining account of travel in French Africa comes from
Mary H. Kingsley, a Victorian lady of ineffable pluck, whose 1897
diary includes advice on how to negotiate a mangrove swamp in
a hoop skirt. She wrote:

> The French officials in Congo Français never hindered me, and
> always treated me with the greatest kindness. You may say there
> was no reason why they should not, for there is nothing in this
> fine colony of France that they need be ashamed of any one
> seeing; but I find it customary for travellers to say the French
> officials throw obstacles in the way of any one visiting their
> possessions so I merely beg to state this was decidedly not my
> experience.

In Gabon, she said, a customs officer

> is courteous and kindly, but he incarcerates my revolver, giving
> me a feeling of iniquity for having had the thing. I am informed
> if I pay 15 shillings for a license, I may have it—if I fire French

ammunition out of it. . . . My collecting cases and spirit, the things which I expected to reduce me to a financial wreck by custom dues, are passed entirely free, because they are for science. *Vive la France!*

The people are seminomadic:

So when a village of Fans has cleared all the rubber out of their district, or has made the said district too hot to hold it by rows with other villages, or has got itself very properly shelled out and burnt for some attack on traders or the French flag in any form, its inhabitants clear off into another district.

Up the Ogooué, past the place where Albert Schweitzer later built his hospital, a French official refused to take responsibility for her traveling the rapids unaccompanied. The last woman through had had a husband. Her Igalwas guides are as good at rapids as any mortal man, she said,

and as for the husband, neither the Royal Geographic Society's list, in their "Hints to Travellers", nor Messrs. Silver, in their elaborate lists of articles necessary for a traveller in tropical climates, make mention of husbands.

She proceeded onward. Praising Brazza, she wrote:

It is impossible for any one to fail to regard him with the greatest veneration, when one knows from personal acquaintance the make of the country and the dangerousness of the native population with which he has had to deal.

She recounted Brazza's speech to Makoko on the glory of the French emblem.

I have no hesitation in saying . . . this high-flown statement is true; and although Brazza did a good thing for France that day, Makoko also did well, for he saved himself from the [Belgian] Congo Free State.

Gradually, needs were met, order was imposed, and roads were built. With the last pieces in place, France established French West Africa, administered from Dakar, and French Equatorial Africa, from Brazzaville.

NEW CALEDONIA had a rocky start. It was designated a penal colony but its energetic and somewhat bizarre governor, Admiral Charles Guillain, wanted more for the place. He designed an emblem featuring a convict, a native Kanak, and the motto "Civilize, Produce, Rehabilitate." He lured settlers from Réunion and elsewhere and urged them to form tight-knit little cooperatives in the manner suggested by his *maître-à-penser,* socialist reformer F. M. C. Fourier.

Arrivals included 5,000 deportees from the Commune of Paris, leftists who had held the capital for a month during the turbulent early days of 1871. They stayed for nearly a decade in a stone village on the luxuriant little Ile des Pins, just off the end of New Caledonia. Most left with an amnesty, and the jungle took back their camp.

And then the Kanaks arose in 1878, in a bloody first act to sporadic rebellion. The Kanaks, native Melanesians, were led by a bearded chief named Atai, remembered now as *le Vercingétorix noir.*

They had welcomed Captain Cook, who discovered and named the island, and the first missionaries. But shiploads of settlers upset the balance. The French took the best land and ran 80,000 head of cattle over sacred places. Missionaries slipped in esteem; they did not want the Kanaks to eat human flesh, but the Catholic God had a poor record for granting miracles. And European men had ungainly appetites for Melanesian women. Guillain, intending to protect Kanak land, had thrown traditional tenure into chaos with a system of titles.

The spark was the murder of a white ex-convict who lived with a Kanak woman. Some chiefs were arrested. Guerrillas attacked a military post at La Foa and killed four gendarmes. Another thirty-nine white settlers were massacred. Commandant Henri Rivière moved in heavy guns. Accounts are grim on both sides. Atai was betrayed; French soldiers overran his camp, cut off his head, and packed it off to Paris for anthropological study. Revolt spread across the island. The *Encyclopédie de la Nouvelle-Calédonie* estimated that 1,000 insurgents and 200 Europeans died. About 200 farms, settlements, and native villages were razed. The revolt ended in 1880 when 110 Kanak warriors from six tribes surrendered.

France now occupied colonies across the Pacific. The Loyalty Islands off New Caledonia were settled, along with other remote bits of coral and volcanic rock. But the prize was Tahiti.

Parisian geography still tends to lump Melanesia with Polynesia. It may be true, as claimed, that the Ministry of Colonies in 1860 refused to build a bakery in Nouméa, New Caledonia, since people there could buy their bread in Tahiti. It was only a 3,000-mile swim.

The first European to sight Tahiti was Samuel Wallis, the Englishman after whom, following colonial logic, the French island of Wallis (pronounced Valees) is named. That was in 1769. Then came Bougainville, the French Quebec veteran, who was pioneering for Choiseul. The next ships were English, including Cook's. In 1789, Tahiti saw Captain Bligh's *Bounty,* more of it than most Tahitians wanted to see. Along with Union Jacks and *fleurs-de-lis,* the ships brought missionaries, habit-forming luxuries, and murderous microbes.

An English missionary, Pritchard, arrived in 1824 and grew close to Queen Pomare IV. He counseled against perfidious Frenchmen, and had two French missionaries arrested and bounced off the island in 1836. Admiral Dupetit-Thouars settled that score in 1838 and gave the queen a treaty to sign. Five years later, Tahiti agreed to be a French protectorate. But Louis-Philippe backed away from the agreement. Thus encouraged, Tahitians rebelled against the French. Blood was spilled, but calm returned in 1846, with a new accord.

Troubles lasted until 1880, when France moved in permanently. Colonial officials divided up the island and gave titles to individual Tahitians, overturning an elaborate structure of common land owned by ancestors. The Marquesas Islands had been French since 1858; the rest of the Society Islands followed.

Glancing today at a Gauguin, or a postcard, it is clear how Tahiti got its reputation as a paradise. But Henri Lebeau, traveling there in 1910, reported, "In this splendid place . . . all is ruin, misery, human decrepitude."

Tahiti, then ravaged by epidemic, would eight years later lose perhaps a quarter of its native population to Spanish influenza. In the Marquesas, according to historian Pierre-Yves Toullelan, the population fell from 60,000 in 1800 to 20,000 in the 1840s and 6,000 by 1874. Half of those survivors died by 1900.

French-born colonists in Polynesia totaled 477 in 1902. By 1926, 1,697 Europeans lived among 35,862 islanders throughout Polynesia.

FROM 1880 TO 1895, the French overseas empire grew from one million to 9,500,000 square kilometers. The population expanded from five to fifty million. The empire was far more than a string of primitive outposts manned by lonely men in scuffed boots. Saigon, by 1887, had already inspired a traveler to write:

> The rue Catinat, with its arcades, is the rue de Rivoli; the quai de Commerce is the quai d'Orsay; our delicious little theater, it is the ex-Folies Marigny. If you have no Bon Marché, here is Civette. The tour d'Inspection, the promenade of the Champs-Elysées. Spend the evening before the cafes of Saigon: the *terrasses* are as thick with people as on the *grands boulevards*. The sound of a piano brings you memories of the absent motherland and evokes sweet impressions in the soul.

Local cooks learned ancient Norman recipes, and added traces of curry and citronelle to develop a cuisine few cultures can match. The cathedral filled on Sunday mornings, but not nearly so regularly as the hippodrome.

In October 1912, Albert Sarrault, later to be minister of the colonies, addressed the Government Council at Hanoi. He was governor-general of Indochina, but he spoke for all parts of France d'outre-mer:

> The work accomplished is really grand, useful, fecund, and it deeply honors the nation that has conceived it. We came here charged with a high mission to civilize; we have now, by far, honored our engagements. We can without boasting, but without fear, face any comparison with other nations that ceaselessly oppose us in the work of colonization. And despite the few certain faults of our action, the few errors, the few organizational

vices, even the abuses not yet completely corrected . . . with what tranquility, nonetheless, can we turn to the indigenous person entrusted to our tutelage to tell him: "Compare your present state with what it was, before the radiance of the French soul in your country."

Sarrault boasted of peace and security, justice, flourishing fields, ports and bridges, schools and hospitals. He concluded, "Look at all this and ask yourself if French protection is an empty phrase, if any other nation of the world could have given you more, and if you, if left on your own, could have achieved this ensemble of progress and benefit."

Twelve years later, a Vietnamese nationalist named Ho Chi Minh took a different view: "Taxes, forced labor, exploitation; that is the summing up of your civilization."[2]

Léon Bloy put it this way:

> The history of our colonies, especially in the Far East, is but pain, unlimited ferocity, and unspeakable turpitude. I have heard stories to make the rocks sigh. The one example suffices, of a poor young man who tried to defend some Moi villages, unbearably oppressed by administrators. The account was soon settled. Seeing him without support or patronage of any sort, the generals set a simple trap . . . and led him by the hand to activities described as rebellious.

Bloy referred to his own brother, Georges, imprisoned in 1886 after defending Indochinese against the administration.[3]

Anatole France, less personally involved, was more to the point: "Will this colonial folly ever end? . . . Colonies are the scourge of peoples."

In a study called *La Décolonisation*, Henri Grimal cites an unnamed French jurist's definition of the phenomenon:

> To colonize, is to establish relations with a new country to profit from its resources of every nature, to develop it in the national interest, and to bring the endowments of a superior race to its primitive peoples, deprived of the advantages of intellec-

tual, social, scientific, moral, artistic, literary, commercial and industrial culture. Colonization is therefore an establishment founded in a new country by an advanced civilization for the double advantages we have thus described.

The greatest colonial figure of his age, Hubert Lyautey, reflected a main current of French thinking for fifty years. As a young officer in Tonkin, in 1895, he advised a friend in Paris to visit England and the United States:

For what is the ensemble of questions of the Far East, whether Japan, Laos, Siam or Afghanistan, it seems that you are in a position to know them as well in Paris as on the spot. There remains only the people to see, but these are no more than curiosities, and in their present slumber, from which they will certainly be awakened, they have nothing to teach us.

Lyautey found the Indochinese ugly but worth saving. At least, he wrote, colonies benefit the army: an ambitious officer learns more abroad in six months than during a whole career in France. He was upset that France messed with the dregs of Indochina but passed up the richest part: Siam. He enjoyed the pomp of colonial office, but was happiest chasing Chinese pirates with the Foreign Legion. At rest, he wrote his brother for a copy of Baudelaire's *Les Fleurs du Mal* and a *Figaro* review of the season's events on the Champs de Mars.

Two years later in Madagascar, he wrote: "It is not the Frenchman that lets down France but rather France that lets down the Frenchman. The *métropole* is decidedly a pain. Parliament seems to see our colonies according to the old Spanish method rather than the good old English method. One depletes and kills colonies by wanting them to be immediately remunerative; one prepares colonial empires for the future in letting them develop freely."

Lyautey decried an "absurd" customs regime, a premature tax system and a corps of officials and magistrates that were not only useless but also damaging. Governments had to invest heavily to earn from their colonies, he wrote, concluding: "Colonial policy is not for the poor, and we are poor."

France paid some heed. Between 1896 and 1900, only 9.8 percent of French exports stayed within the empire; colonial imports were 7.8 percent of the total. But investment was heavy. In 1914, 2,500 miles of road were built in Tunisia alone.

But in 1925, as governor of Morocco, Lyautey made a speech in Rabat that more Frenchmen should have heard:

> It is to be foreseen—and indeed I regard it as a historic truth —that in the more or less distant future North Africa—modernized, civilized, living its own autonomous life—will detach itself from metropolitan France. When this occurs—and it must be our supreme political goal—the parting must occur without pain and the nations must be able to continue to view France without fear. The African peoples must not turn against her. For this reason, we must, from today, as a starting point, make ourselves loved.

THOSE WHO DEFENDED colonialism as noble, and those who rejected it as immoral, each saw their view vindicated. At war with Germany, one Frenchman died every minute from August 1914 to February 1917. In four years, 75,000 Senegalese, Algerians, Indochinese, and others died for France, along with 1,126,000 Frenchmen. They were heroes rallying to the motherland—or luckless dupes forced to fight. Altogether, 607,000 colonial soldiers took up arms: 294,000 North Africans, 189,000 black Africans, 49,000 Indochinese, 41,000 Malagasys, 23,000 from the Caribbean, and 11,000 others.

The war bled France almost to death, but the allies won. Germany was stopped short of Paris this time. The Third Republic survived the war, and the empire emerged stronger than ever. Alsace and Lorraine were restored to France. The German colonies of Togo and Cameroon were absorbed into French Africa.

And in 1919, the League of Nations gave France trusteeship over Syria and Lebanon, which became the first French holdings in the Middle East since the Crusades. Almost immediately, France was at war with Moslem Syrian nationalists, and skirmishes continued off and on for years. But many welcomed the Tricolor. Before the war, France had 500 schools in Syria, with 50,000 students, from an "intellectual protectorate" dating back to Père Joseph in 1617.

Debate has been constant—and it rages still—over the cost of empire. A colonial zealot can show that France might have sunk into bankruptcy without assured markets and raw materials; a hostile legislator can demonstrate how colonies dragged France into a fiscal quagmire. Accounts are likely to be in the black, taking in the indirect returns. By 1933, a third of French exports were sold in the colonies, which produced a quarter of France's imports. But all of that misses the point.

Under Louis XIV, the population of France was twice that of any European power. In 1800, only the Russians outnumbered the French. A century later, there were more Austrians, Germans, and Britons (and, by 1933, Italians) than French. *La Grande Guerre* had killed 10.5 percent of the active male population, and it disabled nearly as many. Farms and industries were wrecked, peasant families shattered.

To a large degree, France owed its freedom to officers trained in the colonies. Galliéni, who tamed Tuaregs and *Tonkinois* with an agile wit, held off the Germans by sending troops in taxis to the Marne.

France could not have purchased the 1931 Colonial Exposition at any price. At the edge of Paris, workmen recreated the empire: Angkor Wat, Tunisian souks, an African village, and more. French people of every shade, in every costume, were brought to the capital. Children's imaginations were fired; chests swelled. Visitors from all over the world watched in envy the fruit of French cultivation.

A handsome *Atlas Colonial Français* was published for the occasion. Its introduction, set in type reserved for formal dinner invitations, was signed by Lyautey, by then Marshal Lyautey, member of the Académie Française, soldier, governor, historian, and empire-builder *par excellence*. Not only were the colonies essential to French grandeur, he wrote, but the war had proved them also vital to French survival. "What would have become of us if we had been reduced to our own means? The colonies are a reservoir where we can always find whatever we need." He concluded:

Must one add these are not the only reasons? Colonization, as we have always understood, is but the highest expression of civilization. We help backward peoples raise themselves up the ladder of humanity. This mission to civilize we have always fulfilled in the *avant-garde* of all nations, and it is one of our most handsome titles to glory.

Leafing through [this atlas] is a veritable voyage around the world, a world where one finds everywhere the flag and the face of France.

Within a generation, the titles to glory would be called into question. But before then, within the decade, France would need every drop it could draw from the rich reservoir in Lyautey's metaphor.

CHAPTER ELEVEN

End of Empire

ADOLF HITLER'S BLITZKREIG swept over the Rhine toward Paris before France recovered from the shock. France, like England, had bent double to appease Hitler, but when Germany invaded Poland, no choice was left. At 5 P.M., September 3, 1939, France declared war. More than with any war since the Gauls resisted Caesar, there were irrefutable reasons of principle. But there was no way to win. On June 22, 1940, France signed an armistice. The Third Republic was dissolved, replaced by the Third Reich.

France was more vulnerable in 1939 than in 1914. Despite all the lessons of World War I, the country was better equipped with glory than guns. European wars would be fought with steel and technique. But in 1927, France spent more on fodder for cavalry horses than it did on higher education.[1]

Sanche de Gramont noted that France, as usual, was one war behind. He blamed the debacle partly on the French penchant for taking words as deeds. Six months before the invasion, he wrote, novelist Jules Romains visited the army's supreme commander, General Maurice Gamelin, in the ancient Vincennes fortress where he sat "like a chief friar in a monastery." The general disliked going to the front, where he might see things that interfered with his opinions. In fact, Gamelin told Romains that the Germans would amass their total power for a swift and horrible assault. "When will it happen? May. Yes, May, it is almost certain." It was then May.

"Here was the French army chief predicting the date and the outcome of the German spring offensive for which France was totally unprepared," de Gramont observed. "For him, it was enough. He could go back to reading Einstein and art books. What did it matter that France did not have the planes or tanks to meet the German offensive so long as he, Gamelin, had an intellectual grasp of the situation?"

France had few friends to count on. Italy was hardly an ally; Mussolini's cheerleaders had crowds chanting, "Nice! Savoy! Tunis! Corsica!" Italy gave Germans access to the southern Mediterranean and North African colonial armies were needed to defend their own coasts. Russia had signed a nonaggression pact with Germany. Belgium was neutral. England, strong at sea and in the air, had few ground troops to offer. That left the United States, which meant almost nothing.

American neutrality laws tied the hands of suppliers who might have sold arms to France as they did in World War I. The antiquated French air force was outnumbered; the impenetrable Maginot Line was outflanked. And no one probed the Siegfried Line to take the war to Germany while Hitler was nailing down Poland. German armor punched through from the north and raced down along the Somme and the Aisne toward Paris. Dive-bombing aircraft softened what little defense could be swung into place. "Not even Joan of Arc could have stopped tanks with a peashooter," an American correspondent observed.

French 75s, admirable artillery pieces though they were, were no match for Panzers. Defending forces enabled Britain to pull 260,000 men back across the channel from Dunkirk. But Hitler boasted, with some reason, that he had captured 1,200,000 French, English, Belgian, and Dutch prisoners during that delaying action. Paris was obviously lost, and so was the war. At that point, Mussolini displayed characteristic courage and declared war on France.

The French government retreated to Tours, afraid that a battle for Paris would demolish the city. Then the bombs rained on Tours. The cabinet, not surprisingly, was divided. No one wanted the French fleet or the air force to fall to Germany; with that extra strength, Hitler could conquer England. Then who could eventually pick up the pieces of France?

Americans, perched squarely on the fence, were in any case short of hardware. Cordell Hull dismissed what he called "extraordinary

. . . hysterical" appeals. France made a final plea to Franklin D. Roosevelt; he said no. Britain would fight to preserve France on one of two conditions: the French fleet must be delivered to English ports; or France could join England in an "indissoluble Franco-British union."

But the French government, already evacuated to Bordeaux, was running out of territory. Algiers was considered but rejected as too far away and with no industrial base for supplying an army. Millions of refugees choked the roads meanwhile, including remnants of shattered armies fleeing the Germans. "Men living in that atmosphere of confusion and horror, had they been hard as flint, could not have remained calm and serene," said President Albert Lebrun.

France surrendered. A "free" zone established a capital at Vichy, and ministries settled into hotels built for ailing tourists coming to take the waters. Marshal Philippe Pétain, a hero of past battles, was head of state. Germany occupied Paris and three-fifths of France.

But in London, two days after the armistice took effect, Winston Churchill recognized Charles de Gaulle as "leader of the Free French."

DE GAULLE WAS the serious-minded son of a family that traced its roots to the medieval sword-bearing officer class. He rose through the ranks of the French army, lecturing at St. Cyr and publishing his thoughts in slim volumes. At the end, he commanded a division and then a cabinet post, seeking to head off the inevitable. Finally, he scrambled into an RAF plane at Bordeaux and went to London. Churchill wrote later, "De Gaulle carried with him, in this small airplane, the honor of France."

There are excellent biographies of de Gaulle, Jean Lacouture's and Don Cook's, among others. The general himself was neither brief nor modest in his memoirs. For quick reference, a glance at his photograph in profile is sufficient. His eyes, wise and worried, gazed loftily over an Alpine nose. He was the picture of immovable France in deep trouble.

De Gaulle spoke of his *certaine idée de la France*." He said he imagined France as the princess of fairy stories, or the Madonna in frescoes, dedicated to an exalted and exceptional destiny. He wrote,

Instinctively, I have the feeling that Providence has created her either for complete successes or for exemplary misfortunes. If, in spite of this, mediocrity shows in her actions, it strikes me as an absurd anomaly to be imputed to the faults of Frenchmen and not to the genius of their land. But the positive side of my mind also assures me that France is not truly herself unless in the front rank . . . that our nation . . . must aim high and hold itself straight, on pain of mortal danger. In short, France cannot be France without greatness.

In London, the general spoke on the BBC, appealing to the French to rally against occupation. Shortly afterward, a telegram arrived from Fort-Lamy, Chad, in the heart of France's African empire. Félix Eboué, the Caribbean-born governor-general, had rallied French Equatorial Africa behind de Gaulle. Bits of the empire followed.

By the terms of title of French overseas property, Eboué's gesture gave de Gaulle a piece of France. The general could argue his legitimacy on firm ground. That was a fine point, however; de Gaulle was not in the habit of arguing.

The general's manner provoked the stiffest of British upper lips to curl in fury; American leaders liked him even less. Roosevelt wrote to Churchill in 1943:

The continual intrigues of de Gaulle upset me more and more. When we actually enter France, we must consider the action as a military occupation organized by English and American generals. . . . I do not know what to do about de Gaulle. You perhaps might want to name him governor of Madagascar.

Churchill, in turn, called de Gaulle "a vain and malicious man" and told Roosevelt, "One cannot truly leave this fool to continue his pernicious activities."[2] De Gaulle placed the cross of Lorraine on his Free French flag. Churchill later grumbled, "The heaviest cross I have to bear is the *Croix de Lorraine.*"

De Gaulle observed that he had no choice. For the survival of his nation, he was destined to act as the perfect symbol of France, of French civilization, and of the French character. His admirers said he was correct. His detractors said yes, that was exactly what Roosevelt and Churchill were talking about.

Brazzaville and then Algiers served as Free French headquarters, along with London. At every stage, de Gaulle made it clear that he was a head of a world power, temporarily dispossessed of his national palace.

Bearing French honor, during World War II, took a strong back. French armies had fought better. A heroic resistance organization harassed the Germans, saved Allied pilots, and laid the groundwork for D-Day. Many paid with their lives. But the hated term collaborator was spoken with grim frequency. Degrees of collaboration varied widely. Many French hated the Germans but silently accepted occupation in fear that their own families might suffer. Nazi records show that 2,200 German Gestapo agents were sent to France. The French working for them were more numerous and, in some cases, more zealous. Forty percent of the industry in Vichy France fed Germany's war machine. De Gaulle was not only disavowed, he was sentenced to death *in absentia*.

A scattered Resistance, later unified under Jean Moulin, sabotaged the occupation. No one's figures are accurate, but activists were few in the dangerous early period. At the height of the war, hard-core *résistants* probably numbered fewer than 75,000, or 0.2 percent of the adult population. At liberation, the total suddenly swelled into the hundreds of thousands.

Jean Dutourd captured the mood in *Taxis de la Marne,* a poignant recollection of his surrendering to the Germans as a young soldier. His ironic title referred to France's moment of glory in the earlier world war, stopping Germany by ferrying troops to the front in taxicabs. He wrote:

> The name de Gaulle seemed bizarre; I did not at all grasp the weight of his proclamation and his decision to pursue the war in the name of our country. My comrades shared my indifference: we were much more interested in Pétain who had ended an untenable situation by signing an armistice. Thanks to him, all was okay and soon our treasured civilian life would be restored. In short, we were, according to the word that had such success

later, realists. We preferred to accommodate to reality rather than change it.

And then he added:

> The word realism is mainly a polite translation for cowardice ... In the best of cases, realism leads to mediocrity; in the worst (the more frequent), it leads to the grave. There are circumstances where prudence is the worst of follies. Almost nothing done by great men is realist. It is by realism—lack of imagination—that men accept slavery. By the maxim, 'Better to be a live dog than a dead lion,' one descends to the rank of dog, which is precisely our case today. . . . One consoles oneself thinking if dogs wear collars and are kicked in the ribs, they are at least fed and sometimes petted. But that is deception, since not all lions die.

Passions distort memories, but facts are established. I discussed them in early 1986 with Serge Klarsfeld, a French lawyer who has painstakingly documented the period. His clinically precise treatment tends to surprise those who know his background. Klarsfeld escaped the ovens because his mother hid him in a wardrobe when police carried off his father. He spent the night listening through the thin wall to French officers torturing two little Jewish girls, neighbors, for information about their family's whereabouts.

Frenchmen delivered 76,000 Jews to the Germans, in cattle cars, along with thousands of Gypsies; only 3 percent came back after the war.[3] Vichy laws were virulently anti-Semitic. Some French risked a great deal to shield Jews; others, however, denounced Jews and then looted their belongings as soon as the police arrested them and took them away.

In a bitter television debate recently, a former French *résistant* quoted a remark of Hitler's: "Pétain, with his police, replaced fifteen divisions for me." At the time, the King of Denmark insisted on wearing a yellow Star of David to symbolize his resistance.

So raw were the wounds that Marcel Ophuls's epic film, *The Sorrow and the Pity,* was banned from French television for half a generation. Certain myths must be preserved, officials argued. It was only in 1981, after an energetic campaign by Klarsfeld, that French schoolbooks began to discuss the Vichy government's treatment of Jews. Later, Klarsfeld helped France to persuade Bolivia to hand over Klaus Barbie, the Gestapo officer in Lyon who tortured to death the Résistance hero Jean Moulin and sent hundreds of Jews to death camps. His trial was delayed repeatedly, to the relief of some Frenchmen not anxious to hear details he might reveal.

Leaks and personal feuds within the Free French organization hurt the war effort. Roosevelt and Churchill made a point of organizing D-Day without de Gaulle, keeping him out of most of the plans for the landing at Normandy. But the token French participation was enough for history: Captain Philippe Kieffer's 177-man commando team upheld France's honor on the Normandy beaches. Soon after, French land forces were again fighting to liberate France.

With Paris delivered, no force on earth could keep France's symbol of the hour, in his khaki kepi, from striding down the Champs-Elysées in a dazzling swirl of blue, white, and red. That de Gaulle was not invited to Yalta to help shape the postwar world was simply one more slight to rise above.

THE COLONIES played more than a strategic role. "Without her empire, France would be today nothing more than a liberated country," Gaston Monnerville said in 1945. "Thanks to her empire, France is a victorious nation."

In 1944, before the war ended, de Gaulle had convoked a meeting in Brazzaville of governors of the African colonies. He praised Brazza for winning Africans' friendship and using that "to advance at the same time the authority of France and civilization." That, de Gaulle said, was France's goal: "It is France, the nation designated by its immortal genius, whose initiatives are steadily raising men toward the summits of dignity and brotherhood where someday we all might come together."

The colonies' loyalty established a permanent link between *la Métropole* and *l'Empire,* he said. The meeting was to discuss carefully measured tangible gratitude. "There would be no progress ... if men could not lift themselves little by little to a level where they would be capable of taking part in the management of their own affairs."

But no Africans were invited, and the ground rules were clear: "The goals of France's work of civilization in the colonies excludes any idea of autonomy, or any possibility of evolution outside of . . . the Empire; the eventual constitution, even distant, of self-government in the colonies is to be excluded."

Resolutions suggested that forced labor be abolished within five years and discouraged polygamy, among other things. They affirmed the Africans' right to education and advancement.

The Brazzaville meeting had shifted away from the term empire. The United States and the Soviet Union each inveighed against empires in the post-war world, and France saw potential heat coming from both extremes. The word, in any case, was not particularly popular since Napoléon III. Instead, de Gaulle laid plans for a French Union.

In Paris, a freshly reconstituted Fourth Republic began putting France together again. One of its first moves was to define the parts of the French Union.

Réunion, Guadeloupe, Martinique, French Guiana, and St. Pierre and Miquelon were folded into the motherland, like the three departments of Algeria. The water separating them from the continent was juridically beside the point. They were not colonies; they were France. The rest of *France d'outre-mer* was divided into various categories of association with futures yet to be defined.

But some leaders in the colonies had already defined their futures without France. Syria and Lebanon, loosely tied to Paris, broke free after some struggle. French troops put down a nearly unreported rebellion in Madagascar, killing anywhere from 10,000 to 100,000 insurgents in 1947. The respected political scientist Alfred Grosser noted in *Affaires Extérieures* that authorities did not acknowledge reports of systematic torture in Madagascar. "But the accounts are precise and not refuted, and the Tananarive prison is certainly not the only place where one inflicted tortures very similar to those used by the Gestapo in France," he wrote. No one was prosecuted, Grosser said, not even a lieutenant who ordered the prison massacre on May 8 of 107 hostages, including sixteen women and four children.

France had a bigger problem with Vietnam. The Japanese seized French Indochina early in the war; it was their granary throughout the Southeast Asian campaign. French colonial administrators helped. Paul Mus, former director of the Ecole Nationale de la France d'Outre-mer, was with French intelligence in India at the time. He described in *Politique étrangère,* how Japan could not have exploited the vast network of isolated hamlets without France's help. In exchange, he said, the French were able to seem masters of their own situation, saving face among the Vietnamese. Collaboration might have gained time, but it was not enough.

Within a year of Germany's surrender, France was at war again. Britain set a precedent by freeing the Indian subcontinent, but France and Holland sought to hold their Asian colonies. According to Swedish economist Gunnar Myrdal, the French and Dutch "did not see their own interests with as much intuitive intelligence." France argued that war was essential in Indochina to hold the line against communism.

Ho Chi Minh, a committed communist since 1917, wanted complete and immediate independence for Vietnam. France refused. Before the war, colonial administrators in Indochina numbered almost 5,000, as many as in British India with fifteen times the population. In 1930 alone, there were nearly 700 summary executions.[4] Had Gandhi tried passive resistance in Indochina, Ho wrote, "he would long since have ascended to heaven." After the war, the Viet Minh pushed hard. Provoked by a series of minor incidents, French naval guns pounded Haiphong harbor on November 23, 1946. Thousands were killed. A month later, General Vo Nguyen Giap waged war on Hanoi. France tried to compromise. In a speech, governor Emile Bollaert promised independence. But he used the words *Doc Lap,* which translate equally to "independence" or "liberty."

France replaced Emperor Bao Dai on the throne in Vietnam, to the satisfaction of few. At an earlier moment of empire, flair and style might have calmed resistance. But the French had not merely lost face, they had had their faces rubbed in mud for four years. The Japanese had pitched aside the Tricolor in Asia.

Vietnamese who fought for France in World War II were infants, or yet unborn, when Albert Sarrault waxed eloquent about the gratitude they should feel. Many of them felt that domination by a capital halfway around the world was not worth a long list of material benefits.

La Guerre d'Indochine was the same sort of bitter, desperate quagmire that the United States stumbled into a generation later. But, in important ways, it was worse. At one extreme, France was at war with itself, committed to bleeding heavily yet again to preserve honor and territorial integrity. At the other extreme, France pursued a vicious colonial war, visiting genocide and torture on a people seeking only to be free. More toward the center, the French were suffering yet more war to hold back communism, spending American money but their own blood.

The war spread quickly in the late 1940s, and Ho Chi Minh sought to negotiate. France pressed on. The Korean War ended, and the Chinese diverted large amounts of aid to the Viet Minh insurgents. French morale flagged badly.

Until 1950, allies considered the French campaign a colonial war. Then China recognized Vietnam. American aid to France began paying for 80 percent of the war costs.

France was disturbed by what was known as the "dirty war," guerrilla tactics answered in kind. Lucien Bodard, in *The Quicksand War,* wrote:

> So often I wanted to ask a French officer, man to man: "Can you defend civilization while you let yourself slide toward everything most inimical to it—violence, deliberate cruelty, torture?" But for months, for a year, I could find no one who would talk. The younger officers of the Expeditionary Force were aware that in France, in their own country, they were unpopular, even detested, and they bore the condemnation in silence.

He found one, however, who talked all night. The officer had been a resistance fighter and hated the idea that the French were acting as the Germans had. But he realized torture was the Asian way and, however Europeans might misunderstand, it saved lives in the end. He said:

> The Viets push us into atrocities. Yet we kill infinitely less than the Viets, and infinitely less than the Americans would. They wouldn't bother to go into details, they'd just bomb whole "zones." Liquidate the population and liquidate the problem.

And at that, international opinion puts up much better with the most lethal wholesale hammering than with the torture of a single assassin.

French efforts renewed under a new commander, General de Lattre de Tassigny. In 1951, he urged escalation of the war, saying, "Nations never die a violent death; their heart continues to beat as long as faith animates it, and it stops only when they refuse to fight and they give up wanting to live."

But, sick and aging, he retired to Paris. The war widened. By 1953, the communist Viet Minh controlled two-thirds of Vietnam. An eager new French military command devised a plan to lure their enemy's main force into a direct assault. The site they chose was a fortified camp deep inside Vietnam, near the Chinese border: Dien Bien Phu.

The camp was in a hollow, dominated by hills. French generals misjudged the guerrillas' ability to muster firepower, and they assumed their air force could keep them supplied. General Giap blasted the camp for fifty-six days, pounding it to rubble with guns his men lugged in on their backs. Dien Bien Phu fell on May 7, 1954, at a cost of more than 1,800 French lives.

With Dien Bien Phu, the government of Joseph Laniel fell. He was the twentieth premier since liberation. Pierre Mendès-France took power June 17, and signed a ceasefire on July 21.

Bodard recalled a conversation with a paracommando captain at the Normandy Bar in Hanoi, when it was all over.

"It was all for nothing," [the captain] was saying. "I let my men die for nothing." His glare was as blind as a sleepwalker's. . . . "In prison camp we faced the reality of the Viet Minh. And we saw that for eight years our generals had been struggling against a revolution without knowing what a revolution was. Dien Bien Phu was not an accident of fate, it was a judgment."

[Bodard added:] In Hong Kong, an American journalist said to me, "You have the most rotten army in the world, but we could have made you win at Dien Bien Phu, and I think we should have." One of his friends said hastily, "But I admire your army. They know how to make a *beau geste.*" It was kind of him, no doubt, but he really meant the French army, like a Louis XV armchair, was the masterpiece of an extinct civilization.

What could I answer? The Americans would never have fought as we did. They would have fought a different war. And by crushing the country and the people under a hail of bombs and dollars, they might well have had more success than we did.

Maybe not. Over eight years, the number of French dead and missing surpassed 50,000, more than American casualties later. Perhaps a half million Viet Minh were killed, along with an estimated 800,000 to two million Vietnamese civilians. The war consumed more than the $2.7 billion France received under the Marshall Plan. War costs each year amounted to 10 percent of the national budget.

France was forced to abandon loyal Vietnamese to their fate, along with a way of life it had sworn to preserve. And there was much more to pay. Less than seven months after the fall of Dien Bien Phu, and in no small way because of it, the Algerian War began.

AS FRANCE FIRST struggled in Algeria to subdue Abd-el-Kadar, Franciade-Fleurus Duvivier wrote: "In spite of the savage war we are waging against them, all natives will be with us in thirty years' time. Let us therefore adopt a policy not of containment but of confidence."

But the more prophetic voices were ominous. Baron Lacuée warned in 1831: "As long as you keep Algiers, you will be constantly at war with Africa; sometimes war will seem to end; but these people will not hate you any the less; it will be a half-extinguished fire that will smoulder under the ash and which, at the first opportunity, will burst into a vast conflagration."[5]

Not long afterward, a conquered chieftain told his captors, "You are merely passing guests. You may stay three hundred years, like the Turks, but in the end you will leave."[6]

In its self-defined mission of bringing civilization to Barbary, France sought to assimilate a new class of brown French. Napoléon III, on a five-week visit to Algeria, had ordered, "Treat the Arabs, in the midst of whom you must live, as compatriots." Since 1847, Algeria had been divided into three departments. Each was just like

Savoy, Corsica, or Bouches-du-Rhône, the history books insisted. By 1954, it was hard to make that point with a straight face.

Boundless energy had been expended. Algeria is the world's tenth biggest country; France built roads and telephone lines across an area four times the size of the *métropole*. Tall white buildings rose over modern harbors. Teachers and doctors reached remote outposts. Marshes and deserts were turned into productive land. Algeria was developed, or as the French would say, *mise en valeur*. But the result was that Europeans streamed in—more Italians, Spanish, Corsicans, Maltese, and Greeks than mainland French—and Arabs and Kabyles were contained ever more tightly.

The native *indigènes* were exhorted to accept full French citizenship and rise to new heights as *évolués* (those who had "evolved"). There was a catch, however. Algerians were Moslem, and accepting French law meant rejecting the laws of the Koran. By 1936, only 2,500 Moslems had applied for French citizenship.[7] Léon Blum urged a new statute to resolve the conflict; the National Assembly refused. In contrast, foreign settlers received French nationality easily, forming a ragbag nobility of cultures with no particular loyalty to Paris. Algeria first stood behind the Vichy government; de Gaulle nearly had to fight his way ashore to set up headquarters in Algiers.

Unlike other *départements*, Algeria came under a governor-general who reported to the Interior Ministry. Legislators were elected by a system heavily skewed toward the *pieds-noirs*, the white settlers. The local assembly was divided into two colleges, one of them all French. Mayors and commanders of outlying districts were also French. Some rich and socially accepted Moslems were active in community affairs. But "assimilation," official policy since 1847, was a standing joke.

Edward Behr, there as a correspondent, noted in *The Algerian Problem* that the majority was dominated by a "a poor white minority, insecure and vociferous." He observed, "It seems to have been a thoroughly evil, as well as a thoroughly inefficient system."

French administrators rigged elections, installing their own Moslem candidates over leaders they considered dangerous. Jacques Soustelle, governor-general and dominant figure of the period, reported to the government in May 1955:

The pseudo-deputies . . . put in office thanks to the electoral fraud, most often illiterate and frequently dishonest, representing nothing and nobody, have no influence in their voting areas and do not even repay the administration for having created them. Few mistakes have been more tragic than that which consisted in distorting our own laws to bring into prominence discredited personalities without any intellectual or moral value.

The argument of Plato's *Republic* was convenient: The masses were not prepared to share power. But little was done to alter the balance between Moslem masses and the Europeans.

In 1954, a group of senior officials and economists under Roland Maspétiol drew a picture of the inequality between 1,070,000 Europeans and more than eight million Moslems.

Ten percent of the population held 90 percent of the wealth. Almost one million Moslems had no work; two million more were seriously underemployed. Eighty percent of Moslem children did not go to school. Three-quarters of all Moslems were illiterate in Arabic; 90 percent could not read French. Yearly income per head of family in Moslem rural areas was sixteen pounds sterling; in the cities, it was forty-five pounds. Official spending, adjusted to inflation, was at the same level as in 1913.

The average European farm was eleven times larger than an average Moslem farm, and it brought in twenty-eight times more revenue. Algeria's main wealth came from wine, which Moslems did not drink.

A second study in 1961 divided the population into three categories: 16 percent had living standards comparable to Western industrialized nations; 26 percent lived at "Mediterranean" standards, those of Greece, Portugal or southern Italy; and 62 percent—all Moslems—were comparable to the rural masses in Egypt or India.

For many Moslems, economic imbalance was not the worst part. Individual attitudes toward Moslems ranged, most often, from condescending to insulting. Back in 1892, Jules Ferry decried the white settlers' discrimination against Moslems:

We have taken a close look at him, and have studied his private and public behavior. We have found him very limited. . . . He lacks what may be described as the virtue of the victor, the balance of the spirit and of the heart, and the regard for the weak which is in no way incompatible with firm leadership. It is difficult to try to convince the European settler that there are rights other than his own in an Arab country and that the native is not a race to be taxed and exploited to the utmost limits. . . . the settlers proclaim that [they] are totally incorrigible and utterly incapable of education, without ever having attempted, over the past 30 years, to do anything to drag them out of their moral and intellectual misery. . . . They fail to understand any other policy than that of containment. To be sure, there are no thoughts of destroying them; it is even claimed that there is no urge to drive them back. But there is no concern for their complaints, or for their numerical growth which seems to increase with their poverty.[8]

The years brought little improvement. The first Moslem colonel to command a regiment was announced with fanfare only in 1959. The races lived in loosely defined separate areas. In Algiers, the European city fronted the sea, with the same terraces and chic store windows found on the opposite rim of the Mediterranean. The Arab quarter, the Casbah, was a medieval rabbit warren of stone lanes twisting up the hills. The fabled invitation, "Come wiz me to ze Casbah," clearly was issued by someone who had never been there.

Germaine Tillion, a liberal sociologist who knew Algeria well, acknowledged France's good intentions, but she tore into the failings of policy which amounted to separate development. In *Algérie en 1957,* she quoted an old man from Kabylia: "You've taken us halfway across the ford and left us."

Resistance rippled from time to time. But the guillotine which Victor Hugo saw arrive tended to discourage troublemakers.

The Algerian time bomb exploded the day after Germany surrendered. While France celebrated liberation, a crowd of Moslems demanded their own freedom in the market town of Sétif, west of Constantine. Crop failures and wartime shortages left people in Sétif miserable. Rich harvests on Europeans' prime land nearby did not help their spirits. The undercurrents smacked of imminent rebellion.

Eight thousand Moslems began to march, ostensibly to lay a wreath for Algerians fallen in the war. The French subprefect decided not to intervene, especially since he had only twenty gendarmes. But the crowd unfurled the green and white standard of Abd-el-Kadar and chanted, "Free and independent Algeria!" He ordered police to stop them. Warned there would be a fight, he replied, "All right, then there'll be a fight."

Someone shot first. A Moslem was killed, and the cry of *jihad,* holy war, arose. Crowds overran the police and fanned out, slaughtering any Europeans they found. On small farms, faithful servants turned on their lifelong masters. In five days, 103 Europeans were murdered. Another 100 were wounded, and the rape victims included an eighty-four-year-old woman. Breasts were slashed off; men's sexual organs were stuffed in their mouths. Then the French army arrived.[9]

A systematic *ratissage* left Moslem villages in ashes; suspected culprits were shot dead on the spot. Bombers flattened at least forty remote hamlets. Gunboats shelled the coast. European vigilantes attacked at random, lynching and stoning Moslems. Official French figures put the Moslem death toll near 1,100. Thirty years later, President Habib Bourguiba of Tunisia insisted it was over 50,000. Objective estimates range between 6,000 and 16,000.

Historian Charles-André Julien described the repression as "ferocious, pitiless, in truth inhuman by its lack of discrimination."

The uprising was barely reported in France, but in Algeria everyone knew about Sétif. A steamy calm prevailed for the next nine years, but nationalist leaders, each fired by memories of Sétif, were preparing the moment. It was to be 1 A.M. on All Saints Day, November 1, 1954.

Rebels targeted the bleak Aurès mountains, bastion of the traditionally fractious Chaouias. They shot two French army sentries in the garrison town of Batna and then two more soldiers. Insurgents stopped a bus and fell upon two French teachers, Guy Monnerot and his twenty-one-year-old wife. The Moslem *caid* of the nearby village of M'Chouneche tried to stop them. In *La Guerre d'Algérie,* Pierre Montagnon records this exchange.

"You cannot kill these young people, come from so far to teach our children."

"Who cares? Our civilization is the Koran, not that of these
Roumi dogs."

The *caid* was shot dead with a machine-gun burst. Monnerot was
executed; his wife was assaulted and left for dead.

In all, separate bands struck in seventy places across Algeria, with
little material damage. But Cairo radio broadcast the first proclamation of the *Front de Libération Nationale,* the FLN. It insisted on
independence, with or without the accord of France.

Rebels organized in cells almost impervious to infiltration; no
guerrilla knew more than four or five others. Algeria was divided
into seven military zones. Scrounged weapons, hidden away, probably totaled fewer than 400 aging rifles, with nothing bigger than
a machine gun. Communist and Arab help would not come for two
years. An amateur factory in the Algiers Casbah produced 200
bombs from oil cans and jam jars.

The French were hardly better prepared. Officers could muster
only 3,500 fighting men; most of the 57,000 troops were needed in
garrisons or were still earmarked for Indochina. Two days before
the war started, a headquarters colonel snorted when told 100 armed
rebels had been seen in the Aurès mountains: "Monsieur le Préfet,
I've been patrolling these roads for a very long time and have never
seen a *fellagha* in front of my jeep." When the assault came, he
insisted on waiting for written orders to sound the alarm. At Batna,
two soldiers were killed even though they saw the rebels approach.
Under peacetime orders, their rifles had been unloaded and their
ammunition had been sewn into their tunics.

In Paris, the first top official to warn of trouble was François
Mitterrand, the minister responsible for Algeria. "I sense something
. . . the situation is unhealthy," he said in the summer.[10] But he did
little about it. Later, Jacques Chevallier, secretary of state for defense
and a *pied-noir,* former (and future) mayor of Algiers, took a long
weekend to go have a look for himself. He chose All Saints Day.

The world mood was against France. The French had already set
free Morocco and Tunisia, after minimal armed conflict. Britain had
given independence to India; Ghana's would follow soon afterward.
The French Union was edging toward new flexibility.

But France rebounded quickly: Algeria was different.

A million white Algerians argued, as other whites did in South

Africa, that their enterprise and achievement outweighed the simple dictates of majority rule. They were not colonizers who could go home; they were home. Governments in Paris were too busy sweeping up debris from fifteen years of war to read the writing on the wall. And many French, along with most *pieds-noirs,* were in no mood for yet another humiliating retreat.

Mendès-France sent Soustelle to be governor-general. Later, Soustelle wrote:

> Algeria! Divided most profoundly within herself, torn between the past and the future, quartered by desires and rancors, she discharged into my face, when I leaned anxiously over her, the ardent and heavy breath of a sorcerer's cauldron. How could one not love her, especially in that ordeal. "When your son has grown up, treat him like your brother," says the Arab proverb; it was certainly painful, but the son had become a man, our equal, our brother. That was what one had to understand.

At first, the *pieds-noirs* hated Soustelle for his liberal approach. He tried to attack the causes of Moslem discontent. His corps of Sections Administratives Spécialisées, the SAS, brought help to neglected areas. School budgets were doubled, and Arabic was accepted along with French. "Assimilation" gave way to "integration," urging Moslems to live side by side with Europeans as Frenchmen.

But attitudes remained basically unchanged, and FLN units grew steadily. The war widened in a series of "incidents." Soustelle issued orders to adhere strictly to Mitterrand's policy: suspects must be handed over to qualified authorities; brutality or any "offense against human dignity" was "rigorously forbidden." But army commanders secretly short-circuited the system. An unofficial policy of "collective responsibility" grew common.

In his *Les Français d'Algérie,* Pierre Nora gave an example. Near Sidi-bel-Abbès, a Foreign Legion patrol executed nine farmhands suspected of helping rebels. The *pied-noir* farmer was outraged. "How could you shoot down workers who saw me born! Without warning me? . . . Assassins, vandals, is this how you pacify?"

The FLN adopted the tactics of Brazilian guerrilla leader Carlos Marighela. They terrorized civilians, bringing widespread repression which, in turn, radicalized the Moslem masses. In August 1955, the little port of Philippeville was awash in blood. Screaming Moslems slashed the throats and bellies of European women and smashed infants' heads against walls. Entire families were massacred. One was the Mello family: the father, the seventy-three-year-old grandmother, and the eleven-year-old daughter were killed in their beds, their arms and legs hacked off. The mother was disemboweled and her five-month-old baby, slashed to death, was placed in her opened womb.

Frenzied revenge killing followed. Official tolls say 123 people were killed by mobs that day, including seventy-one Europeans. The French said they killed 1,273 "insurgents." FLN officers estimated their dead at 12,000.[11] Soustelle surveyed the carnage and decided that his only course was to crush the rebellion.

"A somber harvest of hatred sprouted in the bloodshed," he said. "Far from being brought together by the ordeal, human beings were going to divide themselves and tear themselves to pieces."

The situation worsened at a tumultous pace. Albert Camus rallied Jean-Paul Sartre, Simone de Beauvoir, and other left-leaning intellectuals to push—in vain—for the liberal reforms Soustelle could not accomplish. In Paris, Mendès-France fell after losing a vote of confidence over his North African policy. Edgar Faure, the new premier, called early elections in hopes that a new National Assembly could be steered toward a solution. Guy Mollet, a Socialist, emerged as premier but two and a half million votes went to the militant champion of the extreme right wing, Pierre Poujade.

Mollet recalled Soustelle, but so many *pieds-noirs* thronged the port to keep him in Algiers that it took him an hour to cover 200 yards. Soustelle's replacement was General Georges Catroux, seventy-nine and a liberal. He was regarded as the man who sold out France in Syria and Morocco. Mollet went to Algiers to install Catroux personally, but the premier had to retreat under a barrage of tomatoes and cabbages. Catroux "resigned" in favor of Robert Lacoste, and Mollet brought French troop strength in Algeria to 500,000.

It was a bad year all the way around. The United Nations debated the Algeria problem, and the FLN's support grew in Asia and elsewhere among new leaders of what would be called the Third World. The French hijacked FLN leader Ahmed Ben Bella on his way to a summit in Tunis, infuriating Bourguiba and Moroccan King Mohammed V. In Morocco, French settlers were killed in bloody reprisals. Fragile attempts to negotiate with the FLN went out the window. And then there was Suez.

Gamal Abdel Nasser nationalized the Suez Canal in 1956. The world, at the time, was in uproar. The Soviet Union crushed an uprising in Hungary and nailed down its bloc. War broke out between Israel and Egypt. The United States was reelecting Dwight D. Eisenhower. France was worried, above all, that Nasser would arm the FLN; a shipload of weapons had been seized already in the Mediterranean. With Britain, France invaded the Suez. General Jacques Massu, with troops hardened in Algeria, was nearly at the canal. But the British, wavering from the start, backed out under Soviet pressure. Then Eisenhower obliged France to retreat—and not happily.

Mollet insisted that his aim was to help Israel, but Algeria was at center stage. Nasser was left free to help the FLN. French relations with Britain, strained since the war, turned acrimonious. London had fallen under the sway of Washington. French politicians excoriated the United States for not helping them fight communism in Algeria.

And, to top things off, there was the Battle of Algiers.

Until mid-1956, the war was mostly in the *bled,* rural mountains and remote plains. Then the FLN murdered French gendarmes in Algiers. A prime suspect's house in the heart of the Casbah was mysteriously blown up, killing civilians. In reprisal, guerrillas used young Arab women to sneak explosives past checkpoints. On September 30, bombs obliterated the Milk-Bar and a popular cafeteria, strewing torn limbs and panic in the heart of European Algiers. Massu's paratroopers, facing a war of urban terror, fought back with interrogation by torture.

The Battle of Algiers was won within a year, but some French are still agonizing over how it was done.

At the time, little was reported about torture. Some—not all— French reporters neglected to pass along what they knew. Foreign correspondents heard stories, but had trouble pinning down names and places. *Les paras* and the police issued no invitations to interrogation sessions. Later, no doubts were left.

Recently, a French journalist I know well told me, "I went in the wrong door at police headquarters [in Algiers] and saw a guy with his hands cuffed behind him. A long tube down his throat was attached to a faucet so they could force water to distend his stomach until he was ready to talk. I didn't say anything about it because it wasn't my business. And besides, I was a *pied-noir*. Of course, the police tortured. They were up against fanatics who were planting bombs. Everyone agreed it was the only way."

A favorite device was the *gégène*, a hand-cranked magneto used for powering field telephones. Attached to ear lobes or testicles, it also powered reluctant tongues. Suspects were sometimes beaten or lashed to poles and left suspended. There were water tortures: prolonged dunkings and water forced down the throat through a funnel. Occasionally there were summary executions.

No one has accurately determined the extent of the practice. Ministers and ranking officials insist that no one ordered torture, but officers privately acknowledge that it was systematic. Some argued that it was a noble necessity: without it, paratroopers could not have stopped the random bombing. Torture, by that reasoning, saved innocent lives. When Paris objected, Behr said in an interview, excesses were simply moved farther out of sight. Jean Larteguy recalled that one officer told Mollet, "If everything has to happen in the basement, it is because of you."

The result was what the FLN sought in using terror; sympathy for their cause grew in proportion to the repression. Paratroopers broke an eight-day strike by smashing open closed shops and forcing people back to work. With the battle over, they exercised virtually unlimited control over Moslem Algerians. But they won few hearts or minds.

Beyond torture, and beyond the Battle of Algiers, was the general conduct of the war. Jean-Jacques Servan-Schreiber jolted the nation in 1957 with a personal account, *Lieutenant in Algeria*.

As an example of day-to-day excesses, he started with a random communique: "Yesterday at Brahim, the occupants of a truck machine-gunned people in the street. Fortunately, only one man was wounded." Then he explained what happened.

A young Arab, nearly run down by an army jeep, started to yell at the soldiers. One pointed a machine gun at him. An old man tried to calm down the youth. In his tension, the soldier shot the old man. The soldiers drove off. A "territorial unit" of local settlers saw the body; they decided the old man had been executed by Moslem terrorists for being pro-French. Just then, a truck rolled by carrying five Arab mineworkers. They stopped it; the driver was too frightened to speak French, and they beat him up. An army truck roared up, and the Arabs, in the momentary confusion, fled. The army patrol was led by a sergeant named Maure, a young married railway accountant from Limoges. His men thought him soft because he didn't get drunk or screw around. Pressured to act quickly, he ordered a chase. His patrol caught the Arabs and shot them all dead.

"Maure thanked God that everything had gone so well, and that his men—reservists like himself—had been able to do their duty as soldiers without a single one being killed or wounded," wrote Servan-Schreiber. "His nightmare was that he might one day have a dead man or a disabled man on his conscience. Good old Maure."

At headquarters, however, a problem developed. No weapons were found on the victims, and a young lieutenant asked his captain, Martin, what to do. What do you think? scolded Martin. But if the report said there were arms, it was decided, they might have to be produced later at an inspection. Sometimes captured arms went unreported and were saved for such occasions, but none were available. Instead, no mention was made of the dead Arabs. Then a Captain Julienne broke in. The dead men would be missed, he said, and Moslems would hate the French for the injustice. "I'm suggesting that it's bad business to kill people who may be innocent, and that it is not what we are here for."

In a condescending but friendly manner, Captain Martin explained that Julienne was right—in theory. Unfortunately, he said, there were two choices. He could risk having his men killed, and people would write to their deputies complaining that he was a butcher. "Or you do your duty honorably, which is to say you put the *fellagha* out of commission and look after our men the best you can. In that case, there's only one way: treat every Arab as a suspect, a possible *fellagha,* a potential terrorist—because that, my dear sir, is the truth. And don't come back at me with words like charity and justice. . . . You can talk about that in Paris with the politicians who got us into this mess."

Later, Julienne told Major Marcus, "I've seen enough here to be convinced that what they're making us do here is leading straight to the loss of Algeria—not to speak of our honor as Frenchmen." Weren't there commanders and leaders who saw that? Marcus replied,

> There are, more than you'd think. It is not stupidity that is destroying us, it's cowardice. They understand, but they don't turn a hair. People are lying, Julienne, they're lying from the top to the bottom of the ladder. . . . People lie so much that they don't know they are doing it. You lie from a sense of duty, you see. Once you've got that far, there's no way out. . . .
>
> What the Arabs hated was the colonial set-up; they didn't really hate France. The army should have been independent of the colonial establishment, separate from the rottenness of the administration, from the settlers, the policemen, the mayors, from everything that the colonial attitude has represented for a century now. . . . It did the very opposite.

Servan-Schreiber describes attempts among the extremists to murder radicals like Marcus and himself. More generally, he was vilified as a traitor by brothers in arms. A great many Frenchmen agreed with him. But little changed.

An English foreign legionnaire, Simon Murray, wrote later:

> The effectiveness of torturing people to make them betray their cause cannot be disputed. But with all the good results . . . was a steady buildup of hatred against the French. And this antagonism drew the Arabs, so often divided among themselves, into a common cause; it made them feel the necessity of combining for survival and it made them finally aware of their own strength. The French became the foreign intruder. . . . I wonder how many more crosses must be struck before the end comes—the end for

the French, when a new nation will be born, conceived entirely through French misunderstanding.

Along with torture in Algeria was the scorched earth policy. As Behr suggests, anyone doubting the ravages of random destruction need only have flown low over mountaintops to see village after village, flattened, burned black and lifeless.

Behr noted that he had seen earlier sporadic examples of French excesses in Morocco and Tunisia. But, he wrote, "it was not until the Algerian rebellion spread that people and army brutality became a permanent and quietly efficient instrument, a weapon of war of the same calibre as the grenade or the mortar-bomb."

In late 1985, a Foreign Legion colonel who was in Algeria told me, "No one ordered torture, but it is impossible to control all individual units. And what is torture, anyway? If you kick in a door and fire off a burst without looking first, it is torture if there are women and children inside, but war is like that."

What about the *gégène?* He snorted.

"The *gégène* is not torture, it is a *rigolade.*" That means, a laugh. "I've tried it myself."

He did not attach the electrodes to his scrotum, of course. And he knew when the crank would stop turning—and what would not come next. Psychological torture, victims say, can be worse than outright pain.

A Frenchman who was a senior civilian official in the late 1950s was blunt:

> Of course, torture was widespread, institutionalized, severe. How could you order an army to win a war and not fight it? We tried to control it after 1958, to fight a cleaner war, but it was impossible. The government sent thousands of letters to local commanders: "We understand Mohammed So-and-So has disappeared in mysterious circumstances. . . ." That sort of thing. It had some effect. Look, we managed to slow down torture. But stop it? Impossible.

At one point, a young official in Algiers named Eric Westphal energized a government review committee to investigate human rights abuses. Disgruntled military officers dynamited his house.

The issue burned in 1985 after Paris newspapers quoted Algerians as saying National Front leader Jean-Marie Le Pen, as a lieutenant, had tortured them. Mohammed Mouley said Le Pen commanded a patrol that tortured and killed his father. Le Pen denied personal involvement but defended rough treatment to obtain information. And then his longtime friend, Dr. Jean-Maurice Demarquet, spoke out. He said Le Pen asked him to testify in his favor. That offended his honor.

> I didn't want to lie [he told *Le Monde*]. I even told him we have brothers in arms who have a perfect memory of what we did with them. I said, it had to be done; you have no cause to blush. It is absolutely evident that Le Pen was a member of teams that tortured personally. Personally. It is like that. I must say that we shared the same episodes. That one tries to pretend that it did not happen when the context changes, I don't accept that.

The revelation, among others, did not seem to affect Le Pen's standing with the extreme right. In fact, a poll conducted by the Louis Harris organization and the magazine *Evénement* among 1,-000 adults showed that 20 percent approved of torture in Algeria if it saved the lives of Frenchmen or friendly Algerians. And 40 percent said that if Le Pen were proven a torturer, it would not affect his qualifications to be a French public official. Apparently not. In the March 1986 legislative elections, his National Front won 9.72 percent of the vote. Le Pen and thirty-four Front members took seats in the National Assembly, equalling the Communist Party's bloc.

Answering another question in the Le Pen poll, 72 percent rejected the use of torture under any circumstance. In an interview with *Libération,* General Massu dismissed the Algerians' testimony against Le Pen:

> There is torture, and there is torture. They weren't so badly tortured because they are doing well twenty-eight years later. If they had been horribly tortured, they would not be in that condition. If we had conducted a classic war against them, and

if they had been wounded by machineguns or artillery, they surely would not be talking like that. Now don't come telling me your stories with your tortures. That is a big word.

Assembling notes for this chapter, I clipped an article headlined "Confessed Torturer." It was, in fact, about an Argentine officer who took part in the torture of two French nuns. France and the French energetically condemned the Argentines' "dirty war" against terrorism. I missed the Battle of Algiers but not the Battle of Buenos Aires. Comparisons are risky, and degrees are always different, but some parallels are inescapable. Argentines are not inherent torturers any more than the French are. But in each case, a certain carte blanche was built into the system and overlooked by those who could revoke it.

Some would take Cardinal Newman's approach of the last century: "A gentleman is one who never inflicts pain." Others might answer that the British prelate never raced against time to find an FLN bomb cache. But extreme methods were used even when time was not particularly of the essence. That French officers tortured does not condemn a society. But, unlike in Argentina, there was no clamor for justice after the dirty war, nor did there seem to be much concern at all.

In late 1985, I met Gisèle Halimi, a lawyer who built a reputation defending torture victims during the war. Simone de Beauvoir wrote a preface to a book Halimi wrote describing the difficulties of making French justice work. I asked her about the period, and she cut me off with a sharp look. "Do you think, Mr. Rosenblum, that twenty-five years later is the time to speak about Algerian torture?" By coincidence, that was the day Argentine courts sentenced five generals and admirals for their depredations of a decade earlier. And in Lyon, Klaus Barbie awaited trial for World War II crimes against the French.

I asked three people why no postwar investigations were made. A former civilian official in Algeria said, "It is a great hole in the memory of Frenchmen. There is a collective guilty conscience, and most want it forgotten. My twenty-four-year-old daughter is just now reading her first book on the war in Algeria."

Barry Goodfield, an American who has spent ten years training

French specialists in psychotherapy and who has examined the effects of war on European societies, was more clinical.

"It is unconscious behavior relating to an identity. The French do not see themselves as being capable of that sort of abuse. You can't try someone for something that could not have been done."

But my friend Claude, the elderly French journalist cited above, responded passionately.

Look, France had just emerged from four years of occupation, where Frenchmen were shot in the back. Twenty dead, fifty dead, in reprisal for one German soldier killed. And then Frenchmen were shot in the back by Algerians. After all that, you think anyone got worked up about a little torture? Besides, no one really knew. They didn't absorb what happened. These are not things that Frenchmen do, torture, murder. . . .

Eh bien, oui, this is a bloody society. Look at the Commune [in 1871]. In six days, no, five days, they killed 37,000 people. The army admits to 17,000. The *communards* say 37,000. Believe me, the French are already immunized against violence. What makes me sick is the hypocrisy, the false principles, with which we cry over abuses in Argentina or Chile. We did the same thing, and I am convinced that we would do it again. It is sad, but *c'est comme ça.*

B Y 1 9 5 8, Habib Bourguiba and Mohammed V were pushing hard for negotiations, but French commanders suspected them of helping the FLN. On February 8, 1958, for a second time antiaircraft fire hit a French plane from the Tunisian border village of Sakiet. Three hours later, a B26 squadron flattened the place. It was a market day. About eighty people were killed: children in a school, patients in a hospital, marketwomen. Bourguiba expelled French troops who were in Tunisia under treaty. Premier Félix Gaillard accepted a "good offices" mission from the United States and Britain to heal the rift. But Paris papers sneered at *"Messieurs les bons offices"* meddling in domestic matters.

An anti-American chorus grew; clearly, it was argued, Americans wanted oil from an independent Algeria. On April 15, the Gaillard government fell and, not long after, so did the Fourth Republic.

René Coty was president without a government. *Pieds-noirs* and Moslems alike rebelled against Lacoste, the lame-duck governor. When Lacoste had three terrorists guillotined, the FLN executed three French prisoners. That pushed the army over the edge.

General Raoul Salan telegraphed Paris that unless a clear commitment was made to keep Algeria French "one cannot predict how it (the army) will react." Salan, in effect, ran Lacoste out of town. The *pieds-noirs,* meanwhile, surged through the streets in cars, bleating out a five-note slogan on their horns: *"Al-gér-ie Fran-çaise."* Housewives rapped out the same rhythm on pots and pans. They mobbed the Forum, a vast plaza in front of the governor-general's offices. Then they seized the building itself, burning files and occupying offices. Salan addressed crowds from the balcony, ending his speech, *". . . et vive de Gaulle."* After that, crowds had a new chant: *". . . de Gaulle au pouvoir."*

For twelve years, de Gaulle had sat out events quietly at his modest home in Colombey-les-Deux-Eglises. In 1948, Janet Flanner wrote, "Time, weight, and, evidently, the general's glands are giving his visage a heavy, royal outline; he looks more like a man of dynasty than of destiny." In April 1958, he told a Gaullist deputy, "They will create a burnt earth, they will wait until there is nothing left before calling for de Gaulle! I shall never come back to power in my lifetime." But a month later, at sixty-seven, grayer, heavier, with failing eyesight, he answered the call.

Coty named de Gaulle premier with wide powers, threatening to resign if the National Assembly did not agree. The vote, on June 1, was 329 to 224. He would rule by decree for six months; the Assembly would recess for four months; and he would submit a new constitution for France.

De Gaulle hurried to Algiers and appeared on the balcony where his name had been shouted repeatedly. Salan said, "Our great cry of joy and hope has been heard!" The crowds roared for three full minutes. De Gaulle stretched his arms to a great *V* and thundered, *"Je vous ai compris . . . !"*

De Gaulle had yelled, "I have understood you," and he likely did. But few understood him. Men and women weeping for joy heard him say that all Algerians would live together as Frenchmen, with full and equal rights. They heard him offer the FLN reconciliation:

"Never more than here, nor more than this evening, have I seen how beautiful, how great, how generous is France!" But in that crucial speech, no one heard him say, *"Vive l'Algérie Française!"* And hardly anyone translated full rights to majority rule.

It was a ruse, pure and simple, to gain time, de Gaulle acknowledged later in his memoirs. That was plain at the time to those around him. On his return to Paris, he muttered to an aide, "Africa is finished, and Algeria with it."

The war had split apart the nation. "France is headed toward a great destiny, " de Gaulle declaimed. "We are all murderers," wrote Sartre.

Later that year, de Gaulle called a referendum on a constitution that would give the president of France sweeping power. Later, he would run for president. Sartre remarked that he would rather vote for God: "He is more modest." But 85 percent of metropolitan France voted, giving the Fifth Republic constitution an 80 percent backing.

Colonies in the French Union were invited to remain associated with the new France as independent nations. Every African state but Guinea voted *oui* by a landslide. De Gaulle reminded Ahmed Sékou Touré that France had lived long without Guinea; he pushed the colony out of the nest that same year, without a franc, and recuperated everything French that could be packed onto ships. The others took independence within the "community" in 1960, in an orderly manner.

Algeria, being France and not a colony, could only approve or reject the constitution. Moslems voted overwhelmingly in favor, trusting de Gaulle to find some end to the war.

In a press conference on October 23, de Gaulle offered his *paix des braves,* a noble peace, with a white flag of truce. Jacques Fauvet of *Le Monde* lauded "the nobility of tone, the harmony of thought." Alain de Serigny, in the *Echo d'Alger,* put it this way: "The white flag means surrender."

The FLN rejected the offer, saying they wanted a political solution, not peace. The left agreed that a cease-fire would mean their capitulation. The army and the *pieds-noirs* saw it as capitulation by France. Projecting the demography, many feared that total integration would change the white-Christian nature of France. But then, turning Algeria loose meant losing yet another war.

De Gaulle pushed ahead. He transferred Salan to Paris and purged other activists. He named a forty-four-year-old technocrat, Paul Delouvrier, as civilian administrator, and a tough general of fifty-three, Maurice Challe, as military commander. When appointed, Delouvrier warned de Gaulle that he felt independence was inevitable. "That is not to be excluded," the general replied.[12] And he let the world know that France was back on the world stage. He told the Americans and the British that unless he had an equal part in running NATO, "France will take no further part." He laid out plans for an independent nuclear force. He rejected Britain's idea of a Free Trade Area. The economy braced for growth; new buildings in Paris reflected a confident new mood.

But the FLN brought terror to Paris. In one month, 423 attacks and bombings in France killed eighty-one people. Countermeasures brought the disquieting feel of a police state. Troop trains, too long a feature of French life, weighed on the spirit. Ted Joans, a black American poet who might be mistaken for an Algerian, remembers bitterly how the *garde mobile* regularly rammed gun barrels in his stomach and insulted him at Paris checkpoints. Real Algerians suffered worse fates.

In *Force of Circumstance,* Simone de Beauvoir wrote:

> The police waited for the Algerians to come up out of the metro stations, made them stand still with their hands above their heads, then hit them with their truncheons. He'd [Claude Lanzmann] seen with his own eyes teeth smashed in and skulls fractured. . . . Corpses were being found hanging in the Bois de Boulogne, and others, disfigured and mutilated, in the Seine.

She said scores of bodies were being found and thousands of Algerians were rounded up "like the Jews at Drancy before." When she and friends sought to demonstrate, she said, police pushed them around. She quoted one as saying, "Ah, you cocksuckers! The cops can go out and get themselves killed and you don't give a shit, but if it's those Algerian bastards who get it, then you start screaming."

Later, she wrote, "De Gaulle spoke on New Year's Eve, and I turned the radio off after two minutes, sick to my stomach with that neurotic narcissism and empty grandiloquence." Then, embittered by Parisians honking horns in joyful abandon despite the tragedy, she added, "I took some belladenal to escape all that hateful gaiety, the gaiety of the French people, of murderers, of butchers."

In 1985, Michel Lévine published a book on the episode she describes. In October 1961, he wrote, 200 Algerians were found dead in Paris and another 400 disappeared.[13] Among others, Lévine quoted a survivor named Khebach who described how police beat him and others and threw them in the Seine. Official records and history books reveal almost nothing about the killings, he said, and no law officer was prosecuted.

MEANWHILE, Cold War tension heightened. China and some Eastern bloc states recognized a provisional Algerian government. The Soviet Union remained aloof, helping de Gaulle just enough to strain the Western alliance. Neither the United States nor Britain took a clear stand for France.

Then terrorism ceased in Paris. Challe hit hard in the mountains —the *djebel*—and ran down broken fragments of FLN forces. *Les paras* and legionnaires pressed a relentless campaign, putting the rebels on the defensive. In response, the FLN again terrorized *pied-noir* civilians. It was clear that even a military victory would not resolve the political crisis.

On September 16, 1959, de Gaulle pronounced the fateful words *self-determination.* Holding the nation spellbound, he said Algerians could choose among total separation, integration with France, or associated independence. He wanted the last. Reaction built slowly but grimly. Challe argued that his men could not die to no purpose. Massu was yanked out of Algeria for criticizing de Gaulle's shift to a German reporter. That touched off yet more reaction.

In January 1960, militant *pieds-noirs* mounted barricades in Algiers. French gendarmes sought to control them. A shot was fired, and the crowd began murdering gendarmes. The 1er REP of the Foreign Legion—a paratroop regiment—and other paratroop units mysteriously failed to protect the gendarmes—or to retaliate.

Frenchmen had shot Frenchmen, and ranking officers were dangerously linked with rebelling civilians. Jo Ortiz, a *bistrot* owner who
led crowds, was heard to boast, "Tomorrow, in Paris, I will be the
ruling power." Premier Michel Debré, visiting Algiers, found what
he called "a soviet of colonels." One of the colonels told him de
Gaulle could either renounce self-determination or be replaced by
Challe.

Military censorship muffled the impact in Paris. But coup d'état
rumors bounced among the circles of power. De Gaulle put on his
general's uniform and addressed the television cameras.

"Well then, my old and dear country, here we are together, once
again together, faced with a harsh test." Who, he asked, could
believe the lies that he planned to abandon Algeria?

Horne recalls watching a bistro crowd breaking into tears at the
"hypnotic wizardry." He wrote, "I do not remember any fighting,
wartime broadcast of Churchill's having a greater effect."

Rebelling *pieds-noirs* dismantled their barricades, dejected and
bitter. De Gaulle had France thoroughly confused. In March, he told
officers in Algeria that independence was "a monstrosity . . . France
must not leave. She has the right to be in Algeria; she will remain
there." But he did not renounce self-determination.

Privately, his memoirs say, he felt that prolonging the status quo
would mean a bottomless quagmire, with a "futile and interminable
task of colonial repression."

During 1960, de Gaulle negotiated clumsily with the split Algerian leadership. Provisional leader Ferhat Abbas agreed to meet
him but talks broke off. The rebels won political advantage, and he
further alienated the army and *pieds-noirs*. Challe, transferred from
Algiers, resigned.

In December, de Gaulle told officers at Blida:

> The work of France in Algeria must go on, and it is only too
> evident that it cannot go on under the conditions of yesterday.
> There is—you are all aware of this—the whole context of eman-
> cipation which is sweeping the world from one end to the other
> . . . which has swept, without exception, over all those which
> once were empires, and which cannot but have considerable
> consequences here.

Assassination plots were hatched. And then former officers and civilians set up the Organisation de l'Armée Secrète, the OAS, to force de Gaulle's hand with French terror against France.

Algiers, at the time, was in chaos. Robert Quiriconi, a *pied-noir* journalist now working in Paris, recalled recently:

> It was absolute madness. The French army went after weapons in French homes. All along the enemy had been the Arab, and people were angry, confused. There were curfews; all night long patrols clanked by. Cars caught in traffic jams honked: *Al-gér-ie Fran-çaise.* On starry, balmy nights, housewives on every balcony banged out the slogan with spoons on pans. There was a constant beat. It was the cry of a people that didn't want to die, and it came from the gut.

In April 1961, Salan and other officers tried a coup d'état.

Challe hesitated until he heard de Gaulle tell reporters: "Decolonization is our interest and, therefore, our policy. Why should we remain caught up in colonizations that are costly, bloody and endless when our own nation must be renewed from top to bottom?" France, the president said, would put no obstacle in the way of Algeria's sovereignty.

D-Day was April 20. The coup was hastily planned, leaked to French intelligence, badly coordinated, and generally improbable, and it went into action a day late.

"It seemed like a million people surged into the street," Quiriconi said. "Their hearts had been gripped by desperation, and suddenly they were free. Like a huge weight had been lifted. It was spring, *la fête,* and everyone was smiling. They couldn't believe the army would not pull it off."

Simon Murray's diary describes the heady feeling of being trucked through the night to Algiers, with legionnaires fully expecting to land on Maxim's in Paris as conquering heroes:

> The prospect of being involved in a putsch, a civil war, has a certain fascination almost. . . . De Gaulle's voice orders the army back into line as it thunders over the French radio—and we wait

for orders, sitting on the fence. Sunday approaches. It looks like a long weekend. . . . We were to occupy the airport, which was held by French marines, and they weren't having any of it. So we were given wooden batons, heavy, with sharp points, and in one long line we slowly eased into the marines, pushing them forward like bolshie rams. They frequently turned and attacked with aggression. This was met in many cases with savage beatings and it became a sad and shoddy business. . . . We were in control of the airport from which we will apparently make the drop on Paris.

It was a delicate balance. Old Sherman tanks had clattered up to protect the National Assembly in Paris, but no one was certain there were enough troops in town to save France. Challe insists he never planned to attack France. In any case, de Gaulle again stared down the opposition. He told the nation:

"*Françaises, Français!* Look where France risks going, compared to what she was about to again become. *Françaises, Français! Aidez-moi!*" De Gaulle had heard the news after watching a performance of *Britannicus,* a play by Racine about treason at the court of Nero. After his speech, Flanner observed: "When he cried three times 'Hélas! Hélas! Hélas!' it was the male voice of French tragedy, more moving, because anguished by reality, than any stage voice in *Britannicus.*"[14]

Rebelling officers had seized all communications. But by then it was the transistor age. Glued to tiny radios, the soldiers knew most of France was against them. Career men tended to lean toward rebellion, but drafted troops doing their time heard their commander-in-chief order obedience. Key units hung back in Oran and elsewhere.

In the midst of rebellion, France detonated its first nuclear device at Reggane, its Algerian Sahara test site. De Gaulle now led an atomic power, not some banana junta to be overthrown by retired generals.

The putsch collapsed. It lasted four days and involved about 14,000 officers and men to one degree or another. Five generals and 200 officers were arrested. Conscripts denounced officers, and officers denounced one another. "It was all a thoroughly nasty episode, bringing out much of the worst in human nature, and for many months its poison lingered in the body of the French army," Horne wrote. The coup leaders were sentenced to fifteen years in prison, or less, and all were given amnesty in 1968. Those who fled were sentenced to death *in absentia*.

The 1st REP, squarely behind the coup, was disbanded. The headquarters its legionnaires had built, brick by brick, was dynamited flat.

France was defeating the FLN militarily, but its will to continue was effectively crushed, and the FLN knew it. De Gaulle negotiated from weakness in the black mood of a world chilled by Cold War. Pushed too far, de Gaulle threatened partition. The FLN reacted violently, and fresh waves of terrorism brought more slaughter among Moslems and *pieds-noirs*. In a speech on July 12, de Gaulle said emphatically that France would accept "an entirely independent" Algeria.

A bitter interlude with Tunisia darkened the atmosphere. Bourguiba suddenly demanded that France abandon the key naval base it had leased at Bizerte. Also, he asked for an important Sahara border adjustment near the Algerian oil fields. De Gaulle rankled at what he called "a threatening letter." After waiting two weeks for an answer, the Tunisians attacked the base. France sent 7,000 paratroopers; aircraft strafed and bombed Tunisian positions; three French warships blasted through the blockade. After three days, Tunisian casualties were 700 dead and 1,200 wounded; for the French, twenty-four dead and 100 wounded. De Gaulle made his point but infuriated a vital North African ally.

Meanwhile, army and Foreign Legion officers in hiding and assorted frustrated extremists fortified the OAS. They tried to kill de Gaulle and break French will with terror. De Gaulle's agents, *les Barbouzes,* tried to infiltrate the OAS, and their war was brutal. OAS squads bombed leftist homes in Paris. When they blinded a four-year-old girl, even French papers that supported *Algérie Française* carried huge photos of her bloody, disfigured face. By then, the OAS had killed 553 people.

Paris crowds demonstrating against the OAS clashed with police, leaving eight dead and 100 injured, and 140 police officers injured.

At the mass funeral, the biggest turnout in Paris since liberation, Simone de Beauvoir remarked, "My God! How I hated the French!"

As the end drew near, Salan committed the OAS to its own war in Algeria. Killings on all sides averaged up to forty a day in Algiers. The OAS executed such moderate Algerians as Mouloud Feraoun, a prize-winning Kabyle author and friend of Camus. He had symbolized a bridge of hope, writing at one point:

"There is French in me, there is Kabyle in me. . . . When Algeria lives and raises its head [again] . . . it will remember France and all it owes to France."

In eleven days of talks at Evian, de Gaulle reached an agreement with the FLN. He had hoped to retain petroleum rights, military accords, and other concessions, but it was too late. A cease-fire began on March 19; a month later, Salan was captured. After a last orgy of terror, the OAS gave up. On July 1, Algerians voted massively for independence in a referendum.

The *pieds-noirs* were left with a symbolic choice: the suitcase or the coffin. An exodus of 1,380,000 Europeans and pro-French Moslems hurried to France, many destitute and broken. Others streamed out to Spain or Canada or Israel. Only 30,000 Europeans stayed behind.

As Challe had feared, *harkis* (Algerians who fought for the French) were massacred by the thousands. Under the Evian terms, French units stood by while *harkis* were taken off to slaughter. Some Frenchmen risked their own lives to protect Moslems who had been loyal to them. In other cases, Horne wrote, French officers disarmed the Moslem troops with the promise of providing better weapons "and then sneaked away in the middle of the night, abandoning them to their fate." He added:

"It was a tragedy even more odious than that of the Russian prisoners of war handed back by the Western allies in 1945. Estimates of the numbers of Algerians thus killed vary wildly between 30,000 and 150,000."

Those who made it to France, he said, "were, for the most part, to live lives of poverty, unappreciated and unassimilated." Some have done well in France, but many still live today in wretched camps, targets of growing racism.

One Algerian deputy, who lost ten family members to FLN reprisals, warned de Gaulle his people would suffer. *"Eh bien,"* the general replied, *"vous souffrirez."*[15]

The war lasted seven and a half years. French figures list their dead at 21,600 (including 7,000 killed "accidentally"); more than 65,000 wounded and injured; and 1,000 missing.[16] For Moslems, they estimate 141,000 male combatants killed by security forces; 12,000 FLN members killed in internal purges; 66,000 Moslem civilians killed or abducted by the FLN. In 42,090 listed acts of terror by the FLN and the OAS, 2,788 European civilians died and 500 disappeared, official figures say. Algerians now put their death toll at a million. No one really knows.

To the French as a people, the war was devastating. *Petits blancs* showed what cruelty they would accept for personal gain or political ideas. No one was equal, a brother, or entitled to liberty if he stood in the way of *l'Algérie française.* Democracy and its institutions were needless obstacles. The society showed itself prepared to condone excesses, willing to look elsewhere until left with no choice. For a France immersed in defeat and dejection for most of twenty-three years, it was a heavy blow.

O N J U L Y 5 , 1 9 6 2, French colors were hauled down and taken home. Some military units stayed behind for a while. But de Gaulle gave up Algeria completely; he was moving France out of the colony business. A modern empire, he understood well, worked in different ways.

PART THREE

THE NEW EMPIRE

France will be swept from the face of Africa.
>   —*Ahmed Sékou Touré of Guinea, at*
>   *independence*

But of course we take francs, madame. This is France.
>   —*Gabonese shopkeeper, twenty-five years*
>   *after independence*

CHAPTER TWELVE

Africa I: Trompe-l'Oeil

WHEN IT CAME time to disassemble the African empire, France went home with all the panache it could muster, which is a great deal of panache. Troops in crimson shakos paraded, sun glinting off their cornets. Snapping flags were lowered and ceremoniously folded away. Brand-new national anthems wafted over the flame trees and bougainvillea in the capitals of brand-new nations. French mills spun out acres of bunting in a dozen bright colors. Cargo flights from Paris shuttled out delicate pastry puffs, choice *foie gras* and ball gowns to the heart of darkness. Freshly installed presidents, stiff with pride and the starch in their immaculate formal shirts, rhetorically turned the page of colonialism toward glorious new chapters of independence.

Then calm settled again on the sleepy capitals, and the sign painters took over.

At each new government headquarters, a door was labeled *Ministre des Finances,* and an African moved in. The office's former French occupant shifted to a smaller, adjoining room behind his own new sign: *Conseiller Technique.* And so on in virtually every important department, including the armed forces and secret police.

France thus went from colonial power, at a time in history when that status inspired no admiration, to mentor and friend of an emergent continent. Territories that had begun to besmirch French grandeur formed the basis of a new overseas empire in which each state was bound to Paris by its own free will. More or less.

The theme of African decolonization was "winds of change,"

from a speech by British Prime Minister Harold Macmillan. Britain nudged its colonies out of the nest, equipping them with cash reserves, well-trained civil services, parliamentary democracies, and best wishes. And the wind currents dashed most to the ground. Ghana went bankrupt and jolted from one military coup to another. Nigeria exploded in civil war and then paralyzed itself with corruption. Uganda fell under the bloody depredations of Idi Amin. Tanzania, Zambia, and Sierra Leone suffered economic chaos. Malawi, abandoning the niceties of Westminster democracy, was known as a "one-man Banda," in the tight grip of President Hastings Kamuzu Banda. Kenya, a relative success story, was fraught with problems. After twenty-five years, some hearts may belong to Britain's Commonwealth but a lot of hard assets are mortgaged to international bankers.

France shielded its colonies from the winds of change with an elaborate *trompe-l'oeil*. It only looked like independence. In fact, it was a windbreak. Africans took cover from the buffeting of world currents. And France made sure its windfall did not blow out of reach.

New governments were in charge. France simply shaped the decisions, made up the deficits, warded off coups d'état and invasions, stabilized the currency, controlled imports and exports at preferential rates, locked up the oil and strategic materials, monitored the politics, stood by during bleak years, and drained profits from the private sector in both good years and bad.

The *trompe-l'oeil* was a masterwork of modern statecraft. On its face, it was decolonization on a grand scale, a lasting monument to the French principles of *liberté, égalité, fraternité*. It was not really a sham; each state is, in fact, independent. "Association" is legally seated in Article 88 of the French Constitution, which allows states to link themselves to France "to develop their civilization."

During a state visit, President Georges Pompidou remarked to Léopold Sédar Senghor of Senegal, "We both come from the same culture." Senghor corrected him: "I come from two cultures, and I would not forsake either one."

Two huge blocs, French West Africa and French Equatorial Africa, were broken into fourteen small states, easily manageable if not each homogeneous. Britain might have done better had it done the same in Nigeria and the Sudan. Or Belgium, in the Congo.

Whether they believed it or not, the French packaged decolonization as a voluntary step toward a better future. As de Gaulle put it, "If I did it, it was above all because it seemed to me to be contrary to the interest and new ambition of France to hold itself riveted to obligations, to burdens which no longer fit with what its power and its glory require."[1] The arrangement served the needs of practically everyone: the French Africans gained independence with a safety net below; the Americans could rely on stability in vast regions of potential upheaval; other Africans could vilify the French, or plead for their help, as domestic politics demanded.

And France, with a faithful bloc, assured its political *rayonnement* in world affairs. Louis de Guiringaud, a former foreign minister, put it bluntly: "Africa is the only continent which is still the right size for France, still within the limits of its means. It is the only one where France can still, with 500 men, change the course of history."

A degree of nobility infused French motives. But order has been preserved by the frank pragmatism and subsurface maneuvering that characterize French diplomacy. Coups d'état not first cleared in Paris face a limited life expectancy. In public, the Elysée listens politely and silently to routine floggings of the three weird sisters of emergent Africa: colonialism, neocolonialism, and imperialism.

France reduced the risk of unpleasant surprise by maneuvering friendly leaders into place before independence. Elections were tailored to suit the circumstances. One-party states emerged, and elites in power made sure no one would unseat them, with little objection from Paris. Sympathetic leaders were easy to find; for example, Senghor and Félix Houphouët-Boigny of the Ivory Coast had served in French cabinets.

And then, to make sure things stayed on course, de Gaulle entrusted Africa to Jacques Foccart and to SDECE.

Foccart, who grew up in Guadeloupe and knew the empire well, was legendary for the twenty minutes every day he spent with de Gaulle. He ran Africa for the Elysée, short-circuiting ministers and military commanders, placing his own agents in sensitive spots. He filtered access to the president and dispensed favors in his name. Little happened that he did not know about. Often things happened because of him.

SDECE (pronounced "ez-dek") was the Service de documentation extérieure et de contre-espionnage. Later, it became the DGSE —Direction générale de la sécurité extérieure—of *Rainbow Warrior* fame. France helped each new state set up its own intelligence agency. Maurice Robert, SDECE chief for Africa, then linked them to France through the PLR (Postes de Liaison et de Renseignement). "That permitted me to weave very privileged relations in all French-speaking African countries," Robert said later.[2] The Africa section, which began the 1960s with 150 agents, became one of the most active branches of SDECE.

France also signed military accords with each of the new states. Terms varied, but most governments were in a position to call on Paris for help, and all allowed transit rights. The French closed down almost all of their 100 garrisons in Africa but left well-armed mobile units at strategic points. And all final military decisions were left to France.

The idea was to protect French interests and keep out the Soviets. SDECE tried to work closely with the Bureau of State Security— BOSS—in South Africa, but the French government kept contacts to a minimum.[3] In Cameroon, the first test came even before independence. French troops fought for five years before putting down the Union of Cameroonian Peoples (UPC), bitterly opposed to Ahmadou Ahidjo. Maurice Delauney, the French commander, boasted in his memoirs: "The most spectacular operation permitted me to entirely destroy the UPC headquarters at Bamenda [in British Cameroon]. One fine night, French and Camerounians, all volunteers, crossed the British border . . . and burned all the buildings, placing out of action several leaders of the party. Moumié, unfortunately, was not there." Not to worry; SDECE was prepared.

In their book, *La Piscine*, Roger Faligot and Pascal Krop give this version of events, based on interviews with French agents.

Félix Moumié, the UPC leader, was in exile, often in Europe. One evening a gentleman known as "Grand Bill," who had a phony press card, took him to dinner in Geneva. Moumié was called to the phone, a little surprised because no one knew he was there. Grand Bill slipped a little thallium in his Ricard. Back at the table, Moumié ignored the aperitif. Ever resourceful, the agent laced his guest's wine. At the end of the meal, having drunk his wine, Moumié also knocked back the Ricard.

Disaster. The dose was supposed to be small. Moumié would have gone to his exile home in Guinea and died there, where Sékou Touré would be accused of murdering him. Swiss doctors diagnosed the poison, and Grand Bill hid out on the Riviera. Fifteen years later, he was arrested in Belgium and extradited to Switzerland, but France managed to quash the proceedings.

Sékou Touré, in fact, was a favorite French target. He went to war with de Gaulle because of what seems to have been a tropical temper tantrum. When de Gaulle toured African colonies to campaign for "association," Sékou Touré considered himself close to France. In his major address, he said: "We intend to exercise with sovereignty our right to independence, but we intend to remain tied to France. In this association with France, we will become a proud, sovereign and free people."

But he went overboard on hyperbole. He hammered away at the theme of independence, to the wild cheering of crowds, as de Gaulle sat stonily behind him, his glower as purple as Sékou Touré's rhetoric. The Guineans had sent de Gaulle the speech, but an aide had not wanted to wake the general to show it to him. Things went downhill from there.

When it came time to vote, Guinea registered a thundering *non*. Guinea took independence immediately and first the Soviet Union, then China, recognized it. France scooped up everything and went home: light fixtures, instruction manuals, civil records. They smashed crockery in official residences. Then SDECE set about sabotaging the new government. When Sékou Touré ordered new currency, secret agents flooded Conakry with counterfeit bills. A string of coup d'état attempts failed, despite help from the Portuguese and West Germans. Guinea expelled all French diplomats in 1965. Sékou Touré grew steadily more autocratic, filling jails in which people often disappeared without a trace.

In 1983, a year before his death, Sékou Touré received Foccart in Conakry; he had already made peace with Giscard d'Estaing. Foccart wanted to talk about the past, Faligot and Krop recount. They quote Sékou Touré as saying, "France had an unqualifiable attitude. Why, on purpose, leave to rot in Marseilles important shipments of food for my people? Not to mention the plots."

MONGO BETI, a noted Cameroonian writer, was not among those dazzled by the *trompe-l'oeil*. He wrote:

> A decolonization which establishes an indigenous tyranny based on the silence of cemeteries or the desert of an indentured population, which is shielded from indiscreet scrutiny of the outside world, cannot escape skepticism. . . . The stability of a Camerounian regime deceives only the village idiots.

Other African nationalists berated Francophile leaders as toadies of a lingering colonial presence. Houphouët-Boigny caught the brunt of their derision, but he laughed it off. In 1968, President Mobutu Sese Seko of Zaire (he was Joseph-Désiré Mobutu of the Congo then, before "authenticity") visited the Ivory Coast for the first time. He was dumbstruck by the smoothly clicking wheels of government and business in Abidjan, a capital of glass, steel, and flowers that would do credit to the Riviera. Ah, he asked his host, but how many Frenchmen are here to make it work? "Fifteen thousand." And how many will you have in ten years? "Thirty thousand."

In fact, there were nearly 60,000 Frenchmen in the Ivory Coast ten years later, six times the number at independence. Eventually Mobutu called in French military officers and financial advisers. Zaire, which was colonized by Belgium, is a member in good standing of the club of former French territories.

AN ENDURING piece of African lore is the bet at independence among Kwame Nkrumah of Ghana, Sékou Touré, and Houphouët-Boigny over whose system would come out ahead.

Nkrumah, champion of Pan-African unity, bartered away wealth for useless Soviet hardware and monuments to his own glory. He was overthrown by the military, and Ghana has suffered economic catastrophe for most of its life as a nation. Sékou Touré's rhetoric went nowhere. Although Guinea is rich in bauxite, iron, diamonds, gold, and fertile land, its Soviet-plundered socialist economy fell into ruin. By 1979, Sékou Touré edged back toward France. When he died in 1984, military leaders who took over urged France to help the country to its feet. Houphouët-Boigny's Ivory Coast, with few minerals and mediocre soil, was a thriving modern state, boasting a capital of twenty-story office towers and fast lanes, rich from cocoa, coffee, and palm oil. (The political and social arguments, of course, were another matter.)

After Sékou Touré died, military rulers turned immediately to France. They negotiated to dump their currency, the syli, for the CFA. France demurred; the syli was so weak it was devalued by 93.7 percent, to a fifteenth of its former value, at the end of 1985. France offered a handful of technical advisers, and the Guineans howled in protest. They wanted the hundreds of Frenchmen whom Houphouët-Boigny had replaced with Ivorians.

France's position seemed about to shift slightly in 1981. François Mitterrand at first paid less attention to Africa than did Giscard d'Estaing. He was not, for one thing, a big game hunter. Socialist ministers seemed less willing to be branded as neocolonialists. More importantly, France was running short of money. But by late 1985, the new president was known as Mitterrand *l'Africain.*

At the annual French-African summit, he told his colleagues, "The colonial era is over, and I will not bring it back even to help you out. You are countries, sovereign states, like France; we speak as equals." But, he added, France would be their *avocat*—their advocate and counsel—in dealing with Western creditors. "France is more sensitive to the needs of your continent," Mitterrand said. "She has no more merits than the others, simply a history, an experience." The summit, originally for former French colonies, was attended by most states on the continent.

Mitterrand's offer rattled the Treasury, caught by surprise. The president volunteered to sponsor a separate meeting on African debt, rather than folding the problem into a more general U.N. session. Treasury officials feared such a conference would endanger individual arrangements made by each country with the creditors' Club of Paris. But the Africans were happy.

Africans had begun to look elsewhere to plug ever more gaping holes in their budgets. Competitor nations faced the same economic pressures as France. Some probed deeply for markets in the *chasse gardée* and were prepared to offer aid to pay for their hunting licenses. French Africans, shopping for lower prices and better terms, sought to diversify.

By 1980, two-thirds of all science and technology doctoral candidates from the Ivory Coast were studying in the United States. In 1985, two Senegalese cabinet ministers had American M.B.A. degrees. The Ivory Coast sent home 959 French-subsidized *coopérants* —teachers, administrators, and technicians—leaving just over 2,000. The French community dropped toward 30,000, nearly half its peak level. In almost every former French colony, government contracts were awarded with increasing frequency to Britons, Belgians, Dutch, Americans, Canadians, Germans, Japanese, and Israelis, among others.

One morning in 1985, I flew from Paris to Libreville, Gabon, on what for twenty-five years was virtually a French domestic route. Only the few foreigners, non-French and non-Gabonese, need visas when they arrive. One chooses UTA, a private French airline, or Air Gabon, which relies on contracted Air France staff. Just after takeoff, two businessmen from the former French colonies of Senegal and Cameroon broke into an argument. In perfect English, they were debating the backcourt offense of the Washington Redskins.

BUT THE FRENCH windbreak survives nearly intact, and no nation, Western or Eastern, seems anxious—or able—to replace it.

The Bank of France guarantees convertibility of the CFA franc, the common currency, at a fixed rate with the French franc. The Africans are assured credits, simplified commerce, and easy travel abroad. For this privilege, African central banks keep two-thirds of their foreign exchange holdings under French control. France gives generously from a dozen pots: budgetary supports, trade subsidies, investment credits, development projects, arms. Africans come to Paris to sign the deals, and Frenchmen remain in Africa to oversee them.

French bankers settle deals over a glass of Pernod, without a lot of the annoying paperwork Americans require. Often businesses generously refund part of their profits back to the man who signed the contract.

Altogether, there are perhaps 300,000 Frenchmen in all of Africa, private citizens and people on official contracts. Airlines, factories, even government departments are run by the French on management contracts. French schools train officials, businessmen, and officers.

French military bases watch the continent. Paratroopers are stationed in Senegal, at the western bulge, in the Ivory Coast, in Gabon, and in the Central African Republic. The Foreign Legion is in Djibouti, on the Red Sea, and at Mayotte, an Indian Ocean island still flying the Tricolor. In 1985, 8,500 men were based in the region, not counting 1,278 French military advisers. Troops stormed down from Corsica twice to help Zaire, a former Belgian colony. And France intervened fifteen times in twenty-five years in its own former colonies.

A total of 1,909 African officers, long a constant number, trained in France during 1984. The published budget for French military cooperation with Africa was 805.9 million francs for 1985, up from 154 million in 1970.

The defense accords are mutual. Thomas Sankara of Burkina Faso made that point at a Paris press conference, and French reporters chortled. "There is not a Burkinabe who does not remember an uncle or a father who died so that France could be free," Sankara said, bringing an awkward silence to the room. "I would advise you to remember that."

Economic assistance comes from too many sources to count. Sometimes it involves elaborate aid programs, with feasibility studies and controllers' reports. Sometimes the Elysée simply writes a check to make up a budget deficit.

Signs of an Anglo-Saxon world muscling in are not yet alarming. There is a Super Chicken in Abidjan, near the Hilton where *USA Today* and *Playgirl* are displayed next to *Le Monde* and *Paris-Match*. But there are also Burger Kings on the Champs-Elysées and a Hilton in the shadow of the Eiffel Tower. To get from the Abidjan airport to the far side of town, you take boulevard Valéry Giscard d'Estaing across the Charles de Gaulle Bridge, on down boulevard Charles de Gaulle to boulevard François Mitterrand.

Dakar, Senegal, the grandfather of French African cities, retains its moldy old flavor.

Moscow has fallen flat in French Africa after pushing hard in

Guinea, Mali, and Madagascar. In Brazzaville, the Congo, or in Cotonou, Benin, the billboard slogans of nominally Marxist governments make no impact on the quantity of fresh oysters flown down regularly from Brittany. When a government's overriding ideology is to stay in power, it looks for convenience from its benefactor. The humorless Russians mix badly in Africa, and they try to take more than they give. France controls subtly; the Soviets prefer ironclad lines of power. Besides, as any African leader can tell you, Red Square is not the place Vendôme.

Tension crackles just under the surface. In the Central African Republic, whites live in villas and downtown Bangui apartments, clustering at night at the Rock Club and restaurants by the river. Kilometer 5 is the *quartier populaire,* a vast African slum. In 1986, a French Jaguar took off on a training flight from Bangui. Something went wrong, and the pilot ejected. The aircraft fell on an Islamic school in the heart of Kilometer 5; it killed 23 people, mainly boys, and injured another 30. Africans stoned whites and stormed through the city. Some of the 4,000 French residents huddled in the embassy. French authorities were shaken. The Jaguars at Bangui make up the strike force France relied upon to hold Libya at bay in Chad.

But after a bitter week, the crisis passed. Victims were flown to France for treatment and the school was rebuilt. But French airmen are now known in Kilometer 5 as *les jaguars.*

An extreme example of *trompe-l'oeil* is Gabon. That bite-sized enclave on the west coast of Central Africa, best known as the forgotten bit of jungle where Albert Schweitzer cured lepers, demonstrates what French diplomacy can accomplish with makeup and mirrors.

Two books are sold side by side in Libreville hotel lobbies. According to *L'Implantation Coloniale au Gabon,* by Nicolas Metegue N'nah, independence was "the fruit of more than 120 years of continuous struggle." But in *Le Colonisateur Colonisé,* the last French governor of Gabon, Louis Sanmarco, leaves a different impression.

Of the fourteen African governing councils offered a choice, only Gabon's chose to join France as a *département,* meaning statehood. Sanmarco wrote:

I considered that a triumph, the triumph of 130 years of French colonization which resulted in this request for integration, the posthumous triumph of sailors, foresters, settlers, administrators who, with all their faults, worked not all that badly in this country to make people love France to that degree. Why not say it?

He described how he flew to Paris to negotiate statehood.

I expected to be treated as a triumphant victor who had added another pearl to the crown. I was received like a dog in a bowling alley. The minister, Cornut-Gentile, was even rude: "Sanmarco, have you fallen on your head? . . . We don't have enough Antilles [small troublesome states]? Go on, independence like everyone else."

Failing all else, Gabonese leader Léon M'Ba designed a flag bearing a small Tricolor in the corner. It was rejected in Paris. Reluctantly, M'Ba took Gabon out of the nest to take its place with the others.

But France left the windbreak. In 1964, a popular political opponent led a successful coup against M'Ba. Within forty-eight hours, French troops rushed in from Dakar and Brazzaville to put him back in office. The rebels suffered twenty-seven dead and forty-four wounded. When M'Ba fell ill, French strategists lined up behind an up-and-coming former postal clerk named Albert-Bernard Bongo (later El Hadj Omar Bongo; the president converted to Islam when Gabon joined OPEC). Legitimized by a questionable election, Omar Bongo took over in 1967. He is still in power, protected from any eventuality by his presidential guard—which is commanded by Frenchmen.

At independence in 1960, there were 5,000 Frenchmen in Gabon. Today, there are 26,000. In a country with 750,000 inhabitants, the ratio of whites to Africans approaches that in Rhodesia before Zimbabwean independence. French teachers outnumber Gabonese two to one. Vital government documents can move from ministry to ministry without leaving French hands. French secretaries and unskilled workers advertise for work in the local classifieds.

I chatted one day in 1985 with a young Gabonese professional,

waiting out the initial period of wariness until it seemed that we
were telling each other what we really thought. "Don't you sometimes feel there are too many white faces around here?" I asked. "On
the contrary," he said. "There are not enough." A minor diplomatic
flap was raging at the time. France had announced that, in the
interest of "Gabonization," it was reducing by twenty-eight the 630
teachers and advisers it partially funded. Hundreds of others, in
different categories, would not be affected. Gabonese authorities
complained that France was abandoning them.

The French-owned Mbolo Supermarket stocks fifteen brands of
Camembert cheese along with eleven kinds of dog food. Libreville's
water supply tastes like a swimming pool, but it is clean enough.
Still, Gabon imports 6,000 tons of water a year from France, and
fifteen tons of *foie gras,* along with almost every tomato, potato,
onion, beefsteak, green bean, and kilo of rice, wheat, or corn consumed in Gabon. On Sunday afternoons, French bankers, civil
servants, and businessmen wait in forty-five-minute traffic jams to
have their boats pulled from the water at the marina. Generations
ago, French missionaries clothed African maidens, but Libreville
beaches are sprinkled with topless, sometimes bottomless French
ladies.

The Scotch Club, across from the French consulate, might be any
late-night boisterous *boîte* in St.-Tropez, jammed to paralysis with
sun-tanned youths in windsurfer T-shirts and long-legged women
with a day's wages invested in their hairdos. The only difference is
that in a St.-Tropez club, there would be more blacks. At the
Bataclan, half the place is black—the women. French marines,
traveling salesmen, and bored husbands drop in regularly for a little
paid temporary miscegenation.

In Libreville, you wake to a tinkling voice on the radio, a dead
ringer for the uniformly sweet voices on Paris' Radio FIP. She reads
the horoscope, the modern version of ghostly superstitions Gabonese
brought from the forest, and plays Michel Sardou. You can hop in
a Peugeot 205 (or a Honda, as in France) and drive down a road
labeled with the same little red "N1" marker you will find in
Réunion or Rouen. There is even a French-style *autoroute* to the
port. For most of the way, it is a regular overcrowded African

two-lane blacktop. You recognize it by the stylized blue and white sign depicting a freeway under an overpass.

At the post office, mailboxes say Gabon, France, and Foreign Countries. Sometimes the television anchorman slips and, after detailing President Mitterrand's movements, says, "And now for the international news." In Gabon, as in the Ivory Coast, newscasters use satellite relays of correspondents' reports from France's TF1 and Antenne 2, but only in the Ivory Coast do they make the cosmetic gesture of slicing off the signature at the end. In the evening, Libreville's *jeunesse dorée* gathers at Le Bowlingstore to watch American films dubbed in French. Or, at the Dragon d'Or Chinese restaurant and bar, they browse among the rack of Astérix comic books, reading about their ancestors, the Gauls.

A friend of mine asked a Gabonese woman in a shop if she could pay in French money. The shopkeeper was amazed at the question. "But of course we take francs, madame. This is France."

The big yellow Hertz sign was not French, but the woman at the counter was. Renting cars is just one of those businesses the French cannot get down, whatever the fancy franchise. It is not in the French commercial spirit to try harder for strangers. The woman was very pleasant and made reservations for me in Togo and the Ivory Coast. I asked for confirmations. "We don't give them." But I needed to know, I explained, so I could make other arrangements if necessary; I depended upon a car. "No rental agency gives confirmations," she explained. "But I rent cars all over the world and . . ." She was still very pleasant but firm as granite. "No, monsieur, car rental companies never give confirmations anywhere in the world." I swear to God.

(For balance, let me add the time I reserved an Avis car in Paris, got a computerized confirmation, and forgot to bring the slip when I went for the car. The woman stared at me as if I were an unprincipled liar trying to weasel away one of her cars. In the end, a friend had to waste ninety minutes bringing the slip to her from my home. When it appeared, the woman was furious at having been shown to be wrong; she made an insulting remark about me to another customer and literally flung the contract at me. I didn't bother with the manager. The time before they rented me a car with a bald short-distance emergency tire on it; I didn't discover it until I had driven on it 1,000 miles over freeways and winding mountain roads. His only response was a shrug and a look that said, with reason, alas: Idiot.)

THE FRENCH, with their own position consolidated, just laugh off Bongo's idiosyncrasies. While I was there, he fulminated against "foreigners": Lebanese businessmen who endangered some of his commercial operations. In a speech repeated half a dozen times on television, he urged police to raid their shops. And, he added, army patrols should take whatever liberties they wanted with prostitutes from neighboring countries. "After they have passed among seven or eight soldiers," he said, "they will learn."

For years, diplomats, academics, and journalists have attempted to work out whether France comes out ahead when the costs of its windbreak are compared to the various financial benefits. Few doubt that France does well for itself. In Gabon, that impression is unmistakable.

"Well," remarked a senior French official who asked not to be named, "our cooperation operates at a loss in some of our other former colonies. I don't see why we shouldn't make a profit in Gabon." He outlined France's view:

> It is only natural that Gabon will diversify its markets and interests as time goes on. As we say in France, you can't put all your eggs in one basket. The military base, that's something else, just an agreement. Like you Americans have in Cuba. But France is so established here that sometimes we ask ourselves if we're not here alone. It is not good to be so present. Certainly there will be fewer French in the future. But I think it is only natural that we do everything we can to protect our position.

I asked how long Frenchmen would continue to run Gabon.

"Well, our position here is not eternal, it must evolve," he said, adding with a hearty chuckle, "Look at it this way: they've resolved the problem of colonialism. Before whites made the blacks work for nothing. Now, they make the whites work for money."

A lot of money. Government people on contract make roughly

twice what they would earn in France. Private businessmen often do better. A carpetlayer from southern France can wing down to Libreville on a contract, charge heavily for materials he can get at a discount, and come out even farther ahead on his taxes. The bigger the company, the wider the possibilities.

Foreigners who have tried say that breaking into Gabon is like setting up a video games arcade on turf controlled by the New Jersey mob. One seasoned African businessman laid out the situation:

> The oil companies manage because they're big enough, and they don't have to bribe. But for most things, it's twenty years too late. If you're ready to pay 15 percent on the side, you might make a deal, but you risk buying the wrong guy. And you've got the whole system to fight. It doesn't matter if you offer something cheaper because it's in no one's interest to lower prices.

Bribery aside, outsiders face a finely woven curtain of supplier contracts, management agreements, distribution networks, bank credit, investment guarantees, and pricing agreements, all controlled by a small group of French businessmen with official support. Interlocking subsidiaries can disguise profits and assign losses to Gabonese government partners. What is legal is all but impenetrable. What is not is impossible to find.

Take chickens. The same French group imports cheap feed, raises chickens, and markets poultry and eggs. With powerful Gabonese partners to protect against imports and local competition, profits are substantial. Or roses. Four Libreville florists sell 1,000 roses a week, flown from Paris, at five dollars each. A local producer turned out hydroponic roses at far less cost, but no one would market them.

Or the water. Gabonese entrepreneurs persuaded a French bottler to join in producing mineral water. An American potential investor decided that even if the plant were located near Libreville or Port-Gentil, by far the dominant markets, the project would be risky. But the plant was to be 500 miles inland, as far into Gabon as possible without leaving the country. It was a two-day drive on a hard road from Libreville. It was also, coincidentally, near Bongo's home village. The investor calculated the transport to Libreville as three times more expensive than flying real Evian water from Paris. But the bank loan would be backed by official French guarantees. The Gabon government would protect the project. Management contracts and commissions meant that private French interests would make their money even if the plant ran at a loss.

In French Africa, the laws of economics are political.

Most of Gabon's oil is produced by Elf-Gabon, which provides a third of the total production of its French parent company, Elf-Aquitaine. Gabon owns only 25 percent of Elf-Gabon. Most such companies share production with local governments, absorbing the costs themselves. Elf shares whatever profits it declares. With special marketing arrangements, and operations between dollars and francs, the margin of maneuver is wide.

"The most incredible thing I've heard in this business," remarked a visiting American oilman, "is that in twenty years Elf-Gabon has never been audited."

But that is nothing unusual; it's the French system. My pal Stanley, a retired multinational president who controlled French companies, explained it this way: "French law requires a *commissaire aux comptes* to make sure accounting is done properly, but he only checks to see that the numbers are in the right columns. He has no responsibility to check against vouchers to make sure the numbers relate to reality."

And a senior French diplomat said, "You Americans, you audit everything. We only audit when something is wrong."

Gabon's uranium, estimated at 20 percent of the West's reserves, is a greater mystery. As in Niger, the French do the mining and keep the books. Since uranium is classified as a strategic material, very little is said about it.

President Bongo, whose personal fortune is deep in the substantial category, seems in no hurry for a public audit of anything in Gabon. With all opposition quashed, and faithful French commanders to calm troubled waters, he rules with leisurely grandeur. The daily paper, *Union,* each day tops the front page with news of his routine appointments. Just in time for the 1977 summit of the Organization of African Unity, he completed an $800 million presidential palace, complete with a marble elevator to lift his Bentley limousine up to his bedroom.

And the president can be generous.

"Once I lost my watch in Gabon, just some cheap watch I left somewhere," a friend in the Quai d'Orsay told me. "Bongo somehow heard about it and sent me a new one. It was worth $3,000. They were upset when I insisted on giving it back. They figure they can just buy people."

Bongo is not a man to appreciate criticism. One book not for sale in Libreville is Pierre Péan's *Affaires Africaines,* which came out in 1983.

Péan, a French journalist who had worked in Gabon's Finance Ministry, aimed a spotlight at the French businessmen, diplomats, mercenaries, and thugs who cohabit in the shadows of Africa. He profiled the "Gabonese clan," a small group of right-wing Frenchmen and Gabonese millionaires who manipulated French policy to their own benefit. He documented secret official payments and cover-ups and traced questionable contributions to French political parties. He revealed how French business interests, with Gabonese connivance, plundered the economy, and he described secret Masonic ceremonies linking Bongo and his Gabonese associates to French partners. Foccart was always in the shadows.

Especially interesting was Péan's cast of characters. After the failed putsch in Algeria, the French dynamited the 1st REP headquarters at Zeralda, but its dust settled all over Africa. Colonel Le Braz from the 1st REP set up Bongo's *Garde Présidentielle* and he recruited ex-legionnaires for its ranks. When he retired he was replaced by "LouLou" Martin, another Legion colonel who holds the rank of general in Bongo's army. Maurice Robert went from African head of SDECE to director of Elf-Gabon to ambassador of France. Maurice Delauney, an old colonial administrator who fought on behalf of Cameroon, took his turn as French ambassador. And then there was Bob Denard and his mercenary buddies.

Denard, a large, flamboyant man with short hair and a meaty jaw, "did" Indochina, went for training in the United States, and in 1952 moved back to Morocco where he was born (unless it was Caen, or near Bordeaux; his past is murky) in 1929. He worked for an American security company and fought with underground groups against the *bradeurs d'empire,* those who would give up the colonies. In 1954, he was linked to the plot to kill Mendès-France. After fourteen months in jail, he joined the police. Then he showed up in Katanga with, as Péan aptly phrases it, "unofficial but effective help from Paris"; we'll get to that later.

"Bob Denard thus 'would work' directly or indirectly during close to twenty years for the Elysée or SDECE without ever appearing officially on personnel roles of any administration," Péan wrote. (In fact, it is closer to thirty years. He is still active, under a different name, in the Comoros.) "A mercenary used for all the *'coups tordus'* (dirty tricks) of the Republic, he would serve as scapegoat, at the right moment, to distract the ire of the press and the opposition."

Péan picks up Denard in Gabon in September 1971, lying in wait for an opponent of Bongo, Germain M'Ba. It was his first job in Gabon after long adventures in the Congo. M'Ba was executed; Péan implicates Denard and then notes that French officials covered him. Later, Péan presents evidence of how Bongo hired Denard and other French adventurers to murder his wife's lovers. At times, Péan points out, French police did not investigate with all the energy that might be expected.

The book shows how several of Denard's ill-fated Bay of Piglets operations were mounted from Gabon, with French help. With help from the CIA, he raised a French mercenary force to operate in Angola. Under Soviet attack, they fled to Namibia three months before the end of their contract. Earlier, a French mercenary operation from Gabon, under Jean Kay, failed in Cabinda. Denard made another disastrous try at Cabinda. And then there was Denard's attack on Benin.

At 7 A.M., on January 16, 1977, an unmarked four-engined plane set down in Cotonou and disgorged about 100 men, mostly white. They grabbed the nearest vehicles, raced into town, and blasted away at the presidential palace. Within three hours, they were racing back to their plane. They escaped a few steps ahead of the Benin army but left behind two dead, some prisoners, and documents describing their purpose. Gilbert Bourgeaud—Bob Denard—had led a mercenary force recruited from Gabon. The aircraft was one of a small fleet used to help break the Western blockade against Rhodesia.

Denard did better in the Comoros, picturesque but dirt-poor little islands near Réunion. Mayotte insisted on remaining part of France, but the other three islands of the group chose independence. In 1975, Denard installed Ali Soilih in place of Ahmed Abdallah. Then, in 1978, he raided the little Indian Ocean island again and put Abdallah back in office. Both coups, wrote Péan, among others, were mounted from Gabon. The second time, Denard stayed as minister of defense. He left his official position to shift to business, drifting back and forth between the Comoros and South Africa. But his associate, Roger Ghis, known as "Commandant Charles," ran the presidential guard of mercenaries with far more power than the official Frenchmen advising the army. French business interests control the economy; many Comoreans keep French passports and commute to Marseilles. "The situation remains particularly troubled and scandalously anachronistic," observed the left-leaning magazine *Afrique-Asie.*

In Gabon, Bongo was outraged that François Mitterrand's government allowed Péan's book to appear. Was there not, he demanded, a French law banning insults to foreign heads of state? For a month and a half, he banned the use of the words "France" or "French" on official media, including the powerful radio station Africa No. 1, which transmits to seventeen million French-speaking Africans. During that time, terrorists bombed the French marines' camp in Beirut, killing fifty-eight, and Mitterrand flew to Lebanon. Africa No. 1 had to mention only the U.S. casualties suffered in a companion assault.

Bongo courted the U.S. ambassador, who carefully avoided offending the French by overresponding. He shopped for imports in other European markets. He did not dismiss the French officers in his presidential guard or send home French advisers.

Hands were wrung at the Quai d'Orsay. Whatever Gabon's value to France in francs and barrels of oil, it is a cornerstone of the empire. Transall aircraft stop for gas at Libreville on their way to rescue Mobutu or to change presidents of the Central African Republic. Jaguar fighters stand by ready for anything. The base provides rear support for operations in Chad. In the late 1960s, when France supported Biafra in a secession that would weaken English-speaking Nigeria, a mercenary air force flew from Gabon. Secret flights to Rhodesia were staged from Libreville. French intelligence loves the place.

Soon after the storm, Prime Minister Pierre Mauroy hurried to Gabon. Other French ministers followed. And then, France produced the *pièce de résistance*. Bongo was brought to Paris with a state welcome reserved for the queen of England and the president of the United States. His arrival was covered live on television. The Garde Républicaine trotted alongside his motorcade, sabers flashing and plumes fluttering. A diva trilled for him at the opera. Reporters followed his every move.

French police had banned a press conference by Bongo's opponents, saying it "might endanger public order and damage international relations." But Bongo skipped his own customary press conference because his hosts could not guarantee that Péan would not be there. France, after all, was a democracy.

That was enough. Bongo kept his four villas on the Côte d'Azur, and relations returned to normal. "It is as when there is a quarrel in a family," a senior Gabonese official told me a year later. "One gets mad, words are exchanged. And then it is over." What else would one expect in a country where the president comes from a town called Franceville?

No one in Gabon is betting that France's unchallenged influence will go on forever. There are rumblings of discontent among younger Gabonese, officials, and people in the street, which reflect feelings across French Africa. Two incidents made clear to me both the depth of these rumblings and the extent to which France is implanted. I'm making no bets in either direction.

At Mbolo Supermarket, where 15,000 items are displayed on shelves in what looks like a gigantic blue tin aircraft hangar, I tried to take pictures of Gabonese shoppers. A large woman caught me by the Camembert rack.

"Why did you take my picture?" she demanded.

"I was photographing cheeses, madame, and you happened to be in the picture." It was a dumb thing to say.

She leaped at me and swatted at the camera, trying to smash it. Batteries spilled out of the flash, clattering on the floor. She screamed at me, and I tried to calm her. With a deft twist, she wrapped the camera strap around my wrist, making a combination of handcuffs and dog leash. She marched toward the cops, dragging me along behind.

It was most undignified. I managed to dig my heels in by the canned corn.

She wanted the film. I could understand her position; I had been sneaky, and she didn't know who I was. But I had some good stuff on the roll and did not want to give it to her. The woman continued shrieking, and a small crowd gathered. I looked at the faces.

A handful of youths stared at me in clear hatred. All they knew was what was evident: the woman had a complaint, and I was white, probably French. One of them grabbed the camera and tried to break it open. I saw no way to save the film without involving the police. In fact, I doubted I could avoid the police, in any case. And I knew enough about Gabonese police not to relish the encounter. I opened the camera, handed over the film, and the matter was settled.

Given the woman's hysteria and the youths' anger, it was a little scary. But only a little. At the height of the fracas, a grizzled French paratrooper materialized beside me. He stayed long enough to ensure that the danger would pass. Then, without a word, he dissolved from view.

ON A FLIGHT to Paris, I sat next to a young Gabonese cabinet minister who, after a half-bottle of Bordeaux, let down his guard.

"You know, we are finally learning to deal with the French, to do these things for ourselves. Until now, we shopped for everything in Paris, even ideas. If the French didn't make something, we paid them to get it for us. They had a monopoly, no service, no choice. Now we go straight to where we can get the best equipment, the best deal. . . .

"Elf, for example. You know, American companies came along and found oil on concessions that Elf had looked at and said were no good. That made a real impact, up here," he said, tapping his head. "It opened our eyes. The president said those guys must be trying to hide something for later. When someone is your friend, and you trust him, and something like that happens, it has an effect. . . .

"The French are always talking about emotional ties. Well, it's emotional one way. From us. They play on our emotions to make money off of us. With a new generation, I don't think it will be that way."

The plane neared Charles de Gaulle airport, and I asked the minister where he stayed in Paris. He looked at me, surprised, as though I were a little slow.

"At my place," he answered. "In the sixth *arrondissement.*"

CHAPTER THIRTEEN

Africa II: Chasse Gardée

ON AN ARCTIC FRENCH afternoon in November 1985, I went to see the emperor. Bokassa I had called a press conference. Several beefy Frenchmen with short hair and lumpy jackets checked my credentials. Then I found a plush velvet chair among the tangle of television cables and waited for his majesty.

I noticed a framed gold medal stamped with the face of Charles de Gaulle. Bokassa had called him "Papa" (de Gaulle hated that) and he wept bitterly at the general's funeral. And there was a photograph of Bokassa inscribed, "To my dear relative and very good friend, Valéry Giscard d'Estaing." Apparently it had been returned to sender.

A darkwood desk sat raised on a low purple platform, under formal portraits of two of the only three French-speaking emperors since Charlemagne. There was Napoléon I, of course, chin firm, nose finely chiseled, and eyes fixed on some distant corner of the world he expected to conquer by dinnertime. And then, with a self-satisfied smirk that made Napoléon seem humble, there was Bokassa.

The second portrait was a photograph, taken in 1977 when Jean-Bedel Bokassa, French army sergeant turned president of the Central African Republic by coup d'état, was crowned emperor of the Central African Empire. The coronation cost somewhere between $25 million and $90 million, most of it in French foreign aid. It looked as though Bokassa's uniform cost most of it. He held a plumed and cockaded admiral's hat, and eight rows of colorful ribbons flashed on his breast. On the left side. The right side was occupied by a huge gold cross of the French Légion d'honneur. Sashes and swords led the eye to his boots: gleaming black, each with a sunburst of gold from ankle to toe.

With a flourish, Bokassa himself appeared, wearing much of the above.

The emperor sat down and read, in a monotone, an eight-page text. France deposed him in 1979, he said, and he was a political prisoner. The government seized all his identity papers, including his French passport. All he had left was his French military volunteer card issued by the Free French Forces in World War II; he had thoughtfully added a photocopy—recto, verso—to the press kit. Police followed him everywhere and obliged him to go home if he spent two nights away.

"Home" is an eighteen-room château dating from 1750 set back in a small park at Hardricourt, west of Paris. But, he said, it is all he has. Three châteaus and two houses were seized for taxes. His accounts are blocked. He lives on a monthly military pension of 5,998 francs but receives none of the social security or family allowances due him.

"Try to raise nine kids on that, plus the costs of the château," he said. Most of his other forty-four children were in Bangui with his seventeen wives, who have all left him. He wanted to be there, too, in the worst way.

He would just climb on a plane and fly to Bangui, he said, but that was impossible. The French had installed Colonel Frédéric Mansion as a "super chief of state" next to the president, General André Kolingba. In a garden stroll afterward, he told me, "President Mitterrand has ordered Mansion and the others to shoot me if I show up in *Centrafrique*." He sent his twelve-year-old son, Jean-Bertrand, to Bangui but Mansion put him back on the plane to Paris.

Bokassa displayed one of the last ten copies of his book, *Ma Vérité*. French authorities had burned the rest. Valéry Giscard d'Estaing was not pleased with some of the crudely phrased—and emphatically denied—allegations: that the former French president had impregnated the Empress Catherine and arranged an abortion; that he demanded diamonds on each of his semiyearly visits to a

200,000-acre hunting reserve kept for him so he could pillage ivory; that he dallied with an ever-changing assortment of local women; and so on.

From his dais, Bokassa declaimed:

"This barbarous act, arrest, illegal detention, hostage-taking, and the seizure of goods and personal archives is an act of piracy in which my people did not take part at all."

France, he declared, violated all his internationally guaranteed human rights. Worst of all, Guy Penne, the Elysée Africa czar, would not return his phone calls.

The press conference ended on a touching note. Bokassa posed with his eight-month-old son, Jean-Bedel. Reporters nosed around the château; it was unheated and the family lived mostly in the kitchen, among an untidy clutter of pots and pans, laundry, and broken toys. On a large stove, gas burners were turned up full blast for warmth.

Bokassa complained about his gas and electricity bill; twice he threatened to demonstrate outside the Elysée palace with all nine kids, and the bill was mysteriously paid. After all, he said, Mitterrand had a *caisse noire,* a slush fund, for such things. Christmas, he said, would be brightened by gifts of food from his few faithful friends in France. Later three of Bokassa's children were picked up for shoplifting records and perfume. "It was sausage," he said. "They were hungry." The state put them in a home when he said he was too poor to bail them out.

"Sometimes God helps poor people," he said, and a thin film of tears formed in his eyes.

It was hard, somehow, to summon up a great deal of pity. This was not my first encounter with Bokassa. I recognized, for example, the heavy ebony cane with which he had laid open the forehead of my friend and colleague, Mike Goldsmith. In 1977, Bokassa's goons had seized Mike when he received a garbled message from Johannesburg; that "proved" he was a spy. He was brought to Bokassa who, without a word, knocked him unconscious, kicked him, stamped on his glasses, and imprisoned him for a month. For much of the time, he was handcuffed too tightly, with little food and no doctor for his festering wounds.

Giscard d'Estaing had put up with that sort of behavior; also with the emperor's arbitrary murders, apparent cannibalism, massive corruption, and flights of bizarre behavior. *Le Canard Enchaîné* and *Le Monde* disclosed that the president had accepted diamonds several times as gifts from Bokassa. However, Giscard d'Estaing contained the scandal in an accepted French manner: he refused to answer impertinent reporters and brought the judicial power of the state to bear on anyone who pushed too hard.

Bokassa was deposed only after he clubbed to death children whose parents protested against buying school uniforms from a factory he happened to own. Eyewitnesses testified later that nearly 200 youngsters were killed in a prison yard; Bokassa took part personally in the massacre, Central African Republic courts determined.

At first a French cabinet minister dismissed the massacre as "a pseudo-event." But it was too widely reported; there was no ignoring it.

Opération Barracuda was smooth and brutal. Bokassa's cousin, former Central African Republic president David Dacko, was awakened at his home in Paris and bundled onto a plane. Maurice Robert, Africa director for SDECE, came along for the ride. French troops, already based at Bangui and Bouar, flashed a little steel, just in case. No problem. Bokassa was in Libya at the time; he got the message. The deposed emperor headed for Paris but was refused permission to land at Orly. *"Bande de cons* (you pack of jerks)," he yelled into his pilot's microphone, "give me clearance, or I'll land on the *autoroute."* He was diverted to the Evreux air base, where his plane was surrounded. Giscard d'Estaing called in a favor from Félix Houphouët-Boigny, and Bokassa accepted exile in the Ivory Coast. Two years later, Houphouët had had enough. You made him, he told the French; you take him. And they did.

GOLDSMITH AND I visited Bangui together, by coincidence, late in 1984. We drove to the villa Bokassa built for his Romanian wife at Kolongo, a little suburb on the river outside Bangui.

The original house was a weekend chalet in French colonial style, with high ceilings, a raised porch, and shutters. But behind it, in the huge jungled park, Bokassa wrought tacky splendor. A one-story mansion, looted and half demolished, rambles aimlessly in long corridors of cramped guest rooms and stingy bathrooms. The splintered wooden frame of Bokassa's massive revolving bed dominates a small bedroom. His secret bedroom, the one his wife didn't know about, is across the courtyard with a hidden entrance for girlfriends. The looters did not deface a portrait of the emperor, in a Napoleonic tunic, set into the wall over a side entryway.

In a center courtyard, Bokassa built a pavilion for private audiences, an island in the pool reached by a causeway in the manner of Akbar the Great at Fatipur Sikri, but somewhat less grand. There he received state guests, such as Giscard d'Estaing. And a few steps away is a large room which now bears an inscription scrawled in chalk on the wall: "Torture chamber and cold room where Bokassa kept human bodies."

Police found Bokassa's walk-in cold locker a few days after the power was cut. Goldsmith, there at the time, said the room reeked of the unmistakable smell of human flesh. A coroner identified the remains of a local professor who had disappeared, according to later testimony. He also found human joints trussed in string like standing rib roasts. At an official hearing, one of Bokassa's cooks swore he knew nothing about the freezer's contents or about any unusual bent to his former boss' dietary habits. A second cook, however, said he had prepared human flesh for Bokassa and, occasionally, for unwitting guests, including two high-level French visitors.

Bokassa added two other touches of his own: the crocodile pond and the lion cages.

An aging guard named Paul showed me around the place, recounting its lore without embroidery in the time-worn patter of a sexton pointing out old gravestones in a churchyard.

Here, Paul said, indicating a gazebo in a clearing, was where Bokassa held his trials until three or four in the morning. Alleged offenses were varied. In one case, three guards were suspected of sleeping with Bokassa's neglected Romanian wife. The guilty were fed to the lions or the crocodiles, depending on Bokassa's mood. One victim was the lionkeeper, accused of taking home to his family some meat meant for his charges. Bokassa, as befitted justice, threw him into the lion cage. He remained unharmed in the cage for twenty-four hours because the lions knew him. So Bokassa tossed him to the crocodiles, who didn't.

Paul yanked on a rusty lever to show how the cages worked. The lions were left unfed and cramped for days in an inner cage before anyone was offered to them. The handcuffed victim was placed in the outer cage, and the latch was pulled.

Bokassa vehemently denies the testimony of his former retainers. But not convincingly. French engineers drained the crocodile pond after Bokassa left the country. They found most of eight human skeletons, their bones marked deeply by crocodile teeth.

The ex-emperor was sentenced to death *in absentia* on Christmas Eve, 1980, on a series of charges including murder, embezzlement, and diamond fraud. Mainly, it was the massacre of children. Bokassa was outraged at the verdict. After all, he told interviewers, he loved children. Hadn't UNESCO's Director-General Amadou Mahtar M'Bow asked him to sponsor the Year of the Child in 1979?

Another charge was cannibalism, although the evidence was not ironclad. French officials who sought to disprove the accusations before Bokassa's downfall suddenly found it in their interest to reverse themselves, to justify the coup d'état. In a front-page comment, *Le Monde* editor Jacques Fauvet asked some pertinent questions.

Why did Giscard d'Estaing persist so long in intimate relations with a tyrant he denounced as "cruel and contemptible" immediately after deposing him? How did Bokassa serve France's African policy? And, as for the diamonds, what was gained by disguising or silencing the truth?

Giscard d'Estaing was voted out of office the next year, but not necessarily because of Bokassa.

For the French, Bokassa was one of the surprises of the system; they had tried to make the best of him. Officers who had known him were not impressed; one reported he was too dumb to do anything but carry the flag. His father had been caned to death by colonial administrators and, despite his twenty-three years in the French army, no one was sure about him. In the mid-1960s, French agents planned a coup against Dacko, who had grown too close to the Russians. As Dacko floundered in power, Bokassa moved in and eliminated the gendarme commander the French had tapped for the job.

After Bokassa, the French took no chances. The Colonel Mansion whom Bokassa mentioned was installed as aide to President André Kolingba, with ill-defined but overwhelming powers. In one case, a private French air charter company had negotiated a contract, and Mansion walked in as a cabinet minister was about to sign it. "Don't sign," the colonel said, according to a French source I trust. The minister looked helplessly at a cabinet colleague, who just shrugged. The minister laid down his pen.

"The Central African Republic is important to us, and that's why we keep a strong man there," a senior French official explained in 1984 to a new man in the Quai d'Orsay.

"You mean Kolingba?"

"No, of course not. Mansion."

OFTEN THE FRENCH system works well, as it was designed. As I drove out to see Bokassa, I noticed red, yellow, and green Senegalese flags lining the Champs-Elysées. President Abdou Diouf was in town. On a continent of catastrophes Diouf, like Senegal, is a symbol of French triumph. Calm and effective, thoughtful and humane, Diouf took over from Léopold Sédar Senghor. He was elected in voting that left little to chance, but you can't have everything in Africa. Senegal is a stable cornerstone of the continent, the first French foothold in Africa, and an intellectual base of *francophonie*. It is still emphatically oriented toward Paris. But it is no economic power. Diouf told Mitterrand he did not have the cash to pay government salaries until the end of the year. There was a little gentlemanly haggling, but he flew home with a check in his pocket.

At independence, a senior French civil servant named Jean Colin took up Senegalese citizenship and a place in the cabinet. For a quarter-century a loyal Senegalese official, he has drafted economic plans and government strategy. His relations with France are also excellent.

In places, the system works but French planners wring their hands in the background. The Ivory Coast is France's showcase in Africa, and the "Ivorian Miracle" is one of those standard phrases of modern Africa. Houphouët-Boigny, loyal to France since the first glimmers of self-rule, came back at each election with majorities approaching 99 percent, but perfect democracy was not the goal. Guided by French advisers, aided by French investment, he produced rich returns from coffee, cocoa, and palm oil in a climate of calm and stability. But in early 1986, the perennial president was deep into his eighties and showed no sign of passing on power. Anything could happen in the vacuum, French analysts knew, especially with a stagnant economy and crippling social problems.

Captain Sankara took power in Upper Volta and changed its name to Burkina Faso. He heaped scorn on the French legacy and struck up a friendship with Libya. But in early 1986, he made his ritual visit to Mitterrand.

And sometimes things go totally awry, but French flexibility finds a way to profit, anyway. In Zaire, for example. When Zaire (then the Congo) took independence from Belgium in 1960, everyone was ready for the spoils. The Russians backed Patrice Lumumba. The Americans were behind Joseph-Désiré Mobutu.[1] And the French gambled on Moise Tshombe. Almost immediately, Mobutu, among others, buried Lumumba. Mobutu was not yet in power, but Moscow was out of the game. Not, however, Paris.

Tshombe had seceded in Katanga (now Shaba), and his Belgian military advisor suggested he raise a mercenary army. So Tshombe hired Colonel Roger Trinquier, veteran of Indochina and Algeria, kindly made available to Tshombe by de Gaulle. With Trinquier came Major Roger Faulques, master interrogator of the 1st REP during the Battle of Algiers, and a score of French mercenaries who edged aside the Belgians. But Trinquier got mixed up in the Lumumba murder. France backed away from the international scandal; Trinquier resigned from the French army and retired with a payoff from Tshombe. Faulques, Denard, and others stayed, however, to fight a pitched battle with United Nations forces. Eventually beaten, Faulques moved on. Denard stayed around to dabble in Congo politics over the next seven years.

By 1964, the Congo was ablaze with rebel warfare. Mobutu, helped by the CIA, seized power and imposed peace. Tshombe, beaten in Katanga, prepared a comeback from Europe. SDECE and his mercenary pals stuck with him. But Tshombe was lured onto an airplane by a French bodyguard named François Bodenan, believed to be working for the CIA; he was hijacked to Algeria, where he died in captivity.

This is where I came in. My first job as a correspondent was to wait in Kinshasa for the Algerians to deliver Tshombe to Mobutu, as promised. Of course, they never did. The Americans, meanwhile, quietly helped Mobutu quell yet another uprising. He had liked the idea of mercenaries and brought in his own under Michael Hoare. "Mad Mike" (he is not so mad any more; I visited him again on a trip to South Africa in 1985) had no great love for French mercenaries. Hoare relied more on Britons, Belgians, Germans, and whites from southern Africa. He put down the rebels and left. Not long afterward, Mobutu's mercenaries rose against him.

Denard and a Belgian planter-mercenary named Jean "Black Jack" Schramme feared that Mobutu was about to disband his white mercenary army. They revolted in July 1967, in the eastern Congo. Denard neglected to warn thirty men under his command in Kinshasa; all were arrested and slaughtered. Only one, an Algerian, was able to talk his way out because he was not European. Denard was wounded and flown out to Rhodesia. Schramme captured Bukavu. In 1968, as Mobutu's troops pounded Bukavu in a final assault, Denard tried to rescue Schramme with a pincer movement from Angola. His men came on bicycles.

It was yet another Denard Bay of Piglets. After an initial success, the thinly armed mercenary column lost time arguing over objectives and making needless feints. Denard had expected Mobutu's troops to run, as usual. When the Congolese fought back, Denard's men fled, leaving some dead and captured behind.

Authorities were so anxious to gloat over Denard's defeat that they flew every foreign reporter in town to Katanga to have a look at the bodies. (Each correspondent was handed a thick envelope of cash to cover expenses; I'll never forget the look on the Information Ministry official's face when I handed mine back to him.) While the press corps was conveniently bottled up in Katanga, meanwhile, the International Committee of the Red Cross evacuated the mercenaries from Bukavu across the river to Rwanda.

A side bit of glory for France: a Corsican photographer from the

Associated Press Paris bureau, Spartaco Bodini, infiltrated the mercenaries' prison compound by looking like one of them. When a Belgian officer asked him to be on the lookout for a "fucking photographer who we're going to take care of," he infiltrated his way back out again.

By then, Mobutu had every reason to detest France. But the French conducted themselves with flair and conviction. Champagne glasses clinked undiminished at the ambassador's splendid residence overlooking the Congo River. And Paris got the message.

The next time Katangans attacked from Angola, Denard was gone and France was on Mobutu's side. In 1977 and 1978, France dispatched troops to protect Kolwezi in Shaba (Katanga) Province. By 1984, Mobutu had placed regular French officers in command of an elite paratroop unit. A small rebellion broke out in the east, and French-led troops quashed it in three days.

Mobutu was a member in good standing of the club of former French colonies; French aid flowed in accordingly. In my two years in Zaire, I saw clear evidence of arbitrary killings, torture, and unjust imprisonment. A mildly critical local editor, a man I liked a great deal, was thrown into jail after I left, and he died from the abuse. Estimates of Mobutu's personal requisition of state funds run to more than $4 billion; they are likely accurate. He regularly creams off profits from the few enterprises that make money for Zaire.

None of that deterred Jacques Chirac from declaring in Kinshasa in 1985 to a conference of forty French-speaking mayors from twenty-six countries:

[President Mobutu] is a respectable and profoundly Francophile man who is ulcerated by attacks of certain media. France has every interest in good relations with Zaire, and I don't understand the morbid taste of some to criticize our friends. The Mobutu myth has been exaggerated by certain media and it is particularly unjust. Zaire was an anarchic country which called for a particular charisma.

Seven months earlier, Mobutu sent the French into a mild panic. Mitterrand visited Zaire just before the French-African summit, and

Mobutu said he was too busy to go. In fact, he was angry that Mitterrand's wife had not come along. She was critical of Mobutu's human rights record, and he took her absence as a political gesture. Hasty negotiations increased French aid to Zaire, and Mobutu's agenda suddenly cleared.

DIPLOMACY IS the preferred French approach. *In extremis,* however, there is still the Foreign Legion. I knew about the Legion, like everyone else, from dim memories of *Beau Geste* remakes and a lot of dubious legend. It came to life for me in a cruddy little bar in Djibouti. (Honest.) It was steaming hot, and I ordered a Coke. Suddenly, a twenty-six-pound ham dropped out of the air and landed on my wrist. *"Unngh,"* came a noise like an ore truck climbing up a hill, "one does not drink Coca-Cola here." OK, I said, watching my fingers turn white from the grip on my wrist, I'll have what you're having.

He was actually a nice guy, I discovered, once I stopped trembling. He looked like a Mount Rushmore carving, but harder. He was short on hair and I.Q., but he must have been four feet across the shoulders. He had no neck; ropy muscles sloped outward from his ears.

"What do you think of those goddamned Commies about to take over in Paris?" he asked, offering me a broad hint about what I should think. It was 1981, just before presidential elections between Giscard d'Estaing and Mitterrand. "We are on red alert," he said. "Don't tell anyone. But if that Commie wins, *paf!* We're headed for Paris." I promised not to tell anyone.

A little later, I met two more legionnaires, or rather ex-legionnaires. They were Britons who had just deserted from Djibouti and had walked three days across the Somali desert. Both were medium-sized and intelligent, but each had burned and chiseled hardwood features. "Fuckin' hell, it was," said one. They described days that started before dawn and ended late at night, jogging with heavy loads of rocks, murderous discipline, crippling marches.

I decided to learn something about the Legion.

Louis-Philippe first commissioned *une Légion d'étrangers* in 1831 to do battle outside the kingdom. In Algeria, for example. An early general defined their mission: "You, legionnaires, are soldiers to die.

And I will send you to where death is." An endless list of names
engraved at the Legion's memorial near Marseilles attests that his
promise was kept.

Volunteers had to be between eighteen and forty years of age,
foreigners, and holders of a good conduct certificate. These days,
those conditions rarely apply.

The Foreign Legion numbers 8,500 men, of 105 nationalities;
about half are French. Their peak strength was 50,000, during
World War II, and they lost 10,483 men in Indochina. After 1962,
Algeria took over their proud camp at Sidi-bel-Abbès. Now they
are based in a drab little enclave in the industrial sector of Aubagne,
near Marseilles, where legionnaires print Christmas cards and run
addressograph machines. In Guiana, they build bridges and tear up
local bars. In the South Seas, they guard nuclear test sites. In Mayotte
and Djibouti and Bouar, they wait.

Sometimes the order comes. The 2me REP (the Second Foreign
Paratroop Regiment) scrambled onto planes at their base in Corsica
to beat back rebels for Mobutu. More often, they do push-ups and
take showers.

"It is crazy, crazy," said a young German on the beach in Corsica,
not yet through with his first year. "After two years in this outfit,
you are out of your fucking mind. Nothing to do. It's not so bad
in summer; you can look for girls. Otherwise, train, jump, work.
It is fucked."

Like a lot of legionnaires, he had had a little police trouble at
home. What? "Oh, I was in jail." Why? He smiled slowly and, as
an answer, smacked his right fist into his left palm. Legion policy
is not clear-cut on this score. Blood crimes are frowned upon, and
an intelligence section tries to weed out the murderers and rapists.
"But a few minor scrapes that prove a candidate is a man," an official
spokesman, a colonel, told me, "well, what the hell . . ."

Calvi, Corsica, is thick with legionnaires. You can spot them in
swimming suits: muscles hard and dark as jerked beef, ramrod
posture, and chests shaped for displaying medals. In uniform, they
stand out like flashing neon lights from lesser beings. You can slice
cheese on the two creases down the backs of their shirts. Their white
kepis, by decree and tradition, are spotless.

A woman I know fell in love with a legionnaire, a Frenchman, on one vacation in Calvi. She flew back later to see him but decided the relationship had no future. He liked to slug her and then lock himself in a room and play Nazi marches. Others, I have been told by women with experience, are real gentlemen.

Each year the Legion takes up to 1,800 new recruits, and 7,000 men apply, the colonel told me. They are asked their purpose for volunteering and given intelligence tests and a rigorous medical examination. Are they checked for AIDS? I asked. The colonel shot me a nasty look and replied that they were.

The deal is simple. They sign up for five years and put up with whatever the noncoms and officers decide to dish out. After that, they can reenlist; maybe 40 percent do. Pay is the same as in the regular army, but boot camp is twice as long, and discipline is a hell of a lot worse. In exchange, the Legion takes them under a new name and France smiles benevolently on their application for citizenship when it is all over. Legionnaires can rise to sergeant, but most of the officers are French army.

"Of course, the officers are French," replied a sergeant assigned to brief me on a visit to Aubagne. "That proves the men are fighting for a flag, not for money." Legionnaires sometimes call themselves mercenaries; that is not recommended, however, for a visitor who enjoys breathing.

Probably no organization reveres its relics like the Legion. There is, above all, Captain Danjou's hand. When Napoléon III seized Mexico, he forgot to send the Foreign Legion. Officers protested, and a contingent was sent west. A unit under Danjou, protecting a French convoy, was ambushed at Camarón, near Veracruz. For hours, sixty-five legionnaires held off 2,000 Mexicans. The last five legionnaires ran out of bullets; they charged with bayonets. Every year on April 30, the Legion eats *boudin* (blood sausage) and gets blind drunk to celebrate the victory. To exhibit blind bravery, in the Legion, is to *faire le Camerone*.

Danjou, who ordered the stiff resistance, had a wooden hand. His body disappeared in the battle. But some time later, someone retrieved the dark wood hand from the Mexicans. It is at the legion museum at Aubagne, right there with the tattered flags and dented medals. On Camerone Day, it is marched along at the Legion's ceremonial cadence of eighty-eight steps per minute.

THE LEGION IS the most colorful of French units in Africa, but it is not alone. At any one time, up to 9,000 men rotate among bases from Dakar to Libreville to Djibouti and points in between. And the Force d'Action Rapide sits in southern France. The navy plies African waters regularly, its ports of call serving as a barometer of French relations. In 1985, the *Jeanne d'Arc* called in Madagascar for the first time since the former colony moved away from France twelve years earlier. On the other hand, the vessel dropped New Zealand from its schedule.

Military accords keep African heads of state close to Paris. Few trust their own armies very far, and outsiders are risky. The Americans will seldom help a president in trouble. The Russians will, but then they tend to stay forever. France, however, is a handy neighborhood cop, asking nothing more than continued loyalty and privileged relations. That is why the abrupt end of *Opération Manta* in Chad was such a jolt to French-speaking Africa.

Chad has plagued France since Major Lamy was killed civilizing it. French troops spent three years in Chad getting independence going. Then they returned, off and on from 1968 to 1975, to suppress rebels and bandits in the north. For France, *le Tchad utile* (useful Chad) is the agricultural south along the Chari River up north to where the great desert starts. For Libya under Colonel Muammar Qaddafi, however, every sand dune and salt flat in Chad is useful.

Qaddafi, with ambitions and oil revenues too big for his underpopulated Mediterranean state, seeks outlets wherever he can. Chad, his southern neighbor, is a logical backyard. Through Chad, Qaddafi increases contacts with French Africa and black Africa. Chad extends his border to the vast Sudan, where he sees Moslem brothers clamoring for his enlightened guidance, and to Nigeria, the giant of black Africa.

When French forces went back to Chad yet again in 1977 for a three-year campaign against rebels, Libya was deeply involved on the other side.

But France, in the meantime, cultivated privileged ties with Libya. True, Qaddafi is an exasperating megalomaniac who burned down the French embassy in 1980. True, he also invaded Chad in 1980 and attempted to absorb the fragile state into Libya before pulling back north. But he carries political and financial weight; he has a $13 billion arsenal and a country full of Eastern-bloc advisers; he controls oil; and he can provoke the Americans. The French prefer not to ignore people like that. Mitterrand, from 1981, sought a balance.

As "Colonel Spartacus" wrote in his controversial book, *Opération Manta*, "a suspicious boiling was heard in the Chad basket." In June 1982, Hissène Habré overthrew President Goukouni Oueddei in N'Djamena. Habré, a bitter enemy while a rebel, was an ally not only of France but also of the United States, Egypt, Sudan, and Zaire. The fortunes of politics. Goukouni moved north and linked up with Libya.

The Libyans had moved into the Aouzou strip, a disputed patch of desert between Libya and Chad that French and Italian colonizers never got straight. In mid-1983, Goukouni's forces, backed by Libya, rolled over the important town of Faya-Largeau, at the center of Chad, 480 miles north of the capital. France gave Habré arms and supplies (385 million francs' worth in 1983) but would not intervene. Goukouni moved south. Habré counterattacked; in July, against French advice, he recaptured Faya. Then Libya strafed and bombed government positions with Soviet-built MiGs. Mobutu had given Habré a few small fighters, but the distances were too great. He pleaded for French Jaguars.

Paris was pissed. If Habré had hung back, France might have negotiated something with Libya. Now there was a war on, and half the world screamed for the French to face their responsibilities. "The Americans," grumbled a senior French adviser to one of my colleagues, "want to defend Chad to the last Frenchman."

Mitterrand demurred. But French intelligence counted eight Libyan raids with MiGs—and with Mirages. France cut off arms sales to Libya in 1980, but not before delivering the last of thirty-two Mirage interceptors and Super Frelon helicopters. Qaddafi, meanwhile, denied any involvement and demanded that the United States withdraw its nonexistent forces. He warned that any "foreign intervention" in Chad would be an act of war against Libya.

Arms were not enough and troops would be too much, so France again called out the dogs of war. René du Lac, Bernard's old friend and colleague, was paid to recruit a small secret force—mainly

Frenchmen—to buck up Habré. They did not tip the balance but made an impact. In one skirmish they recovered ten machine guns from the Libyan-backed rebels; du Lac had sold them earlier to Qaddafi.

In Paris, mention was made of the Dey of Algiers' fly whisk. The French found themselves in yet another of those situations where the familiar terms "honor" and "responsibility" made collars itch. In postmortem debate, national assemblymen roasted the Socialists for not backing Habré with more vigor. Newly appointed Foreign Minister Roland Dumas reminded them of Major Pierre Galopin, "murdered in conditions you know by the one whose cause you today espouse." Galopin was executed in 1975 under the command of Habré while seeking to free two French hostages they held. Nonetheless, one deputy told Dumas, "It is shameful to be governed by such men [as you]. You are dishonored." Before the debate, human rights workers had shown that Habré was responsible for massacres of civilians in the south.

Meanwhile, back in Chad, France decided at the last minute against a plan to bomb Libyan aircraft in the poorly mapped Aouzou strip; what if they inadvertently hit Libyan territory? Goukouni's forces pushed east, backed by Libyan T54 and T55 tanks. Defense Minister Charles Hernu suggested that France ask the Americans to protect its Jaguars with F-15s from Sudan. No Americans, Mitterrand said.

There had already been several flaps with Washington. The Americans offered AWACS and waited for a French response. Senior U.S. and French diplomats told me later what had happened. The Americans needed an urgent reply so they could install a ground support force. It was late in Washington and after midnight in Paris. Finally, a top French aide told the Americans to go ahead; Mitterrand had approved. The next morning, Mitterrand was furious. He had not approved, and the operation was called off.

From the beginning, according to well-placed French sources, the Americans had pushed arming Habré as a means of striking hard at Qaddafi. The French argued that only Goukouni could persuade the Libyans to leave; if Habré hit too hard, Goukouni would be forced to rely even more heavily on Qaddafi.

Habré, embittered by the delay and battered by Goukouni,

snarled at the French. On August 9, he was told about *Opération Manta*. France was sending in *les paras*. Habré wanted planes, not troops, but he was in no position to argue. The next day, Faya fell again.

Opération Manta halted Libyan advances, but the price was staggering. The money was one thing; for a long time, it was estimated to cost up to $400,000 a day. But it also inspired fury among the officer corps and pointed out some severe weaknesses of the French military.

Despite their world-ringing field of action, French forces depend on an aging fleet of small Transall C-160s. Committed to buying French, they shun the workhorse U.S. C-130 Hercules used by NATO partners. For their dramatic assault on Kolwezi in 1978, the 2me REP was flown down in U.S. Air Force transports.

Forced to carry fuel, a Transall could carry only ten tons on the 3,000-mile trip from France to N'Djamena. Then Algeria forbade overflights; transports had to stop at Casablanca, Dakar, and Abidjan to refuel. The air force had bought some secondhand DC-8s from UTA, but passenger door configurations limited their use.

Communications were another problem. International telephone lines went through Libya and Algeria. All messages went by a rattling old teletype to Bangui for relay into the French military network. Flash messages could take more than ten minutes; routine traffic took days.

By August 23, the French had 1,525 men in Chad prepared to head north, to be followed by huge shipments of ammunition, videotapes for the officers' mess, and bottled Evian water. The number grew to 3,000 men and stayed near that level.

The adventure was not popular. In a poll by *Paris-Match,* 52 percent of the sampling thought France had special responsibilities in its old colonies; 32 percent did not. But 63 percent said that that did not justify risking French soldiers. Half opposed the war, and as many feared it could turn into a new Algeria or Indochina. And 46 percent, against 39 percent, felt France did not have the means to fight it.

As the war dragged on, N'Djamena was its old self. Alan Cowell of the *New York Times* went to dinner at a new restaurant on avenue Charles de Gaulle, and the waiter apologized, "I am sorry, sir, the

Beaujolais is finished, but there is Côtes du Rhône." There was also ice cream flown from Paris at $9 a quart, Charolais beef, and Pont l'Evêque cheese. In the crumpled, bullet-pocked ruins of their capital, some Chadians missed the people who had put in the electricity and telephones two decades before. One accountant told Cowell, "We were civilized by the French."

After fifteen months of a standoff, Mitterrand decided to declare a victory and leave. But he had some trouble pulling it off.

On November 11, French foreign minister Claude Cheysson sent this pleasant little telegram to his Libyan counterpart, Ali Triki, at the Organization of African Unity summit meeting:

> My dear Ali, your message of November 10 just reached me. It is that of a friend, and I am very touched. I, too, like the direct relationship between us. It has been effective; you recognize it, and it is clear. It is also pleasant. How many times and from how many cities of four continents have I heard your voice on the telephone: *"Alors, Claude, ça va?"* . . .
>
> We will have more frequent and imperious reasons to communicate in this way, but I hope that our ties will remain close. Because what you wanted—in a way that is too flattering to me —to take from our efforts, our policy, requires numerous exchanges of views between us; perhaps even joint actions. . . . Have I been indiscreet in writing you this way, in Addis? I did not want to wait for your return . . . to thank you for your message.[2]

That day, France and Libya announced a joint withdrawal from Chad. A statement said, "The evacuation operations of French forces in Chad and the Libyan units ended today, following the intervention of mixed teams of observers as foreseen under the agreement signed between the two continents."

"The purpose of the operation [Manta] was to make the foreigner leave," Cheysson said in a television interview. "He has left. Chad is once again in the hands of the Chadians." And he added one of those formulations that make other diplomats sit at French feet to learn wisdom: "If they stay, we will stay; if they go, we will go; if they come back, we will return."

At that point, Mitterrand flew to Cyprus to meet Qaddafi, against

the advice of practically everyone. Mitterrand argues that it is best
to reason with adversaries face to face. The French president, per-
spiring in a suit and tie, sought to persuade Qaddafi to move his
troops out quickly. He threatened and pleaded. Qaddafi was relaxed,
in his habitual mocking manner.

Three days later, the Americans muscled into the picture. A senior
U.S. official briefed reporters on satellite intelligence: "We share our
information with the French, and we both know that most of the
Libyan troops with their equipment are still in Chad."

A Foreign Ministry spokesman said the government stuck by its
statement and had nothing to add. Then Cheysson and, finally,
Mitterrand had to admit that, yes, the Libyans were still there, but
. . . A commentator on the state-owned TF1 television newscast
summed it up nicely. Of course the French knew the Libyans were
still there, but that was supposed to be a secret; the Americans had
no business embarrassing their allies that way.

Mitterrand had to suffer a gleeful round of editorials in European, American, and some French papers under headlines heavy with
the word "humiliation." The problem was most serious in Africa,
however.

When the 1983 French-African summit ended at Vittel, Mitterrand asked what other country could summon so many African
nations to such a meeting. The strength of the community was that
so many heads of state turned up. In 1984, attendance was lousy.
Seyne Kountche of Niger went to Washington to see Reagan.
Houphouët-Boigny did not feel like traveling. Other leaders had
pressing business elsewhere. The message was clear: France had been
made to look ridiculous, and Mitterrand had failed to protect the
family.

Winding up the summit, however, Mitterrand was clear. France
had respected its engagements. It would not be an all-purpose gendarme, fighting everyone's battle to the hilt. Mitterrand gambled
that time would be on France's side. Qaddafi's oil revenues dropped
from $22 billion to $9 billion in a year, diminishing his taste for
foreign adventure. Goukouni lost power among the rebels; Habré
bought off some of his own enemies. Africans grumbled some more
and then dropped the subject. After all, what choice had they?

In 1985, in Paris, attendance improved. Sankara skipped the meeting, but he sent word through his embassy that he held "a great deal of friendship" for Mitterrand.

The Libyans, meanwhile, were still there. Mitterrand had vowed not to accept a de facto partition of Chad, but that was what developed. Qaddafi proposed a novel idea: a buffer force should occupy the disputed zone where France and Libyan troops once faced off. A buffer of Libyans, that is. War, he warned, was not a good idea. If France tangled with Libya in Chad, Libya would stir up trouble in New Caledonia and Guadeloupe and elsewhere overseas.

Early in 1986, Chad flared up again, just in time for elections. Goukouni pressed Hissène Habré's forces, attacking below the "red line" drawn at the 16th parallel. The French estimated rebel strength at 4,000, along with 4,500 Libyans, against 5,000 government troops. Qaddafi was calling Mitterrand's bluff.

On February 16, 11 French Jaguars peppered BAP-100 bombs on a concrete runway the Libyans had built at Ouadi Doum, in northern Chad, after the withdrawal accords. The dramatic gesture was costly; the French jets were refueled in midair and protected by Mirages. But the papers were full of praise. Mitterrand had saved French honor and reassured the Africans without another Manta. It was a blow that could not be returned. Some commentators recalled Margaret Thatcher's rewards from the Falklands War.

On February 17, a Libyan Tupolev 22 placed three bombs square onto the runway of N'Djamena airport and flew off unopposed. French Defense Minister Paul Quilès called it a "blind"—read, cowardly—attack from at least 10,000 feet, out of reach of French ground defenses. Reporters who saw it put the altitude closer to 300 feet.

Both runways were working again within days. The unending match game on again, tied, 1-1, in yet another quarter. France set up a logistics team of 500 men. Still plagued with transport limitations, the French swallowed pride and called on giant U.S. Air Force C-5 Galaxies. Qaddafi did not push the showdown, but France would have to stay on guard in Chad. Such are the burdens of power.

France managed to recoup some prestige in 1985 with a fresh attack against a favorite old target: South Africa. Violent repression and a state of emergency offered new grounds for condemning South Africa, and African governments appreciate outside attacks on Pretoria, toward which their own position is ambiguous. When I first arrived in Kinshasa in 1967, Mobutu excoriated white racism at a news conference, demanding a total boycott of South Africa. I glanced down to look at the refreshment he had offered: grape juice from the Cape. The Togolese joked about ships that made the world's fastest trip to Yokohama. They left Togo with phosphate for Japan and came back, days later, laden with South African goods. At the time of this writing, every country in black and Arab Africa is consuming South African goods, directly or via some ruse.

After South African police cracked down hard on black townships in 1985, Prime Minister Laurent Fabius led the European Economic Community to take measures against South Africa. However noble his intentions, the policy provoked a snort from the French in South Africa.

In Johannesburg, I met Jacques-Yves (this is not his real first name), a Frenchman working for the South African government. "It just means things will take a few days longer, and some middleman will make a little more money," he said. "If there is money to be made, no sanctions will work."

France embargoed arms sales in 1977. But in the four previous years, Paris sold $450 million of South Africa's total $622 million arms purchases, including 95 Mirage IIIs, 48 Mirage F-1s, 155 Aérospatiale helicopters, and at least four Daphne-class submarines.[3] South Africa still makes effective use of carefully preserved Mirages, kept aloft with black-market or homemade spare parts. They are so valuable the South Africans won't even fly them in bad weather.

Jacques-Yves was in Rhodesia when a white-minority government fought a bitter battle, theoretically isolated by outraged Western governments. "The Rhodesians were supposed to have only seven Alouette helicopters," he said, with a laugh. "I counted forty on one mission alone. The stuff would come in brand new, in crates, from Paris. De Gaulle just wanted to annoy the British. He sent huge amounts of supplies, munitions. You could see it stacked on the tarmac, in plain sight, imported through the oil people and others who had regular commercial dealings with Rhodesia."

That was when de Gaulle also helped Odumegwu Ojukwu maintain his secessionist state of Biafra against a heavy Nigerian on-slaught. Shadowy French pilots ran an air bridge between Rhodesia and Biafra via Libreville, Gabon. Weapons and supplies from Biafra also came down to the Ivory Coast. De Gaulle is reported to have said to Foccart, "These *braves gens,* we must do something for them." Coincidentally, he was helping to weaken a powerful English-speaking state in the center of French Africa. France did not recognize Biafra, but Gabon and the Ivory Coast did. French interests, meanwhile, had oil rights in part of the breakaway eastern region. Faulques turned up in Biafra to raise a mercenary army, but he did not last long. Ojukwu counted heavily on Rolf Steiner, a German former legionnaire who marched in Biafra under Legion colors with their motto dating back to Louis-Philippe: "Honor and Fidelity." In his memoirs, Steiner says that France supplied him until he refused to push its interests with Ojukwu.[4]

I was covering that story and, routinely, would trip over French blockade runners who regaled bar girls, colleagues, and occasional journalists with their exploits.

Ojukwu escaped by flying secretly to Libreville; then he settled into exile in Abidjan. (From where he made a great deal of money running taxis and trucks in Washington.)

When the war ended, Nigeria took its revenge on the French, but not for long. By the end of 1985, France was Nigeria's best customer and was just passing Britain as leading supplier. Nigeria was the number two oil supplier to France, and 130 French businesses were established there. Even during the war, SCOA and CFAO, French trading companies, thrived in Lagos. Peugeot sales in Nigeria helped the French automaker survive a tough period in France. In Kenya, another former British showcase, the Peugeot dealer is President Daniel arap Moi. Business is business.

Mitterrand's first African guest of 1986 made the usual speech: "We have a future without limits." Roland Dumas remarked, "When times are difficult, you know who your friends are." The visitor was Foreign Minister Bolaji Akinyemi of Nigeria.

Soon after the March 1986 elections, policy began to shift. Jacques Chirac, as prime minister, sent the French ambassador back to South Africa. He named as cooperation minister Michel Aurillac, a conservative who had kept close tabs with Maurice Robert, Foccart and former SDECE people. Bongo was in deep financial trouble because of plummeting oil revenues, but Aurillac assured him France was there.

Mitterrand continued his interest in Africa, but socialist ideology was in short supply. France, in any case, had been old-line Gaullist in Africa since Jean-Pierre Cot made a vain attempt to break the old patterns as cooperation minister during the early 1980s. "We tried to be even-handed and deal directly with human development," a close Cot aide told me at the time, "but we just could not do it."

WHEN JACQUES Foccart left the Elysée in 1974, seven pickup trucks carried off his secret files to three carefully prepared hiding places, according to Patrice Chairoff, who devoted a 42-page chapter to him in *B . . . Commes Barbouzes*. His only official function was director of a lobby group called the French Banana Committee. "Foccart awaits his moment," Chairoff wrote. He quoted a close aide of Foccart's:

Giscard's victory is only a respite and the victory of the Union of the left [under Mitterrand] is inevitable. Backs to the wall, the government will face a situation [where] neither the police nor the army are sure, and they will have to repress, toughly and crisply, selectively but massively, and then, they will all come to eat out of our hands because only we can do that work, a job that once done will not keep us from sleeping.

After the March 1986 elections, Chirac made his first African trip as prime minister to the Ivory Coast. He emerged, grinning broadly, to embrace Houphouët-Boigny. Behind him was his new adviser on African affairs, grinning just as broadly. It was Foccart, seventy-three and full of spirit.

CHAPTER FOURTEEN

North Africa: Beurs and Beaufs

THE FORT IN *Beau Geste,* P. C. Wren's 1924 novelized paean to the French Foreign Legion, might be the 300-year-old Turkish outpost at Bou Saada. The Legion lived there, with their camels and kepis, on the edge of the Algerian Sahara. One night legionnaires painted three-foot-high white letters on an outside wall: *"Ici c'est la France à tout jamais."* This is France. Forever. In 1962, when the French slunk away from Bou Saada and the rest of Algeria, the letters were left in place as a symbol of victory. By now, wind and sand have rendered the words almost unreadable, and time has worn down the irony.

A quarter-century of love-hate relations between France and Algeria suggests that the legionnaires were somehow right, after all. France marked Algeria indelibly, but Algeria has made its mark on France. When the flag came down, a million European French— that is, whites—lived in Algeria. Now a million Algerians live in France.

Islam is the second religion of France; the 2,400,000 faithful include 800,000 Moslems of French nationality.

The accords that created *Algérie Algérienne* foresaw a symbiosis that each side needed. Despite the bitterness, Algeria wanted economic and technical help. And France wanted the *dialogue privilégié* it seeks in every region shaped by French civilization. Beyond that, the political geography that once made them so close suggested that they could each be dangerous enemies.

At first, there was free movement between the two countries.

Moslems who decided to try their luck in France were welcomed. Diehard *pieds-noirs* could take their time coming home. Moroccans and Tunisians had been granted easy access to France, and large numbers moved north with few problems.

In 1968, France and Algeria negotiated an accord: Algerians could work in France, but they needed papers. Still no problems. During the 1970s, France boomed; its crops needed picking; its assembly lines needed unskilled labor; its streets needed sweeping. Recruiting teams rounded up Algerians by the thousands. When the going was good, 700,000 workers, together with 300,000 family members, moved into France.

It was the European pattern. West Germany had its Turks; Belgium and Switzerland imported foreigners by the trainload. And France, after all, was the *terre d'asile,* land of asylum. France had 181,354 refugees in 1986, more than any country in Europe.

Immigrant workers were not exactly the same as political refugees, but the rhetoric was the same. France, the universal nation, was generous. I had seen it myself, from Latin America. Virtually every leftist revolution in South America—and a great deal of right-wing plotting—was rooted to some degree in Paris. Open French borders saved thousands of Latin American lives and nourished intellectuals crushed by censors. For centuries, France had sheltered refugees from European courts.

In 1985, the French government organized a festival of the "liberties and rights of man." Bishop Desmond Tutu, recently awarded the Nobel Peace Prize, flew up from South Africa. Lech Walesa, an earlier Nobel laureate, couldn't leave Poland. But he sent a message: "France is the natural place for such a debate."

The 1980s, however, had brought recession. Up to then, the self-enriching value of sheltering the homeless outweighed the impact on the economy or the society. And with any luck, internal strife in their home countries ended before refugees attracted the attention of neighborhood vigilantes and ended up as a sore point in *Le Figaro.* But by 1985, there were 2,400,000 French out of work, and few people missed a simple calculation: the immigrant work force totaled about 2,400,000.

Suddenly, few issues generated more heat than *les immigrés.* The Poles and Portuguese were not really at issue; *les immigrés* was

mainly code for North Africans. And North Africans, numerous
Moroccans and Tunisians notwithstanding, meant Algerians.

Racism is an unpopular word in France, but racists abound. No
one knows how many blacks, browns, or yellows are in the civil
service; personnel records don't record race. But people notice.
Tennis star Yannick Noah, with an African father and a French
mother, was "the Cameroonian" until he started winning big; then
he was French. In a *Paris-Match* poll in late 1985, 71 percent of
respondents thought the French were racist toward immigrants. A
smaller percentage would call themselves racists.

There is, therefore, a subtle lexicon for making one's point. Used
properly, it allows one to welcome outsiders who fortify France's
reputation as a land of *liberté, égalité, fraternité,* but not those who
carry a cost.

After a brief course in conversational racism, I went to Marseilles.
It is France's second city, with a million inhabitants and the busiest
harbor in the country. An old Phoenician trading port, Marseilles
was already in need of urban renewal when the Romans appeared.
How French can you get? Pastis, a stroll down the Canebière, the
French Connection, *la Marseillaise.*

A French colleague had just come back. "It is incredible," he said
unhappily. "You walk around downtown at night and all you see
are Arabs and blacks and things like that."

At the old port, I worked my way through a bouillabaisse of five
kinds of fish and lobster and then approached the owner. He had
thirty years in the business, and he looked as if he had spent every
day of all of them leaning on his zinc bar, drinking Ricard to his
customers' health.

I began, "Marseilles has changed, hasn't it?"

That might have meant, of course, that the city had modernized;
or that the Germans had leveled much of the old town; or that there
were a lot of American tourists, like me. In code, however, that
meant: "There are too damned many Algerians, right?"

He shook his head in profound grief. "Six million immigrants,
c'est trop. France can't take that many. Two million, okay. But six
million? It is ruining us. They are taking the jobs. They cost money,
Social Security."

Numbers are a key to conversational racism. He was a sixmillioner, a hard case. Jean-Marie Le Pen, of the archly conservative National Front, uses that figure. You get it by adding up all the immigrants, all North Africans with French nationality, all dark-skinned people from the overseas departments and territories, and everyone just back from holiday having spent too much time on the beach.

Official government figures for 1985, based on residence permits, totaled 4,450,000 immigrants, including 860,000 Portuguese, 780,000 Algerians, 520,000 Moroccans, 425,000 Italians and 135,000 black Africans. INSEE, the national research institute, prefers 3,600,000 since some people with residence visas have gone home. There are perhaps another 500,000 clandestine immigrants (or half that or double that, depending on your politics) equivalent to the Mexican "undocumented aliens" in the United States. Because of strict limits imposed, the figure grew by less than 1 percent over that of 1984. More Algerians left than arrived because the government helped 20,000 workers (45,000 people, counting families) to go home.

MANY ALGERIANS IN France cannot return; their property was confiscated and they were sentenced to exile for fighting to help keep Algeria French. Among them are sons of men who died for France.

Harkis sometimes find themselves in pathetic circumstances. Captain Paul Barril recounts, in *Missions Très Spéciales,* how his elite gendarmes took all night to dislodge Ahmed Bouhzan from his house in a village in eastern France. He refused to pay his electric bill and then barricaded himself inside. "He was a former *harki* who wanted to settle the score," Barril wrote. "He had a very fine service record, with the French army. He was all alone in this village, without friends, without a companion, and he fell back on himself, on the battles he had fought on his native soil. I think he decided to die in a last barrage of honor. He wanted, like the Legion, to *faire Camerone.*" Bouhzan held out against tear gas and hails of bullets. At dawn, a sharpshooter finally dropped him.

BY MOST CALCULATIONS, immigrants make up just over 7 percent of the national population, less than in West Germany, Belgium, or Switzerland. Three-quarters of all immigrants have lived in France for ten years or more. Those who make a point of looking, however, can scare themselves to death.

In places, Marseilles might be Algiers. I leaped aside to avoid a Mercedes with Algerian plates near the Porte d'Aix and almost landed in a sidewalk souk of embroidered robes and veils. Old men bent over Korans in doorways once trod by bourgeois merchants rich from the colonial trade. On Fridays, the mosque overflows onto the street.

The heart of Marseilles is the Canebière, a Mediterranean Champs-Elysées, lined with trees and the signatures of the usual gang of Frenchmen: Daniel Hechter, Ted Lapidus, Christian Dior. The avenue was decorated for Christmas, and I saw a sidewalk Santa. He was a slim, short North African, awash in the billowing folds of a red suit. A white cotton beard hung unconvincingly under his own black mustache. Later, I saw a newspaper article headlined, "They have stolen the Canebière from us."

In the Marseilles district of Belsunce, a street market turns over $1.5 billion dollars a year in radio and electronic gadgetry, clothes and textiles and other items; 80 percent of the customers are Algerian tourists. They arrive on an average of 35,000 a week at the airport, and each spends an average of 10,000 francs. Belsunce is the Maghreb's biggest market, with many items found nowhere in North Africa.

In the March 1986 elections, Le Pen's National Front took 25 percent of the vote in Bouches-du-Rhône, which includes Marseilles.

And it is not only Marseilles. Or Lyon, or Paris.

The northern city of Roubaix, near the Belgian border, is crippled by unemployment. Some residents call their city Algiers, or the Medina; 20 percent of the population has a foreign nationality, and half of those are North African. In the 1985 local elections, the National Front polled 20.86 percent. And the trend was not encouraging. The first baby born in 1986 was named Kaci Khouidni.

One Sunday, I drove up to the main *place* at Savigny-les-Beaune, in Burgundy, as deep into *la France profonde* as you can get without drowning in pinot noir. The first person I saw was an Algerian, cheerfully hawking rugs and sheepskins loaded over his shoulder.

Some French rejoice at the new texture added to their culture. Damned few, however.

At Radio Gazelle, a Marseilles FM station run by immigrants for immigrants in a half-dozen languages, I talked about racism with Boualem. He is French, by law and by right. His father bled for France in World War II but preferred to take Algerian citizenship when offered the choice. Boualem was born in France, and his nationality is French. In practice, he is a *Beur.* The *Beurs* are children of North Africans who migrated to France in the 1960s and 1970s, a generation that is neither Arab nor French. The word is a short form of *Arabe,* spelled backward and jumbled in *verlen,* a popular street argot.

Their nemesis is the *Beauf,* short for *beau-frère* (brother-in-law), from a comic book satire of a vulgar, narrow-minded, and bigoted type of Frenchman. Time, it seems, is widening the circle of people the *Beurs* call *Beaufs.*

"Look," said Boualem. "Last night I left the radio, and there was a French woman closing her shop. She took one look at me and slammed down the grille, grabbed her keys, and huddled in fear over her purse. These people think automatically we are thieves and criminals. That is racism."

Ah, but crime statistics show that a lot of Algerians do steal, it is argued. But that would not be necessary if they could get jobs on an equal basis with white French, it is answered. The polemics are less important than the perceptions. A large percentage of the French feel that foreigners—essentially North Africans—are deforming their culture. And an equally large number of North Africans feel that the average French person makes their lives miserable.

Boualem is hopeful. "Every generation has its racism, and we are the latest to come. Last time it was the Italians. Next it will probably be the yellow man, the Asians."

Curiously, I had just found a report on immigration by the French Ministry of Social Affairs and National Solidarity. It included a speech by the minister, Georgina Dufoix. She began by citing a telegram to Paris from the little Crusader port of Aigues-mortes, down the road from Marseilles:

Effervescence somewhat calmed by presence of troops. . . . Six dead and twenty-six injured, including four or five mortally. Investigation continues. It will be very difficult.

That was the result of race riots on August 17, 1893, against Italians brought to work in the salt marshes at wages French laborers would not accept. Three years later, the newspaper *La Patrie* observed of Italian immigrants:

> They arrive like locusts from Piedmonte, Lombardy and Venice, Romagna, Naples, even Sicily. They are dirty, sad, ragged; entire tribes migrate north, where the fields are not devastated, resting strangers to the people who receive them, working at reduced rates, alternately playing with the accordion and the knife.

From time to time, excess foreigners were packed off. In 1935, one million were sent home—largely Italians—and 8,405 foreigners were jailed for not having papers.

Madame Dufoix's position, the government's and the mainline opposition's, is that immigrants must be welcomed as part of the society. "My objective," she told the National Assembly, "is that by this policy for all people we have in our charge, more truth will surround that ideal which makes France at once more French and more universal: Men are born and die free and equal in right."

Mitterrand was clear at a news conference in late 1985: "Immigrants who have been given papers, who bring their work here, are at home in France. . . . Any other sentiment is racial hatred."

But who had scrawled on the side of the train station, *"Trop de bicots, je vote Le Pen"*? Why did Le Pen's National Front win 11 percent of the vote for European Parliament elections in 1984, more than the Communist Party, which had scored at least 20 percent in other elections? Why did a 1985 poll show that 40 percent of France agreed with Le Pen's call for a referendum on immigration? That is code for wanting fresh laws against foreigners.

He could hardly be more clear on his position. Early in the European Parliament election campaign, he said, "Tomorrow, if you don't stay on guard, they will install themselves at your place, eat your soup, and sleep with your wife, your daughter . . . or your son." His slogan is "The French First." Historian René Rémond describes Le Pen's vision as a poor man's Vichy.

Despite the *terre d'asile* mythology, individual French have never been wildly tolerant of outsiders. Xenophobia remains, normally, at a quiet chill, lurking behind the code words and subtle actions. At such times, it can be approached with humor.

My friend Annie's mother is from the Vendée, a region of people so old-line French that they were all but wiped out for supporting the Bourbons. Her father, from Pondicherry, has been a French civil servant all his life. Annie thinks *Vendéenne* and looks like an Arab princess. One of her great joys is to nod toward a passing Algerian and remark to anyone of the bourgeoisie within earshot, *"Tsk, on n'est plus chez soi,"* one is no longer at home here. "They see my face and don't know what to think," she laughs.

When her parents were married, racial mixes were a curiosity; Asians, Arabs, and Africans were exotic to some and easily isolated nuisances to others. They were hardly numerous enough to ruin a neighborhood. Mixed families could integrate well as long as they ignored the injustice and humiliation that inevitably intrudes. Her mother caused a major ripple bringing home an Indian to the Vendée, where even the cows bear uniform markings. But he was cultured, without complexes, and thoroughly housebroken, a product of French schools and colonial governments in Pondicherry and Indochina. He found tight jaws, but he loosened them by being French down to the finest Rabelasian touches. "No one could believe this dark-faced man sitting at the head of a table in La Coupole singing 'Le Curé Pinot.' "

He had to give up his appointment as station manager for Air France in Niamey, the capital of Niger. Form demanded a lighter shade of pale. But there were other jobs.

The exoticism changed with decolonization and the independence of Algeria. It is one thing to heed the satirical call of Americans who fought the civil rights battles of the 1960s: take an Indian to lunch. After all, if a French Indian makes you lunch in return, you will never eat better. It is another when six million people of the darker persuasion muscle into your parks and cafés, praying to Allah while waiting to move into your job or your bedroom.

Le Figaro magazine, almost a parody of itself as a house organ for the far right, published a dossier entitled, "Will France still be French in 2015?" Its cover showed Marianne, the symbol of France (the current model is Catherine Deneuve), swathed in an Arabic veil affixed by a rosette of blue, white, and red. According to its demographic projections, in thirty years there would be 46,200,000 "real" French and 7,900,000 ENE, that is, non-European foreigners: 90 percent Islamic.

Madame Dufoix called the article "reminiscent of the wildest Nazi theories." She said the calculations assumed that immigrant women's fertility rates would remain constant at 4.69 per thousand and that French women's would continue to drop. The facts, she said, were that French birth rates were stable and immigrant rates were dropping steadily.

The *Beaufs,* however, seized the study as proof that France was in for a permanent crime wave and an ever louder wail of the Moslem call to prayer.

Seen from the other side, of course, the view is different. *Beurs* are even less happy than white French that so many immigrants take drugs and knock old ladies on the head to steal their purses. Ethnic background, however, does not impart shared responsibility. Their dues are paid in full. Whoever else forgets, they remember the 35,000 Moslems in French World War II cemeteries. For 150 years, French authorities have told them they were part of France. The law says that when someone is born in France, his passport is blue whatever color his face may be.

It does not always work that way. "I will call up about an advertised job, and things will be going fine on the telephone until I give my name," Boualem said. "Then the guy suddenly remembers the job is already filled." We were still at Radio Gazelle. A young man from Martinique had come in and sat down. I asked him if it was the same with black French. "Hah, are you kidding?" he replied. "Black is black. I usually get farther than the Arabs; my name is not Mohammed, it is Jean-Marc. That means I have to show up so they see my face before they remember the job is filled."

Jane Kramer, in *The New Yorker,* observed that white Parisians have seized upon *le black feeling:* African food, music and clothing. But *le black feeling,* she noted does not extend to the subject of real estate.

In a widening mood of frustration, conflict can take nasty turns. French police have some blacks in their ranks, but not many; there are few Moslems. Their methods are not known for inspiring love among immigrant communities. On September 3, 1985, *La Marseillaise* reported that a man was shot dead by police in the ghetto of La Paternelle. "One body, two versions," it said. Police had chased some armed youths robbing a hi-fi delivery truck. They caught up with one. The police said the man pumped shotgun fire at them, and he was killed in a gunfight. Witnesses said the man tossed away his gun and yelled, "I give up," before two officers shot him at point-blank range. "Like a dog," said one. The victim, and the witnesses, were *immigrés;* that is, ethnic North Africans who may or may not have been French citizens. The incident sparked two hours of rock-throwing and tear gas assaults. A visit by the regional perfect and the Algerian consul calmed feelings.

But the tension is electric.

Three weeks later, Kader Gasmi, twenty-seven, complained to the court about what is known in France as a *passage à tabac.* He said police stopped him on a routine identity check and took him to the station to check on his car registration. During questioning, he said, a policeman suddenly said, "Hey, we've got one from La Paternelle." He testified:

> He insulted me in front of ten officers . . . taking me as responsible for the events. . . . He and some of his colleagues jumped on me, hitting me so hard I fell against the cabinet. I was dead of fear . . . I thought my last hour had come. Then they put handcuffs on me and locked me up. I shouted for them to tell my family and get a doctor. I had several broken teeth, a broken nose, general contusions, and a broken arm. I don't know how long it was before they decided to do something. They wrote a report that I refused to sign because they wouldn't let me read it.

Gasmi insisted that he had no police record, had done nothing wrong, and was nowhere near the La Paternelle rioting. But his affidavit said:

> Kicking me, they put me into a car and took me [to another jail]. I think it was 3 A.M. I yelled for a doctor. To get one, I had to sign their deposition without reading it. I suffered enor-

mously and was dead of fright. A doctor finally came and demanded I go to a hospital. . . . An intern examined me and made X-rays. Then I was taken back to jail where they only gave me aspirins. Only the next morning, I was taken again to the police station where one of the more generous policemen advised my family and my lawyer.

His doctor admitted him to the hospital where his injuries were confirmed. His lawyer brought suit and, at last check, the matter was under investigation. Often such investigations come down to conflicting testimony with no result.

At Radio Gazelle, Boualem had a newspaper clipping that began, "Once again, it has been shown that police are not safe entering . . ." and it described how four officers were injured by young toughs as they arrested a drug dealer. Boualem, who lives nearby, has a different account. He said the suspect had fled to a neighbor's apartment, and police kicked down the door in pursuit. The neighbor was a woman with a pregnant daughter and a ten-year-old son. Police slugged the woman, who happened to be in their way, according to Boualem. The daughter rushed to intervene and she, too, was beaten. The son, watching his mother and sister brutalized, hit one of the policemen with a rock.

Police deny the witnesses' account, and local newspapers lean toward official reports. But the Arab telephone works in Marseilles and Paris even more efficiently than it did in Algiers. True or not, residents believe the witnesses' version.

It is similar in Paris. Most incidents go unreported, but *Libération* pursued the case of Micheline Koubi, who left a Paris nightclub at 5 A.M. near where a man had been stabbed. Police grabbed her. "They threw me in the van. A peace officer called me dirty Jew, dirty Arab, whore. And he slapped me viciously four times." At the hospital, doctors ordered her to bed for ten days because of her injuries. Her father came to get her, bringing along his military honors from the war. "Get out of here, or we'll throw you down the hole," police told him. That was in the eleventh *arrondissement*.

Mrs. Koubi tried to file a complaint but police would not record it. When a reporter intervened, an officer told her, "Be nice. Don't complain right away. We have to find the man in question. This is the first time this has happened." In fact, *Libération* noted, police from the same station had beaten up an African cab driver and wouldn't register his complaint. Madame Koubi is French, but her skin is dark.

Each incident is one more shovelful of coal under a boiling pot in which little melting is going on. At times, the pot boils over.

One Sunday morning in 1985, an unemployed twenty-two-year-old walked into a café in the Brittany village of Chateaubriand and pumped his shotgun at a group of Turkish workers. Two died on the spot. The killer, Frédéric Boulay, told police, "I don't like foreigners." And he added, "Non-European foreigners." He was sentenced to life imprisonment. But twenty-two of the 300 Turkish families in Chateaubriand left France. "They went to find a little more security and respect in the country under . . . the bloodiest dictatorship in Europe," *Libération* wrote.

Later on, at Le Puy, Charles Mandon ignored the little sign in his building asking tenants to be quiet after 10 P.M. At 9:45 P.M., he and his son walked downstairs and emptied rifles into a roomful of noisy Moroccans. Two were killed and five were wounded. Eyewitness accounts vary on the details. A small march protesting racism broke up in disarray, harassed by townsfolk yelling, "France for the French."

Elsewhere in France, a café owner refused to serve Algerian youths. One of them shot him to death, and police had to rescue the Algerians to prevent a lynching.

Three young Frenchmen, turned down by the Foreign Legion, beat up an Algerian and threw him off a moving train. In Lyon, three punks offered a young Algerian a whiskey. When he did not chug it down, they stripped, burned and cut him. "The Arab's head bounced off the wall like a punching ball," one witness put it.

Obviously enough, among four million people, many of them destitute, there is crime and violence. In back streets of Paris, Africans and Arabs deal openly in drugs, with a system of lookouts to warn against police raids or suspicious strangers.

And there is abuse of official hospitality. One youth from Niger was caught collecting support checks as a political refugee from six regional social security offices.

Beurs and others formed SOS Racism, a nationwide group to

promote goodwill among immigrants and the French. The group was launched with a march of 300,000 people into the Place de la Concorde for a rock-against-racism concert. Everyone turned out on stage: the Djurdjura Sisters, Fine Young Cannibal, Carte de Séjour, Indochina.

A godfather of SOS Racism is Bernard-Henri Lévy, a young intellectual superstar, who told a reporter:

> In 1981, I published *l'Idéologie Française,* a book that was bludgeoned by critics, buried under insults, in which I said the French were profoundly racist, that our national fascism is only asleep and Petainism only interrupted. I was called paranoid, a *provocateur.* Alas, my book seems today to have been terribly prophetic.

Lévy said he and his friends were alarmed by the "banalization" of racism. "We saw the possibility of creating the first great youth movement since May 1968." Marek Halter, a prominent critic of anti-Semitism, joined the movement, calling it the new revolution. "Music," he said, "has replaced the guillotine."

SOS Racism's spokesman, Harlem Désir, lives in Chinatown near the porte d'Italie. He is the French equivalent of a South African colored: his mother is from Alsace and his father from Martinique.

The group sold two million badges showing an open hand, palm facing outward, with the slogan, *"Touche pas à mon pote"* (don't touch my pal). The *Beurs* had a rallying symbol, and the *Beaufs* had a new code word: *pote.* At five francs each, the badges paid for rallies and publicity. But the fad wore off, leaving SOS Racism in debt. Politics split the movement, and activists argued over what was racism.

Role models are giving some identity to the *"Beur* generation." Mehdi Charef, who arrived in France at age ten, wrote a best-seller at age thirty-one called *Le Thé au Harem d'Archimède.* That translates to *Tea in Archimedes' Harem.* But it also plays on words, as in Archimedes' Theorem. Radio *Beur,* covering the Paris area, has 400,000 listeners. It launched a voter registration campaign aimed at an estimated 1.5 million French of North African extraction. A few *Beur* politicians have won municipal posts; some ran for the National Assembly in 1986 despite some gratuitous beatings in the street.

TF1, one of three state-owned networks, broadcast in 1985 a dramatic program entitled "We Are All Immigrants." It noted that most French had roots that were other than Gallic or Frankish. At one point, a young Algerian mother recounted how her eighteen-year-old son was murdered in a racist assault. A majority of callers, however, complained that they felt they were no longer in France.

The president of the FAS (Fund for Social Action for Immigrants) argued that the amount of money spent helping immigrants was greater than the national budget of Mali. He neglected to mention that the funds were contributed by immigrants themselves.

In a curious switch, *Actuel* magazine ran a poll in 1985 asking immigrants what they thought of the French. North Africans found the French to be straightforward but racist; one out of two did not want his daughter to marry one. One in three North Africans would not come back; four out of five did not want French nationality. The French, North Africans said, were self-centered and ungenerous. A thirty-five-year-old woman remarked, "When my French neighbor receives her mother, the mother brings her own steak. If I did that, my mother would bury me alive."

Among North Africans, 76 percent have French friends; only 60 percent of blacks and 54 percent of Asians do. Among all immigrant groups, 38 percent felt France had too many immigrants.

"The spirit of tolerance," my journalist friend Claude puts it, "lives mainly in the Frenchman's image of himself. It is *de la littérature.*"

In Marseilles, conflict is plain between the official wish to do the right thing and a heavy racist public opinion. Perhaps 12 percent of the city's one million inhabitants are immigrants. Marseilles shares with the national government the costs of a *Maison de l'étranger,* an active and cheerful center to help immigrants handle their paperwork and fit into the community. Algerian film festivals alternate with original theater productions. Paintings and drawings hang on the walls. But in the excellent little library and documentation section, cuttings from the Marseilles press reek of hostility.

When will we stop excusing ourselves? [asks an unsigned letter to *Le Méridional*]. Have we forgotten we are at home in France and we are citizens of an independent and sovereign nation? Have we forgotten we have the right to accept or refuse to shelter whomever we want on our national soil? Must we fight to prove that we refuse the Arabization and the Islamization of our country, cradle of Christianity? When will we admit that in times of crisis, priority must be to aid our nationals and firmly ask those that have nothing to do here with us to return to their country which has such need of the "richness" they carry—which must be cruelly lacking in their country of origin?

Our pride to be French, European, and Western is degraded every day in the name of anti-French racism carried by a mass of useless people who pass their time with invectives, parades, festivities, and in vacation camps. *Messieurs les potes,* who forget the dignity of the French people, at least accept the facts: France has rejected you. If you have a little dignity, shut up, one has seen and heard enough of you. Forget us and go join your roots. What enrichment for those roots and what happiness for France!

Another said, "I would be very grateful if you could tell me how I might find the badge, 'Don't Touch My Pal.' But written in Arabic so that the poor people who do not understand the subtleties of our language might realize that reciprocity is equally valid."

Le Pen's partisans, meanwhile, came up with their own variation: "Don't Touch My People."

Despite official assurances, there is concern in government circles. Edouard Bonnefous, chairman of the Senate finance committee, noted in *Le Monde* that two million foreign workers came to France since the boom of the 1960s. They performed a service to France and were paid for it. Now, he said, the state should help unemployed foreigners go home. Under legislation he sponsored, immigrants leave France voluntarily with an indemnity averaging 100,000 francs to cover the expenses of establishing themselves at home. Tough new measures were imposed to prevent them coming back illegally. The families of legal immigrants are often turned back at the border.

Racial tension grates on relations between France and Algeria, strained at the best of times. The 1968 agreement gave Algerians a privileged status. But the new French law of July 17, 1984, which many Algerians fought to see passed, left them in the cold. It took eighteen months to bring Algerians under the new provisions.

The legislation is clever. When it was first passed, 2.5 million foreigners—not Algerians—received ten-year residence permits. They can stay, whether or not they have work. Newcomers are given temporary visas; if they lose their jobs, they are out. Algerians' permits were linked to employment. If they lost their livelihood, they fell into limbo. If they left France for six months, they started from zero. After Algerians were brought under the law, new permits for any foreigner were very hard to get.

Algerian authorities argue that immigration is a natural right because of French colonial policy. They would just as soon have their unemployed on French rolls rather than their own. Wage remittances are a welcome source of foreign exchange.

As the 1986 National Assembly elections approached, politicians spoke with conversational racism dictionaries at their elbows. Raymond Barre, like Mitterrand, was crystal clear in defending immigrants. Some others skirted the edges; everyone shunned Le Pen, but the anti-immigrant vote he attracted was tempting.

Catholic and Protestant hierarchies sat down with Freemasons, Jews, and orthodox churches, in a common stand against racism, saying that "discriminatory, extreme ideologies find each day a stronger hold in our country.... These attitudes generate incomprehension, hate, and too often murderous violence."

Pierre Simon, grand master of the Freemasons, said, "There are people less to the right than Le Pen who are beginning to turn their language a little in hopes of draining away votes."

Jacques Toubon, speaking for the neo-Gaullist Rally for the Republic (RPR), responded, "We refuse a chilly or mean France [*frileuse ou méchante*], but we want a French France." Didier Bariani, who wrote the UDF's report on racism, said that refusing to talk about immigration was substituting one intolerance for another. "There is no indecency in having a debate about the future of French society."

After the election, rhetoric hardened. Tough new security laws gave police wide powers to hold foreigners and, with few formalities, expel them. Complaints of brutality burgeoned. Freelance violence continued. In May, a "French Commando Against the Maghrebian (North African) Invasion" blew up a Turkish bath in Marseilles.

And the incidents continue. A Congolese official, Benjamin Tsila, on a study leave in Paris raced for his commuter train with no time to have his ticket punched. He asked the inspector to punch it. Instead the inspector tried to fine him. They argued as the train reached Tsila's stop. The inspector tried to hold him on board. The train started up again and Tsila fell to the track. He died waving his ticket to mortified witnesses.

André Santini, the new minister for repatriated citizens, estimated unemployment among 80,000 children of *harkis* at 85–95 percent. He offered incentives for employers to hire them, but it was not clear who would pay the cost. He also assured *pieds-noirs* they would finally be looked after adequately.

The program for "assisted return" continued, not to everyone's delight. In the town of Montbeliard, nearly 6,500 immigrants went home. Schools closed for lack of pupils, taxes plummeted, and merchants found themselves hurting badly. Only the Front National rejoiced. Mysterious tracts circulated reading: "Only one choice: the suitcase or the coffin."

At one point, Jack Lang, as minister of culture, said that forcing out immigrants would be bad for the reputation of France. At the level of individuals, France's reputation has already suffered. Subtracting the Portuguese concierges tucked away behind doors and the retired Americans lost in the bushes and Frenchified foreigners who pass unnoticed in the stuffiest of circles, France's immigrants amount to a paltry few percent. The *Beaufs* who abuse them in the name of national honor do far more to spoil the society than a few more spoonfuls of couscous in the French pot-au-feu. Tolerance, it seems to the outsider, is a vital element of the French mission to civilize.

THE IMMIGRANT issue is, in fact, only one hoop the French must keep aloft in their high-wire balancing act of a North African policy. Algeria and Morocco are mortal enemies with clashing ideologies. Tunisia's Westernized socialism with a firm hand can veer toward Morocco on the right or Algeria on the left. Libya, never French and hardly a historic *pote* of the French, is always ready to give the tightrope a yank when Paris least expects it. And France usually manages to keep a *dialogue privilégié* going with each of the four.

The French know that privileged friendship has more to do with privilege than friendship. A common language, and shared history that has not always been bitter, form a basis for negotiation. The rest is a matter of balancing mutual advantages.

France is Algeria's best customer and biggest supplier. Most of Algeria's other exports go to the EEC via Paris. France buys a third of its natural gas from Algeria at prices sometimes 25 percent above the open market. That deal alone, according to *Gaz de France,* cost the French balance of payments two billion unnecessary francs in 1985. There is other aid, either overt or hidden in a dozen separate state accounts. Paris, more than Washington or London, coexists with Algeria's East-bloc tendencies.

In exchange, the French profit. They build the Algiers subway and sell *L'Equipe,* a sports newspaper that is wildly popular in Algeria. They export wheat, Chanel, and wheel bearings. And France carries weight in a pivotal Arab state, a Third World leader. For a modern-day seat of empire, influence amounts to what possession used to be. The less defined the influence is, the less vulnerable it is to attack.

Giscard d'Estaing was the first French president to visit Algeria, in 1975, but he did little to move relations beyond a slightly chilly balance of mutual interest. Mitterrand pushed hard to warm them up. In 1981, he brought to Algeria twenty-eight crates of historical documents, from water surveys to family records. President Chadli Benjadid came to Paris in 1983 and laid a wreath on the tomb of France's unknown soldier at the Arc de Triomphe. After all, for all anyone knew, the hallowed remains might be those of an Algerian rifleman.

But there is also Morocco. The word friendship is a little more apt between France and Morocco. Less blood was spilled in colonial times. Moroccans integrated more easily into France. And King Hassan II is the sort of dictator that Western leaders like: committed to capitalist enterprise and political stability with a minimum of disruptive rhetoric. His territory covers the strategic shoulder of Africa, across from Spain and Gibraltar.

French *rapprochement* with Algeria spurred Hassan to widen his options. The Reagan Administration became interested. Republican strategists determined that Morocco was America's neighbor, a little water notwithstanding. With long runways and spacious harbors, Morocco was a perfect staging point between the United States and the Middle East. Rummaging around in history, Reagan's diplomats found all sorts of historic ties.

French teeth gnashed; this was not Gabon. France had paid heavily for decades to retain its friendship with Morocco. There was *l'affaire Ben Barka,* for example.

Mehdi Ben Barka, popular leader of the Moroccan opposition, was bundled into a French police car on October 29, 1965, on his way to lunch at the Brasserie Lipp in St. Germain-des-Pres. He was driven outside of Paris, executed, and buried. It was soon clear that thugs linked to Service 7 of SDECE had joined Moroccan agents in the kidnap and murder. French police covered up clues. Eighteen months later, de Gaulle declared, "This must finish. The real culprits must be found. Oufkir and Dlimi [Moroccan officials] must be convicted. The king [Hassan II], of course, is an accomplice, even the instigator, of the crime."[1]

De Gaulle dissolved Service 7 and placed SDECE under the control of the defense minister. But neither he nor any of his successors shed light on the French agents' involvement, or on who gave the orders. SDECE, later DGSE, remained under the defense minister's control for twenty years until unidentified agents were once again caught killing in the name of France, in New Zealand.

With Reagan courting Hassan II, the French shifted their balance slightly from Algeria. They continued to supply three times more military hardware to Morocco than did the United States. Mitterrand tacitly backed Hassan's claim to the Western Sahara, thus outraging Algeria, which supports the Polisario movement's push for that territory's independence.

In 1984, the tightrope twanged dangerously.

Mitterrand visited Hassan's summer palace at Ifrane. He was looking for help in ending the Chad war. Libya had just "merged" with Morocco, the seventh time Qaddafi had attempted to enlarge his stage with ill-fated unions. Before the merger collapsed, the French hoped to work a deal: Libya could stop supplying arms to the Polisario against Morocco in the Western Sahara; Morocco would help Libya—and France—find a face-saving way out of Chad.

The visit was supposed to be secret, but Hassan announced it. The Algerians reacted bitterly. By his presence, Mitterrand had blessed the merger, which was a threat to Algeria. A month later, Mitterrand flew to Algiers to cut his losses. The official daily, *El Moudjahid,* carried no comment, just photos of the two smiling chiefs of state and a caption: ". . . the exchange of views is the embodiment of the dialogue which Algeria and France wish to conduct, in serenity and confidence."

France's *beau geste* followed within days. Foreign Minister Claude Cheysson attended ceremonies for the thirtieth anniversary of the All Saints Day uprising that started the Algerian War. Opponents invoked the frightful word *forfaiture,* tantamount to treason among generals. "A shameful and scandalous blunder," said Michel Poniatowski. "This government has not even honor." Michel Noir, deputy from the Rhône, called it "a crime against the memory of French assassinated that day." *Le Recours,* which groups *pied-noir* organizations, denounced an "indecent affront to the honor and dignity of France." Edgar Faure, a major figure of the period, evoked the pain he felt that France might associate itself with an episode "marked by the massacre of a family of teachers."

Cheysson replied that deserting Algeria would be treason to those who fought so that France could remain a presence. After twenty years of independence, he said, "France no longer has the possibility of conducting itself differently from others."

Chadli called the storm an internal French matter. But it bore a cost. In the weekly *Jeune Afrique,* Abdelkader Chanderli observed, "The derision . . . and stupidity unfortunately tarnish the image of a people and a nation one might have thought could still teach the world elegance and generosity." He suggested that under this new code of honor of "infantile grudges and susceptibilities of badly raised children," Frenchmen had best avoid Waterloo Station or Trafalgar Square in London. "I fear the glorious past of France has left just about everywhere souvenirs that are best forgotten. . . . if there is a country rich in memories of defeats and humiliations inflicted on others, it is the Hexagon that no longer extends from Dunkirk to Tamanrasset. Britain never would have objected to its government taking part in celebrations of American independence. . . . the English have kept their sense of fair play, even when they draw first."

Clever, if a cheap shot. The Algerians had little claim to elegance and generosity after their fierce settling of scores in the 1960s. FLN leaders fought among themselves for supremacy and waged war on dissenting factions. At independence, with a nationalistic flourish, leaders tore down every trace of France, including road signs and traffic markers. It was chaos, since most literate adults read only French, not Arabic.

The French signs came back. Today, from a distance, Algerian towns seem transplanted from the Midi: neat lines of trees, a substantial *hôtel de ville* (town hall) on shaded central squares, rows of shuttered shops. But the time has been hard on Algeria, with a struggling economy and grave social problems.

In any case, the waters calmed. After Cheysson's trip, the president of Algeria's legislature said, "Bilateral cooperation is going well, and relations are very good." France sent down fifty-eight more crates of documents despite protesting *pieds-noirs*. "At least leave us the Algeria of old papers," said one. Another suggested that at least France should send back an immigrant with each box.

Then it started again. Prime Minister Fabius, in Morocco, said, "This is my first visit to a Maghreb country, and I wanted it to be Morocco." Before he could make it to Algiers, the state-run media dragged out the war and aimed it at France. On the fortieth anniversary of Sétif, Algerian television told in bitter detail how 40,000 Moslems were killed in repression. It showed a 1961 sequence filmed by an East German alleging that the French had tied 150 Moslem prisoners to stakes near its first nuclear test at Reggane to measure the effects of radiation on humans. The source was an unnamed German former legionnaire. Algérie Presse-Service, lauding the production, denounced "a crime against humanity, among so many others, of French colonialism."

France denied the "insulting and lying allegations" and said it "regrets anything that might damage the quality and future of

Franco-Algerian relations." Life-sized dummies were used, it said, not people. The statement ignored an APS remark that France ran Algeria like a concentration camp and practiced genocide.

Fabius reached Algiers in June and evoked "completely privileged relations." It was the thirtieth or the thirty-fifth time a senior official had flown down since 1981 to strike that note. Racism was a constant problem, but the list was long: not enough gas and oil purchases; not enough aid; not enough technology was being transferred; no help on the Western Sahara; overall, an apparent lean toward Morocco.

Fabius's visit was reported dryly and briefly, in contrast to the enthusiastic coverage of the Swedish leader Olof Palme. He, according to *Moudjahid,* knew how to reconcile his convictions and his actions and Sweden was "the only one of the small circle of the richest countries that was credible when it proclaimed its solidarity with the South."

The Algerians demurred on major contracts sought by France. In Paris, *Gaz de France* accountants grumbled privately about "horribly expensive and increasingly unrealistic" prices to Algeria. Holland and the Soviet Union were dropping their rates. But, they said, for Mitterrand the issue was taboo.

The FLN weekly *Révolution Africaine* published a fifteen-page report on torture that likened French generals to Nazi executioners. It was time, it said, "that France overcome its complex as a former colonial power and judge with serenity the truth about the colonialism imposed on the Algerian people." And, "Algerians should not be condemned to amnesia while France continues to cultivate . . . the memory in its youth by the constant recollection of the facts of Nazi Germany and the war of 1939–1945."

The Algerians argued that those who demand punishment for Klaus Barbie should understand the bitterness felt toward French torturers. To make that point, *Révolution Africaine* compared the murder of Resistance leader Jean Moulin by Barbie's Gestapo agents in Lyon to that of Larbi Ben M'Hidi by the French.

The tone eased, and the rhetoric died away. Few French leaders expected it to be gone for good. To some extent, it was a useful political device. But more, it was a lingering pain, on both sides, that would not soon disappear.

Slowly, differences are being settled. Algerian authorities, for example, finally agreed to let children of divorced couples spend a few days' vacation with their mothers in France. That took a summer-long sit-in by French mothers at the embassy in Algiers and repeated visits by two French cabinet ministers.

After thirty years, the revolution is slipping into the past. An Algerian filmmaker reconstructing the war used a cast born mostly after independence. The old figures are coming home. Ben Bella, the first president and leader among the nine revolutionary fathers, was restored to honor after fourteen years of imprisonment and then exile. Belkacem Krim and Mohammed Khider were executed by FLN agents abroad in the 1970s, but their bodies were finally brought back. Algeria has more pressing economic problems that can no longer be blamed on the French: You cannot find orange juice in a country that was once France's orange grove.

Youngsters are still taught to remember grandfathers whom the French threw off cliffs and left to die—or those who were forced by the FLN to swallow their French military medals. But a senior Algerian leader summed up the feeling to a French reporter, late in 1985: "When we speak of foreigners, that might mean Germans, Americans, or Spaniards, but not the French. For us, they will never be foreigners like the others."

CHAPTER FIFTEEN

Middle East: Hall of Mirrors

A STRING OF crumbling French crusader forts rises from high ground across the Levant. They protect nothing and represent little power; but they are still there, after eight centuries. Like France. In North Africa, the French loom large, balanced precariously at center stage. But in the Middle East, they are nowhere and everywhere, moving within a hall of mirrors that only the architects of Versailles could have fashioned.

An Arab intellectual can argue that France has passed from the Middle Eastern theater. But he will likely adorn his discourse with the thoughts of Camus. No matter who is responsible for the morning's acrid odor in Beirut streets, it is the Lanvin sold from the back of decrepit Renault station wagons that masks it. The Arabic tongue is enriched regularly with new nouns: Exocet AM39, Mirage 2000, Super-Etendard, Super-Frelon. After the damage of classic power is done, it is often French engineers who clean it up.

King Hussein of Jordan was motivated by more than a shopping list when he said during a 1984 trip to Paris, "France has an important role to play in the Middle East in search for a solution to the problems of the region. I have said it often." That role is not clear, least of all to the French. But the Middle East is like that.

France is marked by its history in Lebanon and Syria. But apart from its weight in the power balance, it plays a vital role in the rush of modern events. Its diplomats and salesmen move easily in societies that baffle others. They understand the power of symbols, the subtle melting away and resurrection of alliances, the flexibility of the spoken word. When you do it with mirrors, you can apply Descartes with empirical pragmatism.

Some anti-Semitism aside, France is a home for Jews and a declared friend of Israel. The French never maintained a presence in the Gulf, and oil sheiks feel little cultural draw to Paris. But no matter. For Islamic politicians, businessmen, warlords, and terrorists who feel hemmed in by the stern lines of East and West, Paris is a secular Mecca. It is the capital of live and let live—or not.

Fanatical factions wage war on Paris streets. The Saudi embassy was seized in 1973, then the Iraqis'. Arabs fired fourteen bullets into a Palestinian envoy; another was killed later by a car bomb. A former Syrian prime minister was murdered in 1980. Someone had killed an Iraqi nuclear scientist earlier. A bomb demolished the rue Copernic synagogue in 1980, killing four.

Intelligence officers had reached informal understandings with some groups that they would not be harassed if they kept terror out of France. In the 1980s, however, there were too many amateurs, fanatics, and governments involved. Terrorists machine-gunned the lunchtime crowd at Goldenberg's delicatessen in 1983, and six people died. Beirut-based Armenians blew up the Turkish Airlines counter at Orly Airport, along with innocent victims. A blast shattered an anti-Syrian newspaper office on rue Marbeuf in 1984, killing one passerby and injuring a score of others. A gunman missed the U.S. chargé d'affaires in 1981, but another shot the U.S. military attaché; later an Israeli diplomat was killed. In 1984, Iranian terrorists killed an exiled general who had worked for the shah. Someone else shot the United Arab Emirates ambassador. There were scores of other incidents. Barriers in front of the American and Israeli embassies bristle with arms. Some plots are foiled in time. Others, undetected, are carried out by shadowy elements who benefit from the *force majeure* of greater policy goals.

Mostly, however, life is pleasant in Paris. Beyond the Eiffel Tower, along the river, is a cluster of high-rises the Parisians call Beirut-sur-Seine. Many of the apartments are owned by Lebanese who have gotten their money and themselves out of Lebanon. Uncounted thousands are French, whose Lebanese roots go back generations, and thousands more are fresh arrivals, floating between Paris and Beirut as combat rises and falls. A Paris radio station, la

Voix du Liban, keeps them informed. A large community of Syrians also lives in Paris.

"My Syrian in-laws just got their French nationality," my friend James told me. "They're going to vote for Le Pen. They figure there are too many immigrants in France. And they don't consider themselves Arabs, anyway. They're Phoenicians."

France, by tradition, is officially tolerant. In 1978, editors asked their Paris correspondents to check out some holy person named Khomeini who was trying to overthrow the shah of Iran with a Sony tape recorder. That seemed normal. Whoever ruled Iran traditionally had a holiday home in France, and Paris was the center for every faction seeking to take over his power. When Shah Mohammad Reza Pahlavi was temporarily forced out of Iran in 1953, he had to go to Rome. Mossadegh, the prime minister who seized power, had too many supporters in Paris.

Ayatollah Ruholla Khomeini turned out to be worth watching; we slower reporters caught up on the background. The shah had prevailed upon Iraq to expel the ayatollah. Neither Kuwait nor Syria would have him. He wanted to stay in Islamic territory, but Algeria turned him down. Sadegh Ghotbzadeh, living in Paris, brought him to France. It took Khomeini a few days to agree to take refuge in a country that had fathered the Crusades and, after all these years, still adored Christ. But, après tout, Iranians did not need visas for France.

Flora Lewis of the *New York Times* already knew about Khomeini. She happened to be calling at the Quai d'Orsay on the day he arrived in France, and she asked about him. "They did not know he was coming," she told me later. "I'm sure he just showed up." After three months, he would need a visa to stay. That would be no problem.

Khomeini settled comfortably into the village of Neauphle-le-Château, west of Paris; he pronounced it "Noffal." He had the plumbing ripped out to install Turkish toilets and bricked off the women's quarters. He was in the heart of a godless country, a long way from Qom and Mecca, but he had direct-dial telephones.[1]

The French let the ayatollah telephone his revolution to Iran; after all, what if he succeeded? Police made sure no one embarrassed France by hurting him. With a little help from the Quai d'Orsay, the municipality granted drivers' licenses in twenty-four hours instead of the usual two months. The local post office supplied two telex and six phone lines. Khomeini brought in fifty security guards. His people were convinced that the CIA had rigged an ice cream truck to eavesdrop on him; he decided not to ask the French to intervene in case they might install their own microphones.

Theoretically, visitors and refugees are supposed to stay out of politics. In four months in France, however, Khomeini gave 132 radio, television, and press interviews, and he made fifty declarations for clandestine broadcast in Iran. He spoke directly to Iranians who thronged the villa daily, by the end a total of 100,000.

In Tehran, meanwhile, the weakening shah swallowed increasing quantities of pills washed down by mineral water from France. President Valéry Giscard d'Estaing was so convinced the ayatollah would triumph that he discreetly persuaded his allies not to overdo their come-what-may support for the shah.

Khomeini did triumph, of course; he loaded his revolution aboard a chartered Air France 747 and flew home with it from Charles de Gaulle Airport.

The shah went to Egypt. An aide later said he was bitter that France kept him out. "I don't think Charles de Gaulle would have acted in that way," the shah was quoted as saying. "But him, he was something else." Nonetheless, part of the imperial family settled in France, where the shah owned chunks of Paris and the Riviera, with other investments no tax authority could trace. Diehard royalists filled French papers with advertisements denouncing the Islamic revolution.

Steadily, the flotsam and jetsam of the Islamic revolution floated back to Paris, which eventually became so full of anti-Khomeini plotters that France earned the title of Satan, along with the United States. A terrorist bombing killed eighteen in Tehran in 1984. With a curious lapse of memory, Ali Akbar Hashemi Rafsanjani, speaker of Iran's parliament, said, "We consider the French government a party to this crime because of its treatment of criminals as political refugees, providing them with all the facilities."

Then the Iraqis admitted hammering Iran with five Super-Etendard jets, equipped with Exocet missiles, borrowed from the French navy. Their new fleet of Mirages was still on the way.

Hundreds of thousands of Iranians mobbed the streets chanting, "Death to Mitterrand. Death to France."

Et alors? Not everyone in the Khomeini crowd would have forgotten "Noffal," and the wheel would turn. Bitterly opposed to the United States, Iran needed France. *Libération* published what it said were minutes of a secret meeting in Tehran to set up "independent brigades" to terrorize enemy nations: Gulf states and France. The Iranian embassy protested angrily, denouncing a plot to sour improving relations. Sure enough, the pendulum swung slowly back.

France sought to keep a relatively even keel with Iran to hedge bets. But Saddam Hussein of Iraq, Khomeini's major foe, was a friend of the French; they had built him a nuclear plant. So were the Israelis, who had bombed the plant, and a French engineer in the process. And also the Palestine Liberation Organization. Its Paris envoy played Christmas carols on his guitar on French television.

Among other modern monuments, Mitterrand put up the Institut du Monde Arabe, a block of glass and geometry at the end of boulevard St. Germain, towering over the Seine just across from the Ile St. Louis. A billboard at the site declares its purpose is to meld ancient civilizations, those of the Middle East with that of France.

It is a noble sentiment, but a tall order in today's climate. As I studied the half-finished project recently, my face—squinting in concentration—must have seemed disapproving. A car passed and its driver, an Arab, shouted to me: "Don't look like that. You are a racist."

FRANCE'S TRACK RECORD in the Middle East suggests little cause for Moslem warmth. With intermittent lapses, the French allied themselves with the Ottoman Turks. French engineers, military strategists, merchants, investors, and teachers went to Turkey. Ottoman legions fought the Austrians. Under the tacit Turkish accord, French missionaries settled among Maronite Christians in Lebanese mountain strongholds and beyond. In the nineteenth century, French and local Christian capital developed a rich silk-spinning industry, helped by a port at Beirut, roads, and a cog railway to Damascus, all built by the French. Beirut grew from a village of 8,000 in the 1820s to a city of 130,000 less than a century later.

Into the 1900s, France was on a full-blown mission to civilize the Levant.[2]

France joined Britain and Russia in the sneaky Sykes-Picot agreement of 1916, with secret terms that assured Russia southern sea passages and divided Arab territories between Britain and France. After World War I, Britain and France legitimatized their presence with League of Nations mandates. General Henri Gouraud planted the Tricolor and set up a government. He wrote shortly afterward:

> I might compare Syria to a little daughter born to France after the war. . . . Without doubt, it is in that sentiment of a mother of a family that Parliament has given me the necessary credit to pursue "the sacred mission of civilization."

Gouraud, devoutly Christian, made it clear that France was no newcomer to the region:

> Without going back to the Crusades, which have left magnificent castles so moving to contemplate for their splendor and force, our missionaries, sailors, engineers have, since long ago, brought their devotion and intelligence to these coasts. . . . There is not a foreign country in the world, except in the south of Belgium, where French is spoken as fluently as in Lebanon.[3]

The Hashemites, under King Faisal, claimed historic rights to Syria. But in 1920 Gouraud swept west from Beirut and ran Faisal out of Damascus. He broke up Greater Syria into autonomous states under French control, weakening Moslem nationalist factions. To Lebanon, he added Tripoli in the north, Sidon in the south, and the rich Beqaa Valley. Maronite Christians held political sway in a Lebanon the Syrians called artificial. Druzes and Sunni Moslems, among dozens of factions, were splintered and balanced precariously against each other.

One day, disenfranchised leaders warned, Lebanon would collapse, and bloody wars would redivide the turf.

Nearly sixty years before Gouraud, a French naval officer named de Chaille had warned, "[The Maronites] have no desire other than to be governed as in the past; they have ancient privileges which they owe to the protection of France and it is a concern of France only to preserve these for them." The Maronite patriarch, he said, "refuses to understand anything, appreciate anything, or even hear anything" about new trends or requirements of the time. But by 1914, the Maronites clung so fanatically to the French that they taught their children to recite *"Inna faransa immana hanuna."* Truly, France is our benevolent mother.

For the French, Maronite loyalty, even if from self-interest, was a sign that their civilizing mission produced a return. Also, the Maronites were a useful force to counter rebellious factions who wanted France to leave.

From the beginning, nationalists harassed the French. Senegalese troops battled insurgents. When dissidents captured Damascus, French forces shelled the city. George Seldes, an American correspondent for the *Chicago Tribune* who reached Damascus, reported the dead at 1,000, but French censors changed the figure to 500. Seldes wrote later that he was the only reporter in town. Because of heavy French censorship, he said, most people believed inflated Moslem accounts of up to 25,000 dead.

France's position, outlined in the *Revue des Deux Mondes* of December 1921, was "to maintain, to improve, the Ottoman Empire which was so favorable a means for expanding our influence." The mandate, it said, "responds marvelously to our past in the Orient, and to our idea for the future in that part of the world. Since the Crusades, our nation never sought a territorial domination in the Levant."

Seldes concluded,

And so France saved the Christian Lebanon and got no thanks. She built schools and roads. She found epidemics and conquered them. . . . Law and order were enforced. Billions of francs were spent. "Imperialism" was at work. What did France take out of Syria? Nothing. It is an almost barren land, spotted with beautiful oases . . . but no cotton plantations, no vast mineral wealth, no agriculture, no oil, no hope of oil. . . . Militarism, exploitation, imperialism? All I found was intense disgust with the mandate on the part of the French while the natives who cried for freedom and independence feared that the enemy religious cult would fight them unless a foreign power spent its money there maintaining order.

Nonetheless, France stayed. In 1936, the Front Populaire government in Paris promised independence to Syria and to Lebanon, after a three-year period. But in 1939, a new government knelt to military pressure and dropped the idea. France lost face, and the nationalists were furious.

With France crippled by the war, Syrian Moslems demanded a final break. Neither Vichy nor de Gaulle found a solution. On May 8, 1945, insurgents began a wave of strikes, riots, and assaults on French garrisons in four cities of Syria. Nationalists rejected a proposed independence that maintained French air and naval bases, schools, and control of the oil pipeline to Iraq.

Fighting was bitter, and French civilians were attacked. Nationalists boycotted French shops, banks, and schools. On May 28, the French bombed a rebel-held sector of Damascus. Then the British moved in.

Britain, still fighting Japan, feared that upheaval in the Middle East could endanger their supply line. In any case, the entente cordiale carried limited weight in the Middle East. London and Paris were rivals in the region, and British troops forced the French to withdraw.

Le Monde estimated the week's casualties at 400 Syrians killed, 100 missing, and 500 wounded. In ten days, the French lost eighty to 100 killed and 200 to 300 wounded. Charles-André Julien, in *Foreign Affairs,* estimated the losses at twenty-eight French and twenty-five native troops killed; the Syrian-Lebanese dead were about 600, with 300 wounded. In 1946, the *Revue Socialiste* carried extracts of Julien's article, which the French government censored, then released. In the original, it began:

> The functioning of the Syria-Lebanon mandate was perverted from the very outset. Neither the English, nor the French, nor the Syrians believed in the value of the obligations it entailed, and none of them played entirely fair. Varied shrewd dealings during the First World War left the Arabs defiant and embittered. . . . French statesmen played a deceptive game. . . . Badly

informed public opinion believed that France had acquired a new colony, and the high commissioners acted in that spirit. They made every effort to paralyze demands for nationhood instead of stimulating and at the same time canalizing them. The attitude of minor officials aggravated the situation still further. Unlike England, France had no corps of specialists in Eastern affairs. . . . She had recourse to a colonial personnel which imposed on the politically advanced Syrians an authoritative paternalism of a sort little likely to gain their support.

The French imposed forced labor, collective fines and imprisonment, and the belief that common faith assured Christian loyalty, Julien wrote.

In fact, even before World War I a French envoy reported back a common expression among Maronite leaders: any one of them would set the country ablaze to light his cigarette. Syria and Lebanon, each on their own, sought to build nations with little hope of communal generosity among religions and factions.

France moved up and down sharply on the Maronites' shifting popularity polls. Sunni Moslems distrusted the Christians and the French alike. They did not want a Christian government of any sort. Their interest was a greater Syria, not a greater Lebanon dominated by Western-oriented Christians. And beyond the Levant, France's standing was low among Moslem leaders.

Partly to spite the British, France helped to launch the new state of Israel. The *Exodus,* carrying Jewish refugees, sailed from Marseilles. Then the French invaded Suez. War and repression were vicious in Algeria. France armed Israel heavily in the early 1960s, providing the Mirage fighters that wreaked such havoc in the 1967 war.

De Gaulle stopped arms sales to Israel after 1967, just before he left office. He decried the Israelis for shooting first, condemned "expansionist ambitions," and made what Israelis called anti-Semitic remarks. All arms supplies were cut off, including spare parts. Israeli foreign minister Abba Eban charged that France's policy toward the Jewish state was "not one iota less hostile than the Soviet Union's."

Five missile-firing gunboats, ordered and paid for by Israel before the embargo, were blocked at Cherbourg. The Israelis howled in protest; Egypt was menacing their waters and the boats were vital to their survival. France held firm.

But before dawn on Christmas, 1969, the boats left port. Before President Georges Pompidou began bellowing orders down the phone line, they were in international waters. According to the French, they had been bought by respectable clients, for cash. A Norwegian gentleman negotiated the deal for the Starboat Company, Box 25078, Oslo. The company was, in fact, registered in Panama; Starboat, as in Star of David. Its principal shareholder was Israel, as might have been obvious. When *l'affaire* took on its capital *A,* which was immediately, the French asked the Norwegians about the company. Starboat? Never heard of it.

Military authorities in Cherbourg had refused to take responsibility for the boats—they were too hot to handle—so it was not clear who was supposed to approve their release. The boats were lined up ready to go for two days, but the local newspaper publisher said he suppressed the news at the shipbuilders' request. He explained, "We were guided by the sole concern of not harming the . . . most important local industry which employs more than 1,200 people." Two generals were fired, and France apologized.

L'Express wrote, "The Israelis have played well and ridiculed the French government."

Arab leaders, gnashing their teeth at photos of Moshe Dayan jumping for joy on the wharf as the boats chugged into Haifa, were not convinced. Nor were many French. The cover seemed too transparent to be innocent of connivance at some level, and public opinion seemed to like that idea. Commercially, trade with the Arab world amounted to a billion francs a year, 1.5 percent of France's total, the same level as with Sweden. And emotionally, the French leaned toward Israel. Jean Daniel wrote in *Le Nouvel Observateur,* "The embargo was decided against the French, and maintained against the will of the French despite promises made to the French; it is today violated by the French."

L'Express concluded its report: "In majority, [the French] prefer Israelis to Arabs, and the *Guignol* [a Punch-like fool] to the gendarme. Especially when the *Guignol* pays cash."

But France assured Gamal Abdel Nasser that he was "among their friends." Israel got the boats. Pompidou kept his job. A few days later, a ship arrived in Cherbourg to load 4,879,000 francs worth of arms bought by Iraq.

And just about then, France sold 110 Mirage fighters to the new leader of Libya, Colonel Muammar Qaddafi, giving firepower to his newly energized air force.

De Gaulle himself had been immensely popular among the Arabs: he had freed Algeria, bearded the Americans, kept Britain out of the Common Market, withdrawn his troops from NATO—and cut off Israel. But the popularity, historians generally agree, did not extend to France.

The early 1970s brought a clear shift. Britain announced in 1971 that it was pulling its armed forces back from east of the Suez. Then the Arabs discovered the power of their hold on the world oil flow. France, already stepping toward the Arabs' camps, quickened its pace, with a diminished chance that *Perfide Albion* would drop banana peels in their way. France moved quickly to fill a void left by Britain among its former colonies. Arab leaders were happy to find a European source of arms and diplomatic support, free of postcolonial complications.

It was a costly policy for the French image. In the euphoria of new Arab strength, Palestinian terrorists pressed their demand for attention. They succeeded at the 1972 Munich Olympics. Black September, linked to Al Fatah, broke into the Israeli compound. Terrorists killed a weightlifter and a trainer and seized nine hostages. After negotiations, German police stormed in; all the Israelis were killed. Three surviving Palestinians were jailed, but the Black September group hijacked a German airliner three weeks later and forced their release. Israel bombed camps in Lebanon and Syria and set about tracking down those responsible. One mastermind was identified as Abu Daoud.

In 1973, Black September raided a garden party at the Saudi embassy in Khartoum; they seized diplomats from the United States, Belgium, Saudi Arabia, and Jordan. Among their demands was the release of Abu Daoud, imprisoned in Jordan. All capitals refused. After killing two Americans and the Belgian chargé d'affaires, they reduced their ransom. But they still wanted Abu Daoud. Finally, they were overpowered. Six months later, Black September seized another Saudi embassy, in Paris. They demanded Abu Daoud, and Hussein freed him.

And then, in January 1977, the French consulate in Beirut gave a visa to a tall man with a distinctive mustache, an Iraqi passport, and a thick SDECE file; he was to attend the funeral of a PLO envoy murdered in Paris. It was Abu Daoud. He and a companion were met by French protocol, given a police guard, and received at the Quai d'Orsay by French officials anxious to play a role in Middle East peace talks. Then he was arrested.

The Direction de la Surveillance du Territoire picked him up at his hotel bar, either to embarrass the rival SDECE or through bad coordination. Interior Minister Michel Poniatowski approved the order. When the Foreign Ministry found out, a duty officer went white. "But why?" he demanded into the phone. "This is a diplomatic catastrophe." It was, of course. The West Germans asked for Abu Daoud; so did the Israelis. Giscard d'Estaing told Poniatowski, "You have made a horrendous gaffe. But the longer we hold this Abu Daoud, the harder it will be to free him."[4] Pressure would mount for his prosecution. Arabs would want him freed. The Palestinians might seize yet another embassy, a French embassy.

The only way out was the courts. The appropriate judge scheduled a hearing for a week later. Impossible, the Elysée objected. Abu Daoud was rushed into court. The German extradition request was rejected on a questionable technicality. The Israelis were turned down on an equally dubious 1927 law. Abu Daoud was freed the next day and put on a plane for Algiers.

Domestic reaction was bitter. In *Le Nouvel Observateur,* the eminent lawyer Jean-Denis Bredin demolished the legal arguments. He noted that judges were furious over the pressure applied to the courts, and he concluded: "Here is a sickening spectacle. A government weak and slippery at the same time! A judiciary without rigor! Ministers too well trained to lie! We are all deprived of justice and humiliated at being made so ridiculous."

But it was worse elsewhere. Ilana Romano, widow of an Israeli athlete killed in Munich, said, "France understands oil more than blood." Israeli foreign minister Ygal Allon added, "Before a minimum of courage and a maximum of weakness, France failed the test." The *New York Times* editorialized, "The decision leaves the sad but inescapable impression of a nation that shows itself willingly senseless, abject and even cowardly in the face of the blackmail of terror." The *Washington Post* said that France had "mortgaged its foreign policy for Arab oil and Arab markets. . . . What does it matter if the fruits of this boot-licking policy are nonexistent?"

And West Germany's *Bild Zeitung* echoed: "The France of grandeur lifted his arms before terrorism instead of against it. . . . France, weak, cowardly and humiliated, is on its knees."

CIVIL WAR, meantime, shattered much of the trappings of France in Lebanon. Luxury hotels along the Corniche were burned and mortared until they resembled blackened slabs of Gruyère cheese. The bankers and the blonde sunbathers hurried off, leaving Beirut to warring militias. But in some ways French political influence increased.

The Maronites, after pinning their hopes on the Americans and the Israelis, returned to the French. There is a cultural, spiritual and emotional holdover. But more, France defends the borders of greater Lebanon, and Christian leaders count on them to stand by their creation. Ghassan Tueni, publisher of *An Nahar* in Beirut and former Lebanese ambassador to the United Nations, outlined this for me in Paris.

> You will hear Maronites say, 'the Americans abandoned us,' as though the United States was some charity organization. Their only hope is France. There is a feeling that Europe is bound to play a greater role, especially France because of its ties with the Arabs. And France can talk to the Israelis with more freedom than the Americans can.

If Lebanon provided a French entry point to the Middle East, however, it offered little else but anguish. With an oil crisis crippling its economy, France needed more tangible benefits for its foreign policy.

Pursuing a reliable supplier of oil, France had settled on Iraq.

Their ties were historic; the French had kept nearly a quarter interest in the Iraq Petroleum Company when they relinquished to the British other claims on Iraq.

Jacques Chirac, prime minister under Giscard d'Estaing, visited Baghdad in 1974. He negotiated a major exchange of arms for oil under terms that were not made public. The deal has linked France and Iraq since then, but it has not always been smooth.

A year after Chirac's visit, three Arabs fired bazookas at an Israeli airliner, missed, and instead took over Orly Airport for seventeen hours. After wounding twenty people and holding, then releasing ten hostages, they flew to Baghdad. In 1978, an Arab commando seized the Iraqi embassy. The terrorists surrendered. But just as French police were putting them into a van, Iraqi guards blazed away at the prisoners from the embassy windows, killing a French police inspector.

Also, the Iraqis wanted a nuclear reactor.

The nuclear dilemma has been hard on France. De Gaulle built his own bomb after the Americans withheld vital technology in the 1950s. Later, scientists perfected small reactors for generating electric power. France spent heavily on research and development; it ended up with a valuable export commodity. But no French leader was anxious to destabilize the world by selling a nuclear bomb.

It was a perfect situation for anyone seeking to build his own Cartesian bridge to a lucrative sale. Those in the atom business know that almost any exported nuclear technology can move a dedicated bomb-maker closer to his goal; the principal safeguard, goodwill, can be ephemeral. But American, Canadian, and other European salesmen work hard to export peaceful nuclear technology to solid citizens in developing nations. There is a Non-Proliferation Treaty and a regulating body. But in practice, everyone draws his own line on what is too much and who is too risky. As one French exporter told a colleague, if you build a steel plant, who is to say someone won't make guns with it?

French diplomats, privately, had no illusions about Iraq. Saddam was a hard man with a grim record, and he was geographically suited to thump his sworn Zionist enemy. He knew Israel had plutonium, using a research reactor the French built at Dimona. (Israel also smuggled enriched uranium from a plant in Pennsylvania with the knowledge of two U.S. presidents, *Rolling Stone* reported in 1977; France has no monopoly on operating close to the line.) The Israelis had demonstrated often enough that their own security took precedence over virtually everything else. Baghdad was not your ideal site for Islam's first Bomb.

France agreed to build a nuclear reactor under carefully negotiated terms, and Frenchmen would remain nearby to supervise its development. At one extreme, some specialists opposed any such risk and left their jobs. At the other, some willfully skirted government safeguards in the belief that science is science and business is business; someone else would fill any void the French left, anyway. More did their jobs with reservations, following policy. And a few leaked secret documents to two journalists, Steve Weissman and Herbert Krosney, writing a book called *The Islamic Bomb*.

My own research was less thorough than theirs, but I crossexamined Krosney, a friend whom I know to be careful and honest. Unless otherwise noted, *The Islamic Bomb* is my source on FrenchIraqi nuclear dealings.

In May 1981, the French were just finishing the Tammuz I reactor at the Nuclear Research Center outside Baghdad. Mitterrand, only days in office, had ordered an urgent, secret review of Giscard d'Estaing's safeguards. "Iraq had no legal obligation not to use the reactor to irradiate uranium," a French Foreign Ministry official told the authors later. "That was a loophole. We wanted to close it."

It was a touchy issue. French diplomats had worked to prevent danger, but some salesmen pushed for new contracts. By 1980, French imports from Iraq were 23.5 billion francs against exports, mainly arms, of 4.5 billion francs. Iraq was a secure source of 20 percent of France's oil. Frenchmen caught contravening official policy risked penalties. But matters of conscience—a different reading of Descartes—did not merit moral outrage.

By Friday, June 5, the report was lying on the foreign minister's desk, ready to be initialed and sent to the president. It was too late.

Early Sunday morning, on June 7, eight Israeli F-16s streaked toward Baghdad, each carrying two 2,000-pound MK-84 iron bombs. Six F-15s escorted them, ready to fight off any Jordanian or Iraqi planes they met on the way. The attack force flew tightly

bunched to look like a commercial airliner on radar screens. The first
bombs hit the lead and concrete reactor dome with delayed-action
fuses. They penetrated before blasting jagged holes. Seconds later,
another wave placed bombs precisely into the openings, destroying
the reactor. The Israelis chose a Sunday when Frenchmen would be
at home. But Damien Chaussepied, a twenty-five-year-old engineer,
was at work. He died under the rubble.

Had Prime Minister Menachem Begin known of Mitterrand's
report, he might have postponed the raid. Perhaps not. Some French
diplomats suspected that Begin did not consult Paris in order to
avoid a diplomatic entanglement. Yuval Ne'eman, an Israeli scientist
and political leader, told Weissman and Krosney, "Why should we
put our faith in [the French] even if they ask us to? Especially after
they have been so careless in this entire matter." And an Israeli
official, who insisted on anonymity, told the authors, "They're
whores. Anything goes in their nuclear industry. Everybody knows
it, even the Iraqis. That's why they went to the French to buy in
the first place."

Mitterrand reacted sharply, but he condemned the raid, not Israel.
He made it clear that the reactor would be replaced only with
adequate safeguards. By 1984, to expedite the agreement, Iraq agreed
to stringent conditions, including the use of low-grade uranium
known as "caramel" to fuel the reactor. But, conveniently, Iraq's
prolonged war with Iran allowed France to keep the issue in limbo.

In 1982, Mitterrand addressed the Knesset, the first French president to visit Israel. The Tammuz raid had delayed the trip once, and
the Israelis had annexed the Golan Heights. But he arrived in March
to declare himself a friend of Israel. Just to keep French credentials
clear, Foreign Minister Claude Cheysson said earlier in Iraq that
France supported a Palestinian state on the West Bank.

France darted among its mirrors but without much success. Le
Monde headlined a dispatch from Beirut: "The waffling of French
policy is seen by Arab leaders as a mixture of naïveté and duplicity."

MIDDLE EAST analysts are divided over what France really
got out of its Middle East oil policy. Iraq fell behind on payments,
and concessions were made. Forward commitments lost their allure
when world oil prices fell. The balance grew steadily more precari-

ous as Iraq continued its quagmire war with Iran. By late 1983, France began paying in blood.

At 5 A.M. on October 23, an explosion demolished the Drakkar building, barracks of France's contingent of the Multilateral Force in Lebanon. Fifty-eight French marines were killed. Back home, their countrymen watched horrified at newsfilm of marines struggling to free a man trapped under giant chunks of cement and steel. Only his hand protruded, and his friends squeezed it to comfort him, weeping in fury. A simultaneous blast at the U.S. barracks killed 241 U.S. marines.

Mitterrand flew to Beirut and climbed in a helicopter to visit survivors, grim in a bright orange life jacket.

French and U.S. officials blamed the attacks on pro-Iranian Shiite Moslem extremists. They planned a joint reprisal assault near Baalbek. Hours before, however, the Americans backed out. Washington was divided over the operation from the beginning. Then, when U.S. intelligence told the French the targeted terrorist camp had been hurriedly abandoned, France went ahead, anyway. Aircraft off the *Clémenceau* pounded an empty barracks and, because of a malfunction, also dropped bombs on a nearby mountainside. In Tehran, leaders of the revolution announced that thirty-four men were killed in air raids. But the successful attack was a separate operation by Israel. In France, there was some satisfaction of revenge. Among their allies and enemies, however, the French had appeared foolish, and the stakes of the conflict rose.

In Lebanon, the pro-Iranian Hezbollah party said Shiite sappers destroyed the French barracks because of continuing arms sales to Iraq. Hezbollah leaders warned more would follow.

The bombing and reprisal complicated yet further French relations with Syria. France has relied upon its dwindling capital of historic links with Syria in order to nudge Baathist leaders toward moderation. For Paris, Damascus represents yet another entry point to the Middle East. But, with alarming frequency, reality shattered the mirrors.

French ambassador Louis Delamare was assassinated in 1981 in the Syrian-controlled sector of Lebanon. French intelligence linked the killing directly to Syria, according to French reporters, and DGSE agents secretly bombed Baathist headquarters in Damascus, killing thirty-eight people. Later, Syria was held responsible—in internal reports—for the fatal bombing on rue Marbeuf in Paris. Some analysts saw Syria behind the Drakkar attack, as revenge for the Baathist headquarters explosion. But Mitterrand chose to keep talking with Syria, and President Hafez Assad was not taxed publicly for any of the actions.

And in late 1984, Mitterrand flew to Damascus, the first head of state in Syria since independence. The ceremony was moving, but Assad's message was brutal: your influence is nothing more than cultural; keep out of the way. Assad was after the old dream of a Greater Syria, and he had little need of France. He spoke directly to Washington and Moscow, the two capitals that directed heavy fire. Assad's French is excellent, but summits on *la francophonie* are not his style.

France kept up its diplomatic campaign in Syria, tailoring its Palestinian policy with Damascus firmly in mind. But in 1985, more mirrors were cracked. Islamic Jihad, linked to Hezbollah, kidnapped French diplomats Marcel Carton and Marcel Fontaine in Beirut, along with a thirty-eight-year-old French researcher, Michel Seurat. And then Jean-Paul Kauffmann, a respected magazine reporter, was added to the group. None would be released until France halted its aid to Iraq, their captors announced.

At the same time, Shiite snipers began picking off French officers and legionnaires of a lightly armed French observer force that was in Beirut at the request of Lebanese authorities.

France dispatched secret envoys to plead with Iranian leaders to find some face-preserving solution. Assad was also asked to help. Even if Syria might not be directly involved, French analysts reasoned, it could influence the captors in Lebanon. Before Christmas, hopes rose. The four Frenchmen were expected to be released along with American hostages from a TWA flight hijacked to Beirut. Details leaked out about a secret deal for France to contribute to Hezbollah and supply some arms to Iran. The arrangement, never made clear, collapsed. And then two months later, as French legislative elections approached, Islamic Jihad put the hostages at the center of the campaign.

The French sparked the crisis with a *bavure*—in the form of a quiet accord—that stunned public opinion. Two pro-Iran Iraqis were arrested in Paris and, screaming in protest, placed aboard a flight to Baghdad. Amnesty International released what it called an unconfirmed report that at least one of the men was executed in Iraq; some French papers reported that as fact.

In Paris, officials blamed the expulsion on a foul-up in communications between ministries. Law required a complex review before any expulsion except in urgent cases where a foreigner's presence endangered the security of the state. The law did not explain why a state that emphasizes its ability to defend its interests might be threatened by foreign prisoners. The procedure would be changed, but the damage was done.

Enraged, Islamic Jihad announced it had put to death Michel Seurat. The remaining three prisoners would be executed if France did not recover the Iraqis, alive. The captors also demanded that France free a five-man squad imprisoned for an attack on Shahpur Bakhtiar, former Iranian premier. And France would have to stop its support to Iraq.

Mitterrand persuaded Saddam Hussein to pardon the two men and let them fly back to France. Nothing was said on the other conditions. As the March 16 elections approached, Islamic Jihad played on frayed French nerves. An officer was shot to death in the courtyard of the French ambassador's residence in Beirut, the seventh observer force victim in a year. Photos were released to prove Seurat was dead. But they showed no wounds, leaving some doubt. And then a videotape followed: the hostages declared themselves to be innocent victims of French foreign policy.

The conservative daily, Le Figaro, editorialized: "It is all of France that has been murdered, humiliated, slapped, because its government, by its clumsiness, its timidity, its faults, its incapacity has allowed itself to be murdered, humiliated, slapped."

Seurat's Syrian-born wife, persuaded that she was a widow, electrified television viewers. "Hezbollah executed my husband, but he was murdered by [French Minister of the Interior] Pierre Joxe." She excoriated the government for insisting that it did not negotiate with terrorists while, in fact, it did. She said, for example, Paris had agreed not to pursue Abu Nidel's Palestinian fanatics if they did not operate in France. Eyes red and glittering with hostility, she concluded: "France is a doormat."

Fabius, however, was firm. "We will not cede to blackmail intended to divide our nation." Political ranks closed behind him. The hostages were not debated as an issue. French television showed bits of the videotape without the Islamic Jihad propaganda that narrated it. As expected, the conservatives won a legislative majority. But their majority was too slim to suggest that Islamic Jihad influenced the outcome.

Soon after elections, kidnappers seized a four-man television crew from the state-owned Antenne 2. Later, there was a ninth hostage: eighty-four-year-old Camille Sontag, a retired businessman about to return to France after forty-three years in Lebanon.

French arms continued to flow to Iraq. The decision was affirmed by the new prime minister, Jacques Chirac, who had forged the alliance with Baghdad a decade earlier. He would not have an easy time. Moments after Chirac was sworn in, a bomb shattered a shopping mall on the Champs-Elysées, killing two passersby and injuring another twenty-eight. It was only the latest in a series, set by Shiite fanatics protesting French Middle East policy.

Chirac pulled the French observer force out of Lebanon and pressed negotiations with Iran. Besides Iraq, there was a problem about a billion dollars paid out by the shah for a nuclear power project; Iran wanted it back. And there were the Iranian dissidents still operating from Paris.

In May, Ali Reza Moayeri, Iranian vice premier, emerged smiling from a meeting with Chirac. Discussions "were in a very friendly climate," he said, and he was delighted. Chirac added, "Iran is an old society, a civilization, a great culture. France is ready to normalize relations with that country."

Shortly thereafter, Massoud Rajavi, leader of the dissident People's Mujahedeen, left France. Officials said that was voluntary, but the pressure was thinly disguised. Abolhassan Bani Sadr, leader of a less virulent dissident faction, remarked, "The French attitude is not worthy of a democracy. At this rate, Iran will demand they dissolve the National Assembly. I condemn all regimes that use human beings as currency." But he stayed in France along with a range of anti-Khomeini Iranians.

French authorities said Rajavi abused his rules of asylum which forbid political activity. He went to Iraq from where Khomeini,

ironically enough, came to France to mount political activity that
overturned the Shah.

FRANCE HAS PAID heavily in the Middle East, but who
hasn't? The Americans left Beirut first, with far greater losses. Paris
cannot write economic plans, or change presidents, as it can in
Africa. Its good offices cannot resolve conflict. But whose can?
President Jimmy Carter's Camp David accords were a mixed blessing for the Middle East, relieving some pressures while increasing
others. For the French, power is based on the assumption of a
powerful stance: conviction and flair.

Before and after Mitterrand's meeting with Assad, Israeli prime
minister Shimon Peres and King Hussein each have come to Paris
to work on their relations.

France, as a cultural power, enjoys advantages denied to military
powers. It can maintain a balance resting on illusion. In the Middle
East, especially, it need only declare friendship; no one expects
proof. France, Mitterrand maintains, is the only power that can talk
to the Arabs and the Israelis with equal objectivity.

Against the fortunes of a chaotic world, Mitterrand explained to
American viewers on "Face the Nation," France would fulfill any
role it agreed to fulfill. Any retreat would, at the very least, be
orderly. In the meantime, France acts the part. When the Multinational Force arrived to supervise evacuation of the Palestine Liberation Organization, the first troops ashore were the French Foreign
Legion. Their colonel strode up to the Israeli officer there to greet
them. "Shove off," he told the Israeli. "We don't need you to show
us how to occupy a position."

Above all, France insists on its independence of action. Politically, it represents some form of middle ground. Few Arab leaders
trust the Soviet Union, however valuable treaties of friendship
might prove. The United States is too big to act as an honest broker.
Britain, in a general way, is seen as being too close to the Americans.

"France can contribute to keeping the Middle East from being
delivered to the superpowers," King Hussein remarked in 1985, a
theme he repeats often. "We expect France to continue defending
the positions she has taken up to now."

Payment is not always in full or on time, but honest brokering can be lucrative in the Middle East. If Iraq can't shop in Moscow and won't shop in London, there is Paris. Saudi princes may prefer Annabel's to Régine's, but Dom Pérignon goes down better than Guinness stout. If some arms deal is too delicate for anyone else to touch, there is always a chance a Starboat Company might find a way to handle it.

And none of that stops Shimon Peres from exulting in Paris about the "closeness of the very special Franco-Israeli relations." On his second trip to France in ten months, he said that if the Soviet Union allowed thousands of Jews to emigrate to Israel, as hoped, France would supply the aircraft. Laurent Fabius spoke of Israel, in ringing terms, not only as an ally but as a friend.

Up to a point, of course. The French were not pleased when Defense Minister Yitzhak Rabin called their soldiers "carrion." Or "bastards" or "manure," according to French dispatches. The word he used was *neveloth,* a biblical term for the slaughter of animals without proper purification. Whatever the translation, the Quai d'Orsay summoned Israel's ambassador to call it "rude, undignified and unjustified." To add to the injury, Rabin was referring to the 1,350-man French detachment to the U.N. forces in Lebanon (UNIFIL). In 1982, Israeli armored columns rolled over French (and other) positions en route to invade Lebanon, so infuriating one officer that he leaped on a tank and brandished his pistol.

When Israeli aircraft battered PLO offices in Tunisia in a reprisal raid during 1985, Mitterrand and the government objected in clear terms. Chirac, Gaullist mayor of Paris and presumed presidential candidate, sent his own telegram, condemning "a murderous military operation . . . an unqualifiable act." Not only were civilians killed in the raid, but also Tunisian civilians. Tunisia is in the family.

The magazine *France Pays Arabes,* published by the Franco-Arab Solidarity Association, carried all messages in full. In the same issue, it profiled Mohamed Sadiq el Mashat, Iraq's ambassador in France. He regretted that Britain and West Germany showed such little friendship when war broke out with Iran in 1980. Relations were very good with the Soviet Union and just warming with the United States. But, he concluded, "Our cooperation with France grows each year in all aspects; we are establishing *relations privilégiées.*"

French connections reach farther into the Gulf. Qatar, reared by the English, has 6,000 British residents and 500 French, but it is mysteriously Francophile. Paris built a large new embassy, with an active commercial section.

And there are the arms. France is the second largest supplier of arms to the Middle East, after the United States. In 1984, Saudi Arabia bought Crotale missiles and an antiaircraft system worth $3.4 billion. The United Arab Emirates ordered eighteen Mirage 2000s, for $530 million. The French also sold manufacturing technology. Egypt exports its own Mirage 2000s and Gazelle helicopters. Brazil is muscling into traditional French markets—Iraq, for example— with weapons of its own.

In the early 1980s, more than three-quarters of French arms sales went to the Middle East. Since 1984, French export strategists have worked hard to sell more weapons in their neighborhood. Atlantic Alliance armies tend to pay on time and stick more closely to agreements. And, unlike many Middle East states, they know who their potential enemy is.

FRENCH ENGINEERING salesmen are also reconsidering their enthusiasm for *gros coups* in Middle Eastern markets. In mid-1985, *Libération* sent a reporter to spend twenty-four hours with French companies building the Cairo subway. Société Générale d'Entreprise, a subsidiary of Saint-Gobain, and nineteen French and Egyptian companies won the contract for more than one billion francs in 1981. The French government financed the project at 3 percent annual interest, with a grace period of five years before payment was due.

The main line from Tahrir Square is charted along the eastern side of the Nile, on land settled within the last century. But local authorities, fearing archeological disaster, have commanded so many route changes and detours that engineers must use a computer to keep track of them. The project was running two years late and was projected to cost three times as much, the paper reported. The planned ten miles of diverted cables and canals reached sixty miles and was still growing.

Internal wars of authority blocked work, tied up equipment, and cost fortunes in fines and bribes, according to *Libération*. One example: For months engineers sought a way to avoid a thick tube of vital cables from the telephone exchange. Someone cut the tube by accident and found it empty.

"German, American or Japanese competitors point to the project —highly unjustly, by the way, but that is good old commercial war —to grab at our expense the rare metro contract now under negotiation, in Caracas, Algiers, Shanghai or Montreal," the paper said. To the point, it said, that one of the French company presidents called a news conference to criticize the project's management. "In brief," it said, "here are our Frenchmen on trial against themselves."

OVERALL, FRENCH POLICY is to keep talking and, if necessary, absorb the losses. The Gaullist view looks at history, not headlines. There are, of course, detractors. After the Beirut carnage, among a dozen pages of color photos in *Paris-Match,* Marc Ullman questioned whether "maintaining dialogue" should replace determining blame. He recalled that France took no action against Syrian terrorism and "safeguarded a special relationship" with Iran despite its taking of U.S. hostages. In the Middle East, he noted, the stronger party is considered right.

In the end, beyond the politics and the profits, there are the words. France knows their value. A lot fewer people speak French in the Middle East than the Alliance Française might think, but the total is no small number. On arriving in Beirut for the first time, I remarked on the perfect French of the office helper who had come to meet me. He was a little wounded. "But," he said, "do you think we are not civilized?"

CHAPTER SIXTEEN

Asia and the Pacific:
Kanaky and La Bombe

FRANCE NEEDS NO mirrors or high wires in the South
Seas. It reaches island backwaters even the *Bounty* mutineers would
not have wanted. From New Caledonia, 800 miles east of Australia,
to the last flecks of Polynesia, approaching South America, there are
two Pacifics: French and the rest. In bare feet or Guccis, the French
live well, with social security, Gilbert Bécaud and all the refine-
ments civilization has to offer. Lately, however, attention has settled
on one word in particular: *la Bombe.*

Atmospheric nuclear tests were shifted from Algeria to French
Polynesia in 1966. Neighbors complained, and testing was taken
underground in 1975. From then until mid-1986, eighty-one devices
were exploded. French scientists report no noticeable effects beyond
a slight heave of the earth at detonation. But the fourteen-member
Pacific Forum, from Australia to Nauru, complains bitterly.

For France, it is a simple case of *j'y suis, j'y reste.* National security
is at stake. If France can stare down a Soviet premier, it will not
bend to a king of Tonga. And the French like their Pacific role.
Even in an age of supersonic Concordes, it takes cabinet ministers
two days to get from Paris to Papeete; they fly over a lot of far-flung
islands on which to stick a flag.

But even the French find it hard to ignore the furor over *la
Bombe,* especially when it is aggravated by yet another word:
Kanaky. That is what Melanesians want to call New Caledonia if
they can wrest it away from France.

Kanaks are ethnic Melanesians; even the spelling of the word is charged with emotion. People who favor the status quo prefer Canaque. Kanak connotes a tilt toward independence. Most Melanesians use the *K,* and so will I, without taking sides.

The island had fallen on hard times when I first arrived in 1972. World nickel prices were down, and prices of everything else were rising fast. An executive of Société le Nickel told me about it at lunch. With the white Burgundy and *fruits de mer,* I heard about local wages getting out of hand. The cost of staples—silk ties and cheeses—was raised over the red Bordeaux and *côte de boeuf marchand de vin.* By the time we finished the *mousse au chocolat,* coffee, brandy, and Cuban cigars, I was all but reduced to tears. The man might have to sell his second cabin cruiser.

The Kanaks were divided. Many were bitter that *Caldoches,* the local version of *pieds-noirs,* had settled on their best land and bulldozed their traditions. Nationalist leaders considered themselves to be under colonial rule, with all its nameless and intangible humiliations. But others, no small number, saw themselves as French. At Le Nickel, Melanesian employees got an annual home-leave ticket to the *métropole,* just like the *z'oreilles.*

The *Caldoches* regarded themselves at home on *le Caillou,* the Pebble, where many traced their roots back three generations. Many have Melanesian blood from the prison colony days when Frenchwomen were few.

After 1981, Socialist authorities in Paris nudged the island toward autonomy. Nickel earnings were down, and subsidies from Paris approached a billion francs a year. A friendly split, before things got nasty, would allow close postindependence ties with France: military base agreements, mutual trade advantages, and protection for French citizens wishing to stay. The risk was small. If relations soured, there was always Wallis and Futuna nearby to complete the global strategic chain. The Socialists scheduled a referendum on self-determination for 1989.

But it was not that easy. People imported over the years had left patchwork demographics. By 1984, of the island's 145,368 inhabitants, only 61,870 were Melanesians, or 42.56 percent. There were 53,974 whites, 37.12 percent. Another 12,175 Wallisians and Futunans, and 5,570 Tahitians, mostly wanted jobs and peace under the

Tricolor. So did the 5,319 Indonesians, 5,249 Vietnamese and others, and 1,212 Vanuatuans.

Many Kanaks demanded that France stay. Others, knowing what had happened to the *harkis* after Algeria, held their peace but planned to vote to remain French.

In Territorial Assembly elections in July 1979, 40.23 percent of the vote went to the RPCR (Rassemblement pour la Calédonie dans la République), an affiliate of the Gaullist RPR. The Front Indépendantiste won 34.42 percent. A third party, with 18 percent, aligned itself with the RPCR. In 1982, prodded by the Socialists, the swing party shifted its support, and *indépendantistes* dominated the legislature.

By January 1983, hard-liners began pushing for faster change. Two gendarmes were killed in political violence. In 1984, the Socialist Kanak National Liberation Front (FLNKS) ordered an "active boycott" of the November 18 elections. Seventeen of its leaders flew off to Libya for a crash course in troublemaking. Graffiti warned of trouble: "Immigrants into the sea!" "Qaddafi!"

The RPCR won 70.87 percent of the vote. Dick Ukeiwé, a Kanak RPCR senator and leader of an absolute Assembly majority, declared victory. So did Jean-Marie Tjibaou, a burly former priest who headed FLNKS.

Only half the registered voters turned out. In one town, someone scrawled on a wall: "I will secretly kill any Kanak who goes to the polls." FLNKS teams firebombed voting booths and hijacked ballot boxes. Incidents were reported at one of every two polling places.

But a legislature was elected. *Le Monde* announced, *"Le Pire Evité."* The Worst Avoided. Not exactly.

The next day, the Kanaks resumed their old war with France. Militants stormed the gendarmerie at Thio, in the north, and seized guns. FLNKS militants besieged police in their barracks and *Caldoches* on their farms. They seized another village and mounted roadblocks elsewhere on the island. FLNKS avoided serious violence; it was testing its strength. The government elected to waffle.

Libération interviewed the subprefect of the Loyalty Islands, a hostage in his own office at Wé, Ukeiwé's hometown. The account was unsettling. *FLNKS vaincra*—FLNKS will win—was scrawled in black on the white prefecture door. The subprefect inside, Jean-Jacques Demar, was black, a French civil servant from Martinique, held powerless along with his white French assistant. They each went home at night guarded by young militants who favored Bob Marley T-shirts and red headscarves.

"I'm all right," said Demar. Mainly, he was bored. "I'd like to have V. S. Naipaul's *Crocodiles of Yamoussoukro* to read."

For six days, the prefecture Tricolor was not the familiar blue, white, red but rather the FLNKS' blue, red, green, with a yellow sun and a stylized totem pole.

The occupation of Thio dragged on, and Paris was getting edgy. Puma helicopters with reinforcements were met with shotgun fire. Police landed and squared off against Kanaks, weapons drawn. But then they lowered their guns and went to await developments with the local gendarme hostages.

Caldoches began oiling their shotguns, furious at official hesitation. They cleared some roadblocks and mounted their own. The mood grew uglier. And then blood started to flow.

First accounts were muddled. "They killed Eugène Guérin and cut up his wife." Newspapers reported the death, but police found Guérin alive, just badly beaten. Within twenty-four hours, however, a crowd of fifty Kanaks approached Emile Mazière's farm on the Col de Crève-Coeur. In a gunfight of confused origins, he was shot in the back, and he died in the ambulance. Six Kanaks were wounded.

Le Figaro, staunchly right wing, carried an enormous headline: "The Rifle Not the Suitcase." Every French person over thirty-five got the message. Here was the agonizing dilemma of Algeria, *le fusil ou la valise.* The paper pictured half-naked militants with wild hair at Thio, lounging against a military helicopter sprayed with graffiti like a New York subway car. Another photo showed a despondent old man named Rouillard, looking like Albert Schweitzer in a straw hat and white moustache, sitting at Kone airstrip with his wife, his dazed little terrier on a leash, and a pathetically small pile of belongings.

Thierry Desjardins, veteran *Figaro* correspondent not noted for affection toward *indépendantistes,* described an angry meeting of settlers forming a militia. They all knew Mazière, whose grandfather had pioneered the farm. He quoted one: "Tonight, I may kill a Canaque pal with whom I've lived forty-five years on this corner of the earth. Or maybe he will kill me."

A commentary entitled "The Old Dream of Decolonization" noted that de Gaulle got credit for giving away Africa and Algeria; the Socialists at least wanted to turn loose the few crumbs left. And an editorial concluded:

> The specter of a colonial war haunts the spirits of the left, although it amounts to reducing to impotence a handful of *excités* —a few hundred at first, then a few thousand—who abusively pretend to represent the Canaque people and who would have doubtlessly been brought to reason by gendarmes if these had not been condemned to kill time in playing *belote* [a card game].

But it was more than *Figaro*. Each night, the television brought angry and anguished scenes to French who were still trying to locate the island in their atlases. The opposition condemned what some called spineless and humiliating laxness. Newspapers picked up the theme. In Milan, *Corriere della Sera* evoked "Mitterrand's Algeria."

On December 1, Nouméa slammed down its iron shutters and declared itself "a dead city" to mourn the first victims. But thirteen remote farmhouses were burned, and many feared worse would come. Authorities held back. They argued that a few thousand gendarmes more would make little difference, and a harsh response would unleash massive retaliation. A special envoy flew out from Paris to make a report.

Paris suspected a Third World/Anglo-Saxon plot. The Quai d'Orsay had already protested after the Australian foreign minister denounced "one of the last vestiges of colonialism in the South Pacific." Reporting on the elections, *Le Monde* declared that the Kanaks were "encouraged in their separatism by the young independent states in the Pacific and by Australia which dreams of imposing its influence."

Thio remained two-thirds deserted, and Kanaks turned back a convoy with food and medicine. *Figaro* found the Douyéres, a couple in their eighties, poor and sick, held prisoner, robbed, and told they would be shot if they did not leave their land within fifteen days. They had spent fifty years in the simple wood farm-house they built themselves. "FLNKS is making it plain that no one, even among the poorest, is safe . . . from revolutionary law," the paper said.

Tjibaou set up a provisional government but told reporters, "We don't have the means to make war. It is not serious, it is a joke to talk of war against France." The roadblocks, he said, were "to protect our militants in the face of colonists who are very well armed." Not all his lieutenants agreed. Attacks continued on isolated farms. *Caldoches,* agitated, eyes red from sleepless nights, shot back.

Giscard d'Estaing, Raymond Barre, and five Gaullist former prime ministers issued a joint statement condemning Mitterrand for failing to deal with "an insurrectional situation" and debasing French credibility.

Mitterrand sent Edgard Pisani, a former minister and confidant of de Gaulle, to pick up the pieces. Pisani promised to restore order and consult all sides. Hours after his first televised speech, two more Kanaks were killed, bringing the death toll to at least five; a second *Caldoche* had been shot dead. Three police had been wounded, as well as six civilians, two beaten and left for dead.

And then, the next morning, news came of the massacre at Hienghene. A planter named Maurice Matride and his neighbors, fed up, laid a coconut tree across a road and stopped two pickups of Kanaks driving home from a nighttime meeting. They blinded the victims with a searchlight and opened fire. Ten were killed, including two of Tjibaou's brothers; a third brother was badly wounded. At first, police said the Kanaks were killed on their way to burn Matride's house. But Matride told gendarmes he had planned it: "We were harassed, threatened, and our nerves cracked."

The killers were *métis,* descendants of settlers who had married Kanaks. But in the racial structure of New Caledonia, they were considered Europeans. That was just one more complexity to baffle the French watching in alarm 12,000 miles away.

Raoul Lapetite and his six sons were among the confessed killers. *Libération* dug up the diary of F. Lapetite, his grandfather, who arrived with a wife and eleven children in March 1899, unable to make a living in France. In Nouméa, he wrote, they found lodging by "dispossessing tribes of spiders. (Our mission is doubtless to dispossess tribes.)" He was given farmland at Hienghene taken from Kanaks. The Kanaks built his home and asked for food. "Poor people, they were the ones who planted all this," he wrote. "We are beginning to get used to these savages who are like children." Lapetite lamented the Kanaks' heavy drinking and indolence. "As for civilization, the Kanaks have taken our vices, and that is all."

After the massacre, the mood darkened. More settlers fled the bush; others bought more bullets. As Kanaks mourned in Hienghene, 5,000 people gathered on a palm-fringed parking lot by the sea at Nouméa. Men in shorts with sunburned knees, women in summer dresses, Vietnamese, Tahitians, bellowed their support for a French Caledonia. They sang the "Marseillaise," adding volume to the part that goes, *"aux armes, citoyens."*

The Melanesians were split. At one rally, a hefty Kanak woman screamed at television cameras, "We are here to show everybody that we want to be French, under no matter who, all ethnic groups together." In the grainy monochrome newsreels from Algeria, Europeans and Moslems had melded together in the crowds. This time, in crystal-clear color, black and white hands rose together in a swirl of blue, white, and red.

Parallels with Algeria were hard to resist, despite the smaller scale and far greater distance from France. Like Algiers, Nouméa tried to live its normal life while rebellion crackled in the *bled.* French wives and Australian stewardesses tanned bare breasts by turquoise water. Kids revved their Hondas and ate elaborate ice cream *coupes* in noisy downtown cafés. The Brie and Brouilly came in as usual on the UTA run from Paris. But, fired by the odd bomb or phone calls from the bush, Nouméa, like Algiers, began to smoulder.

There were none of Massu's *paras,* but along with Pisani, Paris sent units of the hard-minded GIGN elite police. Transports ferried heavy equipment from Tahiti and France; order was to be reestablished.

When Algeria broke, however, the minister in charge had been François Mitterrand. This time Mitterrand was president, and he was not about to let history repeat itself.

When Giscard d'Estaing argued that New Caledonia be made a department, Fabius delivered his own version of the Maspétiol report. Of the 972 top-ranked civil servants, Fabius noted, six were

Melanesian; 900 European families owned more land than all the Kanaks combined. Melanesians had not been given the vote until 1956. The territory had to be offered self-determination. "You say self-determination," Giscard d'Estaing countered, "but the echo comes back independence."

Pisani freed seventeen Kanaks arrested for disrupting the November elections. Despite his brothers' deaths, Tjibaou lifted the roadblocks to await a political settlement. His minister of security, Eloi Machoro, held out at Thio, but later converted his barriers to checkpoints. But Tjibaou insisted to reporters: "Peace and security in Caledonia are called Kanak independence." In three months of existence, FLNKS had become the main arbiter of Kanak aspirations; its strategy was to keep up the pressure until France pulled out.

But a power struggle loomed within FLNKS. Machoro, who swaggered before the cameras in a fatigue cap and bare chest, predicted violence. Most French first saw him in a photo on November 18, demolishing a ballot box with an axe. FLNKS might send more militants to Libya or Cuba, he said, and establish relations with the Soviet Union and Vietnam, mainly, he told reporters, to piss off France.

On January 7, Pisani revealed his plan: a referendum in six months to ask 75,000 voters—Kanaks and anyone with more than three years' residence—what they thought of independence. If they voted yes, France would withdraw on January 1, 1986, but a treaty would cover military bases, aid, French rights, and internal security. Paris would stay in spirit, supported by more tangible evidence of friendship. He urged a yes vote for both France and independence. No one was happy. Tjibaou said a vote was beside the point: "We are the rightful owners of the country." Ukeiwé said, "We are French and we want to stay French. We cannot discuss independence."

In Tahiti, Gaston Flosse, political head of the French Polynesian Government Council, objected that "independence would be a catastrophe" for both New Caledonia and Polynesia.

Four days later, blood flowed again. A *Caldoche* farmer named Tual left his lunch table to find out why his dogs were barking. He took along his seventeen-year-old son, Yves, to investigate. Tual heard a noise and fired into the bushes. The bushes shot back, killing the boy.

Nouméa erupted. Crowds gathered at the iron gates of the High Commissioner's office, chanting, *"Pisani Assassin!"* *Caldoches* set alight the nearby home of Jean Guiart, an ethnologist who had spent forty years in New Caledonia and was widely believed to have inspired the FLNKS' radical tactics. The building was the island's oldest structure, an officers' mess built in 1854. Rioters hijacked the fire truck and turned hoses on gendarmes in battle gear who watched, immobile.

When crowds marched on the government headquarters, police charged. Gendarmes pumped 137 tear gas canisters and swung truncheons all night long to quell rioters. Sirens screamed. Dentists and shopkeepers shouted that they were ready to die for a French Caledonia. The elegant little tropical capital choked in smoke. Angry men ripped out parking meters and heaved paving stones at police. One youth shouted, "They're firing on us because we want to be French."

Later, Guiart shook his head. "I don't understand how they could have let this happen," he told *l'Agence France-Presse.* "These people try to destabilize the territory. It is not the Melanesians, who only respond to provocations of the over-armed right."

While Nouméa rioted, police combed tribal areas near Tual's farm at Bouloupari, sixty miles away, kicking open doors and interrogating Kanaks. Patrols moved north toward La Foa, Machoro's stronghold. *Libération* interviewed Victor Moindou, a FLNKS hard-liner, who said, "It had to happen. Tual occupied land stolen from the tribe, and he knew it. We've had ten dead, and there will be dead on their side." Tjibaou's moderation was his affair, Moindou said. FLNKS would decide its policy at a congress the next day.

But at dawn, the GIGN cornered Machoro, Marcel Nonnaro, and thirty-seven of their men on a ranch near Thio. What happened then is confused. Police first attributed all deaths to a heavy exchange of fire. Then officers said that Machoro would not surrender, and a sharpshooter with a precision scope had tried to drop him with a shoulder shot. FLNKS insisted that Machoro was coming out, his rifle trailing at his side. But the result was clear. A bullet had struck him full in the sternum, and he died shortly afterward.

Rumors reached Nouméa almost immediately, and new crowds formed outside the High Commissioner's office near the place des Cocotiers. At 10 A.M., the news was confirmed over a loudspeaker. Some roared approval, their fists thrust into the air; some did little dances of joy. Satellites relayed the scene to French television sets that evening. It might have been a film clip from the Forum in Algiers.

Tjibaou called it murder and accused Pisani of complicity. Gendarmes reenacted the episode for reporters to show how the tall grass had limited their options. But *Paris-Match* quoted an unnamed ranking officer: "Let's remove sentiment and be frank. We had to 'neutralize' him before the media made him a star . . . he wanted his war and he got it." Just eliminating Machoro would be suspect, he said, but in a large operation . . . "You know what I mean?"

In *Des Affaires Très Spéciales,* journalists Jacques-Marie Bourget and Yvan Stéfanovitch assert that Machoro was shot dead by a sharpshooter "on loan" to the gendarmes from a specialized paratroop unit, using a deadly 5.56 caliber cartridge. The paratrooper's presence was kept secret. The authors say that officials wanted Machoro dead, but they wanted the gendarmes to think the death was an accident.

Pisani declared a state of emergency and ordered a 7 P.M. curfew. FLNKS said that the "barbarous act" brought the situation back to zero and demanded "the pure and simple restoration of Kanak people's sovereignty over their country." That overworked formulation, "tense calm," was never more apt. The *paras* were called in to protect docks and airfields. Altogether, there were 6,000 police and troops on the island, one for every twenty-four civilians.

Mitterrand himself came out a week later, flying for fifty hours only to spend twelve hours on the ground. Pisani kept him indoors for security. But outside, a crowd of 35,000 people, some with their faces painted in blue, white, and red, clamored for the right to keep their flag. Mitterrand ordered negotiations but also announced that the island's military installations would be expanded.

He promised that Le Nickel would soon reopen its Thio mine.

Within days, seven giant ore trucks were burned, along with commercial fishing boats, apparently by *Caldoche* extremists. Kanaks accused them of trying to sabotage employment. But FLNKS hardliners destroyed 90 percent of the vehicles at Kouaoua, paralyzing the only nickel mine still in operation.

Tjibaou and Ukeiwé each went to Paris to lobby. So did François Neorere, local leader of Le Pen's *Front National,* who showed up in a blue, white, and red vest and said, "Sixty years of France in my heart, believe me, that leaves traces. My education with the Marist brothers gave me a love for French culture, for France, civilizing and generous."

Tjibaou said that he was a man of peace, representing peaceful people, but that "France is the *patrie* of the French; it is not the *patrie* of the Kanaks." On the way home, he stopped in Algeria to denounce French colonialism.

For the next months, Pisani kept on talking. But he insisted, "Change is unavoidable and irreversible." In April, Fabius altered the plan. The referendum was put off until after the March 1986 legislative elections. Voting would be held no later than December 31, 1987. Meanwhile, the island would elect four separate regional assemblies. Nouméa was expected to vote European; the rest, Kanak.

Tjibaou said the plan at least would allow the *indépendantistes* to prepare a more effective takeover later. With its militant wing crippled, FLNKS had little choice. Ukeiwé dismissed the plan as racist, but he had no choice, either.

Then FLNKS decided to take over education. "The school problem is tied to the colonial problem," said Yeiwene Yeiwene. "We have enough texts that talk of trains and snow and our ancestors the Gauls." Also, he said, Kanak children were not safe at school.

Sporadic clashes kept tension high. A Melanesian hacked to death Roland Lecomte on March 9, the twentieth death since November. Melanesians rose against police raids into villages. On April 8, a white teacher, Simone Heurteaux, was hit by a rock and killed as she drove along a mountain road. Nearly 3,000 teachers marched in the capital, demanding protection. Journalists had to rescue the resident correspondent of the *Melbourne Age,* whom *Caldoche* fanatics accused of leaning toward the *indépendantistes.* "Let her go get raped at Thio," shouted one.

On May 8, 200 Melanesians defied a ban on public gatherings and marched into downtown Nouméa. *"France dehors!"* a leader bellowed into a megaphone. Quickly, a crowd of 150 *Caldoches* formed around RCPR leader Jacques Lafleur. The two groups met head on, threw rocks, and fell into a pitched battle. Célestin Zongo, a nineteen-year-old Kanak, was shot dead; ninety-five people were injured, including thirty-eight policemen. Four days later, someone tossed a bomb into the only school on the island that trained Melanesians for a senior certificate. Seven people were hurt. Moments earlier, forty Melanesian children had passed by the spot.

Defense Minister Charles Hernu arrived on May 10 on a nuclear-powered submarine, only hours after France set off its biggest test ever of *la bombe* at Mururoa. He said he wanted "to show the world we are here." He also discussed plans to spend 300 million francs on military bases at Nouméa to increase troop strength by 50 percent to 4,500.

A Paris court convicted Tjibaou of threatening French territorial integrity; Ukeiwé brought the charge. He was given a year's suspended sentence. It was appealed.

In June, Pisani moved to Paris as minister for New Caledonia. Paris papers nicknamed his job Mission Impossible. Fernand Wibaux, the new high commissioner, told Kanaks, "Our objective is to prepare New Caledonia for the accession to independence. Independence is a right, I understand, and the Kanaks have a right to a legitimate existence. What I seek is the way to bring this about."

French authorities reformed land tenure; Kanaks were given back land which they could lease to *Caldoche* farmers. The *Caldoches* responded by twice burning down the land records office.

FLNKS put up new barricades at Thio to protest police methods; *Caldoches* bulldozed them. Both sides met to talk but ended up shouting insults. Incidents peppered the papers. Kanaks stoned the car of a twenty-two-year-old white public works employee; he fired at random and wounded an eight-year-old girl.

In Paris, opposition leaders lost a legal battle to block the elections, which were scheduled for September 29.

Le Pen landed on the island just in time for the September 24 anniversary of its occupation by France. He brought Algeria with him. Before an enormous crowd, he jabbed the air with his finger and bellowed, "In the streets of Algiers, on January 26, the same demonstration under the *drapeau tricolore* clashed with the machine guns of troops who fired for minutes. I hear it now, 'Hold your fire, lieutenant. Hold your fire.' Five minutes later, there were 100 bodies in the street. . . ." Then, slamming the podium with an open palm, he yelled: "And these people now don't have the right. . . ."

But Le Pen agreed to give way to Jacques Chirac, the opposition's main gun, to avoid splitting the pro-French vote. Chirac visited an RPCR Kanak stronghold, bringing as a gift a video recorder and films, including one called *The Moment to Kill.* His big moment was before a roiling, heaving, chanting crowd in Nouméa, at the place des Cocotiers.

Chirac shifted from somber to raucous to thundering. New Caledonia belonged to France, and he would block Socialist efforts to give it away. "By the preconceived engagement to move at any cost toward independence, spurning the most evident realities, the Socialists have a heavy responsibility before history, and they will have to face that." Building to a pitch, he belted out his conclusion over a sea of waving Tricolors and banners:

"When a people is on its feet, as you are; when a people resists, as you have done, its destiny faces no doubt. Tonight, I tell you . . . you can be confident. You are innumerable. You are strong and determined. You are France."

No one needed a translation: *Je vous ai compris.*

Voting went smoothly. The *indépendantistes* won majorities in three of the four regions, as expected. Eighty percent of all Kanaks showed they wanted independence. FLNKS-dominated regions controlled the mines and richest land. But anti-independence candidates got far more votes, 61.21 percent to their adversaries' 34.82 percent. They won a twelve-seat edge in the forty-six-seat Territory Congress elected as well as in the regional assemblies.

And each side dug in to wait for a new French National Assembly. A right-wing majority in Paris could reverse the Socialists' plans and forestall independence. But Tjibaou counted on his own new strength to make that impossible. He sought to prove that his people could govern responsibly and control their extremists. He banned alcohol for his leaders until independence; it was time to work, he said. Meantime, opposing forces would have to talk.

The situation was more tense than calm. White farmers, finding horses murdered and corn fields burned, took their revenge as they could. French gendarmes dotted the roads trying to keep order. A *Libération* reporter interviewed one at a checkpoint: "We can't watch everything; we don't stop the buses, it takes too long to check everyone. And we come from France and don't know the faces. Besides, even if we stop them . . . *bon, allez,* I've said enough. Move along."

Soon after Chirac's government took power, Thierry Desjardins was back. "The Tricolor Floats Over the FLNKS Stronghold," a *Figaro* headline screamed. Bernard Pons, the new conservative DOM-TOM minister, flew out to New Caledonia in April. In a forty-five-minute speech, he mentioned neither Kanaks nor Melanesians but railed against a "minority" that sought to impose its will. FLNKS called it a provocation; he replied, "You can't satisfy everyone."

Pisani's plan for independence-association was scrapped. Instead, Pons proposed a referendum on self-determination in 1987, with Kanaks and Caldoches voting. He undercut the four assemblies, giving budgetary power to a viceroy from Paris. And he reversed Kanak land tenure measures "so limited space could be put to best use." His goal was economic development, not institutional change. France would bring in about $55 million to prime the pump.

FLNKS militants loosened their ties to Libya. The spasm of violence had passed, but tension remained. Tjibaou worried over a French military build-up; he smelled Algeria. The Pons plan, he said, "only confirms what the Algerians have told me: 'Never trust the French, they are all liars.' "

He added: "To speak of marines and paratroopers, that is the permanent colonial mentality. France would always be the apostle of Good bringing light to the savages. Perhaps people will only move from this thinking when there are deaths, like in Algeria. It is a shame."

POLYNESIA watched New Caledonia closely. But a domino would have to fall hard to make waves 3,600 miles away in Tahiti. The societies and situations are different. There is ferment on Tahiti, the urban center of paradise. Seventeen separatists were arrested in late 1985 for skirmishing with police and burning a building. Independence-minded parties poll up to 15 percent in some elections. In 1986, Oscar Temanu's Tavini Huiraatira No Porinetia won two territorial legislature seats, the first for an independence party in twenty-eight years.

But Polynesians mostly shrug at the idea of driving out France. *Indépendantistes* are scattered among 166,800 inhabitants spread on 130 islands over 1.5 million square miles, an area larger than Western Europe. The islands' main resources are France itself and the CEP, the Centre d'Expérimentations du Pacifique. Paris spends fifty million dollars a year subsidizing the territory.

In places, Polynesia still qualifies as paradise. One morning I stood among the hibiscus in a Mooréa cove and watched an old four-master under full sail appear from the mists and tack in toward me over the reefs. It was Captain Bligh, back for more breadfruit. Actually, it was the Spanish navy on a training sail. But only a calendar could have identified the century.

But along with the lush splendor that captured Gauguin are beaches closed by pollution, parking meters, Big Burgers, video arcades and smog, club sandwiches and Club Meds. And on the palm-fanned atoll of Mururoa, paradise is lost completely.

MURUROA MEANS "place of the big secret." It houses 3,000 French specialists and legionnaires, all men but for a score of women. A plant desalts drinking water; just in case, the navy brings in 1,500 gallons of mineral water a day. Testing is done in holes bored underwater, down to 1,200 meters, in the basalt of a dead volcano. No one is ever blown up watching them, French officials like to say. But that is not the problem.

Visiting teams of scientists from New Zealand, Australia, and New Guinea found that humans were exposed to less radiation in Mururoa than in Paris. But they could not assure themselves about the eventual risk of leaks. They had to depend on French statistics, largely controlled by the military, to measure medical effects. Some areas were banned to them, and they were not allowed to witness an actual test.

A Greenpeace briefing paper noted that a bomb exploded in 1979 halfway down an 800-meter shaft, causing a local tidal wave. "Some observers" believe radioactive tritium contaminated the sea, Greenpeace said. In 1981, the *Guardian* quoted "authoritative reports" that radioactive material had been leaking for years through a crack fifteen to nineteen inches wide and a half-mile long. A storm in 1981 dispersed some plutonium into the lagoon, according to Greenpeace. And, the paper adds, scientists worry that each new blast weakens the basalt formations, increasing chances for some future catastrophe.

French specialists deny that any danger exists and discount the possibility of any leak before at least 500 years. Their safety record is impeccable, they argue.

Not everyone agrees. In 1961, the minister of overseas territories, Louis Tacquinet, promised that "no nuclear tests will ever be made by France in the Pacific Ocean." By 1963, the Foreign Legion began occupying the atoll. The Commissariat à l'Energie Atomique assured that "not a single particle of radioactive fallout will ever reach an inhabited island." Scientists promised that tests would take place only when the winds were blowing the other way. De Gaulle went to see the first atmospheric test in May 1966. He was late arriving, and the winds had changed. According to Greenpeace, he demanded that the test take place anyway; he was busy. As a result, a 120-kiloton blast dusted traces of fallout as far as Western Samoa, 1,800 miles downwind.

Nagging questions arise, such as the letter from Mayor Lucas Paeamara on Mangareva, a simple plea for someone to come look at the worrisome rates of cancer and infant deformities among his 582 people. Mangareva, 260 miles from Mururoa, is the closest inhabited atoll. It suffers from Ciguatera disease, traced to eating fish that feed on damaged coral. It causes unbearable itching. The people had to cut out fish, their staple. Paeamara blamed no one, but he hoped someone would come look. A planeload of French journalists came out from Tahiti six weeks later. They focused on the Ciguatera which, experts said, had nothing to do with *la Bombe*. One headline: "It itches but it doesn't glow."

Alan Rusbridger of the *Guardian* spoke to John Doom of the Polynesian Protestant Church who has been studying cancer problems. "We can only trust our own observations that more and more people are sick now—cancers, leukemias, all sorts. The problem is getting the proof."

Oscar Temara, mayor of the Papeete suburb of Faaa, said, "I have seen a lot of people dying of cancer in recent years. . . . But nobody can prove anything."

Among other things, Greenpeace was after proof. Each year, its tiny flotilla pushed the French limits, not only protesting nuclear tests but also bringing back water and mineral samples for analysis. Who knows, the French worry each year, what Greenpeace might find or concoct? France was shifting into a new nuclear generation. The M4 submarine missile needed a new 150-kiloton warhead. And there was the Hades missile. Besides, it was enough that other governments butted in. Greenpeace was a ragged band of *écolos* telling Paris to test its devices in Montpellier, not Mururoa. France is not anxious for advice on what it should do on French territory.

For twelve years, Greenpeace had come back each year. Once the French rammed them. Greenpeace chairman David McTaggart nearly lost an eye in a savage beating that embarrassed the government. Greenpeace was not just a pain in the ass; it was a threat to the *rayonnement* of France.

South Pacific support for Greenpeace seemed to grow each year, and trouble in Kanaky made matters worse. Mitterrand warned of "exterior appetites" and said, "France must preserve in this distant region . . . a position which it must not lose." To ensure that his subtlety was not lost on the Anglo-Saxons, he added, "If natives no longer pose a problem in Australia . . . it is because they have been killed off. That is not the way chosen by France."

On July 10, 1985, the tension exploded, literally. Two underwater charges tore a six-by-eight-foot gash in the hull of the *Rainbow Warrior* in Auckland harbor. The fourteen-man crew was making their last preparations before steaming toward Mururoa. At the first explosion, Fernando Pereira, chief engineer and photographer, raced below for his cameras. The second blast killed him. The 150-foot trawler sank like a stone.

Only by chance, five crew members decided at the last moment to sleep in town. The blasts destroyed their bunks. An hour before the attack, eight to ten people were meeting below decks in the fish hold.

"Who Is Making War on Greenpeace?" asked a large black *Libération* headline. New Zealand prime minister David Lange called the bombing "a major criminal act" with "political and terrorist implications. . . . Greenpeace has millions of friends and a few dozen enemies." He named no names.

France recorded its outrage. Environment minister Huguette Bouchardeau expressed sympathy for the crew. The French embassy in Wellington issued a condolence statement: "It would be terrible if a criminal act was at the origin of the double explosion and the death of a man." Charles Montan, political counselor, said, "France was absolutely not responsible. The French government does not act in this manner with opposing parties." France had not been concerned about the impending protest, he said, because Greenpeace had promised to respect international law.

A Greenpeace spokesman noted only that the sinking would save France a lot of trouble, since the fleet could not sail without the *Rainbow*. McTaggart said later that he did not immediately suspect the French: "I did not think they could be that stupid."

Within three days, police arrested a French couple with false Swiss passports on an extended honeymoon in the New Zealand winter. Allowed one call, they rang 846-8790 in Paris, a panic number of the Direction Générale de la Sécurité Extérieure. Police traced the number through Interpol, situated just outside Paris. Interpol went to the French police. Within five days of the explosion, the international police network implicated five French counterintelligence agents.[1] Police told the Interior Ministry, which, it is believed, told the Elysée. No one, of course, told reporters. New Zealand police continued searching out the missing pieces, and French authorities feigned ignorance.

Two weeks later, the French weekly *VSD* carried a full-page photo of the arrested woman: big round plastic glasses, Audrey Hepburn hair, towel clutched to her face with both hands. Its story began like the Gérard de Villiers thrillers sold by the stack in any French airport:

A fogless *quai* in the port of Auckland. With a cliff at the end of the jetty. Above, there are a few little houses and a large white building. A trawler the color of night, the *Rainbow Warrior* is attached to the dock like a goat to its stake. A solid boat, decorated with a white bird, that no longer smells of mackerel since the ecologists of Greenpeace decided to make it the flagship of their protest campaign. *Rainbow* is there when it is necessary to save whales, baby seals. . . .

A headline read: "Who is Sylvie-Claire Turenge, arrested after the attack of the ecologists' boat? Neither Swiss nor a teacher, as her passport says, but, according to the British, a French secret service officer with the rank of captain. . . ."

And at the top, in huge black letters, the label that would obsess the French press for the next two months: *l'affaire Greenpeace.*

L'Evénement du Jeudi broke the same story. It said officials feared that Greenpeace would spy on a secret airfield France built to back up the U.S. space shuttle program. *VSD* said that Greenpeace had special gear to measure the force of France's neutron bomb. Privately, experts laughed off both ideas. More likely, the French were just exasperated by the yearly hassle, especially since they were testing a new generation of warheads. The *Rainbow Warrior* might have put small boats ashore. France could have used more conventional—and honorable—means, some suggested. But McTaggart told *Le Monde,* "We were getting more dangerous. This year, we had a transmitter that could send satellite photos. Pictures of French sailors beating up on Greenpeace people could be very embarrassing."

The details were enticing. A mysterious yacht, *L'Ouvéa,* disappeared in the Pacific. The French doctor who chartered it had gone to ground in Dieppe. A pleasant-looking French woman ecologist, after cozying up to Greenpeace, had slipped off to Tel Aviv. An old deputy of Bob Denard's, a mercenary wholesaler named René Dulac, had recruited thugs for the mission. Someone left behind a Zodiac, a French-made rubber dinghy, and French diving gear. The accused couple was picked up when they returned a rented van they had used ostentatiously around the port.

It seemed more like the work of the Katzenjammer Kids under Inspector Clouseau than an operation worthy of France. All that was missing, one agent grumbled in Paris, was a beret, a *baguette,* and a bottle of Beaujolais.

Quickly, insiders with axes to grind helped reporters chop away the underbrush. Individuals followed their own scruples. If the original target was Greenpeace, some also took a whack at rival secret agents, the British, the Socialists, and Mitterrand himself.

The French press tried out investigative reporting with mixed results. Facts appeared, changed, receded, and surfaced again. *Le Canard Enchaîné* broke some new ground, as usual, but it revealed the Turenges' true identity incorrectly. *Le Point* suggested that the missing *Ouvéa* crew was hiding in the Gabonese presidential guard. *VSD,* boasting later about its scoop, quietly corrected Madame Turenge's name to Sophie and named her Françoise Prieur. Then she was Captain Dominique Prieur. A small slip. But *VSD* had also linked the operation squarely to senior Elysée aides, and the government filed suit. The magazine admitted casually that a source had mixed up a date—two key people had met after the operation and not before—but its story stood.

In the end, France admitted responsibility but gave no details. The arrested couple pleaded guilty to manslaughter, cheating the curious out of a trial. Newspapers accused Mitterrand of lying and covering up the facts. This was *Warrior* gate. Or Waterloogate. Or Watergaffe. Or Underwatergate. But the bang ended in a quiet whimper. The French, who never understood how the Americans could toss aside a perfectly good president over a minor scandal, took a different approach.

Watergate was abuse of internal espionage and a coverup; in the end, a president fell. *Warrior* gate was foreign espionage in a friendly nation, with an innocent victim and a sunken ship; in the end, reporters noted, French secret police were able to increase fivefold their wiretaps on political opponents and civil servants of questioned loyalty.

Some questions remained unanswered, such as who did it, and why? No one established what Mitterrand knew, or when he learned it. When the trail grew close, people stopped asking questions. France appeared callous, bumbling, and deceitful. But the ship of state steamed on, the whole business amounting to a hard thump in the hull from floating debris. American columnist William Pfaff wrote:

Nobody wanted it to become a French Watergate. The reason would seem to be a sense of national vulnerability, outweighing partisan interest in the government's humiliation. The United States could go to the bitter end in the Watergate affair, driving Richard Nixon out of the White House, because Americans believe that the United States is invulnerable. No one considered the costs of pursuing an abstract justice to whatever end. This is a luxury which, it seems, the French collectively concluded they cannot afford.

Authorities searched the *Ouvéa* at Norfolk Island, but Australian law did not allow the crew to be held without charge until New Zealand detectives and police chemists could get there. The yacht headed for Noumea and disappeared forever. A ranking official in a past government remarked bitterly, at the end, "At first I thought the press had grown intoxicated by a Watergate role and would follow this to the end. But then I realized it was a *coup monté*— a setup—like everything else."

Le Monde split hairs. In Watergate, Nixon's goal was personal; in *l'affaire Greenpeace,* whatever French officials did, even if it was "stupid and criminal," was meant in the interest of the state. The entire episode, including that explanation, said a great deal about France.

Only after the story broke did Mitterrand order a rigorous investigation of the "criminal and absurd" incident. He asked Bernard Tricot, a trusted aide of de Gaulle, to issue a report. Tricot had a drawback: *tricoter* means "to knit" in French, and few commentators would resist the pun. The DGSE, nicknamed *la Piscine* after the public pool across from its imposing headquarters, was already the butt of ridicule.

Defense Minister Charles Hernu, responsible for the DGSE, told reporters, "I have a clear conscience. My position is clear: I want all the truth to be known."

Awaiting the official word, reporters dug hard. They retraced DGSE agents' steps. The Turenges reached Auckland on June 22 and went north. At the Beachcomber Hotel in Paihia, the honeymooners slept in separate beds and gave a Paris address. *L'Ouvéa,* meanwhile, pitched up there from New Caledonia, in difficult water and bad weather. The crew filled a page in the guest book of a local pizzeria. The captain, Raymond Velche, rented a Ford van and left a roll of electric bomb wire inside. He bought a pair of New Balance run-ning shoes which left incriminating tracks. Other purchases aroused the suspicions of a local ship chandler. The Turenges were seen again on July 10. Two hours before the blast, yacht club guards saw a frogman ditch the Zodiac and climb into their camper.

Major Alain Mafart—Turenge—would complain later about nosy islanders who spied on suspicious characters.

The couple would have gotten away in the end except that they waited around a half hour for a small refund on their rented van. Police found on them clumsily altered receipts—obviously for pad-ding an expense account—which further weakened their flimsy honeymoon cover.

The mysterious mole was unmasked. Frédérique Bonlieu—Lieu-tenant Christine Cabon—had infiltrated Greenpeace and staked out the trails. Within a month, New Zealand police had 1,000 pieces of evidence against the French agents.

Three New Zealand detectives came to Paris and got nowhere. Opposition senator (and future interior minister) Charles Pasqua complained, "This is shameful. How long will we tolerate this unacceptable New Zealand interference on our territory?" Another politician demanded an end to meddling into services meant to assure the security and independence of France.

Greenpeace, meanwhile, said it was not giving up. The 200-foot tug *Greenpeace* was diverted from Antarctica to Mururoa to join a ketch, the *Vega,* and two other boats. Mitterrand ordered the navy to keep them out of French waters, with force if necessary.

Libération put it, "The hour is grim in the gutters of the Repub-lic: *petit pipi* threatens to become *grand caca."* Immediately after-ward, the *caca* hit the *ventilateur.*

Tricot produced twenty-nine pages on August 26, after seventeen days of investigation. He found that neither the government nor the DGSE had given any order to sabotage the *Rainbow Warrior;* six DGSE agents had gone to New Zealand only to spy on Greenpeace, with the approval of the Elysée; no clues suggested who sank the boat or why; he believed that all witnesses had told him the truth. He said Mitterrand's military chief of staff, General Jean Saulnier, had approved the expenses, estimated by other sources at about $225,000. But the money was only for spying. The saboteurs, Tricot said, might be "isolated men, moved mainly by political passion, or rather one might suspect others' secret services." In sum, France was blameless.

With a flourish of style, he added that the French agents did their assigned job well. "I believe to have understood, but this applies of course only to the bachelors, that our compatriots applied a sustained attention to the feminine sector of the population."

The *Libération* headline was "Tricot Washes Whiter." Editor Serge July suggested that Tricot might be the Lewis Carroll of French espionage. Alain Madelin of the UDF said, "Tricot takes the French for imbeciles." Prime Minister Lange observed that the report was too transparent to be called a whitewash. He said spying alone was a grave violation of international behavior. And he was angry that only Tricot was given access to three men wanted for murder in Auckland. The *New Zealand Herald* added that if splashed with all the perfume in Provence, the scandal would still smell like a skunk.

Tricot acknowledged in interviews that witnesses might have lied to him.

The next day, Fabius asked Hernu to correct "substantial failings" in the DGSE. He asked New Zealand to provide "proof" against the French agents. And he announced a tighter legislative control over French secret services, saying,

> The identification of the culprits remains to be established. We hope that New Zealand authorities reach the truth as quickly as possible. Our condemnation is not, as one has sometimes heard, against the poor execution of a dubious project; it is an absolute condemnation of a criminal act. The guilty, whoever they are, must answer for this crime.

Opposition response was muted. "My country, right or wrong," said Giscard d'Estaing. (*Le Monde* identified that as "a British formula whose author is a certain Steven Decatur, an American major who lived between 1779 and 1820." A *Monde* reader later recalled how the rest went: "Right or wrong, my country. If it is right, keep it right. If it is wrong, make it right.")

Greenpeace had a few questions. Why five combat divers for an information mission? Why did the agents leave before Greenpeace sailed and abandon their photos on the *Ouvéa?* Why did the *Ouvéa* leave on July 9, in terrible weather, through dangerous water, with reported structural damage?

Defense Ministry officials told selected journalists it was the British; DGSE agents had bought their Zodiac at Barnet Marine in London. French papers said the owner was a former British spy who warned his friends who, in turn, tipped the New Zealanders. The owner himself said he confirmed to police that a Frenchman bought the boat after officers traced it back to him from its markings. The Foreign Office was upset. And the *Daily Mail* dismissed the whole thing as "Bonapartist insolence."

The DGSE liked best the hypothesis of *Le Soir* in Brussels: Greenpeace did it themselves to make the French look bad.

A *Sofres* poll suggested that only a third of France was interested in *l'affaire Greenpeace.* But the press kept up the pressure. French correspondents covered the New Zealand courts. In France, a *juge d'instruction* builds a dossier against a suspect, combining the role of police, prosecutor, and judge. People stay locked up until this is ready, even if it takes years. The French had trouble with curious points of Anglo-Saxon law, notably that suspects answer only for what is proven against them in court, and are considered innocent until then. Or that courts, diplomacy, and executive decisions are kept separate.

And the press reported the color. Florence Décamp of *Libération,* who referred five times to the "deposition earing," ridiculed the New Zealanders' spelling of French dishes which continued to sell like hot croissants. She was also not fond of the frog legs wrapped in apricot with Camembert sauce. Another reporter was amazed that people bought newspapers by leaving money in an open box.

The papers noted international hostility and scorn. In West Germany, Greenpeace membership rocketed. "In no other country is the idea of *raison d'Etat* so widely held as in France," said Werner Holzer, editor of *Frankfurter Rundschau.* The French public, more revolted by the clumsiness of their spies than the act itself, banded together to cover an inexcusable act, he said, "as if France could never lose."

In Paris, a steady stream of leaks continued, but the Tricot report stayed afloat. Then Mitterrand seized the initiative. On September 12, he climbed onto a Concorde and flew to Mururoa. He established a center for advanced French studies in the Pacific, and he invited heads of government in the region to come watch the tests. Australian prime minister Bob Hawke replied that if Mitterrand was so interested in proving the tests' safety, he should "have those absolutely safe tests in metropolitan France."

Lange was also hostile. He said the sabotage was akin to an act of war. He called the Quai d'Orsay pompous for summoning his ambassador to demand fair treatment for the Turenges under international law. The French consulate had not even contacted the couple, Lange said.

Mitterrand asked Lange to cease his "unfounded accusations" against France. But no sooner had the president returned to Paris than Le Monde fired its broadside. It reported on September 18 that a third team, two French navy divers apart from the Turenges and the Ouvéa crew, had sunk the vessel. They had been trained at the secret base at Aspretto, in Corsica, where Mafart had been an instructor. Hernu, or his top aides, ordered the mission, or at least knew about it. Le Monde used the conditional tense so favored by French reporters: "might have sunk" or "should have sunk." That was good enough. Le Canard Enchaîné had already broken the "third team" story. Now it was confirmed by the archbishop of the French press.

Edwy Plenel revealed in Le Monde the Turenges' last mistake. They rang the DGSE, and New Zealand police listened in on an extension. When Interpol went to the French police to trace the number, Interior Minister Pierre Joxe was informed. And, Le Monde said, he told Mitterrand about July 18, a week after the explosion.

The weekly L'Express substantiated the account. It said that Mitterrand was advised of French involvement on July 17, and the president demanded the details. According to L'Express, senior military people, possibly Hernu, lied to him at least until August 7. General Saulnier had "signed the budget estimate" on the operation beforehand, L'Express said, adding that such expenditures would have to be approved by the defense minister as well as a ranking Elysée official.

Libération weighed in with another huge headline: "Mensonges."

Lies. Others followed. At a stormy cabinet session, Mitterrand demanded of Hernu, his friend for thirty years: *"Je veux savoir."* I want to know.

Among French officialdom, passing the franc was easy enough. The affair began with a memo from Admiral Henri Fages, commander at Mururoa. He said France had to *anticiper* Greenpeace. When the memo, moving from Hernu's office through channels, reached the DGSE high command, that word was underlined twice. That is one of those subtleties of French: *anticiper* can simply mean anticipate, as in "be prepared." Like the English equivalent, it can mean forestall. But it can also mean: prevent, at any cost.

On September 18, Hernu insisted that no one under his command had received orders to sabotage the *Rainbow Warrior.* He denounced "rumor, insinuation, and slander" and said, "I know that in this affair, in the shadows, there is malignancy, and that forces me to bring this to light." The next day, Mitterrand ordered Fabius to clean house. "This cannot last," he wrote. The day after that, Fabius asked Hernu for his resignation. The DGSE chief, Admiral Pierre Lacoste, refused to name the French agents sent to New Zealand; he was fired. And on Sunday, September 22, Fabius addressed the nation in a funereal monotone:

> The new Minister of Defense has informed me of the first conclusions of [his] investigation. . . . It was agents of the DGSE who sank this boat. They acted under orders. This truth was hidden from Counselor Tricot. . . . The [agents] evidently must be cleared of blame because it would be inacceptable to expose military people who must obey orders and who have sometimes in the past accomplished very dangerous missions for our country. *Mesdames et messieurs,* the truth of this affair is cruel but it is important that I am engaged in assuring that it is totally and clearly established.

Reaction was harsh. Lange called it a sordid act of state-backed terrorism. Pfaff wrote:

> What official with the slightest sense of political, or of human, realities could possibly have believed that to sink a Greenpeace

ship would deter the anti-nuclear movement? To sink the boat was to present . . . a gold-plated public relations gift. To do it in such a way that a man was killed was worse. To tell convoluted lies about it all was simply suicidal.

The loss of Hernu crippled Mitterrand, who had counted on his prestige with the right to help in the March legislative elections. For the president, it was also a tragic personal loss. His goodbye was touching, but it was unavoidable.

In a television interview, Fabius laid the blame squarely on Hernu and Lacoste. He—and certainly the president—was innocent. "My conviction is that the responsibility was at their level," he said. "In a democracy like ours, the responsibility rests at the political level, that is, the minister."

Fabius was roasted for kicking a fallen scapegoat. Why a minister and not the prime minister? some editorialists asked. One wondered about the value of the convictions of a prime minister in peril. Most agreed that Hernu simply wore the hat, as the French say. "Hernu Sacrificed," *Libération* put it in heavy type. What about Saulnier and the president's inner circle? With the government's credibility near zero, the truth was hard to find. Reporters learned that the new defense minister, Paul Quilès, found vital documents missing. Lacoste threatened to reveal embarrassing details if his former men were implicated, another report said.

"Democracy supposes transparency in public affairs, authority and responsibility," wrote Max Gallo, editor of *Le Matin* and Mitterrand's former spokesman. The right-wing *Le Figaro* and the radio station Europe 1 reported that Fabius had known the details since July 17. *Figaro* persisted: Mitterrand had to have known.

"This is not a government," fumed François Léotard, an opposition leader (and minister of culture in 1986), "this is the Raft of the Medusa." French political crises are at least elegant. He referred to the Géricault painting in the Louvre showing frantic shipwrecked passengers and crew members scrambling over the dead for a place on a life raft.

But the case was closed. "There are no government lies," an Elysée spokesman announced. Five military people were arrested for leaking secrets to the press. French officials told New Zealand they regretted that the sinking had damaged their relations, but they avoided a full apology. Nor did they promise to punish any agents. A month earlier, Fabius had promised legal action if it appeared that Frenchmen were involved.

Within a week, the new director of the DGSE, General René Imbot, announced that he had sawn off all rotten branches. A Foreign Legion veteran, sixty and hard-minded, he declared he had crushed a sinister plot to destroy French secret services. Now, he said, the DGSE was "bolted shut" and above reproach.

Among the tide of letters to *Le Monde* was one from Colonel Trinquier, the former legionnaire and Congo mercenary: "France is not America where the press can launch a new Watergate-type affair. The mass of French people, all political nuances combined, remains patriotic and knows by instinct where the real interests of our country lie."

Pfaff accurately gauged public reaction.

France is a cynical nation where international politics are concerned. The crime, in French eyes, is that those responsible have made France look ridiculous before the world. They have made France seem incompetent and mendacious; and this is unforgivable.

About then, Bernard Tapie was a guest on *"Sept sur Sept,"* a Sunday evening television program on which public figures comment on the news. Tapie, who made millions buying up failing companies and steamrolling them into the black, is one French ideal: an amateur boxer and singer with Rambo frown lines, a *bon vivant,* rich and pushy, brimming with style and conviction. He put it this way:

It is unimaginable, the disproportion between the event and the reaction that followed. . . . I am proud to be French, to belong among the five most powerful countries in the world, and I am ashamed to have a secret service incapable of carrying out this sort of operation. I always believe in results. If as one of the five most powerful nations, we haven't got people who can sink a boat without everyone knowing about it, we are really the bottom.

Then they tell me it might have been on purpose; that is even worse. . . . And I am ashamed at all these rats who come out of their holes to feed on this without giving a damn about its effect abroad. To show the government as liars, poltroons. Even if it is true, the honor of France is at stake. There must be a measure of *pudeur* [decency]. They don't have the right to make us look like a country governed by jerks simply because they might win three more percentage points.

But soon enough, Hernu emerged a hero. He received thunderous applause at the Socialist convention in Toulouse and headed the list of candidates for the Rhône district. Mitterrand received Mikhail Gorbachev in Paris before the Geneva summit, and appeared once again like a president of France.

Greenpeace went to Mururoa as promised; the French kept them clear of the tests, as threatened. The *Greenpeace,* stricken with a faulty generator, was repaired by two French technicians; the boat was banned from Tahiti. The navy boarded the *Vega* and turned it around, but no one was roughed up. The sailors promised to bring champagne the next time. On October 25, the French exploded yet another nuclear device. "The sovereignty of France is not open to discussion," Fabius said, no longer on the defensive. "The nuclear tests are necessary to us. We will conduct them as other countries do."

The thirty-eight-minute trial on November 4 brought one last flurry. Prosecutor David Morris could not prove that Mafart and Prieur placed explosives on the hull. Although Mitterrand and Fabius had each called the act "criminal" and promised that the guilty would pay, France would not deliver the four key suspects or answer vital questions. As a result, the murder charge was dropped to manslaughter. ("Man's laughter," *Le Monde* misspelled it inadvertently.) Both defendants pleaded guilty. The French claimed a victory.

Le Figaro reported snidely: "In English, one would call this brutally a deal. Almost a contract. In French, one would say a tacit accord, a compromise, a consensus." Conviction would be followed by expulsion within weeks, if not days, the paper said. France would

quietly compensate New Zealand. "Looks like we'll be eating a lot
more lamb chops," remarked one radio commentator.

Libération, in an editorial, was ironic:

> At the sunset of this serial, at times *rocambolesque,* sickening or
> sordid, one doesn't know whether to heave a sigh of relief—all's
> well that ends well—or be contented with writing off the list of
> fallen as settlement: a minister, a few officers. . . . In the end, a
> lot of people for a simple Portuguese photographer. But wasn't
> he the only sticking point in the whole affair?

The word was that France would help New Zealand sell dairy
products and lamb in the European Economic Community. "Butter
and *gigot* for spies," Michel Rocard, the Socialist leader, was quoted.
Lang was furious:

> They are not for sale. The question of a plea is a matter for
> the solicitor-general. The system of justice in this country is not
> a matter of convenience for the government. It is a system of
> justice. That is why they are not for sale. . . . This is a process
> of law, not for sordid haggling, selling of prisoners.

Chief Justice Sir Ronald Davison echoed his irritation: "People who
come to this country and commit terrorist activities cannot expect
to have a short holiday at the expense of our government and return
home heroes."

Most French commentators snickered. When New Zealand asked
for damages to cover the enormous cost of investigation and trial,
French papers called it "ransom."

Prieur and Mafart were each sentenced to ten years in prison.
Contrary to expectations in Paris, they were not home for Christmas.

By then, the world had lost interest. Many people never paid
much attention, like the American schoolkid interviewed on French
television who confused the *Rainbow Warrior* with the *Titanic.*
French teachers abroad did not insist on two of the universal words
their language has produced: *chauvinisme* and *sabotage.* The U.S.

government never did work up to a condemnation. Vice President George Bush, heading a study group on terrorism, would not comment. In the United Nations, U.S. ambassador Jeane Kirkpatrick said the act was obviously not terrorism since France clearly did not intend to "kill, maim, or torture" anyone.

Paris-Match offered yet another scoop in early 1986: the third team was deliberate disinformation; the *Ouvéa* crew sank the *Rainbow Warrior*. Yawn.

In New Zealand, people still walked around displaying the slogan "You Can't Sink a Rainbow." But in France, where *l'affaire Greenpeace* quietly died, the Cartesian method required more proof of that than a lapel button.

Two months after the Turenge trial, Fabius told correspondents that negotiations were frozen because New Zealand insisted on holding French citizens. I asked him if *l'affaire Greenpeace* would have an impact on the crucial March legislative elections. "No," he replied. "I don't think so." He was right.

But nagging concerns remained. State agents had threatened to reveal damning secrets if their colleagues were unmasked. Lacoste refused to give his ministers operational details, saying his "duty" prevented it. He said the order came from a "political authority," presumably a minister. No one was punished. Jean François-Poncet, foreign minister under Giscard d'Estaing, said, "No minister has the right to mislead the president." If *Le Monde* was correct that Hernu knew, "This is not a matter for resignation, but a case of treason."

Other secret excesses were scrutinized at least in half light. Magazines reported that Yves Bonnet had been forced to resign as head of the DST because he resisted political pressure to increase wiretapping and smear writers who annoyed authorities. For a while, the ugly DGSE building evoked tourist curiosity.

The key questions remained unanswered. Who gave the order? Who knew? André Fontaine, editor of *Le Monde,* worried that no one had the courage to take responsibility. "Too many people who might have been responsible acted like the schoolchild caught in the act who points to his friend and says, 'It wasn't me, it was him.' " A government in such a situation cannot exercise serious controls; he called it terrifying to hear a president say he learned of his agents' excesses from the newspapers. That, Fontaine said, could undermine confidence between the army and the state, or shatter the national consensus over nuclear dissuasion.

At one point, Lange touched a raw nerve: "If there is one little thing ticking away for France in the issue, it is the corruption of civilized standards."

Other condemnations stung as much from their source as their content. *South* magazine, favored in the Third World circles France likes to frequent, rubbed salt in the wound. And one editorial observed: "This betrays a degree of paranoia, ruthlessness and cynicism which is staggering. It splashes blood on innocent hands. It ranks as one of the most execrable of dirty tricks in recent times." That was the *Cape Times* of Cape Town, a paper more accustomed to attacking the South African government which Fabius had just denounced for state terrorism.

In a major French poll, half the respondents said that a country like France had no right to use such means. Sociologist Alain Touraine noted that the French were prone to shrug off *l'affaire Greenpeace* for reasons of state. It touched their ultimate umbrella, the independent nuclear force that assures their international political role. But, he said:

> It should have made us realize the profound degradation of our political life, which is dominated by a little *raison d'Etat* and a lot of social vacuum. Isn't it high time to renew the life and the dialogue of society and its actors to put the state and its perverse reason under examination?"

But at the height of the New Caledonia crisis, Jacques Chaban-Delmas, a Gaullist and former prime minister, a Resistance hero and stalwart of the political landscape, put the nuclear question in its French perspective:

> If France disappears in New Caledonia, Polynesia (and the test sites) will be next. . . . Your children will be poor little nonentities after the year 2000, because if France ceases to be a nuclear power, it ceases being any sort of power at all.

The whole business almost started again at Queen's Wharf in Auckland just before New Year's Eve, 1985. Customs inspectors found 5,500 rounds of ammunition and disassembled machine pistols hidden near the engines of the French freighter *Ile de Lumière*. Mercenaries were preparing to blast the Turenges out of prison, one New Zealand paper guessed. A judge thought differently. He fined the ship's cook, who admitted to having bought the munitions in Australia; he said he had planned to sell them to the highest bidder in New Caledonia. His captain laughed that off. The cook, settled in New Caledonia after a brief stretch in Chad, was an ardent anti-*indépendantiste*, he said. He was helping to stock the loyalist arms chest.

With some rue, the French recognized the 1,500-ton vessel. A few years earlier, the *Ile de Lumière* had been chartered by A Boat for Vietnam, a committee composed of Jean-Paul Sartre, Yves Montand, and Simone Signoret, among others. It was a hospital ship for the Vietnamese boat people.

The incident quickly faded, but not without some grumbling in Paris. A television commentator observed that inspectors only found the ammunition because of an extrathorough search; New Zealand was picking on France.

TO AN OUTSIDER in France, the aftermath of the *Rainbow Warrior* was nearly as astounding as the event itself. Mitterrand drew a clear line in a foreign policy statement: "No one can argue that France should diminish its surveillance of the atolls and renounce its tests on the strength of an act that does not morally engage our country."

New Zealand, somehow, had become the bad guy, and France was quietly boycotting its meat, fish and fruit until it released the two French citizens it was holding. Import licenses were refused without explanation; cargo was turned away as incorrectly labeled. Complaints to the French foreign and agriculture ministries brought no reply.

French television reported, briefly and offhandedly, that New Zealand courts issued arrest warrants for the *Ouvéa* crew.

"The French have a curious way of looking at things," Lange told

Le Monde in a discreetly placed interview. "We appreciate France's diversity, its sophistication, its qualities and its culture, but perhaps we are wrong."

He called it extraordinary that New Zealanders had been painted as abnormal Anglo-Saxon monsters. He said:

> This has became a matter of national pride, a political symbol, much more than a military imperative. France wants simply to buy back two prisoners who have pleaded guilty to murder. The sabotage can be easily presented as an act of international terrorism perpetrated with the support of a state, for political purposes. What New Zealanders have the most trouble understanding is that the French government, which at first denied any involvement and then condemned the act, promising to do all possible to punish the guilty, suddenly decided to turn around and change the status of the guilty to that of good, loyal soldiers following orders. I don't doubt they were, but for us, they are criminals.

He hoped, despite it all, "to maintain civilized relations between two countries."

The new government in Paris discreetly sought to freeze New Zealand butter and meat sales to the EEC. Negotiations broke down. New Zealand wanted reparations and France wanted back "the hostages." In May, authorities indemnified Pereira's family but not Greenpeace. Edouard Leclerc, the supermarket magnate, pushed a boycott of New Zealand products under the slogan, "Let's not be sheep." He decried "odious blackmail." (His gasoline-mogul brother, Michel, who had whipped up fury against Middle Eastern Arabs over oil prices, was otherwise occupied, sentenced to prison for fraud and abuse of confidence.)

With stone walls in France, New Zealand did not pursue investigations. Police and legal costs had already run deep into the millions. Lange acknowledged that many millions more in export earnings were at risk, but that was a price small nations had to pay for their sovereignty and dignity.

He told a BBC phone-in program in April, "We have no prisoners for sale, thank you very much." That, for most French commentators, meant the price was not yet high enough.

Hernu won his National Assembly seat easily and discussed the possibility of running for president in 1988. Just before the vote, he lunched with correspondents and shrugged off the affair. Why did France do it? The Pacific nations were ganging up on France. Wasn't it a little extreme? Every government defends its interests. How many take their quarrels to the *place publique?* That one stopped him. He smiled engagingly and replied: "Good question." Then he added: *"Oouuf,* whether this damaged France's image in the world, I'm not sure."

Later, I went to a demonstration demanding the release of French hostages in Lebanon. A speaker had said: "No cause is worth the taking of innocent lives." I mentioned this to a table of writers and intellectuals at a Paris dinner party that evening, and I brought up the *Rainbow Warrior.* "How can you make a comparison?" demanded one man, to general agreement. "France had no intention of killing anyone. That silly fool ran back for his cameras. He should have fled after the first warning blast." Here was the ultimate in French wrongfooting. Fernando Pereira had killed himself.

LOST BETWEEN Kanaky and *la Bombe* was a quiet mouse roar from independent Vanuatu, until 1980 called the New Hebrides. France and Britain ran it jointly by what they called a condominium; islanders called it the pandemonium. There were three governments: French, British, and local. Prisoners could pick their jails. British jails were nicer, but the French served wine. Britain seized the higher ground for the governor's residence. The French governor ran up a higher flagpole so the Tricolor could be the same height as the Union Jack.

At independence, a Presbyterian preacher named Walter Lini was elected prime minister. But in the northern island of Espíritu Santo, French planters and merchants backed Jimmy Stevens. He was defeated and jailed; 1,000 French were expelled from the island.

In 1983, after England fought its Falklands War, Vanuatu clashed with France over two tiny uninhabited islets off New Caledonia. It sent its entire navy: one yacht. Crisis was averted.

France and Britain struggle quietly here for influence. French aid, at nine million dollars a year, is slightly higher. Half the 3,000 whites in the capital of Port Vila are French, and the Alliance

Française works overtime to teach the language. Australians threaten to tip the balance. But neither side makes waves. A "green letter" from the government can expel a foreigner overnight.

GLOBAL strategists say that the Pacific is especially important to France because of lost ground in Asia. Paris once dominated the South China Sea, and its political influence bore heavily northward to China and eastward to Japan. But French economic roots were never deep in most of Asia.

Sudest-asie magazine quoted a French industrialist: "Our trade with Asia is derisory. Our products are too expensive, our protectionism is outrageous, and our industries are incapable of competition." The remark was made just after 1900.

By the time France was ejected from Indochina, its *rayonnement* was a weak glow. "France is a ghost in this region," observed a senior Singaporean official. France competes hard in Southeast Asia but lags behind most industrial nations. In 1983, 12,100 French lived in the region, the lowest number for any area of comparable size.

But French cultural residue is thick and rich. Marguerite Duras writes with passion of her youth in Indochina. Edouard Axelrad writes of the war. Sections of Left Bank Paris, redolent of *citronelle* and *nuoc mam,* might be Cholon or Vientiane. Despite the long American war, most Vietnamese, Cambodians, and Laotians see the West through optics ground in France. When Truong Nhu Tang went to Albania for the Viet Cong, he spoke in French.

Prince Sihanouk, deposed as ruler of Cambodia but figurehead of an exile coalition government, remains close to France. He speaks to Mitterrand often in his high-pitched and eloquent French. When peace meetings collapsed, they were usually to have been held in Paris. And when Sihanouk took diplomats inside the Cambodian border in early 1985 to fete his coalition, the toasts were drunk in champagne. Just before this, Foreign Minister Hun Sen of the Vietnam-dominated Cambodian government, on a "private" visit to Paris, had described ties with France: "We have a proverb in Cambodia: if you cannot build a concrete bridge, you can always throw across the river a bamboo walkway."

Vietnam bases few political decisions on sentiment. But in January 1985, Hanoi made a simple, cold gesture to France. Five Vietnamese were condemned to death, accused of spying for China, Thailand, and the West. One was Mai Van Hanh, a retired Royal Air Maroc captain who took French citizenship after leaving Vietnam. Another was Tran Van Ba, who claimed to be French but had no proof from Paris. Fabius appealed for clemency for all. Mai Van Hanh and another man received life imprisonment; the other three were executed on schedule.

In China, France presses a slight advantage. The old French Club in Shanghai was torn down to make room for a Japanese hotel. But French telephones, textiles, Peugeots, profiteroles, engineering projects, and armaments move steadily into the Middle Kingdom. Thirty thousand French tourists a year visit China. Pierre Cardin led the way, but Yves Saint-Laurent dazzled the Chinese with a retrospective of his designs. "I think we have a mutual interest in simplicity," he said, adding that without Chinese silk, he likely would not be in business.

Ten leading Chinese cadres came to France to study public administration in 1985. "The French are teaching us method," one said. In Peking that year, Foreign Minister Roland Dumas happily heard the Chinese tell him France's world role was steadily growing. Five months later, he was even happier. The state enterprise Framatome had finally nailed down a contract to build an elaborate nuclear power plant near Canton.

To the east, France has joined the pack seeking a foothold in Japan. But the balance tilts in the other direction. At one point, so many Japanese video recorders flooded France that officials made importers clear them at the obscure customs post in Poitiers, where paperwork moved at a snail's pace.

To the west, in India, France pulled out all stops, evoking its old grandeur. Pondicherry was handed back in 1954. But Raymond Magry, in his seventies, still welcomes guests on the airy veranda of his Grand Hôtel d'Europe. He reminisced in 1985. "Imagine, when the French ships came in, the parties and grand balls, women in long dresses and generous décolletés, men in evening dress or braided uniform. . . . Right here, you had to see how everything shown like a thousand diamonds."

France suffered in India for selling nuclear technology to Pakistan, but not seriously. In January 1985, Indian papers splashed news about a spy ring that trafficked in documents wholesale, to the West and East. Ten Indian officials were involved, and three Frenchmen were implicated. A French military attaché was suddenly yanked back to Paris; it was for consultations, officials explained. Press reports said he was expelled. Two mysterious French businessmen fled the country. In India, that sort of affair could go either way. A billion dollars in arms deals, among other things, hung in the balance.

"They treated the French with velvet gloves; it was amazing how the Indians hushed it up and smoothed it over," a correspondent friend in Delhi told me later. "The newspapers talked about France, but not Rajiv Gandhi. In Parliament, it was always 'the foreign this' and 'the foreign that' with no names. If it had been the British or the Americans, it would have gone a lot differently."

Six months later, Gandhi ascended the Eiffel Tower with Mitterrand to inaugurate the Year of India in France. India, an emerging power and a Third World champion, was an attractive friend for France. And for India, tiptoeing twixt East and West, France was a natural ally.

"Your passion for liberty and reason, your contribution to the arts and good taste, the work of your thinkers, scientists and technologists cannot be easily matched or surpassed by any other nation," Gandhi said. Pondicherry had sheltered Indian freedom fighters, he recalled. And he noted:

> Victor Hugo, who died 100 years ago, has said, "I represent a party which does not yet exist: the party of revolution, civilization. This party will make the twentieth century." Perhaps not without significance, my party, the Indian National Congress, was born the year Hugo died.

On live television, elephants lumbered by the Trocadero. Dancers swayed to sitars. Ladies in saris dumped rose petals and a flask of Ganges water in the Seine. The water was brown. But the Indians signed a contract for French engineers to build twenty-seven purification plants along the Ganges for five billion francs. They also bought telephones, helicopters, and Airbuses.

The euphoria even survived *l'affaire Munna*.

Mohammed Munshi had come to Paris from Jaipur with Munna, the eight-year-old bear he had raised since it was two days old. Mitterrand welcomed Munna with an official pat on the head. When Gandhi left, bear and handler stayed to open an Indian restaurant on a barge in the shadow of the Eiffel Tower.

But the "Victor Hugo Brigade" did not like the ring in the bear's nose or the small cage in which he lived. One night a commando of French animal lovers chloroformed a watchman and bearnapped Munna. Two weeks later, police found the bear in a zoo. He was nearly dead, depressed without his master and disoriented without his ring. Reunited, Mohammed and Munna went home. Franco-Indian friendship lived on.

CHAPTER SEVENTEEN

Canada: A Few Acres of Snow

THE COLORS OF France snap in the North Atlantic winds over Place Charles de Gaulle, St. Pierre, just about where Cartier planted his flag in 1535. From the rocky little islands of St. Pierre and Miquelon, tucked away off the Newfoundland coast, France built the empire that spanned the St. Lawrence River and snaked down the Mississippi to New Orleans. Except for the nine times English gunboats seized the place—and the four times England deported all the residents and burned St. Pierre to the ground—the islands have been France's anchor in North America. Now they are all it has left.

For more than two centuries, France in North America has amounted to 60,000 raw and rocky acres, peopled by 6,100 descendants of cod fishermen from Brittany, Normandy, and the Basque country. Cartier today is just another name on the duty-free watches. St. Pierre and Miquelon is the oldest and smallest bit of overseas France. And it exhibits all the problems of keeping a sailing ship empire in a satellite age.

A Paris-appointed *préfet* represents France, and islanders elect assemblymen and senators. Two councils, with divided authority, make local decisions. Just like the Haute-Savoie, French officials like to say. That is not exactly true.

The blizzardy day I arrived, in 1985, a mob of fish packers seized the *préfet* by the armpits, frog-marched him along the frozen quai to his official launch, and ran him out of town. Gendarmes sat peaceably at headquarters, not even directing traffic around the tumult. The issue at hand was who got to unload a new factory trawler when it put into port six times a year. But no one missed the wider significance.

France has worried over its American holdings for nearly five centuries. Even after Napoléon sold off Louisiana, passionate voices rose in favor of a North Atlantic base. For strategic purposes, for trade, and for *rayonnement,* they argued, France belonged in North America. For 180 years, the last little French toehold has played a role surpassing its size.

ONLY THE MORE serious geography students have ever heard of the islands. A St. Pierrais in Paris was stung when a postal clerk asked a fortune to mail a package home. In St. Pierre, a *département,* domestic rates applied. But the clerk thought St. Pierre was in Greenland. I spent thirty-five minutes on the phone in New York trying to determine the direct-dialing code. Operators could not find St. Pierre. "Canada?" repeated one when I explained it was a French territory located within Canada. "What province?" Finally, a supervisor came on and announced, "It is a new country in Europe."

Getting there was harder still. Flights go from Halifax and St. John's, Newfoundland. In the summer, they are daily. But there is the fog; an overnight trip can take a week. In winter, flights are three times a week unless there is (and there usually is) too much icy wind. Ferries run sporadically from Newfoundland, but the port is a five-hour drive from the nearest airfield. Paris is never closer than two days away.

The town of St. Pierre is a tight cluster of shingled and wood-slat buildings, painted in yellows, reds, mauves, greens, blues, cheerful even under muddy ice. The old stone structures might be on the French north coast but for the lack of hedges, trees, or flowers. Merchants don't bother with the charming little signs of most French villages; everyone knows where he is. The Biarritz, a raucous, high-tech disco, is an unmarked little gray house. A shingle hangs outside Le Caveau, a Basque-flavored restaurant in a converted bank vault and rum-runner's warehouse, but winds tend to blow it down.

On narrow streets heading uphill, rough-hewn walls and foundations suggest permanence. But gales and fire prevent buildings from lasting long enough to age gracefully. St. Pierre's landmark is the dockside post office; with parrot's-beak gables and weathered old sidings, it is like nothing North American. The islands' features are bare rock, sandy beaches, and a few wind-ravaged trees.

Peugeots and Renaults crowd the few roads, but St. Pierre claims the world's oldest Ford agency, with uninterrupted sales and service since 1919. A hardware store is emblazoned "Affiliated with Handy Andy," pronounced Andy Andy. Cajun plink-plank flavors the music at the AIDs Bar in the Hôtel Ile de France, owned by an Algerian. In the Bar Le Relais, Eric Clapton is Living on Tulsa Time, and Freddy Fender sings in Spanish. Canadian quarters work interchangeably with francs in the video games. Snack bars sell "oignons rings."

Still, a quick sniff tells you it's France: warm croissants, Pernod, *sauce Béarnaise,* Joy. As everywhere else in France, the menus make the best of local specialties. Cod guts are *fraises de morue.*

On my flight in, among the bearded faces and battered parkas, I saw an impeccably shaved caricature of old France: gleaming gold-rim spectacles, burgundy silk tie, midnight-blue suit with a blue Legion of Merit ribbon in the lapel. Another was a butcher from La Rochelle, on his own mission to civilize. He was on loan to local butchers to teach them how to cut meat. "They do it like the Americans," he explained in a solemn tone, reflecting pity and disbelief. "With a saw."

The Catholic church, with its little stone steeple, dominates St. Pierre. Its influence is declining, residents say. But at the Biarritz, in full 2 A.M. liquefied debauchery, the disc jockey stopped to announce that a small cross had been found. The young woman most likely to win a wet T-shirt contest, with the widest wanton leer in the place, raced to reclaim it.

Downtown, a *pétanque* pitch sits just behind the Basque *fronton* court where players with little baskets slam handballs at unbeliev-able speed.

Above all, St. Pierre and Miquelon acts French.

I had a morning appointment with Gérard Lefèvre, the *préfet.* On the way, I stopped to see the head of Interpêche, the fish plant around which the islands turn. He was worried about a docker's strike, which paralyzed his exports. The dockers were fighting with his packers. Each claimed the right to unload the *Bretagne,* a newly commissioned factory ship on which the island depended. Interpêche was in danger of going under, he said. Without it, the only employer would be the government.

Then an aide rushed in and murmured something in his ear.

"You must excuse me," the director said. "All my workers have just left the plant to expel the prefect."

French overstatement, I thought. But just in case, I hurried over to the *Préfecture.*

Had the people who stormed the Bastille smelled like fish, what I found might have been a rerun in miniature of 1789. No one seemed about to lose his head, but there was the unmistakable scent of French revolution.

Crowds roiled outside the little wooden building. An angry few with a grievance were diluted by the curious, enjoying a break from life on an island where nothing ever happens. Inside, the rabble ruled. Men in parkas streaked with fish slime jammed the narrow hallway. Some joked and laughed; others spewed curses and smacked knuckles into calloused palms. In the dead of the North Atlantic winter, a *complexe d'Astérix.*

In the prefect's office, workers sprawled on upholstered chairs and on the floor. A loutish youth in a filthy knitted green wool hat thumbed through a coffee-table book. They tracked fish scales and muddy snow across the green carpet, pacing back and forth to the windows to shout to others below on the street.

Lefèvre, in a dark gray suit and bordeaux tie, sat stiffly behind his desk under a somber portrait of François Mitterrand. He affected interest in a sheaf of papers on the desk. From time to time, he gazed at nothing in particular, light glinting off his metal-rim glasses.

A hall door opened and a voice said, "Monsieur Rosenblum?"

An aide pulled me inside and closed the door. It, uh, did not seem, er, as if the *préfet* could keep his appointment. The aide was polite and controlled, but his fingertips fluttered like aspen leaves.

"I'm certain you won't think badly of St. Pierre because of this," he said. "It has its good side." He then outlined a few of them. But people grow excitable over small things, he explained. After all, unloading the *Bretagne* amounted to only twenty hours of work for twelve men, six times a year. Why all the fuss? "You see how they are here," he said. "Small things become important."

It was, of course, impossible that they would expel the prefect. It would blow over; they were just worked up. After all, he is the representative of France. He was trying to reach a compromise solution and all would end happily.

I asked why the gendarmes did not simply clear the building. No one was armed with so much as a codfish, and only a few dozen workers formed the kernel of protesters.

"Oh, no," he said. "Our twenty-five to thirty gendarmes are not the force necessary to hold back a civil outbreak of 100 people. What can we do?"

He shook my hand and urged, "I would advise you to treat this as an anecdote, not an event. It really doesn't mean anything."

In fact, it meant a great deal. Lefèvre was not only the personification of France, he was also the director of 1,000 civil servants on the islands—half the work force. (In Miquelon, the number of government workers per inhabitant is as high as fifty times that of French villages.) He also controlled French subsidies in a state where imports exceed exports by four to one. By one set of figures, France spends $4,200 a year per inhabitant.

I asked how much of the national budget was spent each year on St. Pierre and Miquelon. His answer was one I had heard often in Paris and around the empire: "We don't know, there are too many factors involved." Surely, I said, such calculations were made. "I suppose one could amuse oneself by doing that," he replied. "But we don't."

In the hallway, I asked for an explanation from an apparent leader, a tall young man, tough-looking in a stained green field jacket. He said it was plain that the fish packers were in the right. An earlier decree had spelled that out. But, he said, Lefèvre had been waiting for months to make a clear statement.

"He has to decide, and if he does not, he's gone on the plane to Halifax," the man told me. *"C'est tout."*

Nothing changed for three hours. Then word came that the Halifax flight had been canceled because of bad weather.

"What now?" I asked the head fish packer.

"The runway is closed, not the sea. We'll use a boat. Or he can swim. We'll take him to the wharf in a wheel chair. But he's gone."

He was enjoying his role as spokesman until I asked his name. "We've seen too much crap in the papers for us to give any names," he said. This was a routine I had heard often enough in Paris but never in a town visited by reporters once a decade. I got his name from someone else, for the form, and then figured what the hell.

True to their word, at 2 P.M. the workers scooped Lefèvre out of his chair, pausing only long enough to let him put on a fur coat against the freezing wind. They hustled him down 300 yards of waterfront, across Place Charles de Gaulle, to the little ferry dock. For half an hour they stood guard as the launch, *Petit Miquelon*, idled in place. Finally, the boat cast off and putted ignominiously out of the harbor.

The *préfet* did not make the two-hour crossing to Canada as ordered. Instead, he made for the less populated island of Miquelon, to the north. He broadcast a victory statement, but his day was lost. Senator Marc Plantegenest, president of the elected General Council, took over negotiations. When the workers tried to push a point, he retorted, "I am not a *préfet* that runs for the plane every time I get a fright."

After much banging of tables and upturning of noses, the fishery workers scored their points. A commission from Paris reached a compromise that recognized the dockers' monopoly on cargo but let the fish plant crews load the containers on board. Lefèvre was summoned to Paris "for consultations." A few days later, he appeared on a list of prefects being reassigned "on a routine basis." No new post was immediately available.

The workers were delighted at imposing jungle rule on the island. Just in case, they took their precautions. They roughed up the cameraman of the government's television station and threatened to attack the newsroom if he did not relinquish his film. The threat proved empty but also needless; the camera was jarred and blocked constantly, and the footage was blurred. A gorilla in a mustache smacked me for taking pictures, and his buddies announced they would toss me into the thirty-three-degree water if I continued.

Later, the spokesman and his pals turned out to be fairly nice guys with selective memories for the facts of the preceding day. They explained their caution. In an earlier disturbance, the government used television film to identify workers who vandalized state property. "Now," announced one of the leaders, indignant, "they face prosecution." Did it occur to them that constitutional republics tended to impose accountability for public disorders? Or that marching down the street in broad daylight, shoving along a kidnapped French *préfet,* would not go unnoticed even if they decided to censor the press? It had, but they did not give a damn. The constitution is a point of principle and, as such, easily elbowed aside when self-interests intervene. It was only logical.

For islanders whose livelihoods depend on Interpeche, any solution that calmed tempers was a happy one. But reflections were bitter.

"There goes order, there goes the Republic," muttered a professional man at the edge of the crowd. "Any jerk can do anything he wants and no one will do anything about it."

A self-employed gentleman who spoke a lot of sense during my visit put it like this:

> The state is afraid to do anything, just like it was in New Caledonia. All it would take would be a few cans of tear gas, and everyone would go home, and there would be some respect for France. Instead, we have this. You watch, someone is going to get pushed in the harbor and frozen, or hit in the head by accident, and we will have violence. Now, with the Change, the local politicians will be able to do anything they want.

The Change was a step away from France—not far—engineered by local politicians and backed by an unofficial poll of voters who seemed to have little idea of what it meant. In early 1985, St. Pierre and Miquelon became a "territorial collective" rather than an overseas department. As a result, it was no longer part of the European Economic Community, and it could deal more freely in the dollar zone surrounding it. But some business leaders, Chamber of Commerce president Louis Hardy for one, saw little practical advantage. The main effect was reducing the power of *les mayous.*

Mayou, a corruption of an old word for carpetbagger, is the equivalent of *z'oreille* in a territory with only people of European stock. The *préfet,* for example, is one. There is no racial connotation.

But a *mayou* is an outsider in a society that would just as soon have its subsidies transferred by mail and not delivered in person.

The Change is a technical one, Georges Lemoine, minister of the overseas departments and territories, explained to me in Paris. "In St. Pierre and Miquelon, we have 6,000 fellow citizens who wish to live under the French flag. We will accommodate them. The cost is irrelevant."

But the new status places more decisions in the hands of the General Council. A lot of St. Pierrais are happier that way.

"We are a peaceful little community, with our own way of life," said Joseph Lehuenen, local historian and museum curator, whose gray lapels are festooned with the red ribbon of the Légion d'honneur. No propagandist, Lehuenen can recount from his prodigious memory every black day of the islands' past.

"They call the coast off Miquelon and Langlade the graveyard of the Atlantic," he said with some pride. Until politely sidetracked, he had launched on a recap of each of the 675 shipwrecks in local waters since 1790.

I asked him about murders. He leaped to a pile of dog-eared notebooks and recited from one marked "1982": ". . . a forty-one-year-old Basque descendant, Edouard Etchéverria, was found dead, stabbed by twelve knife wounds. . . ." If you don't count the 1929 shooting of a Norwegian sailor by an American rum runner, it was the only killing of this century. In the 1800s, there were only three, including one St. Pierre has not forgotten.

In 1848, Joseph Néhel stabbed a man in a bar. French law prescribed the guillotine, so one was brought up from Martinique. The only executioner to be found was a local drunk, who panicked at the last moment. He finally released the blade, but in the meantime, Néhel's struggling had twisted the frame, and the blade stuck. Horrified authorities finished the job with a butcher knife.

Lehuenen brightened when the subject shifted to the islands' heyday, from 1919 to 1933, the period of American Prohibition. Rum runners in eighty fast craft sneaked up to 300,000 cases of booze a month into the United States, from black French Caribbean rum to Scotland's finest whiskeys. There were reverses, such as when the U.S. Coast Guard blasted the *I'm Alone* out of the water. A Frenchman on board froze before he could be rescued, and an international incident lingered for six years. But St. Pierre's fortunes of today were made by converting fish freezers, basements, and bank vaults into liquor warehouses.

The traffic started when Bill McCoy, the original "Real McCoy," selected St. Pierre as a jump-off point for his quality contraband. Al Capone spent a night at the Hotel Robert and left his straw boater as a souvenir. Local archives contain a complaint from an American bootlegger:

> Queer, you people down there, a French colony, don't keep a decent brandy. You can buy it all right, but I am damned if one can get a decent drink of brandy in St. Pierre. Brandy is one thing that can't be imitated. Any amateur can tell a good drink of brandy from that rotgut they sell down there. I am afraid you fellows want to make too much money. A puncheon of alcohol and you're all set! Color, and flavor.

With the slightest encouragement, Lehuenen produces his treasure: a mantel clock engraved with the signature of Charles de Gaulle. He was mayor when de Gaulle sanctified the islands by a visit in 1967. That, he pronounces, was the greatest day of St. Pierre and Miquelon history.

De Gaulle—and what he stood for—has loomed large in the islands' lore since Christmas Eve, 1941, when France invaded the French colony. It was over this invasion of St. Pierre and Miquelon that de Gaulle first incurred the wrath of Franklin D. Roosevelt and his secretary of state, Cordell Hull, which colored American attitudes toward him, and his toward America, for decades.

After Germany occupied France, the islands' governor declared his loyalty to the Vichy government, but few St. Pierrais were happy about it. Many had volunteered to fight the war, enthusiastic even after they were billeted with black troops from the French Caribbean by officers who knew little of the islands' ethnology.

De Gaulle sought to rally the islands. He argued that radio transmitters off Newfoundland could aid Nazi ships in the North Atlantic. But Roosevelt trod a careful line during the war's early years, and he insisted on de Gaulle's assurances that he would do nothing to provoke the Vichy government.

On the day de Gaulle promised U.S. envoys he would take no action, he secretly ordered an assault. The submarine *Surcouf* and three corvettes, lying off Halifax, took the islands without a fight. Hull railed in public against the "so-called" Free French Movement. Words like "duplicity" peppered his private documents.

De Gaulle's 1967 visit shone warmth on a population which, however much it refers to "the French" as if France were a foreign country, clings tightly to the emotional and financial comfort of the motherland.

And de Gaulle, more than anyone before or since, bridged the gulf between the last bit of France and the vast territory that Louis XV abandoned. But on that North American trip, he tightened jaws across English-speaking Canada. From a balcony of the Montreal Hôtel de Ville, facing the column commemorating Lord Nelson, he bellowed, *"Vive le Québec Libre."*

A generation of French and Canadians have debated his meaning. De Gaulle made no move to reclaim Quebec after two centuries nor to incite a war of independence. His cry was rhetorical and symbolic, but in France those are no small adjectives. Spoken at the height of a quiet revolution among Quebecois, his words pounded themselves into history.

Feelings have since calmed. But France and Canada, under elaborate wraps of courtesy and gentle diplomacy, are at war. France claims a 200-mile territorial limit around its islands which, in places, are fifteen miles from Newfoundland. The practical issue is codfish. But surveys suggest that offshore oil lies within the disputed boundaries, as well as extractable minerals. A popular theme in St. Pierre is the Falklands War between Argentina and Britain.

"Canada is not Argentina and will not invade," observed Louis Hardy of the Chamber of Commerce. "But they have other ways of pressuring us. We are a foreign power in their midst." A local official put it, "Oh, we irritate them, all right. We are, as we say in France, a thorn in their foot."

Senior officials of France and Canada were about to take their dispute to a third party in 1986. "We have no designs on St. Pierre and Miquelon, which have been French for a long time," a Canadian negotiator told me. "But a 200-mile limit is a little excessive when it reaches into Canada, and there are problems with fishing rights. Let us just say the French make life interesting."

At times, there is more hostility between St. Pierre and Paris over Canada than between Paris and Ottawa. In early 1985, the Socialist deputy from St. Pierre, Albert Pen, suggested to an aide of Fabius that France send warships. Later, he wrote a blistering letter to the prime minister:

> Negotiations after negotiations, and the Canadian position hardens ceaselessly, while our economy declines inexorably: 26 percent growth in unemployment in a year. You refuse to take into account our budgetary difficulties, sheltering behind a decentralization that could not be applied here. . . . What good is a new statute recognizing we are neither the Côtes-du-Nord nor the Seine-Maritime? . . . Must we wait, arms crossed, for Paris to finally agree with Ottawa behind our backs? I fear . . . it would be better for us, St. Pierre and Miquelon, to deal with Canada ourselves. . . . *Outre-mer,* apparently, fidelity does not pay.

FROM THE CANADIAN side, the picture is different. In the Maritimes, few Canadians are sure where the islands are, let alone worry about them. Ottawa holds all the cards on any procedural question. And in Quebec, where the roots are French, Quebecois see themselves as no more tied to France than the St. Pierrais see themselves as French-Canadians.

People on both sides insist that only language links the French and French-Canadians. For the rest, ties are historical and sentimental. And even to say common tongue is pushing it slightly.

The French like to point out that their language is free of the awkward corruptions of Quebec. If, for example, the Quebecois insist on saying *magasiner* for "to go shopping," the St. Pierrais prefer the pure Parisian usage: *faire le shopping.* In Quebec, a weekend is a *fin de semaine.* In St. Pierre, as everywhere else in France, it is *un weekend.*

More important than vocabulary, though, is accent. Quebecois tend to sling around their syllables like bundles of beaver pelts or sawn logs. They waste little effort routing vowels through tortuous nasal passages. Rather than savoring consonants and releasing them gently, they hammer them out, adding a brief drawl for good measure. It is cold in Quebec, and the language that developed reflects the life of those who spoke it. It is hard and practical as a double-bitted axe.

The French could not imagine Canada's weather. Rabalais, depicting the winter, reported that it was so cold, sailors' words froze in mid-air. In springtime, crews on passing ships could hear the conversations of the previous winter. Some French of the time weren't sure he was exaggerating.

The extreme is a colorful argot called *joalle,* or horse; that's how *cheval* comes out at forty below. But higher Quebecois is pleasant and pure, tinged with *z* sounds where the French would put a *d.*

"The French always compare, and say, 'Well, in France, we do it this way,'" said my friend Hélène in Montreal, whose French sounds like tinkling bells. "They go on until you say, 'Well, fuck, go back to France. We don't need you.'"

But she loves France, from where her grandparents migrated. "I am French-Canadian but when I go back, I am from Normandy," Hélène said, pronouncing it "Normanzie."

Quebecois is rich in references to the church, and only the reckless risk offending the faith. Few curses are worse than *tabernac,* taking tabernacle in vain. "Catholicism," says Hélène, educated by the good sisters, "has the same hold here as voodoo in Haiti."

Hélène remembers that ten years ago, working for Bell Laboratories in Montreal, she was forbidden to speak French with friends in the cafeteria. Law 101 of 1975 changed all that. Now Bell Laboratories, and everyone else, has to use French for all signs, public notices, and official communications.

In Montreal, Law 101 seems a bit forced. On television, "Three's Company" becomes "Vivre à Trois," with clumsy dubbing that misses the word play. Kentucky Fried Chicken is somehow not *poulet frite.* The city feels French, with its wrought-iron exterior staircases. And its churches; Mark Twain once observed that you couldn't point a canoe in Montreal without running its bow through a church window. But it is also heavily Victorian and modern American. After a decade of Law 101, some English merchants had enough and reverted to their old signs, and the law was in court.

In the narrow, winding eighteenth-century streets of Quebec City, however, French is the natural language. And in the back-woods and on farms, the question does not arise. Few rural people can stumble through the most rudimentary English.

"People around here know they trace back to France, a long time ago, but they never think about it," remarked Pierre, a graphic artist I met in the upcountry village of St. François de la Rivière du Sud. "They don't think of it as the language of France. They speak their language."

In sophisticated circles, France is a constant. "Intellectuals who want to increase their cultural impact have to pass via Paris, like it or not," observed Sylvie Maes, a French psychologist married to a Dutch-Canadian in Montreal. "At the same time, they want to be on their own." Young professionals avidly watch rebroadcasts of France's beloved "Apostrophes," a weekly clash of authors' wits. Families on remote farms tap heavy boots along with Michel Drucker's Saturday night special, "Champs-Elysées." *Paris-Match* sells out quickly. A quarter-million French-Canadians a year vacation in France for holidays, admitting to a certain pleasure at being referred to as *nos cousins*.

France is a cultural ally to people in an ostensibly bilingual nation who, from time to time, still hear "Speak white!" when they travel out of Quebec.

A French diplomat with ample Canadian experience said:

There is a deep love-hate relationship, no question about it. After the Plains of Abraham, French officials went home. All that were left were the priests. Many were bitter at separations be-tween the French church and state, and they projected a certain image of France. A lot of French-Canadians have not gotten over how Louis XV abandoned them. They have had a different development, obviously, and their way of life is completely different from that in France.

But there is an attraction to France, a fascination with it, and the young French working here push this to the hilt. It's a huge team effort to sell France, to rekindle feelings of attachment. Not political, but cultural and emotional.

I don't think the Quebecois think of themselves as French in

any way. But I'll tell you one thing: when someone is invited
to the consul general's residence—even for the most boring of
ceremonial events—he comes.

The lingering Quebecois dream of independence from Canada
seems to be over. In 1984, René Lévesque ended a sixteen-year battle
to separate Quebec from Canada. The mood shifted; members of his
Parti Québecois, like those in the opposition, were more worried
about jobs and salaries. But the idea of a Quebec linked culturally
to France remains entrenched, nurtured by vigorous official campaigns.

In 1965, a poll showed few French even knew where Quebec was;
many placed it in South America. At the time, a cultural accord
appropriated the equivalent of $2 million for exchanges and educa-
tion on both sides of the Atlantic. Twenty years later, resources were
eight times greater.

Eighty thousand French live in Quebec, and most have taken out
dual citizenship. A thousand French students study in Canada.
Under an exchange program 600 professionals from France and
another 600 from Quebec work on technical assistance contracts.

But a reverse spin works against Franco-Quebecois cooperation.
In 1984, the Quebec government bought 9,000 computers designed
in France and built locally. That touched off a storm between those
who decried a sentimental purchase, without regard to quality, and
others who denounced a prejudice against French technology. As a
result, officials in Paris complained, Quebec shunned France's best
technology. The Renault Alliance caught hold, according to the
French, because it was made in the United States.

Nonetheless, Canadian politicians ignore the French factor at
their peril. John Crosby of Newfoundland blew his chances some
years back when someone asked him how he would speak with
French Canadians. He said he would do what he did when speaking
with the Chinese ambassador: use an interpreter.

For decades, Canadian prime ministers were hostile to any direct
cultural link between French-speakers and Paris. Brian Mulroney
changed the pattern, clearing the way for the 1986 *francophonie*
summit. He came to Paris with Quebec premier Robert Bourassa,
who promptly invited everyone to Quebec for the next summit.

Prime Minister Richard Hatfield of New Brunswick also led a delegation because of all the Acadians in his province. He could speak no French, however, and he had no interpreter.

In fact, Canada is moving in on the mission to civilize. "There they were, selling like crazy and pushing their own cultural leadership among Third World delegations," a Canadian journalist told me. "On one hand it was shocking, and on the other, funny as hell."

Mulroney noted in his address, "It makes us a unique country, to be nourished by two cultures which are among the richest in modern civilization. . . . For us, *la francophonie* is more than being pro-French and defending linguistic purity . . . it is fundamentally for us the sharing of our existence and of our possibilities for growth."

In 1986, Canada put $280,000 in trust so that the Académie Française could each year honor someone for contributing to "the *rayonnement* of universal *francophonie.*" The grant was announced with an almost comical fanfare in simultaneous news conferences linked by a scratchy telephone line. "It is marvelous that by modern technology we are speaking across the ocean," Maurice Druon of the Academy told Canadian culture minister Benoît Bouchard, "and our language is French."

But the lines may never be clear. When Prime Minister Pierre Mauroy visited Canada in 1983, protocol demanded a long goodby. He left Quebec with a ceremonial send-off, officially ending his state visit. But before returning to Paris, he stopped in Ottawa to leave Canada.

CHAPTER EIGHTEEN

United States: Les Amerloques

CANADIANS MAY BE mixed in their feelings for France, but Americans career wildly twixt phobia and philia. Almost anyone who has stopped briefly in Paris can wrap up the French in a few stereotypes. Those who have not usually harbor ironbound prejudices anyway, for or against. And any American who knows the French well tends to love them and hate them with equal passion.

In France, where Americans—*les Amerloques,* in slang—are seen in the same extremes, such ambivalence seems only natural.

French–American relations have varied sharply at every level since before the United States was a country. How you see them depends on where you pick up the thread. History is the worst place to start.

French teeth gnash at Americans' somewhat selective view of the past, which tends to date Creation from somewhere in the eighteenth century. By then, the French had shaped modern philosophy and perfected 340 different ways to make cheese.

If it weren't for us, Americans constantly remind the French, you would all be speaking German. If it weren't for the French in the 1780s, of course, Americans would be paying a stamp tax to Queen Elizabeth II. Families who suffered German occupation in the 1940s, or who were bled white between 1914 and 1918, do not feel that the United States breezed in and won either war alone.

The two societies are hardly strangers.

American pioneers moving west were not grateful to the French for inciting the Indians to massacre them in their sleep. Back in 1727, a merchant named David Coxe warned:

> The French, who all the world acknowledge to be an enterpriz-ing, great and politick Nation, are so sensible of the Advantages of Foreign Colonies, both in reference to Empire and Trade, that they use all manner of Artifices to lull their neighbors A Sleep, with fine Speeches and plausible Pretenses, whilst they cunningly endeavor to compass their Designs by degrees, tho' at the hazard of encroaching on their Friends and Allies, and depriving them of their Territories and Dominions in time of Profound Peace, and contrary to the most Solemn Treaties.[1]

But then there was Walt Whitman: "Again thy star, O France, fair, lustrous star, in heavenly peace, clearer, more bright than ever, shall beam immortal."

Only a few hundred Americans a year visited France in the mid 1800s, but travel writers loved the place. "We shall always remem-ber something of pleasant France and something also of Paris, al-though it flashed upon us as a splendid meteor, and was gone again," Mark Twain wrote in *Innocents Abroad*. One detail: "In Marseilles they make half the fancy toilet soap we consume in America, but the Marseillaises have only a vague, theoretical idea of its use, which they have obtained from books of travel." But at Versailles, Twain waxed lyrical over the people who showed the world the way.

In his last years, de Gaulle noted that France's independence might displease "a state which might believe that because of its power it is invested with a supreme and universal responsibility." He added, "The reappearance of a nation whose hands are free, which we have again become, obviously modifies world politics which, since Yalta, seemed to be confined to two partners only." American statesmen were repeatedly tempted to remind him how France managed to reappear with untied hands.

Across an ideological gulf, Reagan and Mitterrand forged some of the closest U.S.–French links ever. The French president repeats de Gaulle's message, that world peace and justice depend on more than two poles. But he is nicer about it. The practical politics change by the month. To look at French-American relations, it is safer to start in the warmth of the rhetoric. And the symbols.

As the Paris metro rattles over the Bir-Hakeim Bridge from the fifteenth *arrondissement* to Passy, a glance to the left reveals the Statue of Liberty: torch, spiky crown and all, a hallucinatory flash of the view from the Staten Island ferry. The original stone lady on the Seine, rarely seen by visitors, is the symbolic godmother of the United States.

France gave the United States a larger version in 1886, a century after French troops helped the Continental Army throw off British rule. Most people had forgotten where it came from until 1986 when the combined hoopla of two nations reminded them. From July 4 to Bastille Day, Americans heard of little else.

At the time of the gift, France was launched full tilt on Jules Ferry's mission to civilize. What greater source of pride than a strong nation that took root thanks to gentle guidance from Paris and the force of French arms? The name of the hour was the same one evoked generations later by Americans storming the beaches of France in peril: Marie-Joseph-Paul-Yves-Roch-Gilbert du Motier, marquis de Lafayette.

Today, forty-two American cities and towns bear the name Lafayette. Some have all but forgotten the "Hero of Two Worlds," the French statesman who served as a major general under George Washington. But Lafayette, Louisiana, is a living temple to the glory of things French. Sort of.

A sign at the airport proclaims Lafayette as the heart of Acadiana, a land of spiritual borders that is home to the descendants of French settlers who were deported from eastern Canada by the British: the Cajuns.

The first families lived isolated in Acadia, in what is now Nova Scotia, from 1604. Then Britain moved in. Acadians would not swear to fight their French kinsmen in Quebec, so in 1755 they were dispatched into diaspora. A few thousand reached New Orleans, but the citified French there regarded them as trash. The Spanish, having just taken over Louisiana, had enough problems. The Cajuns and their ancient Norman ways were shuffled off to the swamps.

The Cajuns became Americans in 1803, like everyone else in Louisiana. To reach America, they only had to cross the Atchafalaya

Basin, so dense with cypress and mangrove it took a week to canoe twenty miles.

Around Lafayette today, the potbellies and pickups, and the polyestered lawyers cruising the Hilton bar, do not suggest anything Louis XV left behind. I-10 slices over the bayous. *Cou rouge* (as in redneck) oilmen swarm overhead in helicopters. Cajuns and outsiders each imbue the other with their strongest traits. But it is soon clear to the visitor that more than the 'Chafalaya has held off 180 years of American colonization.

I had a telephone number. Mike Doucet—Beausoleil, as he appears on records and at Carnegie Hall—responded in good cheer, gamely receiving yet another Anglo probing the Cajun craze. When I got to his house, he brightened. *"Ah, mais tu parles français?"* Then I blew it by differentiating Cajun from "pure French." He heaved a sigh, and I realized language was no simple matter in Louisiana.

Doucet is a master fiddler, but in the bayou country, musician is not a category. Music is not for making money; it is for two-stepping and the *fais do-do* (meaning "Go to sleep," as in "Get the rug rats to bed so we can party.") In real life, Doucet is a writer, historian, and teacher.

He and his wife, Sharon, live on the last two acres of what was his family's 900-acre soybean farm. The handsome, ramshackle wood house, built in 1820, is a French-American history lesson in itself: Canadian lines, a Haitian-style porch, tucked back in the Spanish moss of southwestern Louisiana.

Doucet, too, is ramshackle and handsome, bearlike, with deep laugh wrinkles and a prematurely graying beard. In English or French, he speaks with a soft how's-your-granddaddy? drawl that conveys the warmth that permeates Cajun territory.

After a bit, the Doucets paid the supreme, if not rare, Cajun compliment: they invited me out for mudbugs. At Alligator Cove, in front of a baking pan piled fourteen inches high with crawfish steamed in cayenne pepper, Mike talked about Acadiana.

"The culture here is Creole, homegrown. It's not so much France. The language is basically the seventeenth-century French the people spoke when they left. That's pure. But it has been a long time. When the Acadians were booted out by the English, France didn't come

to their aid. There's no great love for the French. Still . . ." He tore
the heads off a few more crawfish and warmed to the subject.

"I went to France in 1974 for a few weeks and stayed six months.
I love it there, and I go back all the time. And the French are
fascinated by our culture, our music. It is a mix, French, people from
Haiti, other blacks."

Was it true, as some argued, that migration from Haiti had
completed France's crescent through America, from the mouth of
the St. Lawrence to the South American coast?

He shrugged and laughed.

"You know, when the British conquered, they made everyone
bow to the crown. The Spanish, they killed everyone. With the
French, they made love to everybody. You can't say, hey, that's it,
anymore." He meant that by now the blood lines are hard to trace,
and cultures are melding.

Doucet worries that the French flavor may die out if children
stop speaking the language. But like many Cajuns, he is skeptical
of an officially backed program that brought teachers from Europe.

"They'd be talking about the Eiffel Tower to kids who'd never
seen anything higher than a grain elevator," he said. "Parisian
French is not what the kids hear outside."

The teachers, 300 at first and fewer now, were brought in by the
Council for the Development of French in Louisiana (CODOFIL).
It is state-funded but more an extension of the personality of James
(Jimmie) Domengeaux, an oilman and former congressman who
organized it.

Tireless, and not one to avoid publicity, he insists that French
French must be the lingua franca for a Cajun cultural revival.
CODOFIL's little building in Lafayette is a shrine to the cause.

In 1975, Domengeaux had stricken from the books a 1921 law
forbidding children to speak French in school. Cajuns recall having
to kneel on corn kernels, their noses pressed to a small circle on a
blackboard, as punishment for confusing "thank you" with *"merci."*

More recently, the state legislature agreed to provide French
instruction in any school where 25 percent of the parents wanted
it. Lack of funds, however, has left that as mainly a good intention.
CODOFIL has a long way to go. French visitors note that Domen-

geaux himself does not read French, and his wife does not speak it.

Many Cajuns speak French without any help from Baton Rouge, or Paris. Russel Dupuis, who describes himself as a Cajun-American Indian born on the 'Chafalaya River, wrote to the *Acadia Times:* "What we do not need, and never did, is Gallic imperialistic meddling. We know and understand ourselves. . . . Imperialism is like a parent who never willingly gives up, even when the child is mature. We want out from your microscope, stop riding our tailgates!!"

Perhaps 800,000 Louisianans understand some form of French, but the range is wide: Creole French from New Orleans, stilted and rare; *français nègre,* a pidgin French evolved by the freed slaves and upper-class whites left too long with their nannies; and Cajun, a blend of early Renaissance French laced with Southern street jive.

And there is the real thing. The week I was in Lafayette, so was Eugène Ionesco, presenting a play. Which one? *Parlons Français.*

One morning, I drove south, pursuing research as a flimsy excuse to kill time before the next meal. At St. Martinville, I visited Father Jean-Marie Jammes and ran smack into the language question again.

The French Foreign Ministry had sent Père Jammes to Louisiana as one of three "animators" to promote French culture. He was a priest, but he also had a doctorate in sociology from the University of Chicago. The program was abandoned, but he changed bosses and stayed. He was assigned to the parish of St. Martinville, once known as *le Petit Paris* for its splendid (and long since forgotten) opera and its coterie of aristocrats who hid there from the guillotine.

"Cajun is not Creole, it is a pure form of French, with some different nuances," Père Jammes assured me. "French people can understand it easily." To prove it, he showed me a Cajun-English dictionary compiled recently by a Lafayette-born priest named Jules Daigle.

Cajun is French, but the nuances are not always subtle. For the verb "to tape record" the French say *enregistrer sur un magnétophone.* Father Daigle's dictionary has it as *recorder sur un tape recorder.*

The dictionary was a smash success, and orders came from across the world. One customer was the Académie Française.

Père Jammes also showed me an article he had published, self-explanatory from the title: "How and Why We Can and Must Save French in Acadiana." He is optimistic.

"It is hard to speak French when the television is blaring English," he said. "You switch to English yourself without realizing it. But people realize the advantages of French, and no one is humiliated for speaking it. Now the American government is protecting minorities, and languages—it is a better time."

On a drive down to New Iberia, I asked Father Jammes if the church played as big a role in preserving Acadiana's French character as it did in Quebec. "Yes, definitely," he said. In case of confusion, he added, "Very definitely." Any doubt was dispelled two minutes later.

We pulled up to a gigantic red brick hangar of a store emblazoned "Rosary House, Wholesale Only," over a five-foot white plaster statue of the Virgin Mary. That, like the two sprawling warehouses behind it and the tin barn across the street, was jammed with every manner of plastic Jesus, kitsch Lord's Prayer lamp, stained glass panel and hymnal.

"People still go to mass here," Père Jammes said. "Every Sunday morning, my church is filled to overflowing."

Heading out of town, I stopped at the *Teche News,* a weekly that happened to be celebrating its hundredth year. The editor and publisher, Henri Bienvenu, breathed gentle Southern charm.

"The language was in terrible danger of fading away," he said. "CODOFIL has given a tremendous impetus. I'm forty, and a lot of people my age were not taught French at home."

Since Cajuns spoke French, he explained, descendants of the aristocracy learned English as their badge of having been civilized. As in New Orleans, French blood and family background were important, not so much the language.

It was lunchtime, and I raced for the nearest thing Acadiana has to the Golden Buddha: Mulate's in Breaux Bridge. At night, its low ceiling bows upward from the raucous chank-a-chank music and the stomping swamp boots. A 1948 "Roy Acuff for Governor" poster peels off one wall near a tattered crawfish net. At midday, there is food: stuffed mushrooms and crab; crawfish *étouffée,* smothered in a brown butter and pepper sauce; gumbo; red beans and rice; Jolie

Blonde beer (which says, "Bottled by Pearl Brewery, San Antonio, Texas" in small print). It is, as the French say, to die.

"Mulate's represents what Cajun culture is all about," said the owner, Kerry Boutte, stating a simple fact. "Cajun has become a catchword for whatever some entrepreneur wants to turn out. It has high visibility. We've been real careful to keep this place Cajun. Cooking is something we don't ever want to lose."

Again, language came up. "Well, I don't feel any particular affinity to the French, or animosity," Boutte put it. "But, you know, CODOFIL, they brought out people from France to teach. It's different here. We're self-conscious when French come and demand that we say something. They ridicule us. If they ask, I say, 'Oh, *on parle un peu.*' Our French is different, you know. If I want to say I'm going back home, I might say, *'je vais back à la maison.'*

"We don't want to talk like the French. We like our language. It's fun."

In Baton Rouge, I stopped to see the governor's brother and omnipresent adviser, Marion Edwards. A successful but lavish gubernatorial campaign had left the governor $4 million in the hole. His brother had saved the day with a novel idea: a trip to France.

He signed up 618 people for a week's trip in a chartered jumbo. Shepherded by the governor, the tour got into the locked back rooms of Versailles, penetrated the circles of power, and ate from star-speckled menus. Each person paid $10,000, and the profit was substantial.

"It was the biggest calculated risk of my life," Edwards said, "but we had a massive turnout. It was because of a feeling people here have toward France. The trip had to be what it was."

Governor Edwards was received into an elite fraternity of wine-tasting *chevaliers.* He seized the ceremonial silver cup and, with a loud whoop, chugalugged its contents. Officials smiled politely at his near-misses with the language. At Versailles, he noted the French had opened for the group parts of the palace rarely shown to visitors. He observed: "My brother must have taken care of someone."

Despite his name, Edwards is from near Lafayette. He believes ties with France are strengthening.

With jet travel, he said, people can see France for themselves. It is no longer an abstraction, kept alive by tradition and folklore. The Cajuns, he maintains, are rooted deeply in modern France.

"It is the way of living," he said. "They live like we live, a *joie de vivre*—you know what that means?—pleasure-seeking . . . more prone to accept life as it is rather than moaning about what it should be."

I tried hard to liken the French *joie de vivre* to the Cajuns'. Somehow, I couldn't picture any Frenchman I knew yelping, "*Eeee-hee-heee,* this'll knock your dick in the dirt." But he seemed convinced.

AFTER CAJUN country, New Orleans seems like a Walt Disney mock-up: Frenchland. The roots are plainly there, but they have grown into something totally different. Most of the French Quarter is, in fact, Spanish. What is French is so aggressively and self-consciously so, the visitor is left wondering, so what? At the old quayside market coffee house, a pompous inscription announces that real French people actually drank coffee on that very spot. The menu includes T-shirts and souvenir mugs.

On the place d'Armes, a painter displayed a portrait of Catherine Deneuve with the added note: "French film actress, internationally known beauty."

Fine restaurants are packed with, naturally enough, American tourists. If New Orleans evokes Paris, it is the Paris of early August when every French person who is not bedridden is somewhere else.

In the sumptuous manors and polished manners of blooded Creole families, the old reality is still strong. The New Orleans Historic Archives documents every brioche ever baked in Louisiana. But a friendly French official gave me a candid view:

"Here, they are trying to keep alive a souvenir. Perhaps 600 French citizens are registered in Louisiana, mostly older people. Unfortunately, it is romanticism not rooted in fact: no French companies, no new blood, no way to keep alive the promise."

The French, he said, were in California and Texas, Florida and Georgia, making money like crazy. From New Orleans, I flew to Miami and saw what he meant even before I got my bags back.

A snotty little white poodle pranced through the Miami airport attached to a blonde lady who could only be described as chic:

sunglasses pushed up onto perfectly shaped hair; a kilo of makeup blended to near invisibility; Parisian sun frock molding very pleasant angles. Her reedy voice spilled across the teeming arrival hall: *"Mais, quel bordel, tu sais. . . ."* Her name was Florence; she was French. Her husband was a perfume executive, and they had been in Florida four years.

"You know, when Mitterrand was elected, the words 'socialist' and 'communist' scared a lot of French people," she explained. "Now we are settled here, and I like it very much. Our economic center is here. But our social life is in Paris."

The 1981 elections sent waves of French—and French money— into the United States, just as aristocracy fled the guillotine two centuries earlier. Most felt right at home.

The French have seasoned the American melting pot from the beginning. Pierre-Charles l'Enfant, the town planner, is why Washington, D.C., is at once so esthetically pleasing and such a nightmare for Nigerian cabdrivers new to the job. Charles Prud'homme, a French-Canadian, was one of the first to find nuggets at the start of California's gold rush. Lazare Frères founded San Francisco's first bank so miners could deposit their earnings. And Jack—as in Jean-Louis—Kerouac eventually wrote about what all that gold did to California's soul.

The historic trivia starts with the word America. French maps first used it, taking the name from cartographer Amerigo Vespucci. Those who prefer the present need only look around. At least 200,000 French live in the United States, and another million visit each year.

Recently I took a back road through the Navajo reservation in northern Arizona. Too long on the road, I wanted to curl up quietly for a while under the big toe of Americana. At a tumbledown trading post, strange tongues reverberated from the saguaro-rib rafters: a family of French tourists were remarking on the fried bread.

IN ATLANTA, the French built the subway. The Bank Indo-suez and Crédit Lyonnais are thriving there. American chefs dip at the knee before La Française in Chicago. With 100,000 French between them, Los Angeles and San Francisco feel as French, in places, as Paris feels American. Large French communities stand out in Houston and Detroit.

But New York? Stand in the heart of midtown at, say, 52nd Street and Fifth Avenue. Cartier, on one corner, faces Piaget across the street. The third corner bears the blue, white, red stripes of Air France. The set is not complete. The fourth corner is Japan Air Lines, right next to La Grenouille.

Just before I first went overseas in 1967, I worked at 50 Rockefeller Plaza and bought my last batch of boxy Oxford-cloth button-down shirts downstairs at an all-American clothing store named Kent. Now the new tenant has put up the same sign displayed below my apartment on the Ile St. Louis: Société Générale. In case anyone misses the point, there are also the words "A French Bank."

And the old French presence is modernizing.

The Librairie Française is still there, as it was during World War II when it was a haven for French publishers evading Vichy's censorship. A poster downstairs bears a tribute from writer Jacques Maritain: "Upon the free soil of the United States, works of French expression could continue to appear, attempting to give a voice to the thoughts of a fettered France." Upstairs, it stocks *Ouest-France* and *Nice-Matin* from the provinces, *Votre Bébé,* Tin Tin, and French bubblegum. When French football teams play in the Coupe de l'Europe, crowds clog the promenade watching the shop window's video monitor. The store is authentically Parisian, down to the sign reading "Positively no refunds."

French products are passing from sophisticated luxuries to basic staples. Never mind the Perrier, which is as American as Michelin tires. Orangina and Bonne Maman jams reach neighborhood groceries.

If you scratch the surface, you still find the French, the best and the worst. In the Manhattan TWA office one morning, a ragged-looking young American came in and asked a woman at the counter to do something with his People Express ticket. I'd noticed her already: tight frown wrinkles, thick makeup, pulled-back blonde hair. French. Taped to her computer was a postcard from a nudist camp in southern France, along with a small Tricolor. She pierced the traveler with a withering stare and let him know that her airline, TWA, did not deal at that class level. As he walked out, crushed, she muttered, "Incredible."

After an initial assault on American cultural imperialism, Mitterrand's minister of culture, Jack Lang, shifted toward energetic proselytizing. He came to New York with a French film festival and paid homage to Hollywood.

Americans dive vicariously with Cousteau. They love it when, in a Charles Boyer accent, he threatens to sink the *Calypso* rather than sell it for commercial exploitation. Reagan gave him a Presidential Medal of Freedom, the closest thing he could produce to the Légion d'honneur; it outranks the medal Lang gave Jerry Lewis.

Cousin, Cousine plays on and on at the cinemas. At American universities, comp. lit. majors follow Jacques Derrida in trival pursuit of Heidegger and Hegel. Not much is new, but there is Marguerite Duras. And there is always Proust—or Albert Whatshisname?

A sizable fringe loves France. And there are the France freaks who show off commendable French, lingering on the flashier dipthongs, until they give themselves away with an Elmer Fudd *r*.

The movement, however, is westward. Hemingway's generation was lost in Paris, but the feast has moved back home. Among French artists, writers, and artisans, the pull of New York, and the United States behind it, has been overwhelming.

"But there is a very good reason," said Martine Vermeulen, a potter who crossed the Atlantic in 1961 and stayed. "In France, the mentality is restricted, blocked, everything is impossible. In France, they close the door in your face and walk away. Here, there is always a possibility. If someone can't help you, he will help you find someone who can."

In the 1950s and 1960s, when Germans leaned toward America, French people like Martine were rare. "The snobs in France loved America but didn't want to admit it, for all their arrogance," she said. "Now all that is gone."

For years now, her atelier and gallery on Bond Street have served the purpose of a colonial cathedral.

"Aha," she said with a bright laugh, when I mentioned the proposed name of this book, "but I have been on a mission to civilize for twenty-four years. That is what we French can do. And I have civilized a lot of Americans, taught them of the beauty of breakfast in bed, to celebrate every day, the pretty little things that make a meal a festival. . . ."

Her floor is set in subtle blue tiles like a carpet. A stylized clay cow's skull perches over a mantel. Her shelves are stocked with delicate but earthy platters and pots, cups and urns. She does a brisk business among French tourists who can no longer find her sort of skills at home.

"It is not that the French are taking over but that the Americans are progressing, becoming sophisticated," Martine said. "When I arrived, they didn't know cappucino from croissants. Terribly backward. Now, the fascination of Americans for all that is French, it is phenomenal. It is passionate. It adds something to their existence, a charm, a joy."

Martine sent me to her friend Alain Delouette, proprietor of La Rousse restaurant on 42nd. He immediately picked up the theme.

"In the last years, such a big change. . . . When I came, Americans knew Brie. Camembert, maybe. Now, you find a gourmet shop on every block. One hundred in New York. And customers who are expert at what they see. Cheese, wines. And restaurants. . . . Before, you served *coq au vin, cuisses de grenouille, escargots, canard à l'orange.* That was it. Not any more. You try to get by with that stuff now, and you're out of business in a week. My croissant supplier makes 15,000 a day and can't keep up. . . ."

French analysts pick to death the new American fascination. Explanations involve Springsteen's Levi's and Reagan's slim grasp of economics. I, for one, am confused. I asked a French friend just back from America. She sounded like a recent escapee from a Manchurian mindwash.

"My God, how can I find words? The energy, the power, the imagination. . . . I went to the Jefferson Memorial at night. I could feel him talking to me. I was so overcome with what I heard, felt, experienced, it took me a week after returning just to absorb it all."

However emotional the draw, it is heavily economic. The art market in New York is well heeled. Jobs pay well, and businesses have flourished. For French industry and exporters, the United States is a huge market they are only beginning to penetrate.

France is second in the world in commercial aircraft production; first in trains; third in rocketry; fourth in automobiles. The French excel in medicine and biosciences. And few Americans know it.

"It is not merely ignorance but rather a psychological refusal to see France as an advanced industrial nation and a leader in technology," said Edith Cresson, then cabinet minister charged with pushing foreign trade and modernizing French industries. "Americans need the image of a France of perfumes and fine food and vacations. They won't believe anything else."

I spoke to Madame Cresson in Washington at the modernistic little city of an embassy France just built in Georgetown. She had come on a trade mission, along with 150 potential investors who were meeting with French businesspeople who had already made it in America. French investment in the United States, at about $6.3 billion, was less than Taiwan's or South Korea's. "We are far behind," she said, "the fourth exporter in the world but the ninth to the United States. It will not be easy."

She did her best. Her voice, in slightly accented English, wafted from radios across the country: "We love the United States, and we think it is a wonderful market."

Later, I met a French textile executive, a veteran of the U.S. market, and told him about the embassy extravaganza. He chuckled. "They think you come here on an official mission, shake hands, and then go home and make money. Hah. The Americans don't buy that way, or do business that way. They want service, action, and they won't stick with you if you don't deliver." Time, he allowed, will tell.

Regularly, one side or the other manages to stir up the basic peace. When a Long Island judge banned the Concorde from Kennedy Airport, Giscard d'Estaing fumed at Jimmy Carter. He would not believe an American president could not deliver an appellate decision. Negotiations over oil supplies, interest rates, currency exchange, and trade balances are seldom pleasant.

In 1985, Reagan's ambassador, Evan G. Galbraith, was quoted in an interview as saying that the French Communist Party was "sort of outside the law" and should not be allowed in the government. The Foreign Ministry protested, calling that meddling in French politics.

What really galls the French, however, is how American leaders look at world power. A senior French official remarked to me, "Do they take us seriously? No, I don't think so. We serve a certain purpose for them, of course, but the Reagan Administration, like others before it, feels they are the cornerstone of Free World security, and the allies should follow along with whatever they feel is right."

I tried this out on an official friend, a ranking State Department man who follows European affairs. "It's true, most Administration people regard France—all allies, to some extent, but mainly France —as a pain in the ass to be placated and kept informed but not essentially a major element in the world power balance. That's a mistake, but it's not new."

A main obstacle lingers from the past. "De Gaulle's understanding of world politics violated fundamentally what George Kennan identified a generation ago as the 'legalistic-moralistic' approach to foreign affairs," wrote Robert O. Paxton in the *New York Review of Books*. Americans see themselves as a chosen people, freed of Europe's corruption, and they see allies as "an army of the righteous in which one enlists once and for all, as in an act of personal salvation." De Gaulle, in contrast, "was in recent European history the boldest and most unsentimental practitioner of traditional national-interest diplomacy. Americans could tolerate a backslider, but not an unblushing apostate." Paxton noted:

> What touched Americans most was that de Gaulle doubted their good intentions. Taking it as normal that all states seek their own interests, de Gaulle saw and proclaimed American self-interest where Americans wanted to see their own idealism and generosity. This was more than a disagreement; it was a moral affront.

Reagan discovered this when he sought to enlist the newly elected Mitterrand in holy war against the Evil Empire; he tried to block the Trans-Siberian gas pipeline via Germany to France. But Paris, and Bonn, saw that as neither effective nor in their own interest.

When the French refused overflight permission and obliged U.S. aircraft to add 2,600 miles to their assault on Libya in April 1986,

Reagan was acid. "I see no justification for this," he said. Across the country, people fumed. One veteran noted that he was happy France allowed Americans landing rights on the beaches in 1944. Families cancelled their welcome for French foreign exchange students. Johnny Carson flung a pie at an actor made up as a Frenchman. But soon afterward, Reagan and Mitterrand embraced. Such disputes were in the nature of things, the French president said. And Reagan produced a hoary, "Let today be the first day of the rest of our lives."

Unruly or not, France has its weight. American strategist planners do not overlook France's nuclear force. France motivates the European Space Agency, which competes with Americans to deposit sophisticated gadgetry into orbit. To Reagan's suggestion that allies subcontract components of his Strategic Defense Initiative, Mitterrand replied, *merde,* with only slightly less tact than de Gaulle might have used. France sought to line up European partners behind Eureka, their own high-technology program with Star Wars potentialities.

Some Americans attribute such duplication to French cantankerousness and an unrealistic, wasteful pride. In France, the optics are different. The French have seen a great deal since Vercingétorix. If a finger is to rest on the button, they want it to be a Gallic finger.

And, stepping back from Doomsday, other questions arise. Is France prepared to lose more scientists to Silicon Valley? Can France, with crippling unemployment, happily sell bloated goose liver and Chanel Number Five to a superpower growing steadily richer and more powerful?

The Gaullist, neo-Gaullist, and proto-Gaullist response is clear enough.

Arriving at the White House in 1984, Mitterrand evoked the warm ties of "brothers in arms who together have shed their blood from Yorktown to Beirut." And he added:

> Because France is strong, independent, and confident in itself, true to its great past . . . and sure of its citizens, my country, within its means, can and wants to engage in discussions with all parties on all subjects.

Later in his visit, he let Americans know why he thought so:

> France is a much older nation and to us the United States
> appears still quite young. . . . I believe that our civilization carries
> a message that is not for us alone, that it can be understood and
> accepted by the greater part of humanity.

But in the realm of symbols, national interests slip away conveniently in the name of historic friendship. And as traffic increases
across cultural bridges, France and the United States seem to be
moving closer together.

In late 1984, a team of ten fine metalworkers came over to fix
the Statue of Liberty's makeup. They were funded privately and
officially from both sides of the Atlantic. The men, from Reims in
the heart of Champagne country, were chosen as among the best
iron craftsmen in the world. They brought two tons of hand tools,
including 100 hammers they made themselves.

They tried to make friends with their neighbors late one night
by rapping on the window with a bottle of wine. Police responded.
Their work was delayed because Iron Workers Local 455 protested
the hiring of foreigners. Jean-Michel Grés, one of the group, told
a *New York Times* interviewer how they spent their time: "We
watch the baseball, and they are with the clubs and the running. And
there is American football and they jump on top of each other and
then get off, time after time."

But, they concluded, the Atlantic was not all that wide. Said one,
speaking of his American colleagues: "We are not so different. Some
of them are so big and have tattoos. But they love the statue just
as we do. I saw one of them kissing her."

CHAPTER NINETEEN

Caribbean and Latin America: La Question

NOT LONG AFTER sending the Statue of Liberty to the United States, the French dispatched another shipment across the Atlantic. A Jewish artillery captain named Alfred Dreyfus was exiled to a rock called Ile du Diable, Devil's Island, off the South American coast. He fashioned a stone bench during his imprisonment, and he sat pondering the vagaries of French character. Today, you can do the same. Around the old bench, it is peaceful and absolutely quiet. Except for the moment, every few weeks or so, when an Ariane rocket streaks off the launchpad nearby.

Until World War II, French Guiana was an impenetrable jungle peopled by primitive Indians. It was a dumping ground for prisoners, men like Papillon, who stood little chance of escape against the sharks, mosquitoes, and smashing surf. It is still an impenetrable jungle, but it is France. The Indians, still primitive, are French citizens. And instead of society's dregs, France ships out the finest scientists and engineers it can get to sign a contract for the space center at Kourou.

French Guiana—*Guyane*—was the only French property in South America, which Spain and Portugal divided up while François I was otherwise occupied. Now it is the only piece of the continent to fly a European flag.

IN CONTRAST, Guadeloupe and Martinique are the sort of islands that send travel writers to the thesaurus. They are run-of-the-mill paradise: fine sand and lush flowers, turquoise waters, lavender mountains, reggae and rum punch. That is the physical part. In every other aspect, there is no mistaking them.

A gigantic building dominates the four-lane boulevard into Pointe-à-Pitre, the commercial center of Guadeloupe. Eleven stories high, it covers an entire block, modern, businesslike, and forbidding. It dwarfs the nearby post office and all else around it.

It is the Social Security building.

"Ah, that," laughed a French official when I asked him about it. "That and the church are the two most visited buildings in the islands."

And more than the church, that building symbolizes why the *indépendantistes* face a long uphill struggle. When unemployment in the *métropole* hovers near 10 percent in France, it is above 30 percent in Guadeloupe. Separatists blame that on Paris. But Guadeloupe produces almost nothing, and what jobs there are come largely from the government. Souvenir T-shirts are made in China; shells are packaged in the Philippines.

"In my heart, I am an *indépendantiste,*" remarked a woman who lives well on her salary. "Probably 40 percent of the people are. But when it comes to reality, we have no choice."

Guadeloupeans live well; only Martiniquais and Puerto Ricans earn more per capita in the Caribbean. When they fall sick, when they lose a breadwinner, when they retire, when they get the sack, they have a friend in the Social Security building. French authorities stretch the limits to include common-law couples because so many children are born out of wedlock.

The giant building is a safety net against the sort of misery suffered in Haiti and other parts of the Caribbean. The airport is another.

Why are Antillean mothers all misshapen? runs a popular riddle, posed with bitter amusement. Because every kid is born with a suitcase in his hand. An estimated 180,000 Guadeloupeans and Martiniquais, a quarter of the islands' population, live in France.

But hard times are squeezing shut the safety valves. Fewer jobs are to be found in Paris, and illegal immigrants from Haiti and Dominica are swelling the jobless ranks in Guadeloupe. Pressure is increasing to limit social benefits everywhere in France.

Guadeloupe, for years billed as a model island paradise, is now, stretching no figure of speech, a tropical time bomb.

Being French, Guadeloupeans have a higher threshold of misery than their Caribbean neighbors. The elevated standard of living is a mixed blessing.

There is a private car for every three people, a higher ratio than in metropolitan France, let alone Haiti and Dominica. The capital's narrow streets are choked solid all day long; overpowering fumes and drivers' curses cloud over the picturesque island balconies.

An overlay of *France moderne* leaves Pointe-à-Pitre halfway between what it once was and Marseilles. A gleaming branch of Société Générale fronts the old open market. The old row houses, with battered shutters and fancy ironwork, stand out like bad teeth among the white and glass of modern structures. A cloverleaf traffic exchange, past computer shops and an overcrowded yacht harbor, feeds into a tin-roofed slum.

In Guadeloupe, as in other DOM-TOMS, official wages carry a 40 percent premium, largely to offset inflation caused by the extra 40 percent. The minimum wage of 3,200 francs a month is six times Haiti's.

"Such a gulf separates those who have and those who don't that there is bitterness, tension, and unhappiness," remarked a tourism executive whose job is to say the opposite. "It is not that people are really poor here. It is the frustration of knowing what everyone can do that you can't afford."

Prospects worsen by the year. Field hands cost too much; farmers make little money from sugar or coffee. About 50,000 acres, a third of all arable land, lie unused. The government spent 90 million francs in 1984 to produce 500,000 tons of sugar and save 600 jobs; beet sugar imported from France would cost one-third of that. "This," one official put it, "is *grand luxe* sugar." Industry is incidental: the odd window shutter factory or cannery.

The state was investing nearly a billion francs a year in Guadeloupe's economy by 1985. In 1981, it was half that. In Martinique, state expenditures account for 80 percent of the gross domestic product.

American economists estimate that for every government franc spent in Guadeloupe, Martinique, and Guiana, 95 centimes are spent on goods and services from the *métropole*. Private French studies suggest that the figures more than balance out.

But that perpetuates a closed circuit, economically and politically unsound. For growth, there is only tourism. And that promises no solution. The French faith in the North American market rests heavily on self-delusion. Guadeloupe is pleasant enough, but it is no rare jewel. The mark of development intrudes on its charm. Pointe-à-Pitre's urban sprawl is ugly.

"Exquisite, no?" asked a friend, pointing out a concrete barracks behind a chain-link fence. "That's a new resort . . . beautiful." It was yet another palm and schlock hotel in the Bas-du-Fort zone outside the capital.

In one of them, the French manager extolled the island in American-accented English. "Once more people in the United States discover the fabulous scenery and the warmth of our people, they will come down in great numbers."

Talking to Americans who had discovered Guadeloupe and Martinique injects some doubt.

"God, they are so *awful*," fumed a New York legal secretary, putting in her two weeks in the sun at a French chain hotel. "They're rude, they ignore you, they cheat you, and they charge you a fortune." Elsewhere, a Canadian woman, herself a hotelier, was less complimentary.

The hotels exemplify the extremes of the Antilles. At the Auberge de la Vieille Tour near Pointe-à-Pitre, one clerk, exuding warmth and gaiety, battled for me against the archaic telephone system. The next snarled like a prison guard with a toothache, refusing to undertake the gargantuan task of changing twenty dollars. It was a common pattern, in hotels and elsewhere.

Normally in France, the desire to please weakens the farther one gets from the cash drawer. Small hotelkeepers tend to like customers, not only for the money but also for the testimony to their *accueil*, their welcome. At medium-sized places, employees risk trouble if they sneer at guests when the boss is around. In the big hotels, however, staffs are motivated only by a theoretical principle that customers should get what they pay for. That does not count for much.

In the French corporate mentality, it is natural to exchange francs at seven to the dollar when the banks give eight. Or to triple the telephone rate—even with direct dialing—as a service charge.

But in the Antilles, a wild card is thrown into the standard French games: social, often racial tension. A ripple of hostility can overwhelm feeble feelings that the customer might be right. Yet the reverse applies. Traditional island warmth can add unexpected humor and joy to simple commercial exchanges.

The result is like traveling in the Soviet Union. You are at the mercy of human nature. If you fall upon someone who is susceptible to your particular charm, you hit the jackpot. If not, may the Lord have mercy on your soul.

Unlike in the Soviet Union, what you get, with or without a smile, is likely to look good, feel nice, or taste fabulous. This is not only France; it is the islands.

One of my happiest moments ever was at Madame Basile's, a little clapboard house on the north coast. My friend René took me there, after a long ride through the pitch-dark canefields. Madame Basile belongs up there with Escoffier. She piles the plate with *poisson court-bouillon, blaff,* and *boudin.* Mounds of beans, rice, and fried bananas flank the plate. I slowed down to catch my breath, and she rushed over. "What's wrong? You're not hungry? It's not cooked right?" Before I could answer, she was howling abuse at the kitchen. Only the modest bill reminded me I was not an invited guest at her home.

But coming and going, I found the other extreme.

I flew into Guadeloupe after two months in Canada, the United States, and Haiti; instantly, I was back in France. At the Vieille Tour, a handsome woman with blonde hair and blue eyelids sat at the lobby tourism desk, beaming warmly at something. My glance crossed hers and I smiled back. The thermostat dropped forty degrees. Eyes narrowed to a blank stare. Mouth snapped to a tight straight line. As in the *métropole,* French outposts are not the place for mindless North American Have-a-Nice-Dayism.

On the way out, at the airport newsstand, I brought some magazines to the woman at the counter and waited for her to finish picking at a fingernail. She scowled briefly, totaled the bill, and mumbled, "Twenty-three francs, sixty." She snatched my fifty-franc note and, without bothering to look up, dropped the change in my direction. The coins missed my outstretched fingers. Not even the spectacle of a sweating, swearing tourist pawing among the bags of mints and heaps of *Le Matin* for his twenty-six francs brought a smile to her lips.

Guadeloupe feels tense. It is hard to pin down, but it is obvious. I went with a friend to the home of Marie-Christine, a government employee of some standing. She had the sort of working person's living room you might find in the fifteenth *arrondissement:* glass-fronted buffet with knickknacks, vacation snapshots, a few books, and a lace doily. She poured a *ponch,* prunes steeped in rum, powerful enough to run a tractor. On French TV, we watched Stacy Keach, in a white linen painter's smock, playing *pétanque* in a Provençal village.

I asked Marie-Christine if she felt she was in the same country as that game of *pétanque.* "Not really," she said. "You know, a country is an organic unit where people feel a certain common tie. This is artificial."

Outside her building, someone had scrawled, *"Mort à la Tornade Blanche."* The White Tornado was an elite unit of head-knockers flown from Paris to investigate persistent bombings.

The island's peculiar overlay of self-satisfaction forms a strong defense against terrorists seeking to destabilize the islands. "Look," a local journalist told me, driving along a ramshackle row of wooden slums fronting on an open ditch, "this is a far better standard of living compared to the English." At the hospital: "Look, the most modern in the Caribbean." At a second yacht harbor: "There is nothing like that in the English islands."

I remarked to him each time we passed some hostile graffiti, which was often. He admonished me not to make too much of it. "You should not exaggerate. We have a capitalist mentality in a country that produces nothing. But everything is fine here. There is some ferment, but, after all, this is France, and people like it that way. Those against it are a very small minority."

I said goodnight and suggested calling him later at the office. "I'm working at home these days. The paper was burned down." By whom? "Probably by the *indépendantistes.*"

The *préfet,* Maurice Saborin, was clear about what he was up against. For one thing, each year more youths seem attracted to extreme positions.

"My greatest worry is over the young people, half desperate, coming out of school well educated onto the job market," he told me. "It is a very serious problem, let's be honest about it."

Saborin was a textbook prefect, charming and crisp, with gold-rimmed spectacles and a nicely cut suit. He had been unplugged from his last job, a department in the *métropole,* and would be connected to another. He called himself an administrator, with no function as a political analyst, and then set about disproving that with an astute reading of the complex situation.

He stressed Mitterrand's policy, that of most governments since Guadeloupe and Martinique became departments in 1946. If a majority of voters want independence, appropriate negotiations will take place. If not, legality and security must prevail.

That last part, the prefect acknowledged, was no small job.

An outlawed fringe has exploded hundreds of bombs since 1981 when the Socialist government promised to increase local leaders' power. Four extremists were blown up by their own bomb in 1984. But another four bystanders died in the violence, including an elderly American tourist.

"The independence movement exploits race to the hilt," Saborin said. "Every conflict ends with a call for whites to go. . . . And among the whites, there is racism against the Antilleans [blacks]. The situation here is capable of growing violent very fast."

Qaddafi, he added, meddled in Guadeloupe the way he did in New Caledonia. "I have new evidence that Libyan involvement goes much farther than simple contacts." Two Libyan delegations visited the island, and Guadeloupeans went to Libya. Outside funds supported two radio stations and a newspaper. "It is not cheap to run media like that, without a scrap of advertising."

Saborin said he was determined to prevent terrorism from causing panic. Someone had tried to kill him the year before. But he shops for his own tomatoes, unguarded in the market. His office in Basse-Terre, a rambling old island mansion set back in a park of palms, is hardly protected. I drove in with a casual wave to a bored gendarme. Another officer cheerfully conducted me to the prefect's office without asking who I was or what was in the odd-shaped black bag I was carrying.

At the airport, security guards often wave passengers through without a glance, not even turning on the X-ray machine.

But terrorism is never far away. An Association of Small and Medium-Sized Industries meeting opened with a minute of silence for bombing victims. "You have to understand, this place is small and everyone knows the victims," said the manager of a large hotel. "One bomb here is equal to 1,000 bombs in New York."

In any case, terrorism is not the major problem.

Independence candidates poll only a few percentage points in elections, but their weight is felt throughout Guadeloupe. I drove half an hour down the road to see Claude Makouke, a physician and leader of the Union Populaire pour la Libération de Guadeloupe. Elections proved nothing, he said; the French manipulated them at will. Terrorism was deplorable, he added, but what did the French expect from frustrated people?

"We feel the people are entitled to use every means available to convince the colonialists to leave," he said.

Makouke's UPLG had just organized what they called an assembly of the last French colonies. Delegates took part from every DOM and TOM except St. Pierre and Miquelon. The French Polynesians sent a message of solidarity but did not attend. The meeting's slogan in Creole: *On Sel Chimen, Lendependans.* In French, that would read: *Un seul chemin, l'indépendance.* A single road, independence.

"As the French government proclaims internationally the rights of peoples to choose for themselves, the political reality in Guadeloupe is the opposite," Makouke told delegates. "Reactionary forces are more and more aggressive. . . . France is the occupying colonial power. Relations are those of domination, subjugation, colonial ties. They are intolerable, and they should be completely destroyed."

François Yves, of the Martinique Conseil National des Comités Populaires, stretched for color:

The French colonists are like professional gamblers on Mississippi River boats. They invite you to play and insist you use their marked cards. They are flanked by servants who reveal your hand

and, at last resort, by murderers to slit your throat on the way
out in case, by some chance, you win. French democracy is a ruse.
The cards are stacked.

The Kanaks pronounced their own struggle a guaranteed success and
exhorted others to follow.

Some French snickered that a simultaneous Jehovah's Witnesses
rally outdrew the *indépendantistes* by a wide margin. Desjardins, in
Le Figaro, hooted, "Flop. There is no other word."

But Saborin was not among those laughing. "Sooner or later,"
he said, "something is going to break loose. It would be a serious
mistake to underestimate the *indépendantistes.*"

Three months later, Pointe-à-Pitre was cut off behind barricades
of burning cars, felled trees, and ripped out toilets. Screaming
youths with Molotov cocktails faced off against riot gendarmes
flown from Paris in Boeing 747s. The riots were caused by a freshly
arrived white math teacher who kicked a rowdy black student in
the buttocks. Slave owners did that, and Antilleans don't like it.
Georges Faisans, a burly *indépendantiste,* whacked the teacher in the
leg with a machete. Faisans, jailed for three years, went on a hunger
strike. After two months, violence exploded.

At the same time, Luc Reinette, serving twenty-three years for
terrorism, escaped from prison. He hid out in the hills, like runaway
marrons of the last century. From hiding, he announced that French
officials had secretly discussed independence with him in 1983. Paris
denied it, but Reinette's followers believed him.

Frustrated youths joined the riots, spurred on by veteran militants. If Faisans was not freed, they warned, blood would flow.
Reinette's banned Caribbean Revolutionary Alliance, after a year
of silence, warned it would terminate "the insupportable arrogance
of French bandits who conduct themselves like masters in our
country." It threatened to punish not only the teacher but also a
dentist accused of anesthetizing and raping a fourteen-year-old girl.

Paris moved quickly to reach some solution. An appellate court
reviewed Faisans's case and then released him. A cry of *"Yo lege!"*
— "They let him go!"—rippled around Pointe-à-Pitre. Barricades
were lifted. After the triumphant chanting and fist-waving subsided,
indépendantiste Amédée Etilce told reporters that the outburst gave

Guadeloupeans a new dignity: "This was a turning point; things will never again be as they were before."

Maybe. There are others who recall that the islands, though left-leaning, voted three to one for Giscard d'Estaing over Mitterrand in 1981. The false rumor went round that Mitterrand was soft on independence.

THE FALLOUT was not violent in Martinique, a short hop south, beyond Dominica. On Martinique, the social temperature is lower, and the small independence movement is split. Still, *l'affaire Faisans* made an impact among youths and the jobless whose patience is wearing thin.

Aimé Césaire, deputy from Martinique, mayor of Fort-de-France and poet of negritude, argues for autonomy. Strong links to France are vital, he maintains, but the island must take its own decisions and shape its own economy and society.

Mitterrand said decentralization had brought that about. In a visit in 1985, he made the same point on both islands. "From now on," he told one crowd, "you can be Guadeloupean, pride yourself as Guadeloupean, conduct yourself as Guadeloupean while being proud and happy to call yourself French, citizens of the French Republic."

Such a dichotomy is hard to put into practice. In Martinique, for example, a colleague of mine called on a local tourism official who insisted on his spiritual independence from France. Just then he answered his phone. The man stood up, brought his heels together, and for the next five minutes repeated, *"Oui, Monsieur le Préfet."*

And in Paris, a nurse from the islands grumbled to me, "They colonized us and told us we're all the same, but in truth you're only French on your identity card." She was bitter because her brother studied until 3 A.M. for months to be a police inspector in spite of a racist superior. Eventually, her brother cracked under the constant riding, and he slugged the officer. Now he is trying to be a gym teacher.

Others are, as the president says, proud and happy to be French. And it is clear that they are. Martinique is France down to the statue of its most famous daughter, Napoléon's Joséphine. She is in the vast waterfront park, right hand clutching a rose to her bosom, left lying atop a relief of the emperor's face. The inland sugar mill at which she was born is in ruins. In a small museum there, her white stockings, with a little red embroidered *J,* and her crown are on display along with chains her family used on the slaves.

Martinique's sugar industry is also in ruins. Wages and costs are too high, so two-thirds of local consumption is of beet sugar from France. And the whole economy is like that. At the *Préfecture,* a thoughtful young official told me:

> We could cut away Martinique with little loss. It has no strategic importance any more. We certainly make no money from it. But France does not exist but for its culture and history. There is a certain naïveté, a certain feeling that we can bring something of importance to people. Our presence in the Antilles is an expression of that. We are here for affection. How could a German, say, understand that sort of thing?

GUIANA, WITH ONLY 80,000 inhabitants, is mostly jungled hinterland sheltering endangered tribes of Indians. French officials restrict visitors and settlers. But the pull is strong for Indians who want to work in Cayenne, the louvered and leafy colonial-style capital. Guiana is the most backward part of France. But at Kourou, the combined French space research center and European Space Agency launch site is the twenty-first century.

The contrast is stark. Kourou, fifty miles west of Cayenne, is a shabby little fishing town across from the abandoned prison islands. Its barroom tables dip at the center from ham fists banging on them for attention; a Foreign Legion detachment lives nearby in concrete apartments left vacant by a first space project that went bust. Kourou reeks of boredom, and tension can hang as heavily as the humid air. The place exploded briefly in 1985 when someone killed a legionnaire.

The victims' friends had no idea who did it, so they systematically smashed whatever they found: car windshields, bar tables, whorehouse doors, windows, and the heads of unfortunate passersby. Townsfolk, fed up, got out their own bats and shotguns. By midnight, two platoons of gendarmes were racing down from Cayenne. Final result: one dead, nineteen injured.

A Socialist politician blamed the extreme right for pushing tension. The Legion colonel said his men acted on their own; they did not need prodding by politicians. "One should not hide the fact that conflicts between legionnaires on the town and civilians have been numerous, but up to now they were settled among individuals and the Legion's own service of control."

Some called it a small race riot. Others said it was simply what happens when you put 600 combat-trained men in a small town where local women are guarded at musket point by their families and the white women are married to computer programmers.

The rocket people live in freshly built suburban clusters which crowd the town. They are linked to the capital by a mirror-smooth, extra-wide section of highway.

"We call that the *Route des Blancs*—the White Man's Road—because they would have never built anything so nice just for us," an engineer-turned-*indépendantiste* named Michel Kapel told me. "It is there so that the Ariane rockets don't get jolted on the truck ride from the port at Cayenne to the base."

Kapel heads a party called PANGA. The acronym means "Attention" in local dialect. I noted that it was also an African word for machete. "All the better," he grinned. Kapel wore a giant straw hat with frayed edges, huge comic sunglasses, a yoked Levi vest with no shirt, and ragged pants; he smoked a fat cigar and carried a guitar. After a few minutes' conversation, it was clear he was no clown.

Before leaving Paris, I had asked Georges Lemoine, minister for the DOM-TOM, about the new independence movement there. He shrugged and replied, "How many are there? What do they amount to? Not much."

Kapel agreed that the numbers were small. "That is not the point. The world does not like colonies any more, and France gets away with it because people don't notice," he said. "How much money and prestige do they get from Kourou? For Ariane, they need peace. We will not give them peace. The Europeans will force them to end their antiquated domination."

Did he mean violence, I asked? Kapel hedged a little. Destabilization was a better word, he said. "If they fight us, we'll fight back."

There is clearly discontent. A wide fringe complains that France has done little to develop the long-forgotten enclave while impos-

ing policies against the people's will. But the *préfet,* Bernard Cour-
tois, was probably right. Few of the malcontents would reject
massive French support to a virtually nonexistent economy. And a
great deal of people in Guiana are happy to be French.

Indépendantistes seize an argument heard elsewhere in the DOM-
TOM: France tries to weaken local societies by moving in other
ethnic minorities and by assimilating local people into the French
mainstream. PANGA objects to the absorption of Laotians while
long-time residents from Haiti, Brazil, and Surinam are expelled.
"We are becoming a minority," Kapel said.

Cayenne is like no place else. Over the Place des Amandiers drifts
the clack of mah-jongg tiles as Chinese merchants win and lose large
chunks of the town's retail trade. Sun-browned Frenchmen organize
commerce and banking at café tables by a park of giant palm trees.
On the waterfront and downtown, the old buildings stand in rows:
handsome white columns among rusted tin roofs; collapsing carved
wood balconies and wrought iron scrollwork. "They will tear down
this town and put up a concrete monstrosity, in this land of beautiful
wood," remarked my friend Edmond. "Look around, it is ghastly."
But there is still plenty left.

I am a connoisseur of such raunchy backwaters as those found in
Manila, Panama City, and Lagos. In Cayenne, I found the Versailles
of raunchiness: Chicago. It is a modest-sized two-story bar in a small
slum just over the stinking canal at the edge of Cayenne. The top
floor is routine raunch. A loud band pumps thunderbolts of reggae
into a sweating, slithering human mass generally enjoying itself.
Downstairs is a simple bar; no hookers, armed bandits, or legionnaires. But there is a way people watch you, through eyes narrowed
with suspicion and rum. I could imagine some Hollywood casting
director gleefully scooping up each patron with a butterfly net.
Halfway through one beer, I realized why Edmond, built like a
truck, had been reluctant to come.

By the old power plant, Brazilians squatted in wood-scrap slums
as bad as anything in a Rio *favela.* It was not what France considered
to be housing.

IN EARLY 1985, France inaugurated in Guiana three 500-
kilowatt transmitters, using eleven antennas, capable of carrying the

faintest nasal vowel to the ends of Patagonia and, of course, north-ward as well. They doubled the potential audience of Radio France Internationale. Communications Minister Georges Fillioud ex-plained, "Neither a tool of propaganda nor an instrument of domi-nation, international broadcasting is a privileged means for France to send to foreign nations a sign of recognition but also an appeal: an appeal for exchange, for a dialogue of cultures."

Beyond radio waves, bank loans, and trade missions, France ventures only spasmodically into the rest of Latin America. Old ties remain with Brazil and Mexico. Venezuelans, Argentines, and Peruvians look to Paris for culture and luxury. Most of the region finds France useful as a non-*Yanqui* Western power. But France has higher priorities.

In 1981, Central America was a major interest for the newly elected Socialist-Communist coalition. It was a painless place to differ from the Washington view that every conflict was part of a grand East-West struggle. Mitterrand's wife, Danielle, was cap-tivated by the region. Régis Debray, a leftist intellectual who hobnobbed with Che Guevara in Bolivia, was brought into the Elysée as a counselor. France joined Mexico to lead efforts toward negotiation with El Salvador's dissidents. France sold low-grade military gear to Nicaragua.

Mitterrand reminded Reagan that anti-Communist forces are not necessarily pro-democratic. He reinforced his credentials by embar-going arms to Chile. But the position was not so painless. The Reagan Administration had enough trouble accepting that a gov-ernment with Communists in the cabinet was a reliable partner. Otherwise, there was little advantage to an energetic Central Ameri-can role, and French attention flagged.

In 1985, a visit to France by Argentine president Raul Alfonsin emphasized that Latin America is not so far away. He evoked his country's old fascination with France; some French have even for-given Ambassador Gainza Paz, of years past, who brought his own cattle to Paris to assure himself of decent beef. And Alfonsin made a beeline for Toulouse, birthplace of Carlos Gardel, the tango king.

FRENCH TRACES are strong on an island that has been out of the empire for 180 years: Haiti. Until Indochina and Algeria, no other colony had managed to throw off France in war. And, some Haitians grumble, they are still paying.

Few countries suffer as much misery per square mile. World Bank figures put per capita income at $200 a year, but most Haitians earn nearly nothing. Of eight million inhabitants, perhaps 60,000 have three-dollar-a-day factory jobs making the major leagues' baseballs or assembling electronic parts. Many farmers, with badly eroded land, cannot afford to grow even basic food crops for their families.

When France settled in two centuries ago, this was the richest agricultural colony in the Americas. Turmoil, greed, and neglect are destroying the land. Of eighteen healthy watersheds, twelve are left. A U.S. government study estimated that only one will remain by the year 2006. Once-thick forests are now deserts where peasants scavenge the last stumps and bushes to sell as fuel. Farmers work slopes so steep that some literally must lash their ankles to stakes to keep from falling out of their cornfields.

A small elite controls the best land and creams off the economy. Their mark is a command of French civilization: culture, language, and manners, kept fresh with regular pilgrimages to Paris.

Some argue that that is changing. "We look to New York now and idiomatic English is valued above elegant French," said a journalist-politician whose English is as idiomatic as his French is elegant. "They might talk about Paris, fashions and all, but France is finished. With all the movement, the immigration, it is New York."

He said the French no longer seemed interested in Haitians (they need visas now to visit France) and, in fact, never mixed much with Haitians from the earliest days.

"Merde," said a Port-au-Prince businessman, with *café-au-lait* skin and *salon* manners buffed to a sheen, an expert in art, music, and noble thoughts. "The truly educated and sophisticated Haitians look more than ever toward Paris. This is a bastion of Frenchness in America. Pure, from the eighteenth century. When a Haitian goes to France, he has the feeling of already having been there. For convenience and business, okay, the U.S. Ah, but France . . ."

Whatever Haitians' feelings toward France, it is clear that, for better or worse, they are out of the empire. A writer named Serge recalled, "I studied in France, and I went there to be a Frenchman.

All Paris would throw open wide their arms to welcome me and, man, I was ready. It did not work quite that way."

Haitians deal calmly in black and white, and racism goes down badly. Serge said that when he applied for a job as a clerk, a Frenchman asked all candidates to line up, French on the right and foreigners on the left.

"I was Haitian, so I went left," Serge said. "But this Martiniquais went to the right. The white guy yelled, 'I said, French to the right, foreigners to the left.' This went on, the guy yelling each time louder, until the Martiniquais said, 'Look, I'm French, from the Antilles.' At which point the man bellowed straight into his face: 'I said, French to the right, foreigners to the left.'"

France is represented from a grand mansion set back in the trees, now as seedy as imposing. Inside, a senior diplomat was cautious. Yes, there were historic ties, and there was the language. France helped all Third World nations. There might be more aid, after increased U.S. assistance, but certainly no struggle to retain influence. Would any of France's constantly traveling leaders be in soon? Well, the minister for cooperation came in 1980. "But," he concluded, "Haiti is very small and far away and people are very busy."

But that was before February 1986 when Haiti rose against Baby Doc. Duvalier, in official French circles, was suddenly a dirty word. The young dictator decided to bolt while he could, and the Americans offered him a ride to anywhere but the United States. Late at night in Paris, U.S. authorities persuaded the French to take temporary charge of the French-speaking pariah. With extreme reluctance they agreed on a week. But frantic phone calls produced no takers for Baby Doc. In Gabon, Omar Bongo replied, "My country is not a garbage can." Only Liberia gave a qualified yes, but Duvalier wasn't interested. On French radio, he said: "France is the only country where I feel comfortable. When I decided to come here, I had not the slightest doubt I would be welcomed." His wife, Michèle, added: "France is the country that most suits us. Its culture, its hospitality." Its boutiques. She had been welcomed often in the past, bringing planeloads of friends and fortunes in overweight on shopping sprees.

Fabius wanted the deposed dictator out of France. Mitterrand waffled. "Our constitution says we must accept anyone who serves liberty, but I am not sure this person best defends human rights," he said. But he added, "He is not such a burden. One must not exaggerate." Shortly afterward, the United States took in Ferdinand Marcos, and French officials simmered; many felt they had been had.

The Duvaliers remained cloistered in a three-star converted abbey at Talloires, on the lovely Lake Annecy, while their lawyers sued French authorities to let them stay. It was embarrassing timing. At the Francophone summit in Paris, speakers harped on the theme of French liberty and *largesse.* Duvalier argued he was under virtual house arrest, with a room bill alone of 120,000 francs a day. In occasional interviews, he repeated the magic words: "We have always looked to France as *terre d'asile,* of refuge." He was certain France would not betray its humanitarian mission. Finally, the French forced Duvalier out of the Alps. He went, instead, to the Riviera. He was allowed to move to a small estate north of Nice, with four acres of grounds, a pool and tennis courts. But, the French added, he was restricted to the Côte d'Azur *département* of Alpes-Maritimes.

Not everyone was happy to see Duvalier deposed. Jean Dutourd, tongue half in cheek, warned that his disappearance might mean the end of French as Haiti's language. *Le Canard Enchaîné* retorted that he should declare Duvalier's victims as *"morts pour la France."* They died for France.

A few thousand French live in Haiti, priests and nuns included. But the little port of Jacmel, linked to the capital by a French-built mountain road, has the unmistakable stamp of a French island colony. The words *Liberté, Egalité, Fraternité* are emblazoned across the town hall. Houses in faded pastels, streaked with mossy slime and chipped with age, rest on fancy iron pillars shipped out as ballast. Cobblestone courtyards and dripping fountains are hidden behind louvered windows. Worn stairs lead to balconies and tiered walkways. Inside, Louis XV buffets and massive provincial tables hold dusty bottles of Bordeaux and pastis.

But a glance at the dates suggests that Jacmel remains French-style by choice. Hurricanes and fires have ravaged the town regularly. Almost nothing, save the ornate iron columns, antedates the bitter revolution.

A Port-au-Prince physician-historian explained his perspective of both sides:

Haitians don't like the French; they like the French language. It is that simple. Like in Canada, the Quebecois only wave the French flag when they want to make a point against the English-speakers. It sets them apart. And the French, they don't like to lose. Look at Napoléon III. His was a great epoch: France exported and produced creative works. But he lost and was forgotten. It is the same here. In Haiti, France lost.

The first omens were not good. At independence, Haitians made a new flag by ripping the white from the center of the tricolor. Every leader since has viewed France with mixed feelings. Intensely anti-Communist, President-for-life (it did not work out that way) Jean-Claude Duvalier was correct but cautious when Mitterrand took office. But Duvalier's extravagant wife, Michèle, took planeloads of friends to shop in Paris. And he spent heavily to seek a favorable press in France.

Haiti has gone through a lot of tyrants since Napoléon, but French remains a court language that sets presidents comfortably above the masses. When Duvalier addressed the nation, he might as well be speaking Korean for many who understand only Creole. But the words were less important than the message. Which is, he was not asking that they vote for him.

The feeling for Haiti comes on the horse trail, a sort of *équiphérique,* to the Citadelle. The road passes the crumbling remains of King Christophe's stone palace, inspired by Versailles and only slightly less grand. The difference, of course, is that Versailles still functions. Christophe named it Sans Souci, but it is hard to imagine him without cares, considering his situation at the time. He must have had a few *soucis,* because he designed one of the most heavily fortified, trickily engineered, painstakingly built—and totally useless—forts in history.

We rode up Joseph-and-Mary style behind our handlers, who trotted along reciting fragments of history. The Citadelle was 21,000 lives in the making. Forced laborers, just freed from French slavery, died of exhaustion; others fell from the cliff face. Christophe heaved people over the edge for minor breaches of code. The mortality rate has since dropped, but our horses were better shod than most Haitians. Our guide climbed the sharp rocks on a few scraps of leather held in place with string.

The Citadelle's stone ramparts form a flat parade ground, with five sharp turns and no railings despite a sheer drop to the rocks far below. Christophe impressed visitors occasionally by neglecting to give the order to turn right. In such instances, troops loyally marched over the edge. The fort was built like a gigantic stone battleship sitting 1,000 yards up on a mountaintop and was just as practical. Fifteen miles from Cap Haitien, the cannon bristling from its walls could not heft an iron ball to the harbor and offered little defense against attack from the sea. Invaders could isolate the fortified peak, and rule the rest of Haiti until only skeletons remained in the Citadelle. I asked our guide about this. "Ah, no. It was very good protection. Christophe had a French architect design it." That might have been the answer. Or Christophe knew something I don't.

It didn't matter. The king died of a stroke before the fort was finished, and the French never came back. Napoléon no longer needed Haiti to protect Louisiana, and he was busy elsewhere. The Citadelle remains an American version of the pyramids, except that the people who built it were newly free.

"Haiti never fully developed into a state; it is a sort of proto-state," remarked an American anthropologist friend who spent years there. "It has the trappings but no inner reality. What was the model at the time? Napoléon. Despotic personal rule. This is France's main legacy, and it has not changed since."

I MADE ONE other stop in the Caribbean. St. Barthélemy, a dependency of Guadeloupe an hour's flight north, is a perfect French creation. The airport snack bar is St. Tropez macho. Local heroes, their chest hair just out of curlers, dazzle lady tourists with early-Belmondo gestures. The tiny Swedish-built port of Gustavia feels Scandinavian in its primness, but its shop windows are France. Its disco, Le Must, is Paris *yé-yé* where only the transients go. *Les gens cool* are at Le Sélect, as they would be in Montparnasse. There are, of course, differences.

In Montparnasse, stuffy waiters in black and white float among the tables, which they flick with a rag at the drop of an ash. The St. Barth version is raucous and raw. Its barman is classic island flotsam: barefoot in torn shorts and T-shirt, an army hat over hair that shoots out in all directions. He runs back and forth, cheerful and rapid, slopping rum into plastic cups and snapping fresh Bankie Banx tapes into the stereo. The Swedish owner has sprinkled memorabilia of Scandinavian royalty among hard-rock posters, scrimshaw, moth-chewed books, and bits of ships that passed in the night. Reggae music pounds, and laughter is loud. A sign outside pushes the bar's famed cheeseburger: "Over 56,000 sold." But in its way, Le Sélect is just like its namesake. A basic clientele lounges around battered tables, inside and out, scrutinizing everyone who comes into view. One is ostentatiously graded and, like it or not, handed a report card.

At Le Tamarin, toward the beach, a hybrid macaw in brilliant reds and blues sits in a giant spreading tree screeching, "Fuck off." The place is run by friendly Parisian dropouts who do an unbelievable red snapper in *beurre blanc*. Paradise might be sipping chilled Muscadet next to an explosion of hibiscus and bougainvillea, in reds, pinks, and purples, stirred by soft, spicy breezes. Minimokes rattle past full of French tourists paying no heed whatever to the sign reading, "Nudism is prohibited in St. Barthélemy."

I met a hospitable French couple; both had grown up on the tiny island. They were furious at developers from the *métropole*. "They bring in every nail, even their own laborers, and take back all the profits," the husband said. "And they are putting up all sorts of garbage, driving up prices, and ruining the island. Even the Americans are leaving."

That night, I went to the Licorne. People crowded a dance floor open to a light, flower-scented wind. Like everywhere in the Caribbean, carnival music thumped, beer flowed, and people "jumped up." But no one laughed or grinned as they do everywhere else. The few blacks seemed self-conscious. The whites had that Castel's mask of contrived boredom. In the islands, strangers dance and mingle with some abandon. But at the Licorne, an outsider asking a stranger to dance risks the reception Jack the Ripper might expect when offering to show his knife collection.

St. Barth is the islands, but it is France.

CHAPTER TWENTY

Europe: In the New Old World

FRANÇOIS MITTERRAND did not make it to the 1985 superpower summit between Ronald Reagan and Mikhail Gorbachev. But France did. At one point, a Soviet official briefing reporters reached into his pocket, pulled out a slip of paper, and read off a snatch of Voltaire: "I have never had but one prayer: O God, make my enemies ridiculous."

The pen is not mightier than the Bomb, but you can get a lot more daily use out of it. With a *force de frappe* that is now structured to project nuclear warheads beyond the borders of West Germany, the credibility of France is based on more than ink. But the French know that megatons are no real measure of power.

Once Reagan or Gorbachev throws his nuclear weight, it is too late to matter. Until he does, what really matters is how he holds his fork. And who invented forks? (The Italians, in fact, but who does everyone *think* invented the fork?)

In the view of some, France's role has changed only a little since Charlemagne defined it a millenium ago. Accidents of history have left France a medium-sized nation; fifty-five million people cannot dominate the world, even if they are French. But they can still guide it. If some less enlightened peoples choose not to follow *la bonne voie,* that does not reflect on those patiently holding aloft the light.

Most French would agree that their light has dimmed. But most would also add that it should beam brightly again, and that it can.

The British once ruled a quarter of humanity. With its navy

under full sail, Britannia unsettled the most powerful of French statesmen. But the British folded up the Union Jack and went home, content to look inward and steadily decline. England has sixteen islands strewn about the globe, and 85 percent of all international telephone conversations are conducted in English. *Et alors?* Who knows that? Germany rose and fell once too often. Now, troubled by an internal political division and a present tainted by the past, Germans focus their attention on living well. Italy dropped out of the empire business with the demise of *il Duce.* The rest of Europe, as de Gaulle once put it, *c'est la verdure.* It is garnish. The superpowers, musclebound, parvenus, obsessed with balance, somehow escape the equation.

That leaves the people who brought you Voltaire. And a rabies cure, and the Cuisinart.

This analysis buckles under the weight of numbers. France's economy is only the fifth largest in the world. West Germans earn more per capita, with lower unemployment and less inflation. The Japanese, dismissed by de Gaulle as "transistor salesmen," steamroll French markets, abroad and in France. Even Britain outsells the French.

But numbers, like megatons, are not the measure. France simply steps to its rightful place at the head of the line. Cool hauteur rises above others' niggling complaints. A bad patch followed the leftists' victory in 1981. As usual, however, France confounded lesser civilizations. As Washington worried over Reds in the cabinet, a new senior minister close to Mitterrand told me, "Americans just don't understand. Only we Socialists can finish off the Communists."

France cleaned up the economic mess made during the first few years of dabbling on the left. The Communists dropped out, and the next Socialist prime minister was a young technocrat whose hobby was show jumping. Inflation was curbed, and unemployment stabilized near 10 percent. The franc had slipped perilously but caught itself. Debt was controlled and the balance of payments remained on keel. Nationalized companies had to show a profit or perish. The fields and farms, France's source of recovery since medieval wars, produced rich export crops. The largest source of foreign exchange came from tourists, attracted as beetles to a flame by *la lumière du monde.*

And, in 1986, France voted right. Mitterrand stayed, but Gaullists ran the government.

De Gaulle saw France as a drawbridge from West to East, anchored on one side but capable of spanning chasms that NATO military partners could not. He recognized Peking in the 1960s, when American maps showed China as a little island off the coast of a massive blank spot. In Peking, I asked a senior French diplomat whether Paris reaped rewards for that foresight. "Not really," he said. "But we enjoy a certain privileged political dialogue. The Chinese tend to see us as a locomotive for the European Economic Community. In a sense, we lead the way."

The French like this idea of being Europe's driving force. It was Jean Monnet who laid the tracks for the Common Market, and de Gaulle who continually derailed it. Three presidents since de Gaulle have wrestled with his devils, seeking a balance between towering French nationalism and a desire for France to forge European unity.

If France is not, in fact, the leader of Europe, the community turns on the short axis between Paris and Bonn. When Reagan first sketched his Star Wars fantasy, Mitterrand refused to sign on as a subcontractor. Instead, he tried to rally Europe behind an idea called Eureka to tackle every problem from space research to AIDS. If Eureka research shaped technology for a Strategic Defense Initiative, its architects said, all the better.

Airbus Industrie, a European venture with its plant at Toulouse, is 35 percent French. In early 1985, Airbus was pressing Boeing, aiming for a third of the $150 billion airlines were expected to spend by the turn of the century.

Ariane and the European Space Agency compete for an expected $52 billion in business by the year 2000. The program is as much a source of pride as income. It is a European consortium, but most Frenchmen regard it as their own. The agency's Paris headquarters approved a game called Spacego, in eight languages, in which players race for riches in space aboard European and U.S. rockets. When a Challenger spacecraft exploded in 1986, killing seven Americans, French newscasters were quick to point out the competitive implications.

French-only projects brighten the aura of European technology. Dassault alone makes twenty-one different models of aircraft, with sales of 15.6 billion francs in 1984. The Mirage 2000 stresses the metal of any MiG on the market. The Train à Grande Vitesse and subway systems are seldom absent from speeches on modern France.

For the first time in 2,000 years, French defense strategy no longer envisions Teutonic hordes swarming over the Rhine. The threat has shifted one border eastward. If the French have no illusions about civilizing Germany, they can at least help protect it. French and other Western strategists fear that an ill-defended West Germany might be tempted to shift toward neutrality. That could mean a separate peace with the Soviet Union, which it cannot discourage militarily.

A U.S. umbrella covers Germany, but the eternal question persists: will Washington sacrifice Hamburg to spare Detroit?

France developed a 47,000-man Force de Réaction Rapide, prepared to strike at any edge of the empire. Its range is limited by too few short-range Transalls. The main purpose is as backup support for Germany, where 50,000 French troops are still based along with U.S. and British forces. A new generation of Hades missiles, with a 200-mile range, will be able to reach East Germany in the 1990s —until a Soviet SDI renders them useless. France developed the neutron weapon the United States turned down.

West Germany, anxious to be more than an expendable doormat for any potential European ground conflict, develops weapons jointly with France. And the French sell them in places Germans fear to tread.

German chancellors and French presidents have been close since de Gaulle and Konrad Adenauer. Giscard d'Estaing and Helmut Schmidt were friends and mutual admirers. Mitterrand and Helmut Kohl installed a hot line between them. But relations with Washington always intercede. Bonn agreed to take part in Reagan's SDI, causing a ripple with the French.

But the Atlantic Alliance works like that. It is a tug of war with the European end of the rope unraveled into disparate handfuls. France merely has to grab hold of a sizable strand, and keep it taut. No one forgets that a half-dozen French nuclear submarines cruise at the will of Paris, permanent wild cards in the delicate balance.

Europe often prefers Gaullist national-interest politics to the moralistic-legalistic sort Kennan defined. Reagan's personal war with Qaddafi demonstrated that. West Germany, Italy, and Britain, like France, deplored Libyan-backed terrorism, but few saw that as a reason to dent their own economies. Each found it easy enough to cite some example of American hypocrisy to justify a policy of business-as-usual.

For all its reputation as a stubborn maverick, France is a solid anchor of NATO. In early 1986, journalist Thierry Wolton revealed that in 1981 Mitterrand delivered to Reagan intelligence from a French mole in the KGB who was known to only five Frenchmen. The agent, "Farewell," delivered to France 4,000 documents in eighteen months and made possible the expulsion of forty-seven Soviet agents in 1983. It was among the most valuable acts of espionage since the war.[1]

European pacifists protested the deployment of Pershing and cruise missiles. Not, however, in France. It helped that no missiles were placed in France, but the French have remained convinced, since de Gaulle, that their lives depend on a nuclear shield which they themselves wield. Beneath *l'affaire Greenpeace* lies a bedrock principle: France is prepared to take extreme measures to defend its nuclear capacity.

Though committed to the West, France treasures its role as a moderating influence between the blocs. Before the summit, Gorbachev spent three days in Paris. It was the seventeenth Franco-Soviet summit since de Gaulle took power.

On French television, Gorbachev said cooperation would deepen in trade, research, space exploration, and cultural projects. It was standard boilerplate, but it had a new ring. The Russians had received fifty French industrialists in Moscow. Crédit Lyonnais, established at St. Petersburg in 1878, was the first Western bank in Moscow, in 1972. It financed much of the pipeline from Siberia to Europe which Reagan tried hard to block.

Mitterrand had explained in Washington that continental neighbors had to talk without hostility. "We have had friendly relations with [the Russians] for several centuries." Not quite, but it was close enough for diplomacy. He skipped Reagan's presummit briefing in New York for Atlantic allies. The short notice smacked of a summons, the French said.

Mitterrand declined to negotiate separately on the *force de frappe,* but Gorbachev's presence in Paris amounted to something similar. Meanwhile, Raisa Gorbachev watched six models show forty-three creations at Yves Saint-Laurent and left with a sizable flask of Opium under her arm.

French police banned demonstrations. Warm speeches did not recall Mitterrand's visit to Gorbachev's predecessor. He had Russians choking on their vodka, discarding the *pro forma* toast to say what he thought about their treatment of Andrei Sakharov.

Two weeks after the summit, Mitterrand's guest was Wojciech Jaruzelski, and much of France was up in arms. No other Western leader would receive the Polish general. France, home to Polish exiles for centuries, had stood firmly behind Solidarity. *France-Soir,* the right-wing daily, screamed, "Visit of Shame." Fabius told the National Assembly he was "personally troubled" by the visit. Polish television showed seventeen minutes of Jaruzelski in Paris: meeting Mitterrand, laying a wreath to Polish war victims, cruising the Seine in a *bateau-mouche.* Somehow, the cameras missed the bitter demonstrations that paralyzed Paris traffic.

Mitterrand explained that a president of France maintains relations among states. Not agreeing with a head of state is no reason not to see him. The issue was touchy, he acknowledged. But, he told reporters, "History will prove me right." History, of course, seldom delivers clear verdicts, as the French understand well. In any case, it did not count as a state visit. Mitterrand marked that point as only a French leader could: Jaruzelski did not enter the Elysée by the main door from the courtyard. He was led through the garden to a side entrance, for tradesmen and dictators.

A FEW DAYS after Soviet planes shot down Korean Air Lines flight 007, I was off to Moscow. Western airlines boycotted the Soviet Union, and governments denied Aeroflot landing rights. Air France, however, had a flight. I rose before dawn to miss the morning traffic. We were kept standing by for hours, and the flight was finally called at lunchtime. Passengers filed on board, each lost in thoughts of a last good Air France meal before the boiled cabbage and rubber chicken of Moscow. "We regret to announce," interrupted a voice reflecting little regret, "that no food or beverages will be served on this flight." Why? I asked the purser. He gave me that gentle smile one gives the slow. *"Mais,* we have to make our protest."

I looked around. Not a Russian in sight. The Kremlin would doubtless tremble in shame on learning that France's state-owned airline expressed disapproval by starving its full-fare passengers en route to Moscow.

THE WEIGHT OF France in the New Old World is less Napoléon than it is Hans Christian Andersen. Today's emperors are short on clothes. In such a situation, they are not in a position to brag too loudly about their tailors. A corps of polished diplomats and politicians manage to clad France in remarkable finery. But Cartesian flexibility, clumsily applied, can expose France to ridicule. In the case of UNESCO, for example.

In the mid-1970s, French editors joined Western colleagues in warning of a threat to reporting. Third World leaders had seized upon Soviet efforts to equip governments with the moral right to ban, expel, censor, or arrest foreign correspondents. Their reason was noble: to improve the often inadequate and inaccurate picture portrayed of their countries. But for many, the purpose was different. For them, objective reporting meant relaying only information they generated themselves.

UNESCO director-general Amadou Mahtar M'Bow liked the idea. Authoritarians outnumbered democrats, and the issue was popular among the Afro-Arab nations that supported him. Soon correspondents felt the results. In Africa and Asia, I was denied visas, or permits for internal travel, by officials who cited UNESCO codes. Many governments, counseled by UNESCO experts, drafted policies that put stumbling blocks between correspondents and reality.

Western diplomats at first made things worse. Rather than refuse any compromise on the principle of press freedom, they negotiated wording. The result was a grab bag of statements condemning censorship while laying out ways to implement it. But by 1983, American editors got through to Reagan. Washington gave notice it would leave UNESCO unless it respected access to information and also trimmed its waste. A General Accounting Office survey found financial scandal, and press controls remained an issue. The

United States withdrew at the end of 1984, depriving UNESCO of 25 percent of its budget.

The next year, Britain gave notice. British journalists and officials had been the first, and the most eloquent, to denounce threats to reporting. The Thatcher government, giving up on reform, said it would spend its UNESCO budget directly in developing countries.

The French were furious. UNESCO was a perfect vehicle for the Socialist government's Third World campaigns: painless, well-funded, and far-reaching. Even better, its massive headquarters was in Paris, a source of pride and income for France.

At the 1985 General Conference in Sofia, the French ambassador to UNESCO was Gisèle Halimi, a lawyer with neither journalistic nor diplomatic background. By custom, geopolitical caucuses select representatives to the Drafting and Negotiation Committee. Western delegates wanted a solid front, argued by cool and seasoned voices. They had five seats and six candidates. Madame Halimi lost. She then took her candidacy to the full membership. Third World delegates, delighted to have a sympathetic spirit in the Western camp, voted her in. "I won by plebiscite," she proclaimed.

According to Western delegates, she then got onto the Executive Board by rallying Africans to vote against the Icelandic envoy tapped to head the Finance and Administration Committee. A Sudanese was elected instead. Africans then supported her for another job. With the Icelandic candidate out, the West had a vacant seat to fill. The Executive Board ended up with fourteen African members: eleven French-speaking states, Ethiopia, and two others. M'Bow is from Senegal.

The British, disgusted by the conference, confirmed their decision to withdraw. French commentators called that slavish obedience to Washington, ignoring Britain's record of criticism. Singapore went, too. That was painted as Commonwealth solidarity although Singaporeans had planned to leave even before the Americans. They waited to avoid any connection with Reagan's decision.

I went to see Madame Halimi in Paris for her version of Sofia and a briefing on France's position on UNESCO. I asked why she had called Britain's decision political if London was to apply the same money to cultural projects. She advised me to ask Mrs.

Thatcher. I pursued the question, and she said, "Nothing that occurred at Sofia justified Britain's decision." Halfway through the
next question, she broke in.

"You're writing a book for whom? What title? When is it
coming out?"

I told her the name of the American publisher and said that a
French translation was under negotiation.

"Aha. So you don't even have a publisher," she said. Before I
finished the next sentence, she cut in: "I don't have time to help you
write a book. I have written books. When I write a book, I go to
the documentation."

We are, therefore, left with the documentation.

Le Monde, under the headline, "Relations between France and its
Western partners are degraded yet further," reported that Madame
Halimi had weakened the Western negotiating team by going to the
full membership. "The composition of the group was thus determined, by the French move, by members not a part of it," the article
said. "Other Western representatives took it very badly that their
colleague imposed herself, with support from the outside, in an
instance where her partners did not want her seated. And some note
that is hardly the sort of gesture to convince those who were
considering leaving to stay in the organization."

She replied to *Le Monde:*

"France, because of the energetic role it plays within UNESCO,
deserved quite naturally to be part of the group. This is the first time
it has been excluded by its partners."

Agence France-Presse quoted a senior official of an unnamed
"powerful East bloc" country as saying that the French ambassador
had provoked a Western consensus against herself. He was a senior
Soviet delegate, in fact, who was steering East bloc support away
from involvement in press controls and from M'Bow's controversial
leadership. His remark, carried by AFP, was: "She does not understand. She knows very well what she wants. But she does not know
what the others do not want."

I reminded Madame Halimi that French editors had pioneered the
debate, and I gave some examples of how UNESCO actions ham-
pered reporting. She cut me off. "I studied the dossiers. There is not

one word, not one sentence in UNESCO documents that endangers freedom of the press."

Just to be sure, I repeated, "You are saying the French position is that UNESCO does not represent any threat to freedom of the press?"

"No. It does not."

BUT THAT IS also one of the strengths of France. It is a serious country, rich in substance and potential, which need not always be taken seriously. A traveler in the Old World finds that no European can mention the French without leaking at least some judgment: an arching of the eyebrows, a licking of the lips, an energetic rubbing of the stomach, or a sharp kick toward an imaginary seat of the pants.

In each country the judgments, if extreme, are never unanimous. Italians tend to like the French, or at least admire them. Except for those who loathe them. A friend of mine in Rome mentioned to Italian friends that he had sublet his apartment to a French couple. "What?" they sputtered. "Are you crazy?" Their prejudice was that French tenants were overbearing, hard on the furniture, and likely to pay with a bad check. Germans must like the French; enough of them come to visit. And so on.

French views toward other Europeans are less violent and less diverse. I met a very pleasant French multinational executive based in Rome who summed up his thoughts on Italians and the rest: "Rather agreeable but, ah, somewhat primitive."

The French and Spanish work hard on friendly relations against all odds. After the European Community extended territorial waters to 200 miles, France claimed much of the Bay of Biscay. Madrid, hoping to enter the Common Market, did not object, but Basque fishermen did. When a French patrol boat fired on Spanish trawlers 140 miles off La Rochelle, wounding at least six fishermen, a storm broke. In one Basque village, crowds screamed, "France, assassin!" In Madrid, people threw eggs and excrement at the French embassy. Near the border, Spaniards burned French trucks, a tactic used earlier by French protesting Spanish vegetables and fruits coming across the Pyrenees. "It's just a fishing incident," a French Foreign

Ministry official remarked in March 1984. "It's unfortunate but we tried to warn them and intercept the boat peacefully." *Cambio 16* editorialized: "Geography condemned Japan to have earthquakes and the Caribbean to endure hurricanes. Our curse has been to be the neighbor of France."

But in 1985, King Juan Carlos visited Mitterrand, who promised harsh treatment for Basque terrorists who seek refuge among French Basques. France had already begun deporting suspected Euskadi terrorists, triggering a tide of Basque vandalism against French interests in Spain. France is Spain's best customer and, like it or not, geographic buffer to the rest of Europe. Just before Christmas, 1985, a new crisis opened painful wounds: France, not Spain, won the contract for Europe's first Disneyland.

For sheer terror and amusement, nothing approaches the mutual regard of the British and the French. Once in a while a commentator remarks, "Relations are more friendly between Britain and France after . . ." Friendly has nothing to do with it. Hot and cold blasts across the Channel (or the Manche; the French have their own word for it) antedate William the Conqueror. French infants are taught *"Perfide Albion"* right after *"Maman"* and *"Ce n'est pas ma faute."* A British child learns only later that a frog is also a small green amphibian.

Horace Walpole, in the eighteenth century, decried France's "insolent and unfounded airs of superiority." More recently, Barbara Cartland, romance novelist in her eighties, said that France was the only place where you could make love in the afternoon without people pounding on your door to ask if you were ill. François Mauriac wrote in 1937: "I do not understand and I do not like the English except when they are dead."[2]

The British middle classes are perhaps unreasonably hard on the French. After French farmers hijacked cheap British lamb (after Britain banned cheap French turkeys), the *Sun* in London ran a contest for the best "Froggie jokes." Some entries:

"First man: 'I managed to get an English dictionary for my French wife.'" Second man: 'That's a good swap.'"

"Why do surgeons hate operating on the French? They only have two moving parts—their mouths and their bottoms—and they're both interchangeable." Or:

"How did France, humiliated in World War II and without a single bomb dropped on Paris, finish up as a great power in Europe?"

"Dunno—I give up."

"So did the French."

But the French take their revenge on *les rosbifs*, often with less humor. My friend Claude, a journalist, found himself in a Normandy bar on his way home from an extended visit to England some years ago. He had adopted London local color: a derby, umbrella, even spats. He ordered *Viandox*, a beef bouillon the French put in white wine. Next to him, a grizzled old Frenchman decided to perform for his neighbors. *"Bah,* he should be drinking tea, this stupid Englishman." Encouraged by the general laughter, and the certainty that a stupid Englishman could not understand French, he rambled on, "What's he coming here for, to bother us, this English jerk . . . why can't he stay home where he belongs, polluting France with his fucking—" About then, Claude turned and broke in. *"Vous voulez fermer votre claque-merde?"* (Would you mind closing your shit-trap?) Remorseful silence prevailed.

There is a certain English implantation past Calais. The French have taken over the word "snob," not necessarily the attitude, but certainly the word, along with fashionably soiled Burberry's trenchcoats and Range Rovers *(les Rahnges).* France knows comedian Benny Hill. But *pub* is a French word all on its own, meaning advertising (as in *publicité*). The real penetration is in the other direction.

A whole fringe of society waits breathlessly at Dover for the *nouveau Beaujolais.* Diners seek out French names on restaurants to escape roast beef and two vegs. Britons may call that rich dark wine claret, but any Frenchman can recognize it as Bordeaux. England has produced a playwright or two, I suppose, but anyone can pronounce Marlowe. The points are awarded for what happens at the roof of the mouth at the end of Molière.

In the 1960s, cross-cultural invasion kept an even balance. The English called their contraceptives French letters; in France, they were *capotes anglaises.* But in the 1970s, French travelers found a great deal of France in England.

And now the 1980s have produced the ultimate outrage. In Sloane

Square, right next to the tube stop, in the very *quartier général* of the Sloane Rangers, there is L'Oriel. It is a French brasserie-café, complete with waiters who deftly sprinkle scorn on the clientele in Charles Boyer accents. There is only one concession to England: the rolls are hard as rocks.

THE SUBSTANCE of Anglo-French relations is deep and wide. France and Britain built the Concorde together and defended their technological masterpiece against the derision of accountants. Their trade has grown sixfold in the last decade, and cross-Channel traffic is heavy enough to justify the 200-year-old dream of a fixed link between them. Both sides have agreed on plans for a railroad joining Britain to the continent. Nonetheless there were members of parliament who objected, as Lord Palmerston did in the last century, to spending money to shorten a distance that was already too short.

Mitterrand visited the queen in 1984 amid the pomp and grandeur only two historic seats of empire could produce. His message was that Europe must push the superpowers toward direct comprehensive arms control talks. He addressed Parliament, protected by Guardsmen in bearskin helmets. On the walls of the Royal Gallery where he spoke were two forty-five-foot-long frescoes. One depicted Waterloo; the other, Trafalgar.

Queen Elizabeth, in diamonds, fed the French president good English beef and scampi with lobster sauce in a grand ballroom under six huge crystal chandeliers. "Ours is the history of unity and diversity, cooperation and rivalry, friendship and disdain, war and peace," she said. "Let us never forget how much we share—a commitment to peace, freedom, and democracy, a stubborn spirit of independence. . . . We have outgrown conflict and disdain."

One British writer recalled an earlier sovereign, King Edward VII, escorted by cuirassiers through Paris in 1903 to formalize the Entente Cordiale. People jeered and shouted, *"Vivent les Boers."* The king remarked, "The French don't seem to like us very much." And an aide replied, "Why should they?"

After World War I, Lord Curzon, then foreign secretary, came to Paris to remonstrate with Prime Minister Raymond Poincaré. The French had pulled troops back from Chanak, leaving a small

British unit alone against Ataturk's raging-mad nationalists. At the Hôtel Matignon, Poincaré lost control and raved for fifteen minutes. Curzon had to be helped into the next room. He collapsed on a sofa, hands shaking violently, and told his ambassador, "Charley, I can't bear that horrid little man. I can't bear him. I can't bear him." Then he wept.[3]

Some years later, Sir Anthony Eden had French hands trembling when he backed down at Suez, with French forces out front.

Competition remains fierce, if sometimes friendly. The British entered the Common Market after de Gaulle died; then they elected Margaret Thatcher, who badgered her partners for a better deal. The *Times* of London observed that many French see Mrs. Thatcher the way the British regarded de Gaulle: a tiresome person to deal with but one whom they wished their own leaders resembled more.

When the Pentagon decided to make its largest ever purchase abroad, a battlefield communications system, the Americans leaned toward France's $4.3 billion offer, the RITA. Mrs. Thatcher, pushing Britain's Ptarmigan, appealed to Reagan to consider who was the more faithful ally. But the Ptarmigan cost $7.1 billion and was not yet in use. RITA won, and a French commentator remarked that that was to be expected "even though some people will stop at nothing."

Even the pomp and grandeur of Mitterrand's visit to the queen ended in a quarrel. French security agents, apparently to prove the British fallible, buried explosives in the French ambassador's garden. English dogs sniffed out the explosives immediately, and English members of Parliament demanded to know what was going on. Mrs. Thatcher's observations were sharp; twelve days earlier she had nearly been blown up by an Irish terrorists' bomb. The French, in heated self-justification, implied that British colleagues set them up. The Britons asked to be tested, according to the French.

That blew over quickly. But the episode of the Exocet had all the makings of a modern-day Fashoda incident.

For people who tuned in late, the Falklands War seemed like a sudden flurry over a needless piece of real estate, seized upon by generals in need of diverting a disgruntled populace. The last part is correct; certainly not the first. From the first grade, Argentine children learn, *"Las Malvinas son nuestras."* At the same time, the

1,800 Kelpers who populate those wind-blown rocky islands center their lives around two pillars: sheep and Queen Elizabeth. I visited the Falklands in 1975 and left amazed. An hour in the pub offers evidence enough, but I scoured Port Stanley and did not find a single resident who wanted to shift allegiance to Buenos Aires. Margaret Thatcher, rooted firmly in empirical principles, could not have avoided war.

The risk was enormous for Britain. Had the Argentines sunk an aircraft carrier, as they repeatedly claimed they had, they might have won. London would have staggered under the loss of life, of military advantage, and of image. The key to the war was air-to-sea missiles. When the war began, Argentina had a fleet of French Super Etendard aircraft and five Exocet AM39 (air-sea) missiles. They had not, however, worked out how to attach, arm, and fire them.

On May 4, 1982, an Exocet sank the destroyer H.M.S. *Sheffield,* with a loss of twenty seamen. At Aérospatiale, which makes the missile, there was some jubilation on the assembly line. Nothing ghoulish over the victims; it was simply pride in a technological job well done. In Paris, meanwhile, British diplomats worked furiously to dissuade France from allowing more Exocets to fall into Argentine hands. The French stopped sales to Argentina but approved a shipment to Peru, and the British learned of the deal only at the last minute. "These days we cannot afford to maintain spies among our allies," a senior British officer remarked to me with a very thin smile. "Only our enemies." At a 4 A.M. meeting with senior French officials, British attachés and the ambassador made a last-ditch attempt to stop the Exocets, already loaded for export. The French argued that Peru had promised not to reexport the missiles. Finally, Thatcher telephoned Mitterrand, and the Exocets were not sent.

Published reports in Paris and London said that French technicians who had not been officially sanctioned had helped the Argentines arm the missiles. In London, I called on a man in a position to know, who asked not to be named. Did French experts arm the Exocets and then, at an official level, assist Britain in working out a defense against them? "Yes," he said. "That seems to be the case." As a strategy, it was only partially successful. When an Exocet was aimed at the British convoy, seamen confused its guidance mechanism (designed, ironically, in Britain) by firing off projectiles of aluminum strips. The Exocet missed its targeted warship. Instead, it sunk the *Atlantic Conveyer,* a cargo ship in the fleet.

Immediately after a ceasefire was signed, but while Britain still had 4,000 troops on the Falklands and feared a revenge strike, France resumed the shipments. In one month, five Exocet air-to-sea missiles were dispatched along with nine Super Etendard aircraft and a another shipload of munitions. Mrs. Thatcher acknowledged that France had contracts to fill but confessed to being extremely irritated. British sailors from the *Hermes* fought a few pitched battles on French docks. And members of Parliament branded the move "near treason" and demanded economic vengeance.

Exocets reached such stardom that their black market price rose to a million dollars, five times their shelf price. But there weren't many around; the Argentines could not find any more.

Two years later, Aérospatiale took out a full-page ad in the *Economist* in London. It was not to apologize but rather to counter damaging claims that an Exocet failed to explode when it hit the tanker *Alexander the Great* in the Gulf War. It boasted: "Exocet is and remains the leader in its category . . . that's why it upsets people so much!" Aerospatiale condemned slander in Britain which claimed that the *Sheffield*'s Exocet had not exploded. As evidence, it quoted published remarks by Captain Salt, the ship's commander.

Aérospatiale noted that an ignorant public does not realize the Exocet's mission is to disable a ship, not necessarily to sink it.

These at times rather unspectacular results have therefore made the non-explosion hypothesis more easy to swallow. But in reality the high number of broadcasted results point to the contrary: from the beginning of the Iran-Iraq conflict up to 10th July last [1984], 112 ships were hit by Exocets (60 confirmed, 52 probable). Out of 103 cases that were analyzed, 57 ships either sank, ran aground or were towed home for scrapping; damage to the other 46 was variable. Out of such a large number . . . only one case of non-explosion was recorded.

As the ad noted, "The Falklands conflict suddenly brought Exocet into unexpected limelight . . . some advertisements for detection systems even refer to the missile using 'Exocet' as a common noun."

Aérospatiale had, it said, 2,000 units ordered, with Exocets in service in twenty-seven countries.

At the height of the missiles' stardom, I went to the ancient little city where they are made: Bourges, the perfect picture of bourgeois France. It was once a stronghold of Vercingétorix; now it is one of the handsomest cities of *la France profonde.* The tourist office boasts of its cheese and Sancerre, of Jacques Coeur, the merchant who enriched King Charles VII, and, above all, of its stunning cathedral with foundations dating back to the Romans. But not of the Exocet. Inhabitants have been wrestling with their consciences ever since Napoléon III moved his cannonworks here a century ago. The fabled French 75s were made in Bourges.

The Aérospatiale public relations man said he could tell me nothing without Defense Ministry clearance, not even his own name. The missile is made at a government-owned plant on rich farmland at the edge of town, masked by trees and guarded by ill-tempered dogs. At a nearby café, a retired hardhat named Arthur told me, "The Argentina junta is terrible, like Hitler. But this is commerce." Deputy Mayor Marguerite Renaudat, a Communist with blued hair and a motherly manner, said, "This is not a simple problem for Bourges, with our old vocation of arms manufacturing. We are for armaments and peace." But at the Chamber of Commerce and Industry, Secretary General Henri Cotte was blunt: "If the unfortunate conflict between Britain and Argentina has allowed the world to discover French arms, I can only rejoice and hope that our business doubles."

In the cathedral, an elderly souvenir seller had never heard the word Exocet (which means, incidentally, flying fish in French). "Exocet? Exocet?" she repeated. Then, glancing down at postcards of Bourges' favorite king, she brightened. "Ah! You mean, Charles *Sept.*"

ARMS SALES offer France a political advantage, but they are also lucrative. After food, armaments are France's biggest selling item, 60 billion francs in 1984. The Socialists announced on taking office in 1981 that they would scrutinize all customers and add an element of "morality" to their arms exports. Only Chile was crossed off the list. Selected gear went to Nicaragua, instead. Once arms go to Belgium or Switzerland, the trail evaporates, and energy to pursue their eventual destinations flags. The system offers ample rationalization for those whose consciences need it.

In late 1985, when Reagan was freezing Qaddafi's assets and ordering all Americans out of Libya, the state-owned French television reported that France had acted secretly as broker to help Libya buy hand-me-down Argentine gunboats.

Looking ahead, the analysts disagree on France's role in the New Old World. Paris has long since lost its role as capital of the universe, but France is no toothless power. The answer, of course, depends on the shape of the world around France.

If the arms race moves into orbit, the French nuclear force could face obsolescence. France's conventional power is questionable. A senior general was censured in 1985 for saying that the French arsenal was inadequate and out-of-date. But that was hardly news. When the rapid-action force prepared to march for the first time on Bastille Day, *Le Canard Enchaîné* noted that the army had requested 154 Transalls, fifty-six for the FAR alone; but there were only sixty-five altogether. The paper recalled Operation Manta in Chad, when it took three months to transport 3,300 men, 12,000 tons of freight, thirty helicopters and 700 vehicles; there were 150 round-trips by DC8s; constant flights by thirty-six requisitioned jumbo jets from UTA; and eighty round-trips by Transalls, which can cover 2,400 miles carrying four tons of cargo. "But, for the moment," *le Canard* said, "at least the Rapid Action Force knows how to march."

But money is pumped regularly into the nuclear program. New technology is pursued, as in biomedical research and the other sciences, with *rayonnement* firmly in mind.

And there are still the intangibles. France adds up to more than the sum of its parts. You can still feel the slight electric charge at diplomatic gatherings when the French ambassador walks into a room. He represents not only the Fifth Republic but also Voltaire.

The Cold War thawed to détente, but that, too, is going. New balances and approaches are forming, and they are not clear. "I'm looking for a new word for 'détente,'" Flora Lewis told me at the end of 1985. She will most likely find one. And my bet is that, like détente—and *rapprochement* and *fin du monde*—it will be a French word.

CHAPTER TWENTY-ONE

A Modern Mission

BACK BEFORE HE hired I. M. Pei, a Chinese-American, to create a reflecting glass pyramid at the entrance to the Louvre, French culture minister Jack Lang enlivened one of those deadly United Nations conferences in Acapulco. He denounced ". . . this financial and cultural imperialism that no longer, or rarely, grabs territory but grabs consciousness, ways of thinking, ways of living."

He meant the United States. The French, in the midst of discovering America the way the Lost Generation found France a half-century before, did not think much of the speech. Judging from his actions in the following years, neither did Lang. But Lang meant what he was trying to say in 1982.

In a world of satellites, transistors, cheap flights, and easy borders, Western nations can do little more than add flavor to an amorphous Atlantic omniculture. In most places, that is a side issue. Not in France. Culture is what makes a nation of fifty-five million sit at the most privileged of tables. Every French person knows that a counter-clockwise twist of the rheostat portends ignominious decline. France might—*que Dieu la protège*—go the way of Britain.

Culture is the Maginot Line. Properly defended, it allows France to radiate civilization, according to its historic mission. But the Anglo-Saxons loom. On top of films, music, and advertising, foreign television is ever more pervasive. There is a nightmarish specter of reality; only a state of mind protects Paris from becoming a suburb of Dallas.

It seems that *rayonnement* might be a diminished priority behind the more pressing pursuits of economic growth and political solidity. Times are hard in Western Europe. Among *les grass roots,* the concern is jobs, not glory. The alarmists wonder whether French democracy will survive its second century, until 1989.

But the radiance of French culture is not a luxury, it is a fundamental point of departure. Without it, *ça, alors* . . .

Each country has its comparative strengths and weaknesses. Sustained competition in unfamiliar markets is not France's forte. The French, by and large, are lousy salesmen; few believe the customer is right. French bureaucracy is hard on international business. But France has two advantages. One is that its products are generally good. The other, far more important, is the heat emitted by a handsome business card that radiates France.

"All forays out of the Hexagon have ended unhappily," Fernand Braudel observed in 1985, "but there is one permanent triumph of French life that is a cultural triumph, a *rayonnement* of civilization. The identity of France is this *rayonnement,* more or less brilliant, more or less justified."

But French grandeur today, he added, rests on past glory. The menace is that the *rayonnement* may grow steadily less brilliant and, therefore, be increasingly less justified. No one forgets de Gaulle: "France cannot be France without grandeur."

THE WEEKLY *Le Point,* in a cover story entitled, "How to Resist the American Cultural Invasion," noted that European culture ministers met at Delphi in mid-1985 to reflect on the transitory nature of *gloria.* Had they switched on the television that day, they could have seen Montpellier by satellite, where 30,000 electrified youths in jeans and UCLA T-shirts, crushing Coke cans with their cowboy boots, were singing along with Bruce Springsteen and the E Street Band, "Born in the USA."

FUTURE FRENCH grandeur will be built largely at home. France is out of the colonization business. Political chaos may force a Sixth Republic, but not a Third Empire; not even the fanatic Bonapartists in Corsica expect a Napoléon IV. De Gaulle defined France's world role, but events beyond French control shape the script. Still, if no longer producer or director, France remains a principal actor. It can at least upstage the cast and bring down the house.

France's modern empire is figurative but substantial, particularly among the vast populations who live toward the bottom of the page in World Bank reports. To developing peoples, America exports red sorghum and money. The Soviets offer ideology and used MiG fighters. But France sends foreign aid shipments of civilization.

As the Algerian War was ending, with French Africa independent, de Gaulle dispelled any nagging fears: "We have always had a humane mission and we have it still; policy must adapt itself to our genius." And: "France comes from the depth of ages . . . the centuries call her. But she remains herself throughout time."

Twenty-five years later, Mitterrand's message was fraught with unsettling defensiveness. English pressed in from all sides. French was nearly absent in the Far East. Even French diplomats sometimes forgot to speak their own language at international meetings.

In defense of Culture, France relies most heavily on the language. French is a fine tongue, and its keepers tremble at the advance of *franglais,* or its insidious offshoot, *framéricain.* But, offensive as it is, English is hardly a threat to the culture. The French do not "borrow" words any more than Napoléon borrowed the obelisk at Luxor. They bring them home, implant them in a figurative place de la Concorde, and drive past them every morning with a self-satisfied smirk of possession.

The French use some English for concepts not readily found in their own language, such as *fair play* and *gentleman.* Other words just muscle their way in. It is perfectly proper French to say, *"Un gentleman en bluejeans et blazer lit un best-seller sur le ferryboat."* But mostly, by the time an alien word earns its *carte de séjour,* the French have colonized it.

In French, *un look,* pronounced "luke," means the image conveyed by careful primping, facial expression, and clothing, as in *un look cool*. The Académie Française accepted *blue jeans* long after French designers created a whole new *look* from the Levi's we wore as kids. Not many American *drugstores* have full-blown restaurants, electronics supermarkets, and movie theaters.

Take *le fast food.* Immediately, the French played on the words: It is, for some, *fast fou.* In French, *fou* means crazy, or soaring far beyond what is seemly. (Or, with real *esprit,* it is *faste fou:* a *faste* is an ostentatious banquet.) They began their own chains and added *herbes provençales* and *gruyère* to the recipes. And application made the concept exclusively French. When the first McDonald's opened just off the Champs-Elysées in 1976, an elegant gentleman ordered: *"Un Beeg Mac, s'il vous plaît. Pas trop cuit."* Not too well done.

Faceless staffs, not having to answer to customers, dealt with unfamiliar pressure by throwing raw patties onto buns. The French lined up at counters according to custom, side by side and shoving, all clamoring for attention. In *The New Yorker,* Calvin Trillin devised the Prix du Hamburger and explored fast food in Paris. He wrote:

> I couldn't imagine that any fast-food outfit could afford to rent a store on the Champs-Elysées wide enough to accommodate more than one or two French lines. Also, it occurred to me that a customer who finally reached the head of a line at a French Burger King might ask for a couple of Whopper burgers, an order of fries, and a chocolate milkshake only to have the counterperson poise a scratchy quill pen over some exceedingly long forms, look up sourly, and say, "Granmuzzer's maiden name?"

Gretchen and I stopped at a service area on the *autoroute* south. *Un fast-food* featuring hamburgers had opened next to *le self,* the traditional self-service cafeteria. Gretchen, reared in Idaho, is of the "catsup" persuasion. She asked for some. *La countergirl* gave her a quizzical look. Finally, Gretchen explained in flawless French that catsup was a sort of tomato sauce applied to *hamburgers* and *hotdogs* and she was certain some could be found behind the counter in foil packets. *"Ahh,"* the young woman said, fixing Gretchen with that piercing stare the French reserve for foreigners who defile their language, "you mean *ketchup."*

Poisoning the language is one thing. But some fear that fast food might do worse. What if, as a result of this trend, the French lost their regard for decent food? What if Hell had ski lifts? The best French chefs still chart their lives by Michelin stars. Most give no more thought to the Big Mac than a ballet dancer would to a jogger. Not long ago, I had a chicken salad at Alain Chapel's near Lyon.

Actually, it was "a salad of *roquette* lettuce, rare mountain greens, and slivers of young Guinea fowl from Bresse with garlic-rubbed crusts in nut oil."

There is fear that foreign hordes might crowd out the French at decent tables. In 1986, the more famous restaurants were filling up months in advance, and cash deposits were required with reservations. Some restaurateurs devised the perfect Parisian solution. They fixed a 40 percent quota on bookings from people with funny accents and non-French names. "As far as filling our *salles* with Americans, we would do better to build annexes under a sign of Uncle Sam," said Claude Terrail of the Tour d'Argent. But he is not unreasonable. Downstairs and across the street from his restaurant, he sells *foie gras de canard frais* and four kinds of honey for American rejects to leave conspicuously around their kitchens. You can even buy a Tour d'Argent ashtray to make it look as if you ate there. In fact, Terrail told one food writer, he put the shop in a vacant location so no trashy *couscous* joint could lower the tone of the street corner.

Other restaurateurs, like Paul Bocuse, reach out to the masses but defend the sanctity of their dining rooms. The balance is delicate, however. Roger Viard, or rather Monsieur Roger, retired in 1985 after forty-seven years at Maxim's, twenty-five of them as head maître d'hôtel. And that's not all. At his last New Year's Eve party, there were more Lebanese and American tourists than *tout-Parisiens*. Rather than the traditional black and white party favors, there were false noses and gaudy hats. Viard told Hebe Dorsey (who is a sort of Eiffel Tower among society scribes), "It is not Maxim's that has changed. It is the world that has changed."

France is keeping pace. Maxim's is now owned by Pierre Cardin, who has placed so many *PC* monograms on bizarre articles in remote places that the initials might as well stand for *Père Civilisateur*.

Electronics help pigs sniff out truffles. Banners exclaiming *"Le Beaujolais nouveau est arrivé"* outshadowed in Kinshasa streets the signs welcoming Mitterrand on a visit to Zaire. And now there is kosher Beaujolais.

Inroads penetrate, however. A classy little *épicerie* on the Ile Saint Louis sells Fauchon's products but also Old Paso chili con carne and two strengths of enchilada sauce. And American chocolate chip cookies. "We make them here, but they are not French copies," the shopkeeper told me. "They are the real thing." She added, "We even have pumpkin pie, *pour le Sanksgiving.*" Papa Maya, a Paris Mexican restaurant with roots in San Antonio, advertises, "The Eiffel Tower now has Taco Power."

Lang worried that French restaurants might slip to the function of those elsewhere in the world: just serving food. In France, he was dead right to insist, food is a pillar of culture. And not only its preparation and presentation. The great Carême codified cuisine in twelve fat volumes, and there were things even he didn't know. That French chefs travel worries no one; Escoffier spent most of his career on a civilizing mission to London. But, just to make sure the pillar is not eroded, Lang organized a school for advanced French cuisine.

Not to worry. You can still get one of the world's finer meals at a Paris train station. At Le Train Bleu in the Gare de Lyon, under baroque gilt-scrolled ceilings, with pastels of cherubs and landscapes and Sarah Bernhardt, you can eat *foie gras* and watch your train load for Milan. On the same plush banquettes, colonels and colonial officers put away their last decent *gigots* before traveling down to Marseilles to board their ships and go off to settle the world.

USING FOREIGN words is hardly new. Lyautey, nearly a century ago, argued that French policy should be, "Le *right man for the right place.*" Nor is it only one way. I've never heard anyone say, *un je ne sais quoi* in Paris. In New York, it is as common as *gwon, get outta heah.* Or, *déjà vu,* pronounced, dayja voo. The *Washington Post* observed in an editorial that languages are like little kids, seizing words that delight them with no thought to origin; banning a word's use merely adds to its flavor. As Truman Capote's Holly Golightly might remark over a *croissants* and *café au lait* breakfast at Tiffany's, "quelle ridicule."

Words go back and forth, like people. Les Ateliers Gaget, for example, built the Statue of Liberty in Paris and then flooded the world with small reproductions of Mlle. Liberté. "Chewing their words like gum," as a Parisian journalist observed, Americans produced the words, *gadget.*

The French love the word *gadget,* and they love gadgets even more. One of Mitterrand's creations in Paris is La Villette, a half-billion-dollar erector set cradling a giant silver golf ball, on the site of an abandoned slaughterhouse. Two and a half times the size of the Centre Pompidou, it is a playland showcase of science, technology and industry. La Villette is to cost $80 million a year to operate as a reminder to the world that France entered the twenty-first century ahead of schedule. And it was opened, on the night Halley's Comet passed, with nineteenth-century French flair. Amid the electronic gadgetry, cellists in tails and the Radio France choir performed Berlioz.

La Villette symbolizes the French concern for its image as a modern innovator—and exporter. France has not registered a year-end trade surplus since 1978. Japan puts twice as many students through the higher levels of education, with emphasis on industrial training. That is no small worry. In a major policy statement, Mitterrand said: "One wins Austerlitz when one takes away a position in electronics or biology. One loses Waterloo when one abandons automobiles or machine tools. These are the real modern battlefields."

This is a principal reason for defending the language. The French devised the word *logiciel* for software and set about writing sophisticated programs in their own language. "Must we translate into English the orders we give our machines?" the president asked.

The Académie Française rails at *le marketing* when *commercialisation* is perfectly adequate. A special commission has actually made it a crime (punished by a fine, not a jail term) for some use of foreign terms in advertising and business when French ones will do. When French words are not available, they are invented. Thus, the English "fuel" is, in French, *fioul.* "Cash flow" becomes *MBA* for *marge brute d'autofinancement.* And, to match the acronym for a type of bond called CATS, the French came up with *fonds d'Etat libres d'intérêts nominaux.* That is, FELIN.

A group known as AGULF took forty-four companies to court in 1985 for violating the 1975 law. TWA, for example, was fined $500 for issuing boarding passes in English at Charles de Gaulle Airport. To protest foreign words in commercials, Lang wrote to the head of the broadcasting authority, in English: "Should we fail to take steps promptly, we will most certainly lose our identity as a nation—give up our very soul."

But the use of Americanisms in business reflects a penetration much greater than linguistic. Whatever the French call it, they are thinking hard about old ways of producing, advertising, and placing goods in the market. A growing number of French executives leave Harvard Business School with a perfect command of American, from computer jargon to corporate sleaze.

"Supermarket" was quickly consumed and digested; the French broadened the concept to the *hypermarché*. French entrepreneurs run Bigg's in Cincinnati, four times the size of most supermarkets, perhaps in revenge for "Dynasty."

Not long ago, Americans had to come up with "smart card" to match the *carte à mémoire*. Once the French decided against turning up their noses at credit cards, they invented one with a microprocessor stamped onto it for fast authorizations and automatic banking. Credit cards are now so common that drivers can pay twenty-cent freeway tolls with any of a handful. This is France, of course. Small-merchant associations howled that banks took too much of a commission. "When we explain to Parisians how much that little insect of a card costs us, they understand very well and take out their checkbook," a hotelier in the south told a *Libération* reporter. But banks ordered twelve million smart cards to be ready by 1988.

Some worry about a brain drain or, more properly, a *fuite des cerveaux*. The French are attracted not only by American concepts, but by America itself. When Mitterrand visited Silicon Valley in 1984, Steve Jobs was brutally frank about the French lag in computer technology. Not long before Jobs got the delete key at Apple, a new, flashy young executive showed up at the company's headquarters: Jean-Pierre Gassée, "the Frenchy," who had directed Apple-France. But brain drain is not terminal. It takes less time to fly home to Paris from the North Carolina Research Triangle than it does to drive from St. Tropez back to avenue Foch. And well-paid French engineers and executives can take only so many hush puppies.

The most serious concern is over television, films, and advertising. And with reason. At 8:30 A.M., there is "Peyton Place," with a very young Mia Farrow. At midday, there is "Starsky et Hutch."

And then "Dynasty" and "Columbo" and the never-ending saga about guess which ranch. One French carmaker sells its latest model on TV, with dramatically done special effects, by driving it into Grace Jones's mouth. On Antenne 2, programming ends with "Les Vidéo Clips." French teenagers who forgot that their uncles died in Indochina thrill to *Rambo*. Fans watching Clint Eastwood point a pistol at someone pondering whether to attack do not need the subtitle: *"Faites mon jour."*

French television bought "Miami Vice," an event worth three full pages in *Libération*. "Intense, man," the paper observed.

On television, France rang in 1986 with, yet again, Springsteen and "Born in the USA." Chauvinists could have changed channels —to a Fred Astaire retrospective, followed by *Three Little Words* in the original English.

France produced a home-grown "Dallas" called "Châteauvallon." It was a national event. For all the critics' wisecracks, it was an engaging program. The opening aerial shot showed, rather than "Souzfork," the stately Berg manor on the Loire. The Bergs had grown rich and powerful from their provincial newspaper. Florence Berg, a chic Paris lawyer who received clients in a pink satin jogging suit, inherited the paper. But the actress, Chantal Nobel, was injured in an accident after the first season. The producers decided not to write her out of the script; instead, they canceled the show.

Mickey Mouse is no longer just a frequent visitor to France; he has been granted permanent residence. Europe's first Disneyland, on 4,500 acres outside Paris, is to receive ten million people a year. It immediately produced a labor squabble worthy of Scrooge McDuck. Developers wanted flexibility to hire and fire according to seasonal demand. French unions called that "a massacre of workers' rights." Authorities were bitter at guarantees developers wanted on paper. "We're not a banana republic," remarked a senior French official. Some French wondered why France was not exploiting Astérix instead of an imported rodent.

The nation's main event is still a bicycle race, up the Alps, along the Riviera, and through the Normandy hedgerows: *le Tour de France*. Its official drink is no longer Perrier, however; it is Coca-Cola. A boastful commentary in the *Wall Street Journal* made too much of that. One French racer remarked, "So? I don't like Coke, and I am not going to pedal any faster to the finish to drink one."

All is not lost. There are still Frenchmen who hear "Rambo" as Rimbaud, the eccentric French poet who assaulted Africa, not Vietnam. An American journalist honeymooning in the Champagne region asked at dinner for Perrier. "Tout de suite, madame," replied the waiter, and he popped the cork from a bottle of Laurent Perrier. It was a $50 drink of water, with no water.

But Americans are coming in from all sides, poking into France's most treasured institutions—and the French psyche.

La Comédie-Française, founded in 1680, offered three one-act farces by Feydeau in 1985. The director, Stuart Seide, was born in Brooklyn. He spent fifteen years in Paris and caught on fast to France; Lang granted him a subsidy. Seide chose to put on Feydeau. He told Mary Blume, in the *International Herald Tribune* Weekend section:

> The plays are very funny but very cruel. People talk about Jewish humor, gallows—in Feydeau someone says, "Your mother is dead" and it's a laugh a minute from that moment on. The production is funny but it isn't gay. French audiences, especially at the Comédie-Française, are very reverential—a lot of them see that Feydeau is cruel, but they don't want to believe it.
>
> What you have in Feydeau is people making totally rational self-justifications in total bad faith. The characters justify themselves with a certain logic and then contradict themselves with equal logic. Everyone talks very fast and no one listens. I guess I've gotten pretty good at that, too.

Americans are affecting French journalism. Christine Ockrent, broadcast superstar, did her boot camp at CBS. Serge July, editor of *Libération,* ordered his reporters to "Saxonize": to dig deeper and write harder. Let loose in France, *Saxonisation* could be poisonous to the beloved rhetoric. A prized skill is the ability to speak eloquently and at length on a subject about which the speaker knows nothing. Gaps in knowledge are spanned with the conditional tense or, *in extremis,* a wild stab in the dark.

The Univeristy of Nantes accepted a thesis in 1986 from a sixty-six-year-old student who "demonstrated" that Nazi gas chambers did not exist.

Masters of French rhetoric seize on an impression and then wing it. Sometimes they miss the mark. Alphonse de Chateaubriant, winner of the Prix Goncourt and the French Academy's grand prize, wrote in 1939: "The physiognomic analysis of Hitler's face reveals . . . his immense kindness. Look at him, in the midst of children . . . he is immensely kind, I repeat it."

French scientists, among the world's most accomplished, often rail at the rhetoric. Claude Lévi-Strauss oversees in France a sociological database produced at Yale University. It contains millions of references with line-by-line indexes of works on every people of the world. Twenty copies exist, eighteen in the United States, one in Japan, and one in France. No U.S. agency makes a move overseas without first consulting the file, Lévi-Strauss said. In twenty years, he added, not one French public official has ever consulted it.

Levi-Strauss, for many young Frenchmen, is more familiar as the name of a San Francisco pants maker.

Some political veterans, such as Michel Debré, warn of total eclipse if France does not beam more brightly. They want more emphasis on cultural heritage. Jacques Séguela, media master and image-maker, fears the past is fading away. He told a reporter, "My son does not know Molière, but he knows J. R."

But even Molière has a shelf life. He is immortal but as much universal as he is French. Cultures are not defended, they are nourished. Shakespeare did not save the English.

In 1944, Georges Duhamel produced a slim volume entitled *Civilisation Française* in which, ignoring the moment's humiliation, he catalogued the countless glories of France. He wrote:

> The traveler who goes from nation to nation encounters everywhere people to learn French, to speak French and to find pleasure in it. France does little, in sum, for such a grand result and what one ordinarily calls propaganda—frightful word—figures little in the cordial favor. If foreign peoples love to learn French, to speak it, to write it, it is that our beautiful language is the key to a great civilization.

Today's mission is to remind the world of that fading reality.

French radiance depends heavily on its source of light, *la ville lumière,* the capital of the world. Only the king of France or the president of the Republic can mess around with Paris. Henri IV, four Louises and a pair of Bonapartes committed grandeur to space and stone. And each modern overlay has a name. The ugly high-rise at Montparnasse: Pompidou. The preserved old roads along the quais: Giscard d'Estaing. Mitterrand himself chose Pei for the Louvre. He also guided plans for an opera at the Bastille and four other major new landmarks.

De Gaulle inadvertently let Paris slip badly. André Malraux, his culture minister, looked after grandeur in a manner rarely seen since Sully and Colbert. Malraux's lofty gaze saw monuments and *maisons de culture.* Meantime, venal and clumsy developers ate away the edges of Paris. More recently, the scourge has struck les Halles, what Zola called the belly of Paris.

I first saw Paris the night they shut down les Halles, in 1968. Almost forever, greengrocers had bought produce there at dawn from wholesalers who rumbled in all night from the farms. Hectic trading was done under elegant iron and glass umbrellas, the Pavillons Baltard. Near Saint Eustache church, a row of brasseries served steaming thick onion soup, paved with melted Gruyère and bread. Workers stopped off at the bars for *un petit coup* against the cold, or for the hell of it. Hookers faced the morning with oysters and absinthe.

But the trucks choked Paris streets. The noise was deafening. The rats had their own *force de frappe.* In the student revolt of May 1968, so many demonstrators hid in its warren of alleys that it became the Casbah of Paris. Les Halles was coming down.

On the last night, young crowds snake-danced through the streets. A pick-up orchestra climbed onto a stone fountain and played "Those Were the Days" with trumpets and tubas, encouraged by a barrage of wine bottles pitched to them at each pause. I was with a friend, and we wanted onion soup at Le Pied-de-Cochon. Do not miss it, we had been told. The place was jammed. Waiters spun among small tables set in a barnlike room. A kindly maître d'hôtel built us a rickety table by the cash register. This was the promised Paris.

In its place, de Gaulle wanted Versailles splendor. Pompidou wanted downtown Chicago. Giscard d'Estaing and Jacques Chirac, prime minister and later mayor of Paris, did not know what they wanted. In compromise, les Halles was a twenty-six-acre hole in the ground. Costly studies were made and filed away. The building dragged on for years.

Today, les Halles is a stark multistory underground shopping mall, sinisterly modern and reeking of hamburger grease, where you can get your body sequined or your wallet lifted. The Pavillons Baltard were trucked off and junked, replaced by featureless plastic and concrete. "A monster," concluded art critic Pierre Cabanne of *Le Matin*. "It is one of the most distressing architectural white elephants ever imagined. The heart of Paris has been forever disfigured and plundered." *Ah, oui.*

Outside Paris, some châteaux and churches edge toward collapse. The skills to repair them are disappearing as fast as the old fortunes necessary to pay for them. The French tax is based on visible signs of wealth. A fat Austrian bank account is less splendid but far easier to keep. The old towns of worn stone and hardy geraniums are increasingly blemished with garish *grande surface* discount stores and sore-thumb housing projects. Parts of modern France bear as much resemblance to classic proportion and style as Athens sprawl does to Ancient Greece.

But there is plenty left of Paris and France. On that first night in Paris, we walked from les Halles to the Ile Saint Louis. Now, from any of the little stone bridges on the Seine, the gentle orange lights still sparkle. The view has not changed much since Sully stood admiring his handiwork more than three centuries ago. You can exit almost any *autoroute* and follow the cobblestones to a France of slow-turning cheeses and wild raspberries.

Some people fear it is the French themselves who are disappearing. They argue that the French no longer live up to France. Young people, traveling and looking outward for nourishment, no longer take the time to worry about curdling sauces. The great figures are dying off, taking their age with them. Polls track a steady decline in values, traditions, and old skills. Pure French people, this argument goes, are destined to live on artificially protected ground, on a sort of postindustrial Indian reservation.

Merde.

It is true, as Steven Spielberg lamented on an Academy Awards night, the coming year would not produce a new Truffaut film. But every Wednesday, *Pariscope* lists the 300 movies shown each week in town. Bardot retired long ago to save baby seals, but a dozen talented young actresses raise box office receipts.

Simone de Beauvoir and Jean Genêt, the grand rebels, died within a day of one another in 1986. But each left a lot behind.

Sartre is no more dead than Marx is, or God. He was fresh in the news in 1986 because of a biography by Annie Cohen-Solal; every second reviewer confessed a desire to nibble the author's neck. *Magazine Littéraire* carried a recent who's who of sixty-three philosophers worthy of argument. The flashy ones are as famous as rock stars. Bernard-Henri Lévi marches against racism. Derrida and his gang of deconstructionists pick apart whatever Descartes left intact.

Even if most French had never heard of him, Claude Simon won the 1985 Nobel Prize for literature; unlike Sartre in 1964, he accepted it. A far better known French author writes Proust-sized novels on a subject long thought pornographic: money. Paul-Loup Sulitzer scorns a hypocritical *bourgeoisie* that uses words like *parvenu* to put down people who make their own fortunes.

Sulitzer is popular in America, where a lot of French artists are now found. Pierre Boulez was music director of the New York Philharmonic until 1977 and he teamed up in concert with Frank Zappa.

That hardly suggests, as some argue, a decline of French culture. The new nature of borders obliterates the old guidelines. It is harder today to base cultural superiority on illusion. But it is easier to exhibit talent (or genius, when it appears) to a lot of people at once.

And the point is not which individuals one can cite. A society's level of *civilisation* is determined not by its summits but by its base camps. It is not easy to measure.

NO ONE TAKES more polls than the French. Since poll-takers cannot correct for the vast number of French who slam doors in their faces, the results are often dubious. But I found at least one useful poll in 1985. *Le Chasseur Français* found that 84 percent of respondents thought contact with nature is essential; 45 percent had left, or were about to leave, the cities to live closer to nature. But only 0.5 percent could identify the leaves of an oak, elm, beech, or birch.

And a Sofres sampling suggested that 82 percent of the French believe their politicians lie to them. In spite of that, 55 percent think politics an honorable profession.

French self-delusion mingles with a devaluation of labels. Politics do not follow a linear concept between right and left. France has red millionaires and downtrodden Fascists. The radicals, *les radicaux,* are moderate.

Alain Duhamel noted, "It is a comic misunderstanding, an ironic mistake of history: the English, Spaniards, Belgians, Dutch, and Scandinavians believe they live in monarchies; the French think they are in a Republic. In reality, the reverse is true." Mitterrand himself remarked that the president of France has too much power. A hostile National Assembly could temper that. But Duhamel is right: France elects a king.

Chirac provoked crisis in 1986, immediately after moving in as prime minister. His constitutional powers rivaled those of the president. He decided to attend the industrialized powers' summit in Tokyo, with Mitterrand. For starters, where would he sit? Anywhere, his aide remarked dryly, but under the table. Unwittingly, he made the pecking order clearer than he would have wished. Mitterrand took the Concorde. Chirac bought a ticket on Air France.

Cohabitation was thus defined. One could cohabit government offices but not a throne.

The French are basically conservative, fond of strong leaders and the status quo, until they decide to change both. A century and a half after the July Revolution, royalists can choose between two branches of pretenders in the wings. The comte de Paris, the uncrowned Henri VI, traces himself back 1,000 years to Hugues Capet.

When Socialists and Communists took power in 1981, Baron Guy de Rothschild checked out of France with a bitter note of goodby. Patriarch of the French Rothschilds, society leader and lover of horses, he was the most famous of financial refugees fleeing the left. His family bank nationalized, he moved to New York. He wrote to *Le Monde:* "A Jew under Pétain, a pariah under Mitterrand

—for me, it is enough. To rebuild on ruins twice in a lifetime is too much."

Rothschild blamed Socialist excesses and other such spasmodic fits on French attitudes toward money. The French, he told an interviewer, love money more than any other people. "They are different from the Americans, who are obsessed with making money. The jealousies, the pettiness of the French are very specific regarding money." His book, *The Whims of Fortune,* began: "[The French] cling to a pathological distinction between their own possessions, which are sacred, and anonymous riches labeled 'finance,' which are suspect."

In 1985, at seventy-six, the baron decided to come home. The government had realized that soaking the rich was not such a great idea; politics had shifted to the right. But mostly he returned because France was still France.

Just before the 1986 elections, I met another former bank director who had been nationalized out of a job. He was not bitter. "The Socialists were needed to unite the country in 1981, and now they are not," he said with a shrug. "That is French politics."

IT COMES DOWN to personal judgment. Like any reporter's, my address book bulges with the names of experts: the historians, the savants of *Sciences-Po,* the French who live the lives I observe as an outsider. My shelves buckle under reports, figures, assessments, and cuttings squirreled away over a decade. I've pondered at length how to track the French mission to civilize with fairness and balance. It was Sempé, who captures France with a few flicks of a brush, who reassured me: "If you drew, you would see this. Someone always says, 'You forgot a young person, or a trade unionist, or a woman . . .' Never mind all that. Go for the feeling."

Sempé asked if I didn't find the French to be pretentious. That was what got to him.

As Descartes would say, yes and no. Sempé is not pretentious, for example. Pretense suggests assuming airs that are not backed by substance. France exudes substance. You cannot fool even some of the people some of the time for five centuries. The French spirit is rich in broad qualities and examples of individual greatness.

But, of course, the French are pretentious. That is their greatest quality, their most exasperating drawback, and their source of price-less natural wealth. Who else could have assumed the posture of universal greatness from the immortal achievements of a few? Who else could have shaped a civilization on refinement and *politesse* and then set off in gunboats to share it with the world?

There is a better term than pretentious. Naturally, it is French, and it defies translation. It is *quant-à-soi,* meaning self-esteem, a sort of confident aloof pride that is shaped and transmitted by a society. When one has it, one can *rayonner.*

Possessed of *quant-à-soi,* a Frenchman can take a position and answer to no one for it. Certainly not to a foreigner. To avoid *malheur,* he might have to keep that position secret. He might have to follow someone else's orders, perhaps under humiliating circum-stances. But he can hold his position and dismiss any contradiction with self-delusion. Defeat and humiliation pass. What matters is conviction, and flair.

In the French *quant-à-soi,* grandeur began at Biberacte, where Vercingétorix assembled the Gauls to defy the universe. Mitterrand, like any French president, is at his best on the ancient sites, claiming his spiritual heritage. Little, in fact, links the smooth intellectual Socialist president to the howling mad Celt with dirty long blond braids. But that is not the point.

A French leader establishes a link with the spirits. Thus il-luminated, it does not matter if the sky falls on his head. The Sun King built Versailles in perfect symmetry so light would radiate from his navel as he slept on his back. De Gaulle communed with the Gallic forest. Others choose more modest symbolism. But their role is the same. *Civiliser,* according to Larousse, means first "to bring out of a primitive state" and then "to polish the mores."

Simple facts do not bear out this leading role. "France is the fifth-ranking power," a friend on the *Wall Street Journal* pro-nounced the other day, whipping out World Bank figures to prove it. Of course, he is right.

Braudel himself agreed, right up to his death. For him, the seats of world commercial power were, in turn, Venice, Amsterdam, London, and New York. France succeeded only by being close to the center. The French blew their one chance to be great, he said, in Canada and Louisiana. Since 1763, it was all downhill. France might have built Europe after the war, Braudel said, but its *quant-à-soi* got in the way. "The sad thing," he told one interviewer, "is that France loses too often."

This proves nothing. Ah, goes the logical reply, but Braudel was the greatest historian of his age. And he was French. Eminent historians simply add richness to the debate. And bean-counting foreigners do not matter. France is great because it is great. An outsider who does not see that is disqualified from judgment because of an obvious failing: he is not French.

That France loses often is easily rectified. A young American I know remarked recently to his nine-year-old French pal that France had not won a war in 100 years. You're crazy, the kid replied. We won both world wars. No one had taught him that Germans had occupied France or that allies helped in the fight.

Traditionally, French reporters have helped along this self-delusion. Sanche de Gramont recalls describing in 1961, in the New York *Herald Tribune,* atrocities committed by French paratroopers on Tunisian civilians. He wrote:

> Michel Debré, then Premier, asked his press secretary whether I was a French national. On being told that I was, he said: "Tell that fellow that he is a very poor advocate of France." I wondered about the fragility of a regime that could only tolerate advocates. The border between criticism and lack of patriotism is blurred. It is considered disloyal to bare French failings to the outside world.

French reporters are starting to poke holes in the self-delusion. Pooled television coverage and computerized news agencies leave them no choice. When Marchand's Tricolor toppled into the Nile mud a century ago, snickers were limited to the immediate vicinity. The BBC would have loved footage on it.

And French governments find that impressing the benighted is no longer a small chore. The cost of trade beads escalates when rivals are handing out pieces of the moon. France's focus on specific high technology has made an impact. Still, it is not easy.

One year, France waited in vain for Mitterrand's New Year message, live from his country home near Bordeaux. The crane that was supposed to lift the antenna was off pruning trees. A year later, during a televised interview, he declared with finality that only state control could ensure technical excellence of television. Suddenly, his face froze in grotesque contortion. The picture flickered, the sound wavered, and transmission ceased for several minutes.

Giscard d'Estaing had his sniffer airplane. France put a substantial sum into a mysterious Belgian bank account for an Italian's dubious invention to find oil from the air. The government enjoined an official investigator to hush it up. Money down the hole is one thing. But *le look* of France?!

These are not sidelights but symbols in a nation whose grandeur is symbolic. Gaullism works for France; but it requires a de Gaulle. The French survived defeat, occupation, and eclipse. Ridicule would be a catastrophe of a different magnitude.

BEFORE FINISHING this study, I took a last plunge into *la France profonde*. First, I saw Jean-Claude and Hélène, both in advertising, world travelers, and the best of modern France. In their old mill house near Vézelay, I watched Hélène's father, Roger, pan-broil a beef rib in shallots. This does not mean putting on a funny apron and flinging a steak on the charcoal. Roger's recipe begins with spending forty-five minutes with the butcher discussing the relative merits of pieces of meat. He uses a splash of vinegar to *déglacer,* gauges the heat like a nuclear physicist, and produces a steak you could fight a war over.

I asked Jean-Claude if his son would be able to produce such a dish at Roger's age. "Look," he said, "Lorenzo will go see how Americans do things, and travel. He's growing up in a more open world. But he is learning where he comes from—and his grandfather's recipes. What I hope is he will have both roots and wings."

We went off to inspect the Burgundy wine country. At Clos de Vougeot, a vineyard so hallowed that French army units salute when marching past, my heart sank. The château's ancient stones had been sandblasted to a sheen. Heavy oaken doors were coated in something like congealed model airplane glue. A sign in four languages commanded: "No tipping." Cheap wrought iron blocked the entrance to a massive vault illuminated by stained plastic windows. A scratchy tape narrated the past. The grand entryway was dominated by a souvenir counter selling pencils stamped with the vine-yard's name at three for ten francs. There was an outrageously priced stamped leather map of the wine country, which would make a Taiwan kitsch king blush in shame. The winery probably still had its heady aroma, but I could smell only exhaust from the tour buses.

We stopped at Savigny-les-Beaune, built around a château deco-rated in a relief of *rocaille* studded in handsome patterns on a perfectly proportioned facade. A sign announced the château's new purpose: a motorcycle museum. Even in 1986 France, it was hard to imagine a fourteenth-century Harley-Davidson. The village square was deserted except for an ambulant salesman: an Algerian lugging a pile of rugs and sheepskins.

But we drove among darkening grapes to Romanée Conti, the world's most expensive rural real estate, just an unassuming little vineyard marked by a 150-year-old Calvary. And thoughts turned to Lunch. An American will buy a house with less time and thought than a Frenchman spends on determining where to eat lunch. Beaune was out: too many tourists. One place was investigated and rejected. Too full? No, too empty. I bordered on despair, sliding deep into crankiness. My friends found the perfect spot. Of course. And then we visited the *caves* of Louis Latour.

Not a symbol was out of place in the village of Carton. The stooped old lady was there with her *filet* shopping bag of onions and macaroni; the men in blue overalls, faces black with grease, bent into the guts of a Citroën 2CV; Jean Gabin, in a frayed flannel suit, ambled down the cobblestones by the old church, *Le Petit Parisien* under his arm. We found only winemakers at the winery. Some flashy technology sped up the process, but the old presses were still there. When biological profusion clogs the old oak vats, an old-timer takes off his boots and climbs in to degunk them. Our host was a young Englishman who used to make dandelion wine; he cared about wine and was studying at the source.

We bumped among dim underground vaults of stacked bottles to a spiral stone stairway leading into blackness. The bottom level was a set for Dracula meets Joan of Arc. Walls oozed green and purple slime. Spooky long beards of mold hung from the prone bottles and scarred wooden racks. Spiderwebs blocked the narrow passages. And we sat down among bottles that were lying there when Americans were fighting over slavery, to sip wine in the deepest innards of France.

Later, I went skiing at Val d'Isère. At a bar called Bananas, Ginny the Australian bartender was warm and efficient. After four seasons at the Val, she had trouble counting to twelve in French. "I panic when a French person comes in," she said, with a laugh. It was not serious; the few French who did come usually spoke English. The best hotel is the Squaw Valley, with the manager's Ford Bronco out front and a giant tin sign advertising Indian Motor Oil nailed to the wall. It houses Val d'Isère's finest restaurant, the White Ocean, which serves flapjacks.

They are not exactly flapjacks. They are *crêpes au saumon Vonnassien,* potato pancakes of fresh salmon, red salmon caviar, and a sauce of ethereal lightness. Didier, the young chef, worked with Georges Blanc, who created the dish.

In Paris, I took a long cab ride and talked to the driver. His taxi was a Soviet-built Lada, rare in France, and I remarked on it. He was defensive. "Yeah, the car is Russian, the driver is French. It's a solid car, good economy." His friends gave him a hard time, he explained. Why a Commie car when there were Peugeots, Citroëns, and Renaults in the world? I asked if the French were like that. His monologue lasted from the Pont-Marie to the place des Ternes, twenty-three minutes.

They are so narrow-minded and small, I tell you. . . . Last night, I had an Algerian in the cab who came for medical treatment. He had no hotel, and it was late. He went into five places. At every hotel, the same story: "Sorry, we are full." So I said, "Let me try; you stay in the car." At the first hotel, I explained I had a fare who needed a room. "But of course." They look at the Americans and say, "Oh, look what those bastards do to their blacks" and never see their own hypocrisy. . . . You're writing a book on the French? You'd better make it a long one.

Then I asked about him. He did volunteer church work to help the distraught. His son fought racism. In a self-effacing way, he conveyed the opposite of every trait he had decried in the French. But he was French, too.

On television, not long after, I watched the Saturday-night shouting match, "Droit de Réponse." For ninety minutes each week, a dozen notables of the present and past ignore one another to shout their own opinions above the general din. The subject that night was the children of Vichy. American historian Robert Paxton mentioned that Pétain led the only energetically collaborationist government in Europe, and he deported Jews even before Hitler asked. A voice, loud and hectoring, cut him off: "I don't butt into his affairs to tell him about the Indians in America." A minister in the Vichy cabinet tried to show how Pétain had protected the Jews. Marie-Claire Mendès-France observed that sending 79,000 Jews to their deaths was not very effective protection.

This was France: forty-five years later, some French were deluding themselves about brutal blackness in their past. And other French were rubbing their noses in it, making sure the record was clear. It seemed to me a better use of the airwaves than tracing the imaginary banalities of some Texas grease magnates.

I took a last flip through the clippings. Dreyfus was back in the news. The government commissioned Tim, a well-loved Jewish sculptor, to do the wronged officer in bronze. All was forgiven. L'Ecole Militaire, however, did not want the statue in its courtyard. All was not forgotten.

In a quick round of French roulette, I chose three last sources. There was Jacqui, a reformed bum at 37: "This country is finished, done. It can't compete. All over the world, people laugh at us. If you fall on your face here, you'll never get up. Look at the government: it's like the Shah of Iran ruling with the Ayatollah Khomeini."

There was an unnamed cab driver. My car had broken down in the middle of traffic; I approached him for help and, as soon as he saw I might mean bother, he sped away, spraying me with gravel. But then there was Madame Tourdes, the garage lady whose lunch got cold as she helped me out of the mess. She is one of those people who motivate outsiders to like the French as much as France. And she is not worried about the future of either.

Finally, I called on *la Vieille Dame du Quai Conti,* which is the Académie Française. I went to a news conference marking its 350th anniversary.

It was here that Cardinal Richelieu struck the match to light the world's path. And ever since, from plush grey and green armchairs under a soaring dome, an ever-replenished body of forty *Immortels* have tended the flame. The writer Michel Mohrt was brought into the circle in 1986, and Jean d'Ormesson welcomed him. Their speeches covered four full pages in *Le Monde.* D'Ormesson declaimed:

> "What purpose the Academy?" is one of those recurrent questions posed by imbeciles when they exhaust the charms of the weather. . . . What purpose? *Mais,* none, like all delicious and somewhat great things. What purposes cats, the Temple of Abu Simbel, the islands of the Italian lakes, the flame roses of the Camargue, military parades and the strutting of animals who wish to dazzle their conquests, the very old oaks of our fields, our memories of happiness? What purpose rites and ceremonies? To the eyes of a world dominated by money, by power in all of its aspects, by collective movements, fleeting and blind, what purpose the Academy? None. None at all. Its purpose is to be *beau.*

Maurice Druon, secretary in perpetuity, entered the room with two other members. We all rose. They sat before a huge Aubusson tapestry: Ceres, goddess of grain, clutching a sheaf of wheat in a chariot drawn by golden lions. Druon embodies French civilization. A dark suit with pinstripes and rich silk tie, mannerly tufts of grey-white hair emitting intellectual energy, charm and *politesse* edged with the subtle hint of potential arrogance. That he used teams of helpers to write often inane historical novels was totally beside the point.

He selected each syllable with infinite care, placing it ahead of him just so and then sinking into it as if it were a velvet cushion. In subtle patterns, he repeated key phrases, his voice booming and then dropping to a barely audible rasp. L'Académie was finishing the ninth edition of its dictionary. It would have 45,000 words. The eighth, published in 1935, had 35,000 words. French is evolving, he said, in its role of providing the means to precisely and clearly define the arts and sciences.

We had a light snack, the usual. Bits of fine marinated salmon on toast, *jambon d'Auvergne,* hazelnut mousse. Druon captivated a small group. He paused to unscrew the metal cap of a fat Havana and lit it with elaborate care. Waving the cigar, he pronounced:

"What is tradition, after all, but progress that has succeeded."[1]

I asked Druon about the phrase *mission civilisatrice.* "But of course it is in use," he said. "I use it myself." And its origin? "I don't know; I really cannot say," he replied. Then he reflected a moment, lifted his chin slightly and added, "It just naturally comes to mind."

WHEN SCHOOL started again in the fall of 1985, 12,300,000 children went back to a new curriculum. An experiment in *éveil* (awakening) to encourage individual expression was junked in favor of basic values: discipline, rigor, effort. Basic subjects were back: French, math, science and technology, history and geography. An emphasis on moral development was added. "Civic education," the government said of the new course, "develops honesty, courage, refusal of racism, love for the Republic."

This was Jules Ferry. The study of colonies was replaced by computer science, but the foundations were the same. In second grade, pupils contemplate a verse from Louis Aragon: "I found my lady by the water, my lady is France and I am her Lancelot." And they sing the "Marseillaise," complete with the impure blood spilled from enemies to drench French furrows. The message is more subtle, but the mission is the same.

Every culture keeps handy a few brief snatches of enduring popular wisdom. America is too young to have proved the value of any truly transcendental saying. But the French have one, nicked and worn from overuse, but apt on a minefield in ancient Gaul, at the court of the Sun King, in a Gabon supermarket, or in the little French village of St.-Paul lost out in the Indian Ocean: *Plus ça change, plus c'est la même chose.* The more things change, the more they remain unchanged.

It is likely there will always be an England. It is certain there will always be a France.

Notes

Chapter One

1. *Nouveau Dictionnaire Etymologique et Historique* (Paris: Larousse).
2. This translated extract is from Sanche de Gramont's *The French* (New York: Putnam, 1969), an amusing but hard-eyed look at France by a correspondent of French and American origin.
3. Emil Schreyger, *l'Office du Niger au Mali* (Weisbaden: Steiner, 1984).

Chapter Two

1. The contrast with Britain was marked. Associated Press correspondent Michael Goldsmith, a Briton, was arrested in the Central African Republic in 1977, as described in Chapter 13. Asked to help, the British government replied, "When a British subject finds himself in difficulty in an area where we have no representation, he must look out for himself." Goldsmith was freed in thirty days after intervention by African heads of state.
2. Jacques-Marie Bourget and Yvan Stefanovitch, *Des Affaires Très Spéciales* (Paris: Plon, 1986).

Chapter Seven

1. This quotation is from Jean Meyer, *La France Moderne* (Paris: Fayard, 1985), who has mixed his own paraphrase with direct citations from Machiavelli's *De Natura Gallorum*.
2. W. H. Lewis covers Challes's voyage in *The Splendid Century*

(New York: Morrow, 1978); Challes tells it himself in *Voyages aux Indes* (Paris: Plon, 1933).

3. Sanche de Gramont relayed this fragment of Racine in *The French*. I presume the translation is his.

4. Meyer, *La France Moderne*.

Chapter Eight

1. Slavery figures are disputed; these are Philip D. Curtin's estimates, cited by Pierre Pluchon, *Histoire des Antilles et de la Guyane* (Toulouse: Privat, 1982).

2. These figure are cited in the massive *Histoire des Colonies Françaises* by Gabriel Hanotaux and Alfred Martineau (Paris: Plon, 1929). Abbé Reynal confirms them in his work, cited in the text.

3. W. C. Stinchcombe, *The American Revolution and the French Alliance* (Syracuse, N.Y.: Syracuse University, 1969). Similar figures and deployments are found in *The War of American Independence: Military Attitudes, Policies and Practices, 1763–1789* (Urbana, Ill.: University of Indiana, 1971) and in Jean-Baptiste Duroselle, *France and the United States* (Chicago: University of Chicago Press, 1976). France's costs were believed to be two million dollars per year for 5,000 ground troops, as well as naval costs. It was never clear what was grant and what was loan. Beaumarchais sought repayment after the war. U.S. authorities finally settled with his descendants for 800,000 francs in 1835.

Chapter Nine

1. Marvin Zahniser, *Uncertain Friendship* (New York: John Wiley, 1975).

2. Henriette Celarié, *La Prise d'Alger* (Paris: Hachette, 1929).

3. Edward Behr, *The Algerian Problem* (London: Hodder and Stoughton, 1961). Behr, an old Algerian hand, dug out Saint-Arnaud's letters.

Chapter Ten

1. Once again, this is Sanche de Gramont, *The French*.

2. Paul Johnson, *A History of the Modern World* (London: Weidenfeld and Nicolson, 1983).

3. Nicole Priollaud, *La France Colonisatrice* (Paris: Liana Levi, 1983). A fascinating collection of thoughts on French colonization.

Chapter Eleven

1. Johnson, *History of the Modern World.*
2. Jean Lacouture, *De Gaulle,* Vol. 1, *Le Rebelle* (Paris: Seuil, 1984).
3. Michael R. Marrus and Robert O. Paxton, *Vichy France and the Jews* (New York: Basic Books, 1981).
4. Johnson, *History of the Modern World.*
5. Alistair Horne, *A Savage War of Peace* (London: Macmillan, 1977). I am especially indebted to this carefully researched account. The Algeria section is drawn from a number of published works, news dispatches, and personal interviews, but I found Horne, and the following cited work of Edward Behr, to be particularly useful.
6. Behr, *Algerian Problem.*
7. Horne, *Savage War of Peace.*
8. Behr, *Algerian Problem,* quoting from Jules Ferry's *Le Gouvernement de l'Algérie.*
9. Horne, *Savage War of Peace,* among others.
10. Horne, *Savage War of Peace.*
11. This is essentially Horne's account *(Savage War of Peace),* which is corroborated by others.
12. A former senior aide of Delouvrier's told me this; he asked to remain anonymous.
13. Michel Lévine, *Les Ratonnades d'Octobre* (Paris: Ramsey, 1985).
14. Again, Horne's careful research turned up this quotation from Flanner.
15. Horne, *Savage War of Peace;* also Johnson, *History of the Modern World.*
16. French military statistics are difficult to pin down. Defense Minister Charles Hernu reported the figure of 21,600 to the Senate on Jan. 20, 1982. Other figures are from Horne, *Savage War of Peace.* For Indochina, an Army spokesman gave me these figures in June 1985: 36,480 French dead; 21,000 missing; 72,200 wounded.

Chapter Twelve

1. Pascal Chaigneau, *La Politique militaire de la France en Afrique* (Paris: Centre des Hautes Etudes sur l'Afrique et l'Asie Modernes, 1984).
2. Roger Faligot and Pascal Krop, *La Piscine* (Paris: Seuil, 1985).
3. Faligot and Krop, *La Piscine.*

Chapter Thirteen

1. The Americans outdid the French in meddling in the Congo. A month after Lumumba was elected prime minister of the Congo, the CIA decided to kill him. An agent brought a specialized poison to Léopoldville, but the job was botched. Events then took care of themselves. A U.S. Senate commission determined that Allen Dulles gave the order and might have had reason to believe President Eisenhower wished him to take such a drastic step; Eisenhower's role was not established. The commission decided that it was in the long-term U.S. interest to admit the facts in the hope that other nations would respect a will to expiate wrongdoing.
2. *Le Monde* carried the leaked text on December 5, 1984.
3. F. Roy Willis, *The French Paradox* (Stanford, Cal.: Hoover Institution, 1982). Willis cites the U.S. Arms Control and Disarmament Agency.
4. Rolf Steiner, *The Last Adventurer* (Boston: Little, Brown, 1978).

Chapter Fourteen

1. *Libération,* citing *Cahier du Témoignage chrétien,* no. 54, February, 1973.

Chapter Fifteen

1. These details are included in Amir Taheri, *Khomeiny* (Paris: Balland, 1985). Taheri is a journalist in exile who knows his Iran.
2. Jonathan Randal covers this material in *Going All the Way* (New York: Viking, 1983), and he kindly discussed his current research on France in the Levant in personal interviews.
3. Gen. Henri Gouraud, "La France en Syrie," *La Revue de France,* April 1922.
4. *Le Nouvel Observateur,* January 17, 1977.

Chapter Sixteen

1. This information came from an Interpol source who cannot be named; later, official French sources substantiated it.

Chapter Eighteen

1. Max Savelle, *The Origins of American Diplomacy: The International History of Angloamerica, 1492–1763* (New York: Macmillan, 1967).
2. Zahniser, *Uncertain Friendship.*

Chapter Twenty

1. Thierry Wolton, *Le KGB en France* (Paris: Grasset, 1986).
2. Johnson, *History of the Modern World.*
3. Johnson, *History of the Modern World.*

Chapter Twenty-one

1. This was a direct quote from Druon's own acceptance speech to the Académie in 1967. In welcoming him, Sanche de Gramont notes, Louis Pasteur Vallery-Radot could not resist quoting some of the inanities in his books, such as: "Like nearly all those destined to the follies of passion, Mary had one eye slightly smaller than the other."

Bibliography

Ardagh, John. *France in the 1980s.* London: Secker and Warburg, 1982.

Atlas Colonial Français. Paris: L'Illustration, 1929.

Balandier, Georges. *Au Temps des Colonies.* Paris: Seuil, 1984.

Baldwin, Marshall. *History of the Crusades.* Vol. 1. Madison: Univ. of Wisconsin, 1969.

Bare, Jean-François. *Le Malentendu Pacifique.* Paris: Hachette, 1985.

Barril, Paul. *Missions Très Spéciales.* Paris: Presses de la Cité, 1954.

Barzini, Luigi. *The Europeans.* New York: Simon and Schuster, 1983.

Behr, Edward. *The Algerian Problem.* London: Hodder and Stoughton, 1961.

Benoit, Pierre. *Océanie Française.* Paris: Alpina, 1933.

Bergot, Erwan. *Gendarmes au Combat.* Paris: Presses de la Cité, 1985.

Blet, Henri. *Histoire de la Colonisation Française.* Paris: Arthaud, 1946.

Bodard, Lucien. *The Quicksand War.* Boston: Little, Brown, 1967.

Bordonove, Georges. *Les Templiers.* Paris: Fayard, 1977.

Bourget, Jacques-Marie, and Yvan Stefanovitch. *Des Affaires Très Spéciales.* Paris: Plon, 1986.

Braudel, Fernand. *La Méditerranée et le Monde Méditerranéen à l'Epoque de Philippe II.* Paris: Armand Colin, 1949.

————. *La Méditerranée.* Paris: Arts et Metiers Graphiques, 1977.

————. *L'Identité de le France.* Paris: Arthaud, 1986.

Brunschwig, Henri. *Noirs et Blancs dans l'Afrique noire Française.* Flammarion, Paris, 1983.

Burin des Roziers, Etienne. *Retour aux Sources.* Paris: Plon, 1986.

Caesar, Julius. *Conquest of Gaul.* Harmondsworth, England: Penguin, 1951.

Caron, François. *La France des Patriotes.* Vol. 5, *Histoire de France.* Paris: Fayard, 1985.

Casanova, Jacques-Donat. *America's French Heritage.* Paris: Documentation Française, 1976.

Celarié, Henriette. *La Prise d'Alger.* Paris: Hachette, 1929.

Cerny, Philip C. *The Politics of Grandeur.* Cambridge: University Press, 1980.

Chaigneau, Pascal. *La Politique militaire de la France en Afrique.* Paris: Centre des Hautes Etudes sur l'Afrique et l'Asie Modernes, 1984.

Chairoff, Patrice. *B . . . Comme Barbouzes.* Paris: Moreau, 1975.

Challes, Robert. *Voyages aux Indes.* Paris: Plon, 1933.

Chamberlain, M. E. *Decolonization.* Oxford: Basil Blackwell, 1985.

Cohen-Solal, Annie. *Sartre.* Paris: Gallimard, 1985.

Cook, Don. *Charles de Gaulle.* New York: Putnam, 1983.

Crété, Liliane. *La Vie Quotidienne en Louisiane.* Paris: Hachette, 1978.

Darcy, Jean. *Cent Années de Rivalité Coloniale.* Paris: Perrin, 1904.

De Beauvoir, Simone. *Force of Circumstance.* Harmondsworth, England: Penguin, 1968.

De Berthier de Sauvigny, G. *La France et les Français vu par les voyageurs américains.* Paris: Flammarion, 1985.

De Gaulle, Charles. *War Memoirs.* New York: Simon and Schuster, 1967.

De Gramont, Sanche. *The French.* New York: Putnam, 1969.

De Grèce, Michel. *La Nuit du Sérail.* Paris: Orban, 1982.

Delale, Alain, and Gilles Ragache. *La France de 68.* Paris: Seuil, 1978.

Delpey, Roger. *Affaires Centrafricaines.* Paris: Grancher, 1985.

De Pourtalès, Guy. *Nous à qui rien n'appartient.* Paris: Flammarion, 1931.

Des Champs, Hubert. *Les Pirates à Madagascar.* Paris: Berger-Levrault, 1972.

Desjardins, Thierry. *Nouvelle Calédonie.* Paris: Plon, 1985.

Dorgelès, Roland. *Sous le Casque Blanc.* Paris: Editions des France, 1941.

Douville, Raymond. *La Vie Quotidienne en Nouvelle France.* Paris: Hachette, 1964.

Duhamel, Alain. *Le Complexe d'Astérix.* Paris: Gallimard, 1985.

Duhamel, Georges. *Civilisation Française.* Paris: Hachette, 1944.

Dumont, René. *L'Afrique noire est mal Partie.* Paris: Seuil, 1962.

Duroselle, Jean-Baptiste. *In Search of France.* Cambridge: Harvard University Press, 1963.

———. *France and the United States.* Chicago: University of Chicago Press, 1976.

Dutourd, Jean. *La Gauche la plus bête du Monde.* Paris: Flammarion, 1985.

———. *Les Taxis de la Marne.* Paris: Gallimard, 1956.

Duval, Paul-Marie. *La Vie Quotidienne en Gaule.* Paris: Hachette, 1952.

Dyson, John and Joseph Fitchett. *Sink the Rainbow.* London: Gollancz, 1986.

Emmanuelli, René. *La Vie de Pascal Paoli.* Calvi, Corsica: Accadèmia d'i Vagabondi, 1976.

Espaces. *L'Identité Française.* Paris: Tierce, 1985.

Faligot, Roger, and Pascal Krop. *Services secrets en Afrique.* Paris: Le Sycomore, 1982.

———. *La Piscine.* Paris: Seuil, 1985.

Favier, Jean. *Le Temps des Principautés.* Vol. 2, *Histoire de France.* Paris: Fayard, 1984.

Flachère, R. P. A. *Sous la Menace des Idoles.* Paris: Plon, 1938.

Garnier, Francis. *Voyage d'exploration en Indochine.* Paris: La Découverte, 1985.

Gide, André. *Voyages au Congo.* Paris: Gallimard, 1927.

Girardet, Raoul. *L'Idée coloniale en France, 1871–1962.* Paris: La Table Ronde, 1972.

Goldschmidt, Arthur, Jr. *A Concise History of the Middle East.* Boulder: Westview Press, 1979.

Gregorj, Ghajcumu. *Chroniques irrespectueuses sur l'Histoires des Corses.* Calvi, Corsica: Accadèmia d'i Vagabondi, 1982.

Grimal, Henri. *La Décolonisation.* Paris: Colin, 1965.

Grosser, Alfred. *Affaires Extérieures.* Paris: Flammarion, 1985.

Grousset, René. *L'Épopée des Croisades.* Paris: Plon, 1939.

Guillebaud, J. C. *Les Confettis de l'Empire.* Paris: Seuil, 1976.

Hamdani, Amar. *La Vérité sur l'Expédition d'Alger.* Paris: Balland, 1985.

Hanley, D. L., A. P. Kerr, and N. H. Waites. *Contemporary France.* London: Routledge and Kegan Paul, 1984.

Hanotaux, Gabriel, and Alfred Martineau. *Histoire des Colonies Françaises.* Paris: Plon, 1929.

———. *La France en 1614.* Paris: Nelson, 1914.

Harmand, Jacques. *Vercingétorix.* Paris: Fayard, 1984.

Heinrich, Pierre. *La Louisiane.* New York: Burt Franklin, 1908.

Hill, John Hugh. *Raymond IV, Count of Toulouse.* Syracuse, N.Y.: Syracuse University, 1962.

Hoffmann, Stanley, *Decline or Renewal? France since the 1930s.* New York: Viking Press, 1974.

Hoffman, Stanley, and others. *In Search of France.* Cambridge: Harvard University Press, 1963.

Horne, Alistair. *A Savage War of Peace.* London: Macmillan, 1977.

———. *The French Army and Politics.* London: Macmillan, 1984.

L'Immigration Maghrébine en France. Paris: Les Temps Modernes, 1984.

Jacquier, Henri. *Piraterie dans le Pacifique.* Paris: Latines, 1973.

Jenkins, E. H. *A History of the French Navy.* London: MacDonald and Jane's, 1973.

Johnson, Paul. *A History of the Modern World.* London: Weidenfeld and Nicolson, 1983.

Jullian, Camille. *Vercingétorix.* Paris: Tallandier, 1977.

July, Serge. *Les Années Mitterrand.* Paris: Grasset, 1986.

Kahler, Miles. *Decolonization in Britain and France.* Princeton, N.J.: Princeton University Press, 1984.

Kennan, George F., *The Fateful Alliance.* New York: Pantheon, 1984.

Kennedy, Ludovic. *A Book of Sea Journeys.* London: Collins, 1981.

Kingsley, Mary H. *Travels in West Africa.* London: Macmillan and Co., 1897.

Klarsfeld, Serge. *Vichy-Auschwitz.* Vol. 1. Paris: Fayard, 1983.

———. *Vichy-Auschwitz.* Vol. 2. Paris: Fayard, 1985.

Knibiehler, Yvonne, and Regine Goutalier. *La Femme au Temps des Colonies*. Paris: Stock, 1985.

Lacouture, Jean. *De Gaulle*. Vol. 1, *Le Rebelle*. Paris: Seuil, 1984.

————. *De Gaulle*. Vol. 2, *Le Politique*. Paris: Seuil, 1985.

Lacouture, Jean, and Simonne Lacouture. *Vietnam*. Paris: Seuil, 1976.

Lamb, David. *The Africans*. New York: Random House, 1982.

Langlais, Pierre. *Dien Bien Phu*. Paris: Editions France-Empire, 1963.

Lapping, Brian. *End of Empire*. London: Granada, 1985.

Lauga, Henri. *De la Banquise à la Jungle*. Paris: Plon, 1952.

Leblond, Marius. *Les Grandes Heures des Iles et des Mers Françaises*. Paris: Colbert, 1943.

Ledwidge, Bernard. *De Gaulle et les Américains*. Paris: Flammarion, 1984.

Le Gall, Joel. *Alésia*. Paris: Fayard, 1963.

Lemoine, Maurice. *Le Mal Antillais*. Paris: L'Harmattan, 1982.

Les Expéditions Françaises au Tonkin par un Missionaire. Société de Saint-Augustin. Lille: Desclee, de Brouwer et Cie., no date.

Lestocquoy, Jean. *Histoire du Patriotisme en France*. Paris: Albin Michel, 1968.

Lévine, Michel. *Les Ratonnades d'Octobre*. Paris: Ramsey, 1985.

Lewis, W. H. *The Splendid Century*. New York: Morrow, 1978.

Loubat, Bernard. *L'Orge de Berengo*. Paris: Lefeuvre, 1981.

Lot, Ferdinand. *La Gaule*. Paris: Fayard, 1967.

Luethy, Hebert. *France against Herself*. New York: Meridian, 1957.

Lyautey, Hubert. *Lettres du Tonkin et de Madagascar*. Paris: Armand Colin, 1921.

Lyautey, Pierre. *L'Empire Colonial Français*. Paris: Editions de France, 1931.

MacShane, Denis. *François Mitterrand*. London: Quartet, 1982.

Mangin, Charles. *Lettres du Soudan*. Paris: Portiques, 1930.

Marcilly, Jean. *Le Pen sans Bandeau*. Paris: Grancher, 1984.

Mariotti, André. *Journal de Campagne en Corse an 1731*. Calvi, Corsica: Casalonga, 1982.

Marrus, Michael R., and Robert O. Paxton. *Vichy France and the Jews*. New York: Basic Books, 1981.

Marseille, Jacques. *Empire Colonial et Capitalisme Français.* Paris: Albin Michel, 1984.

Maurois, André. *A History of France.* New York: Farrar, Straus and Cudahy, 1948.

McDermott, John F. *Frenchmen and French Ways in the Mississippi Valley.* Urbana, Ill.: University of Illinois, 1969.

Mercier, André François. *Faut-il Abandonner l'Indochine?* Paris: Editions France-Empire, 1954.

Mermet, Gerard. *Francoscopie.* Paris: Larousse, 1985.

Meyer, Charles. *La Vie Quotidienne des Français en Indochine.* Paris: Hachette, 1985.

Meyer, Jean. *La France moderne.* Vol. 3, *Histoire de France.* Paris: Fayard, 1985.

Michel, Henri. *Histoire de la Résistance.* Paris: Presses Universitaires de France, 1950.

Mitterrand, François. *Réflexions sur la Politique Extérieure de la France.* Paris: Fayard, 1986.

Mockler, Anthony. *The New Mercenaries.* London: Sidgwick and Jackson, 1985.

Montagnon, Pierre. *La Conquête de l'Algérie.* Paris: Pygmalion, 1986.

Murray, Simon. *Légionnaire.* London: Sidgwick and Jackson, 1978.

Myrdal, Gunnar. *Asian Drama.* London: Allen Lane, 1968.

Parkinson, Wenda. *This Gilded African: Toussaint L'Ouverture.* London: Quartet, 1980.

Parkman, Francis. *The Parkman Reader.* Edited by Samuel Eliot. Boston: Morison, Little, Brown, 1955.

————. *France and England in North America.* Vol. 2. New York: Library of America, 1983.

Paris, Paulin. *Guillaume de Tyr.* Paris: Firmin-Didot, 1879.

Péan, Pierre. *Bokassa Ier.* Paris: Alain Moreau, 1977.

————. *Affaires Africaines.* Paris: Fayard, 1983.

Pernoud, Régine. *Les Hommes de la Croisade.* Paris: Tallandier, 1982.

Peyrefitte, Alain. *Le Mal Français.* Paris: Plon, 1976.

Pierre, Andrew. *The Global Politics of Arms Sales.* Princeton, N.J.: Princeton University Press, 1982.

Pluchon, Pierre. *Histoire des Antilles et de la Guyane.* Toulouse: Privat, 1982.

Priollaud, Nicole. *La France Colonisatrice*. Paris: Liana Levi, 1983.

Proust, Louis. *Visions d'Afrique*. Paris: Aristide Quillet, 1925.

Randal, Jonathan. *Going All the Way*. New York: Viking, 1983.

Raynal, Abbé Guillaume. *Histoire philosophique et politique des Deux Indes*. Paris: François Maspero, 1981.

Rocolle, Pierre. *Pourquoi Dien Bien Phu?* Paris: Flammarion, 1968.

Rodman, Selden. *Haiti*. Greenwich, Conn.: Devin-Adair, 1984.

Rousset, Paul. *Les Origines et les Caractères de la Première Croisade*. Geneva: University of Geneva, 1945.

Runciman, Steven. *A History of the Crusades*. 3 vols. Cambridge, England: University Press, 1951.

Saint-Hamont, Daniel. *Histoires Algériennes*. Paris: Robert Laffont, 1979.

Sanmarco, Louis. *Le Colonisateur colonisé*. Paris: ABC, 1983.

Sassier, Philippe. *Les Français à la Corbeille*. Paris: Robert Laffont, 1985.

Schlarman, J. R. *From Quebec to New Orleans*. Belleville, Ill.: Buechler, 1929.

Schreyger, Emil. *L'Office du Niger au Mali*. Weisbaden: Steiner, 1984.

Seldes, George. *You Can't Print That*. Garden City, N.Y.: Doubleday, 1929.

Servan-Schreiber, Jean-Jacques. *Lieutenant in Algeria*. New York: Knopf, 1957.

Smith, William H. C. *Napoléon III*. Paris: 1982.

Sofres, *Opinion publique 1985*. Paris: Gallimard, 1985.

Spartacus, Colonel. *Opération Manta*. Paris: Plon, 1985.

Stacey, C. P. *Québec 1759*. Toronto: Macmillan, 1959.

Stasi, Bernard. *L'Immigration, une Chance pour la France*. Paris: Robert Laffont, 1984.

Steiner, Rolf. *The Last Adventurer*. Boston: Little, Brown, 1978.

Stinchcombe, W. C. *The American Revolution and the French Alliance*. Syracuse, N.Y.: Syracuse University, 1969.

Strachey, John. *The End of Empire*. London: Gollancz, 1959.

Sunday Times, The. *Rainbow Warrior*. London: Arrow, 1986.

Taboulet, Georges. *La Geste Française en Indochine*. Vols. I and II. Paris: Adrien-Maisonneuve, 1955.

Taheri, Amir. *Khomeiny.* Paris: Balland, 1985.

Tallant, Robert. *Voodoo in New Orleans.* Gretna, La.: Pelican, 1974.

Tharaud, Jérôme, and Jean Tharaud. *Alerte en Syrie.* Paris: Plon, 1937.

Tillion, Germaine. *Algérie en 1957.* Paris: Minuit, 1957.

Tilly, Charles. *The Contentious French.* Cambridge: Belknap, 1986.

Trial, Georges. *Okoume.* Paris: Je Sers, 1939.

Tulard, Jean. *Les Révolutions.* Vol. 4, *Histoire de France.* Paris: Fayard, 1985.

Van Loon, H. W. *The Story of Mankind.* New York: Washington Square Press, 1939.

Versini, Xavier. *La Vie Quotidienne en Corse au Temps de Mérimée.* Paris: Hachette, 1979.

Vie, Jean-Emile. *Faut-il abandonner les D.O.M.?* Paris: Economica, 1978.

Villère, Sidney Louis. *Jacques Philippe Villère.* New Orleans, La.: Historic Collection, 1981.

Weissman, Steve, and Herbert Krosney. *The Islamic Bomb.* New York: Times Books, 1981.

Werner, Karl F. *Les Origines.* Vol. 1, *Histoire de France.* Fayard, Paris, 1984.

Weygand, Général. *L'Arc de Triomphe de Paris.* Paris: Flammarion, 1960.

Willis, F. Roy. *The French Paradox.* Stanford, Cal.: Hoover Institution, 1982.

Wolton, Thierry. *Le KGB en France.* Paris: Grasset, 1986.

Yost, David S. *France's Deterrent Posture and Security in Europe.* London: Adelphi Papers, International Institute for Strategic Studies, 1984.

Zahniser, Marvin. *Uncertain Friendship.* New York: John Wiley, 1975.

Zeldin, Theodore. *France 1848–1945: Anxiety and Hypocrisy.* Oxford: Oxford University Press, 1981.

———. *The French.* New York: Pantheon, 1983.

Zumthor, Paul. *Guillaume le Conquérant.* Paris: Hachette, 1978.

Index

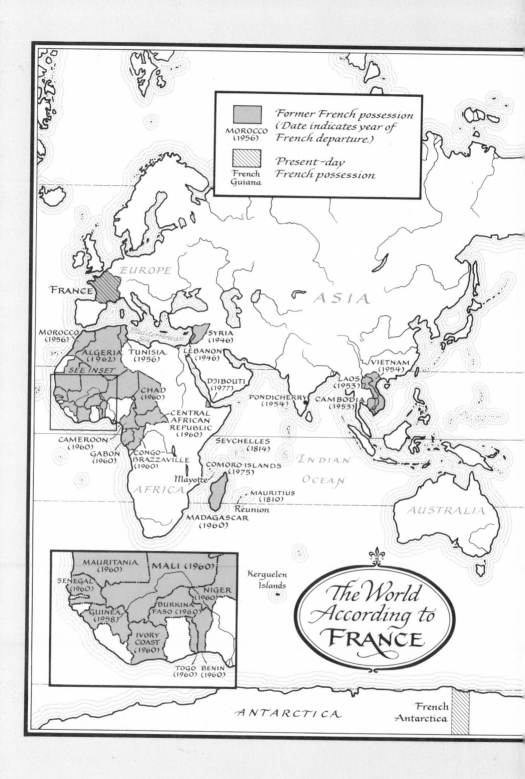

Former French possession
(Date indicates year of
French departure.)

MOROCCO
(1956)

Present-day
French possession

French
Guiana

EUROPE

ASIA

FRANCE

MOROCCO
(1956)

ALGERIA
(1962)

TUNISIA
(1956)

SYRIA
(1946)

LEBANON
(1946)

SEE INSET

DJIBOUTI
(1977)

CHAD
(1960)

PONDICHERRY
(1954)

LAOS
(1953)

VIETNAM
(1954)

CAMBODIA
(1953)

CENTRAL
AFRICAN
REPUBLIC
(1960)

CAMEROON
(1960)

GABON
(1960)

CONGO-
BRAZZAVILLE
(1960)

SEYCHELLES
(1814)

COMORO ISLANDS
(1975)

INDIAN

OCEAN

AUSTRALIA

Mayotte

AFRICA

MAURITIUS
(1810)

Réunion

MADAGASCAR
(1960)

MAURITANIA
(1960)

MALI (1960)

Kerguelen
Islands

SENEGAL
(1960)

NIGER
(1960)

GUINEA
(1958)

BURKINA
FASO (1960)

IVORY
COAST
(1960)

TOGO   BENIN
(1960) (1960)

The World
According to
FRANCE

ANTARCTICA

French
Antarctica